G000272978

Hilla

LATIN COMPENDIUM

Hillard & Botting's
LATIN COMPENDIUM

BY

THE REV. ALBERT ERNEST HILLARD, D.D.
(1865–1935)
LATE HIGH MASTER OF ST PAUL'S SCHOOL, LONDON

AND

CECIL GEORGE BOTTING, M.A.
(1870–1929)
LATE ASSISTANT MASTER AT ST PAUL'S SCHOOL, LONDON

SECOND EDITION

COMPILED AND REVISED
BY
NIGEL WETTERS GOURLAY

Hillard & Botting's Latin Compendium, Second Edition

Printing History

February 2016	First Edition, ISBN 978-981-09-5211-2
February 2017	Second Edition, ISBN 978-981-09-5210-5 ⟵
TBC	Second Edition with Answers, ISBN 978-981-11-2618-5

National Library Board, Singapore
Cataloguing-in-Publication Data

Names: Gourlay, Nigel Wetters, compiler. |
    Hillard, A. E. (Albert Ernest), 1865–1935. |
    Botting, C. G.
Title: Hillard and Botting's Latin compendium /
    by The Rev. Albert Ernest Hillard and Cecil George Botting ;
    compiled and revised by Nigel Wetters Gourlay.
Other titles: Latin compendium.
Description: Second Edition |
    [Singapore] : Nigel Wetters Gourlay, [2017] |
    Text in English and Latin.
Identifiers: OCN 970009772 | ISBN 978-981-09-5210-5 (paperback)
Subjects: LCSH: Latin language--Problems, exercises, etc. |
    Latin language--Translating into English. |
    Latin language--Readers.
Classification: LCC PA2087 | DDC 478.6421--dc23

melius est prō patriā morī quam vincī
Hillard & Botting (1910)

My friend, you would not tell with such high zest
To children ardent for some desperate glory,
The old Lie: Dulce et decorum est
Pro patria mori.
Wilfred Owen (1917), quoting Horace

TABLE OF CONTENTS

EX.   GRAMMAR INTRODUCED

7

Table of Contents

PREFACE

The purpose of this book is to enable the student to become fluent by employing the most direct approach—translating English into Latin, and Latin into English. If the reader takes this task seriously, then these 384 exercises will take a little over a year to complete, two years at a more pedestrian pace. At any rate, such practice will commit a large chunk of Latin grammar and vocabulary to long-term memory.

Since publishing the first edition of this book, I have been writing an answer key to be published shortly after the second edition. Compiling the answer key, together with teaching Latin to my boy, caused me to make several changes. Some exercises which had been impossible using the given vocabulary are now possible, and errors in vowel length have been corrected.

A larger issue was the necessity of studying a Latin grammar guide alongside this book. For a long time I considered including a short grammar section of noun and verb tables as frontmatter, but I think even this would have been insufficient. In the end, I have opted to include the whole of *The Shorter Latin Primer* (1896) as an appendix. This was the grammar guide that Hillard & Botting used with their own students, and 120 years after publication it still stands as a testament to the liberal genius of its author Benjamin Hall Kennedy. Other grammar notes have been added alongside relevant exercises.

I have often been asked by teachers or parents why children should continue to learn Latin. It's a question I struggle to answer. I know why *I* love Latin, but there are a dozen or more reasons why other people's children should follow my example. If caught off guard, I flap around searching for one my interlocutor might prefer to hear.

In England in particular, Latin has a strange vestigial link to social class, along with cricket and the school song. It is to my shame that I play on that link with middle-class parents, emphasising the cultural benefits of studying the Graeco-Roman world, and its influences on our art, literature, and government. It's not really an argument about the benefits of learning Latin as a language, but it seems effective.

Some teachers love constructivist arguments, and so I've used them freely when interrupted in the staff room or library by a curious passer-by. Latin is a difficult subject, and studying difficult subjects adds new pathways in the brain, so the pupil has alternative ways of thinking about the world. Thus Latin is merely the intellectual scaffolding used to build a child's mind-palace. Again, it's not an argument about Latin, but it seems to please some listeners.

Ann Patty, the American literary editor, has written a humorous memoir *Living with a Dead Language* (2016, Viking) about learning Latin in her adulthood—the transformational power of an ancient literature read in the original, and the sudoku-like mental challenge of a strongly inflected foreign language. If an adult ever asked me for reasons why they should learn Latin, I would point them towards Ann Patty's book. Adults don't ask though: you either want to learn Latin or you don't; there is no uncertainty.

My own reason for studying Latin is rather embarrassing to put down on paper, and so I've never used it on a casual acquaintance. At my core, I am a misanthropist who despairs at the frivolity of modern life. Most people I find impossible, and even those in the educated set seem to say the same things, think the same thoughts, follow the flighty whims of social media, ovine, transitory. A New York Times writer will condense last week's dinner-party banter into an essay and the readers will regurgitate the main points as their own thoughts. A week later, no one remembers their opinion on any matter of importance. It's all just froth.

The Victorians were deeply pragmatic and serious people. Hypocritical too, but they tried to think profound thoughts without the barest hint of irony or nihilism. It wasn't uncommon for a boy to leave school having composed ten-thousand verses of original Latin poetry, and so the reading and writing of English poetry held no fear—it was simply the medium of condensed thought. All this is dust now, just as T. S. Eliot predicted in *The Wasteland,* and civilisation is in a long, terminal decline. These exercises were themselves aimed at prep-school boys of around eleven years of age, who were just starting on their journey towards fluency, whereas now they reflect the standard at which most pupils will leave their study of Latin. No doubt, in the future, technology will continue its improvement, but the imagination and confidence are disappearing, just as they disappeared at the end of Rome. Who now amongst our leaders is considering the sweep of history? I'm sure pockets of liberality will survive longer than anyone would predict, but the war for the supremacy of Enlightened Values is lost along with the Victorians.

This book is the first in what will become a series of early-twentieth-century guides to Latin and Greek. My next volume is a revision of North & Hillard's *Latin Prose Composition,* to be published in 2018; the book you're holding should be seen as the natural prelude to North & Hillard. Resurrecting these books is my response to the sense of loss I feel for a more serious world. As you can imagine, my reasons probably wouldn't convince many others of the benefits of "trudging" through their conjugations and declensions, which is why I will continue to flap around when asked the question.

N. W. G.
Singapore, Dec. 2016

Grave men, near death, who see with blinding sight
Blind eyes could blaze like meteors and be gay,
Rage, rage against the dying of the light.
                                        D. M. Thomas (1947)

ABOUT THE AUTHORS

Hillard and Botting worked at St Paul's, a school founded in 1509 on humanist principles. The school's most illustrious former pupil was the 17th-century poet John Milton, and St Paul's continues to this day as one of the leading schools in England.

ALBERT ERNEST HILLARD (1865–1935) was High Master of St Paul's for 22 years. An Anglican clergyman and talented classicist, he ordered three immediate innovations, the holding of Confirmation classes, the introduction of the 'modern' pronunciation of Latin, and the institution of the prefect system. Dr Hillard also encouraged the teaching of English Literature to pupils, as there had previously been no provision for any specialist English teaching, and many boys were failing their university entrance exams. At the time, one teacher noted it was ironic that schoolfellows of Milton should in the matter of English be "the hungry sheep who looked up and were not fed".

Collaborating with Michael Arthur ('Neddy') North of Clifton College, he wrote *Latin Prose Composition* (1895) which remained the standard textbook in English grammar schools for much of the twentieth century; this, more than his leadership, was his legacy to education. Hillard was profoundly shy, and avoided both teachers and pupils alike, only on the rarest of occasions visiting a classroom. Staff salaries stagnated during his time in charge of St Paul's, and this, combined with his social difficulties, meant he had few admirers. A history of the school written a quarter of a century after his retirement glosses over Dr Hillard's 22 years as a stepping-stone between two personality-driven leaders.

CECIL GEORGE BOTTING (1870–1929) was educated at Dulwich College and Cambridge University before teaching Classics, first at Colet Court Prep School and then at St Paul's itself. In all, he spent 37 years at the schools, and was known as the "supreme scholarship winner", having coached more boys to success in university entrance exams than any other teacher. It was written later than he was driven to augment his income with out-of-school coaching, "to the grave detriment of his health", and the blame for this was pinned squarely on Hillard's salary policy.

Cecil converted to Catholicism at the age of 36, and forced his wife and seven-year-old daughter to do the same. By his admirers he was said to have found the perfect flowering of his beloved Greeks within Catholic philosophy, and to him it seemed the spirit of Plato, even more than that of Aristotle, informed Catholic thought. His daughter, the author Antonia White, suffered mental illness for a large portion of her life. According to her autobiography, her disciplinarian father did not get the son he had hoped for, and she implies in her semi-autobiographical novels that he saw his conversion as salvation for sins of forbidden love.

NIGEL GOURLAY lives with his family in Singapore.

HILLARD   BOTTING

SOME HINTS ON TRANSLATION

With the longer passages that start to appear at Exercise 37, a few pieces of advice will be helpful for the beginner and more experienced student alike.

Unseen translation is the process of taking a passage of Latin that has not previously been studied, and writing a translation without reference to the vocabulary list at the back of the book or other reference material. Practising unseen translation is the fastest route to fluency and, of course, examination success.

First read the piece through: the meaning of some sentences will probably be clear at once, that of others doubtful, the rest unintelligible. Then read it through again; probably, the knowledge of the general sense of the passage gained from what you could interpret in your first reading will make what was before doubtful now clear, and what was before unintelligible now partly intelligible. Read it through again and again, and do not set pen to paper until you have decided how you are going to translate every word in the passage; otherwise you will stick in the middle and fail to finish the piece in the time given. If you have three-quarters of an hour in which to do the piece, spend at least twenty-five minutes in reading it through and the remainder in writing it out.

There will be some words that you do not know, and some passages of which you are not certain. Do not leave blanks; guess the meaning. Not only will a sensible shot be better marked by your examiner than a blank, but it is only by having the courage to make guesses that you will acquire the power of doing unseen translation at all. It is like learning to swim; the hardest thing is the first plunge.

In making a guess at the meaning of a word or sentence certain rules must be rigorously observed. Never make your author violate a rule of accidence or syntax, and always assume he is writing sense. Above all, never guess the meaning of a word until after you have made out what you can of the sense from the words that you do know. Otherwise you may start off on a wrong trail at the outset, and get a hopelessly wrong idea of what the passage is about. If you commit yourself to nothing except what you are certain of until your final reading, you will not go far wrong in your guesses. If you were steering a ship, a slight error in the compass at the beginning of your voyage would lead you miles away from your destination, whereas the same error near the end of your course might make only a trifling difference. It is a good idea to read the passage through to yourself in English, substituting 'x' for any word that you do not know. Often the correct translation of the word will flash into your mind as being the inevitable one.

It is hardly necessary to point out the invaluable assistance afforded if a strange word occurs twice in the passage given for translation. The number of ways in which it can be translated, so as to suit both places in which it occurs, is so restricted that it is usually quite easy to conjecture the right meaning. It is recommended that the pupil, on receiving back his version corrected, should enter in a note-book kept for the purpose all words that he did not know, with their meanings, including those whose meaning is given at the bottom of the page. These should be learnt by heart, as they will prove invaluable in doing future pieces.

ACKNOWLEDGEMENTS

I would like to thank the following individuals for the help and advice they provided during the production of this book: E. J. Aherne, P. A. Cartledge, J. Dodgson, L. Georgulas, J. W. Gourlay, N. M. Gwynne, J. Hayes, P. R. Hardie, A. Meskens, C. A. Stray, C. L. Taylor, T. G. Wilson, E. C. Yong (楊京達).

SECTION 1

See Grammar Notes №. 82,
Present and Future Indicative Active of amō.

TENSES

When we speak of an action, we must speak of it happening either in the Present time or in the Future or in the Past.

In all languages therefore, the Verb which expresses an action will have three different sets of forms for these three times. These sets of forms are called Present, Future, and Past tenses. Thus, *I love* or *he loves* is said to be a form of the Present Tense, *I shall love* or *he will love* is said to be a form of the Future Tense, *I loved* or *he loved* is said to be a form of the Past Tense.

THE PRESENT AND FUTURE TENSES IN LATIN AND ENGLISH

In learning the Present and Future of amō, notice these things:
1. In English we say *I love* or *I am loving* for the Present Tense. Latin has one form only for both of these, amō.

    So we also say *I shall love* or *I shall be loving* for the Future Tense. Latin has one form only for both of these, amābō.
2. In English we always express the Subject of the Verb. In Latin this is not necessary if the Subject is a Personal Pronoun. Thus amō means *I love,* amāmus means *we love,* amant means *they love* without any separate word for the Subject.

    The reason for this is obvious if you compare the Latin and English tenses. In English the Verb is *love* for the 1st Person Singular and for the 1st, 2nd, and 3rd Persons Plural. In Latin every one of these has a separate form, and thus the form of the Verb makes it clear whether the Subject is *I, we, you,* or *they.*

Exercise 1.

1. I work.
2. We love.
3. He hastens.
4. We hasten.
5. You work.

6. They love.
7. I hasten.
8. He works.
9. We work.
10. You hasten.

I work labōrō 1. **I love** amō 1. **I hasten** mātūrō 1.

Exercise 2.

1. We shall hasten.
2. I shall work.
3. He will love.
4. You will work.
5. They will hasten.

6. I shall love.
7. We shall work.
8. They are fighting.
9. He will hasten.
10. They will work.

I fight pugnō 1.

Exercise 3.

1. He will fight.
2. They are hastening.
3. I shall fight.
4. She works.
5. We hasten.

6. You will fight.
7. I shall hasten.
8. We are fighting.
9. She hastens.
10. She will work.

Exercise 4.

1. amābit.
2. labōrat.
3. amant.
4. mātūrābō.
5. pugnābimus.

6. mātūrat.
7. amābunt.
8. mātūrābit.
9. pugnābis.
10. labōrās.

amō 1. I love. **labōrō** 1. I work. **mātūrō** 1. I hasten.
pugnō 1. I fight.

See Grammar Notes №. 82,
Perfect and Imperfect Indicative Active of amō.

THE PAST TENSES IN
LATIN AND ENGLISH

It has been explained that in English we can say *I love* or *I am loving* for the Present Tense, *I shall love* or *I shall be loving* for the Future Tense, and that Latin has only one form for each of these Tenses.

In the same way we can say *I loved* or *I was loving* for the Past Tense. But here Latin is like English in having two forms, that are amāvī (which is called in the Grammar the Perfect Tense) and amābam (which is called the Imperfect Tense).

In the following exercises wherever the English has the simple Past (e.g. *I loved, we hastened, they fought*) use the first of these, the Perfect Tense; whenever the English has the longer form (e.g. *I was loving, we were hastening, they were fighting*) use the second, the Imperfect Tense.

N.B. The form *I was loving* (like *I am loving* in the Present and *I shall be loving* in the Future) is used to make it clear that we are speaking of an action as continuing or in progress. Think of the sentence *I was climbing a tree when the branch broke* and ask yourself whether it would be as well expressed by *I climbed a tree when the branch broke*.

Exercise 5.

1. He fought.
2. You hastened.
3. She wanders.
4. They work.
5. I fought.
6. You fight.
7. We shall wander.
8. We worked.
9. She will hasten.
10. He fights.

I wander errō 1.

Exercise 6.

1. He hastened.
2. He will fight.
3. You fought.
4. We hastened.
5. You worked.
6. She fights.
7. I shall wander.
8. They fought.
9. We shall fight.
10. I worked.

Exercise 7.

1. I hastened.
2. We fought.
3. She will fight.
4. They hastened.
5. He worked.
6. You will hasten.
7. She loves.
8. They will fight.
9. They worked.
10. They will love.

Exercise 8.

1. errābit.
2. amāvit.
3. pugnāvimus.
4. labōrāvī.
5. errāvērunt.
6. pugnābunt.
7. mātūrāvistī.
8. errāvistī.
9. mātūrāvimus.
10. amāvistis.

Exercise 9.

1. He was working.
2. He is wandering.
3. We were fighting.
4. She worked.
5. They were hastening.
6. He wanders.
7. I was fighting.
8. You are wandering.
9. We wander.
10. They were working.

Exercise 10.

1. They are wandering.
2. She fought.
3. You will wander.
4. I am fighting.
5. They will wander.
6. She wanders.
7. He was hastening.
8. We love.
9. He will wander.
10. We were hastening.

Exercise 11.

1. He will wander.
2. You love.
3. I was hastening.
4. She will love.
5. She hastened.
6. We shall wander.
7. You were hastening.
8. You will wander.
9. You were fighting.
10. They were fighting.

Exercise 12.

1. mātūrābat.
2. labōrāvī.
3. pugnābant.
4. mātūrāvit.
5. errābam.
6. amābāmus.
7. mātūrābitis.
8. errābamus.
9. labōrāvērunt.
10. pugnābātis.

See Grammar Notes № 82,
Perfect, Pluperfect, Future Perfect
Indicative Active of amō.

THE PERFECT, PLUPERFECT, AND FUTURE PERFECT TENSES

In Exercises 1–12 we have practised the simple ways of expressing an action in the three times (Present, Future, Past), these are:

	ENGLISH	LATIN
Present	*I love—I am loving*	amō
Future	*I shall love—I shall be loving*	amābō
Past	*I loved—I was loving*	amāvī—amābam

But sometimes we want to make it clear that we are speaking of an action as completed at a certain time, and this gave rise in all languages to some different sets of forms which are also called tenses.

In English we say *I have loved, I had loved, I shall have loved.* The Latin forms are:

I have loved	amāvī	Perfect Tense
I had loved	amāveram	Pluperfect Tense
I shall have loved	amāverō	Future Perfect Tense

It is most important to notice that the first of these Latin tenses is the same as that which expresses the simple Past. In fact the Latin "Perfect Tense" has to do double duty; for example:

amāvī = *I loved* or *I have loved.*
pugnāvērunt = *they fought* or *they have fought.*

Exercise 13.

1. I have worked.
2. You will sail.
3. I had fought.
4. He sailed.
5. We have hastened.
6. She sails.
7. She had hastened.
8. They sailed.
9. He has hastened.
10. You have worked.

I sail nāvigō 1.

Exercise 14.

1. I had worked.
2. You had fought.
3. We sailed.
4. He has worked.
5. He was sailing.
6. You have hastened.
7. He had fought.
8. I was sailing.
9. They have hastened.
10. They were sailing.

Exercise 15.

1. He will sail.
2. We were sailing.
3. We have worked.
4. You sailed.
5. I have hastened.
6. You have worked.
7. We shall sail.
8. You have wandered.
9. We had fought.
10. They are sailing.

Exercise 16.

1. pugnāverat.
2. mātūrāverāmus.
3. mātūrāvimus.
4. nāvigābit.
5. labōrāvit.
6. labōrāverat.
7. pugnāveram.
8. nāvigāverās.
9. mātūrāvistis.
10. pugnāverātis.

Exercise 17.

1. We shall have worked.
2. I had wandered.
3. You will have fought.
4. He had sailed.
5. He will have worked.
6. You had wandered.
7. He will have fought.
8. He has wandered.
9. He had wandered.
10. They will have hastened.

Exercise 18.

1. We had sailed.
2. We shall have fought.
3. You will have worked.
4. We had wandered.
5. She has sailed.
6. You will have fought.
7. I have wandered.
8. She had sailed.
9. They will have worked.
10. They had sailed.

Exercise 19.

1. She has wandered.
2. They will have fought.
3. We have wandered.
4. He has sailed.
5. You will have hastened.
6. You had sailed.
7. They have wandered.
8. He will have hastened.
9. They had wandered.
10. I had sailed.

Exercise 20.

1. mātūrāverimus.
2. mātūrāverāmus.
3. errāveris.
4. nāvigāvit.
5. nāvigāverit.
6. pugnāvī.
7. errāvistī.
8. nāvigāverāmus.
9. pugnāvimus.
10. pugnāverimus.

SECTION 4

See Grammar Notes №. 18,
Nouns of 1st Declension.

NOMINATIVE AND ACCUSATIVE CASES—
AGREEMENT OF VERB WITH ITS SUBJECT

If we take the simplest English sentence with a Transitive
Verb we learn in English Grammar to divide it thus:

	SUBJECT	VERB	OBJECT
e.g.	*The King*	*rules*	*the city.*
	We	*honour*	*him.*

and with regard to these three parts of the sentence we learn
these rules:

1. The Subject is in the Nominative Case.
2. The Object is in the Objective or Accusative Case.
3. The Verb agrees with its Subject in Number and Person.

These rules apply to Latin also;

> e.g. *You love your fatherland.*
>   amātis patriam.
>
>   *Cotta announced a victory.*
>   Cotta victōriam nūntiāvit.

N.B. Remember (Section 1) that if the subject is a Personal
Pronoun it need not be expressed in Latin, as in the first of
the above examples.

Exercise 21.

1. They will love their* native country.
2. They were attacking the Belgians.
3. The Belgians report the victory.
4. Cotta will attack the Belgians.
5. The Belgians had loved their country.
6. We shall attack Cotta.
7. He had reported the victory.
8. The Belgians loved battles.
9. Cotta has attacked the Belgians.
10. He will attack the forces.

country, native country patria, -ae 1. f.
I attack, assail oppugnō 1. **the Belgians** Belgae, -ārum
1. m. pl. **I announce, report** nūntiō 1. **victory** victōria, -ae
1. f. **Cotta** Cotta, -ae 1. m. **battle** pugna, -ae 1. f.
forces, troops cōpiae, -ārum 1. f. pl.

*In this and the following exercises, the possessive adjectives *my, your, their,* etc., need not be expressed in Latin.

Exercise 22.

1. They had reported the victory.
2. Cotta had attacked the Belgians.
3. The Belgians love their country.
4. They are attacking the Belgians.
5. Cotta will report the battle.
6. The Belgians attacked Cotta.
7. You will report the victory.
8. We had reported the victory.
9. The Belgians attacked the forces.
10. Cotta will have reported the victory.

Exercise 23.

1. We shall have reported the victory.
2. You will attack Cotta.
3. Cotta had attacked the forces.
4. I shall announce the victory.
5. The Belgians will have attacked Cotta.
6. Cotta was attacking the Belgians.
7. You will report the battle.
8. Cotta loved his country.
9. He had attacked the Belgians.
10. Cotta had reported the battle.

Exercise 24.

1. Belgās oppugnāverō.
2. Belgae cōpiās oppugnāvērunt.
3. Belgae patriam amābunt.
4. pugnam nūntiāverātis.
5. Cotta victōriam nūntiāverit.
6. Belgae pugnam nūntiābant.
7. mātūrābat Cotta.
8. Cotta Belgās oppugnat.
9. patriam Belgae amant.
10. Belgae Cottam oppugnāverint.

Belgae, -ārum 1. m. pl. Belgians. **oppugnō** 1. I attack, assail. **nūntiō** 1. I announce, report, give information. **Cotta** 1. m. Cotta, an officer in the Roman army. **victōria, -ae** 1. f. victory. **pugna, -ae** 1. f. battle, fight.

Exercise 25.

1. cōpiās parant.
2. ad Asiam nāvigant.
3. diū pugnant.
4. fāmam comparant.
5. Trōiam expugnant.
6. cōpiās parābunt.
7. ad Asiam nāvigābunt.
8. diū pugnābunt.
9. fāmam comparābunt.
10. Trōiam expugnābunt.

cōpiae 1. f. pl. troops, forces. **parō** 1. I prepare. **ad** (+acc.) to, towards. **Asia** 1. f. the Roman province of Asia, now part of Turkey. **nāvigō** 1. I sail. **diū** for a long time. **fāma** 1. f. fame, glory. **comparō** 1. I gain, win. **Trōia** 1. f. Troy. **expugnō** 1. I take by storm.

Exercise 26.

1. lātē per Graeciam errat.
2. inter incolās fāmam comparat.
3. cōpiās parābit.
4. ad Asiam nāvigābit.
5. incolās oppugnābit.
6. tandem incolās superābit.
7. Trōiam expugnābit.
8. fāmam comparābit.
9. hodiē regnat.
10. diū regnābit.

lātē far and wide. **per** (+acc.) through. **Graecia** 1. f. Greece. **errō** 1. I wander. **inter** (+acc.) among. **tandem** at last. **incola** 1. c. inhabitant. **superō** 1. I overcome, defeat. **hodiē** today. **regnō** 1. I reign.

SECTION 5

See Grammar Notes №. 18,
Nouns of 1st Declension.

VOCATIVE, GENITIVE, DATIVE, ABLATIVE CASES

A Latin noun has six Cases, i.e. six forms of the word to be used according to the part the word takes in the sentence.
We have already seen (Section 4) that

1. The NOMINATIVE form is used when the word is the Subject of the Verb.
2. The ACCUSATIVE form is used when the word is the Object of the Verb.

In the next set of exercises, the other cases must be practised according to the following rules:

3. The VOCATIVE form is to be used when we address a person directly;

   e.g. *Labienus, you will fight.*
   Labiēne, pugnābis.

4. The GENITIVE form is to be used to express the Possessor, like the English *Possessive Case;*

   e.g. *They were attacking* { *the Belgians' forces.*
   the forces of the Belgians.
   Belgārum cōpiās oppugnābant.

5. The DATIVE form is to be used to express what we call the Indirect Object.
   This is best understood by thinking of some English sentences; e.g. *We gave the beggar money.* The Verb in this sentence appears to govern two objects. But what we gave was *money,* and this word is the real object of

the Verb (to be expressed by the Accusative Case). The word *beggar* explains to whom we gave money, and this is called the Indirect Object of the Verb. So in the sentence *Tell the king the news,* the word *news* is the real Object, the word *king* is the Indirect Object.

In English we have only one form for the Objective Case, and therefore we most often use a Preposition to express the Indirect Object; e.g. We gave money *to the beggar,* Tell the news *to the king.*

But in Latin there is a separate case, the Dative, to express the Indirect Object;

e.g. *They report a victory to the Belgians.*
    victōriam Belgīs nūntiant.

6. The ABLATIVE form is to be used to express the instrument by which or with which we do something. In English we can only express this by Prepositions.

e.g. *They wounded the Belgians with arrows.*
    Belgās sagittīs vulnerāvērunt.

Exercise 27.

1. We love our native country.
2. They are attacking the forces of the Belgians.
3. We reported the victory.
4. Cotta will wound the Belgians.
5. The Belgians love their country.
6. They wounded the Belgians with their arrows.
7. We had reported the victory of Cotta.
8. Cotta attacked the forces of the Belgians.
9. The Belgians reported the victory.
10. The Belgians had attacked the forces of Cotta.

I wound vulnerō 1. **arrow** sagitta, -ae 1. f.

Exercise 28.

1. They reported the victory of the Belgians.
2. He assailed the Belgians with arrows.
3. Cotta will save his country by his wisdom.
4. They will wound the Belgians with arrows.
5. They have attacked the forces of Cotta.
6. We shall report the battle to the Belgians.
7. They had attacked the forces of the Belgians with arrows.
8. He had reported the battle to the Belgians.
9. We attacked the forces of the Belgians.
10. He reported the victories of Cotta.

I save, preserve servō 1. **wisdom** sapientia, -ae 1. f.

Exercise 29.

1. We reported the victory to the Belgians.
2. They attacked the forces of the Belgians with arrows.
3. They will report the victory to Cotta.
4. He will announce the victory of the Belgians.
5. Cotta has saved his country by his wisdom.
6. They will attack the forces of the Belgians.
7. They will save their country by their wisdom.
8. They will announce the victory to the Belgians.
9. The Belgians saved their country by wisdom.
10. We were attacking the forces of the Belgians.

Exercise 30.

1. Belgārum cōpiās oppugnābis.
2. Belgae victōriam amābant.
3. Belgārum cōpiās oppugnāverāmus.
4. Belgae Cottam sagittā vulnerāvērunt.
5. Belgārum cōpiās oppugnāverat.
6. Belgās sagittīs vulnerāverant.
7. Belgārum victōriam nūntiābit.
8. victōriam Belgīs nūntiāvit.
9. Belgae patriam sapientiā servāvērunt.
10. victōriam Belgīs nūntiābimus.

sapientia 1. f. wisdom. **servō** 1. I preserve, save.

Exercise 31.

1. ōlim in Graeciā regnābat.
2. inter incolās fāmam comparāvit.
3. cōpiās parāvit.
4. ad Asiam nāvigāvit.
5. inter incolās Asiae fāmam comparāvit.
6. Trōiam oppugnāvit.
7. tandem Trōiam superāvit.
8. posteā ad Graeciam nāvigāvit.
9. hodiē inter incolās Graeciae regnat.
10. semper in Graeciā fāma dūrābit.

ōlim once upon a time, formerly, once. **in** (+abl.) in.
posteā afterwards. **semper** always, forever. **dūrō** 1. I
remain, last.

Exercise 32.

1. ōlim in Asiā pugnābam.
2. saepe Trōiam oppugnābant.
3. tandem Trōiam expugnāvērunt.
4. lātē per Asiam errābam.
5. ad Ītaliam nāvigāvī.
6. inter incolās Ītaliae fāmam comparāvī.
7. diū in Ītaliā pugnābam.
8. tandem incolās Ītaliae superāvī.
9. semper fāma in Ītaliā dūrābit.
10. Aenēadae Albam Longam aedificābunt.

saepe often. **Ītalia** 1. f. Italy. **Aenēadae** 1. m. pl. the
descendants of Aeneas. **aedificō** 1. I build.

Exercise 33.

1. in Asiā saepe pugnāverās.
2. advenae Trōiam saepe oppugnāverant.
3. semper cum advenīs pugnāverās.
4. advenās prope superāvistī.
5. tandem Trōiam expugnāvērunt.
6. diū inter incolās Asiae errābās.
7. tandem ad Ītaliam nāvigāvistī.
8. ibi fāmam inter incolās comparāvistī.
9. Aenēadae Rōmam aedificāverint.
10. semper Rōmae fāma dūrābit.

advena 1. c. stranger. **cum** (+abl.) with. **prope** (adv.)
almost. **ibi** there. **Rōma** 1. f. Rome.

Exercise 34.

1. diū inter incolās Graeciae regnābam.
2. cōpiās parāvī et in Asiam nāvigāvī.
3. ibi diū prope Trōiam pugnāvimus.
4. fāmam in Asiā comparāvimus.
5. saepe Trōiam oppugnāverāmus.
6. saepe incolās Asiae prope superāverāmus.
7. tandem Trōiam expugnāvimus.
8. diū in Asiā fāma dūrābit.
9. semper in Graeciā fāma dūrāverit.
10. lātē per Ītaliam fāmam comparāverimus.

et and. **in** (+acc.) into, against. **prope** (+acc.) near.
prope (adv.) almost.

Exercise 35.

1. in Asiā ōlim habitāverat.
2. patriam semper amābat.
3. advenae Trōiam expugnāvērunt.
4. procul ā patriā errābat.
5. tandem in Ītaliam cum advenīs nāvigāvit.
6. contrā incolās pugnāvit.
7. fāmam ibi comparāvērunt.
8. fāma semper inter incolās Graeciae et Ītaliae dūrābit.
9. hodiē patriam amāmus.
10. semper patriam amābimus.

habitō 1. I dwell. **patria** 1. f. fatherland, native land, own country. **procul** far. **ā, ab** (+abl.) from. **contrā** (+acc.) against.

Exercise 36.

1. incolae Ītaliae semper patriam amāverant.
2. advenae contrā Ītaliam propter invidiam coniūrāvērunt.
3. incolae Ītaliae advenās sagittīs vulnerāvērunt.
4. ē terrā advenās fugāvērunt.
5. lātē per Graeciam errant.
6. crās ad Asiam nāvigābunt.
7. iterum contrā incolās coniūrābunt.
8. iterum incolae advenās sagittīs oppugnābunt.
9. tandem advenās superābunt.
10. iterum ē terrā advenās fugābunt.

propter (+acc.) on account of, because of. **invidia** 1. f. envy. **coniūrō** 1. I conspire. **sagitta** 1. f. arrow. **vulnerō** 1. I wound. **ē, ex** (+abl.) from, out of. **terra** 1. f. land, country. **fugō** 1. I put to flight, drive. **crās** tomorrow. **iterum** again.

37. The Founding of Rome

ōlim in Graeciā regnābant Agamemnon et Menelāus: cōpiās parābant et ad Asiam nāvigāvērunt.

cum incolīs Asiae diū pugnābant: Trōiam oppugnāvērunt et tandem superāvērunt.

inter incolās Trōiae pugnābat Aenēās: ubi advenae Trōiam expugnāvērunt, Aenēās lātē errābat et tandem ad Ītaliam nāvigāvit. cum incolīs Ītaliae pugnāvit et superāvit.

Aenēadae Albam Longam aedificāvērunt.

posteā Rōmūlus Rōmam prope Albam Longam aedificāvit et ibi regnābat.

incolae Rōmae lātē per Ītaliam fāmam comparābant. cum incolīs Ītaliae pugnābant et saepe superābant.

fāma Rōmae hodiē dūrat et semper dūrābit.

Aenēās (nom.) Aeneas, the Trojan hero. **ubi** when, where.

38. Aeneas Addresses His Followers

patriam ōlim amāvimus, ubi in patriā habitābāmus: hodiē procul ā Phrygiā errāmus. advenae Trōiam expugnāvērunt et nōs ē patriā fugāvērunt: nōs patriam in terrā advenārum explōrāmus, et Trōiam iterum aedificābimus. ad Ītaliam tandem nāvigāvimus. incolae Ītaliae contrā nōs coniūrant et cōpiās parant: crās oppugnābunt. sagittīs nōs vulnerābunt, fortasse prīmō fugābunt; nōn tamen superābunt. sī prīmō nōs fugāverint, nōn vōs ā pugnā revocābō: iterum oppugnābimus, tandem superābimus. ōlim vōs inter incolās Asiae fāmam comparāvistis: sī fāmam amātis, servābitis.

nōs we, us. **explōrō** 1. I seek to find. **fortasse** perhaps. **prīmō** at first. **nōn** not. **tamen** however. **sī** if. **vōs** you. **revocō** 1. I recall, summon back.

SECTION 6

See Grammar Notes №. 19,
Nouns of 2nd Declension in *-us*.

Exercise 39.

1. The barbarians loved their native country.
2. We overcame the Romans.
3. The Romans did not like the Belgians.
4. They wounded Labienus with an arrow.
5. They announced the victory of the Romans.
6. They wounded the barbarians' horses with arrows.
7. The Romans will defeat the barbarians.
8. Labienus attacked the barbarians.
9. Cotta will announce a victory to the Romans.
10. The barbarians have wounded Labienus with an arrow.

barbarian barbarus, -ī 2. m. **I overcome, defeat** superō 1.
Roman *noun* Rōmānus, -ī 2. m. **not** nōn. **I like** amō 1.
Labienus Labiēnus, -ī 2. m. **horse** equus, -ī 2. m.

Exercise 40.

1. The Romans will have defeated the barbarians.
2. Our men attacked the forces of the Belgians.
3. Our men overcame the barbarians.
4. Labienus saved his country.
5. Our men were wounding the barbarians with arrows.
6. The Romans and Belgians will fight.
7. He will defeat the Romans.
8. Labienus, you do not love your country.
9. We had saved our country by our wisdom.
10. The Belgians will attack the Romans.

our men nostrī, -ōrum 2. m. pl. **and** et.

Exercise 41.

1. Our men had wounded the Belgians with arrows.
2. Labienus, you will not defeat the Belgians.
3. Our men are wounding the barbarians' horses.
4. Our men will overcome the Belgians.
5. The barbarians assailed our men with arrows.
6. Our men will attack the forces of the barbarians.
7. The Romans had assailed the Belgians with arrows.
8. You had announced the victory of our men.
9. We attacked the forces of the barbarians.
10. The barbarians attacked the forces of the Belgians.

Exercise 42.

1. barbarī patriam amant.
2. barbarī Marcum nōn amant.
3. Labiēnum sagittā vulnerāverant.
4. Labiēnus barbarōs nōn amat.
5. Rōmānī Labiēnum amāvērunt.
6. Rōmānī et barbarī pugnābunt.
7. Rōmānī barbarōs superāverint.
8. barbarōrum equōs sagittīs vulnerant.
9. Rōmānī barbarōs superant.
10. Rōmānōrum victōriam nūntiābunt.

barbarus 2. m. barbarian, foreigner. **Labiēnus** 2. m.
Labienus, a Roman legate. **Rōmānus** 2. m. a Roman. **equus**
2. m. horse.

43. The Seven Kings of Rome

regnābant inter Rōmānōs Rōmulus, Nūma Pompilius, Tullus Hostilius, Ancus Marcius, Tarquinius Priscus, Servius Tullius, Tarquinius Superbus.

Rōmulus et Rēmus geminī erant.

Rōmulus mūrum aedificat.

Rēmus propter invidiam trāns mūrum saltat.

Rōmulus Rēmum necat et inter Rōmānōs regnat.

post Rōmulum Nūma regnāvit.

Rōmulus propter mīlitiam, Nūma propter sapientiam fāmam comparāvit.

Tullus Hostilius saepe contrā finitimōs pugnāvit.

Albānōs superat et Albam Longam expugnat: posteā cum Albānīs amīcitiam confirmat.

Ancus Marcius cum Latīnīs prīmō pugnābat, posteā amīcitiam confirmāvit.

Tarquinius Priscus Circum, Servius Tullius mūrum aedificāvit.

tandem Tarquinius Superbus inter Rōmānōs regnāvit: post Tarquinium Superbum nēmō regnāvit.

geminus 2. m. twin-brother. **erant** were, there were. **mūrus** 2. m. wall. **trāns** (+acc.), over, across. **saltō** 1. I jump. **necō** 1. I kill. **post** (+acc.), after. **mīlitia** 1. f. warfare. **finitimus** 2. m. neighbour. **amīcitia** 1. f. friendship. **confirmō** 1. I establish, strengthen. **circus** 2. m. circus, racecourse (here, the Circus Maximus at Rome, where chariot races were held). **nēmō** (acc. **nēminem**) no one.

44. The Greatness of Rome

Rōmānī in Ītaliā habitābant; patriam amābant et saepe contrā
fīnitimōs pugnābant.

nōn sōlum fīnitimōrum sed etiam barbarōrum cōpiās
oppugnābant.

lātē per Ītaliam colōniās collocābant: in Galliā victōriam
saepe reportābant: Graecōs superāvērunt, etiam ad Asiam
nāvigāvērunt.

nōn sōlum propter victōriās sed etiam propter sapientiam
fāmam comparābant: ad philosophiam et litterās animōs
applicābant.

cum fīnitimīs, ubi superāverant, amīcitiam confirmābant:
barbarōs ad disciplīnam informābant.

nōs procul ab Ītaliā habitāmus: fāma tamen Rōmānōrum
etiam hodiē inter nōs dūrat et semper dūrābit.

sōlum (adv.) only. **sed** but. **etiam** also, even. **colōnia** 1. f.
colony. **collocō** 1. I place. **colōniam collocō** I plant a
colony. **Gallia** 1. f. Gaul. **reportō** 1. I carry back. **victōriam
reportō** I win a victory. **Graecus** 2. m. a Greek.
philosophia 1. f. philosophy. **litterae** 1. f. pl. literature,
writing. **animus** 2. m. mind. **applicō** 1. I apply. **disciplīna** 1.
f. discipline. **informō** 1. I train.

45. Our Country's Greatness

patriam nostram amāmus: patriae fāma diū dūrābit. saepe
cum fīnitimīs, saepe cum advenīs pugnāvimus; semper tandem
superāvimus; ubi superāvimus, amīcitiam et cum advenīs et
cum fīnitimīs confirmāmus. victōriās procul ā patriā repor-
tāvimus; barbarōs ad disciplīnam informāvimus, colōniās et
in Asiā et in Āfricā collocāvimus. fāmam tamen nōn sōlum
propter victōriās comparāvimus: ad philosophiam et litterās
animōs applicāmus. sī iūstitiam amābimus, sī iūstē regnābimus,
nēmō nōs propter invidiam oppugnābit.

noster, -tra, -trum our, ours. **et … et** both … and. **Āfrica** 1.
f. Africa. **iūstitia, -ae** 1. f. justice, fairness. **iūstē** justly.

SECTION 7

See Grammar Notes №. 19,
Nouns of 2nd Declension in *-um*.

Exercise 46.

1. The barbarians were preparing war.
2. Our men overcame the barbarians.
3. They assailed the forces of the barbarians with weapons.
4. They saved the town by their plan.
5. The weapons were wounding the Romans' horses.
6. The stratagem of the Romans saved the towns.
7. Labienus, you avoided the dangers of the war.
8. The barbarians assailed the towns.
9. Cotta saved the towns by a stratagem.
10. Labienus, you will not avoid the danger.

I prepare parō 1. **war** bellum, -ī 2. n. **town** oppidum, -ī 2. n. **weapon** tēlum, -ī 2. n. **plan, stratagem, advice, device** cōnsilium, -ī 2. n. **I avoid** vītō 1. **danger, risk** perīculum, -ī 2. n.

Exercise 47.

1. The Belgians attacked Cotta's camp.
2. The weapons of our men are wounding the Belgians' horses.
3. The Romans will overcome the Belgians.
4. The barbarians defeated our men by a stratagem.
5. Our men are assailing the camp of the barbarians.
6. The forces of the Romans will save the town.
7. You will not overcome the Belgians.
8. Our men assailed the Belgians with their weapons.
9. We shall not overcome the Romans by stratagem.
10. The Romans loved wars and battles.

camp castra, -ōrum 2. n. pl.

Exercise 48.

1. Our men had assailed the towns of the barbarians.
2. Our men will attack the camp of the Belgians.
3. We shall attack the camp of the Romans.
4. Labienus had avoided the dangers of war.
5. The Belgians are assailing the camp with arrows.
6. The barbarians assailed the towns of the Romans.
7. We announced to the Romans the victories of the barbarians.
8. The victory of our men saved the camp.
9. Romans, you will prepare war.
10. By your wisdom you avoided the dangers of war.

Exercise 49.

1. barbarī perīculum vītābunt.
2. Rōmānōs tēlīs vulnerābunt.
3. barbarōs cōnsiliō superāvimus.
4. Rōmānī bellum parābant.
5. equum tēlō vulnerāvistī.
6. oppidum Labiēnus oppugnāvit.
7. castra cōnsiliō servāvit.
8. Rōmānī cōnsiliō barbarōs superābunt.
9. castra barbarī oppugnāvērunt.
10. bellum parābant barbarī.

perīculum 2. n. danger, risk. **vītō** 1. I avoid. **tēlum** 2. n. weapon. **cōnsilium** 2. n. plan, stratagem, advice. **bellum** 2. n. war. **oppidum** 2. n. town. **castra** 2. n. pl. camp.

50. The Expulsion of the Tyrant

Tarquinius Superbus templum in Capitōliō aedificāvit et colōniās in Ītaliā collocābat.

bellum contrā fīnitimōs parāvit: Volscōs saepe superābat et oppida expugnābat.

sed Rōmānī nec Tarquinium nec fīlium Tarquiniī Sextum amāvērunt.

itaque populus contrā tyrannōs coniūrāvit.

Tarquinium et filiōs in Etrūriam, ubi ōlim habitāverant, fugāvērunt.

nēmō post Tarquiniōs inter Rōmānōs regnāvit.

imperium administrābant Brūtus et Valērius.

Brūtus filiōs necāvit quod prō Tarquiniō contrā populum coniūrāverant.

Valērium Rōmānī "Poplicolam" vocāvērunt quod populō amīcus erat.

diū inter Rōmānōs dūrābat Brūtī et Tarquiniī fāma.

templum 2. n. temple. **Capitōlium** 2. n. the Capitol (the citadel of Rome). **Volscī** 2. m. pl. the Volsci, an ancient Italic people. **neque (nec)** nor, and not. **neque (nec) … neque (nec)** neither … nor. **filius** 2. m. son. **itaque** therefore. **populus** 2. m. the people. **tyrannus** 2. m. tyrant. **imperium** 2. n. supreme power, rule. **administrō** 1. I administer. **quod** because. **prō** (+abl.) for, on behalf of, instead of. **vocō** 1. I call. **amīcus** 2. m. friend. **erat** was, there was.

51. Greek Tyrants

ōlim in Graeciā tyrannī regnābant. saepe bene regnābant; fāmam propter victōriās et sapientiam comparāvērunt: cum finitimīs amīcitiam confirmābant: mūrōs et templa aedificābant: ad philosophiam et litterās animōs applicābant: contrā barbarōs pugnābant et patriae incolās ā perīculīs servābant. Graecī tamen tyrannōs nōn amābant, quod saepe crūdēliter administrābant imperium. itaque contrā tyrannōs coniūrāvērunt et ex oppidīs fugāvērunt.

nōs Graecōrum exemplum hodiē laudāmus: nēmō hodiē tyrannōs amat. etiam sī bene regnant, sī patriam ē perīculō servant, populus nōn libenter vītam et bona tyrannī arbitriō mandat. hodiē ferē ubique imperium administrat populus.

bene well. **crūdēliter** cruelly. **exemplum** 2. n. example. **laudō** 1. I praise. **libenter** willingly. **vīta** 1. f. life. **bona** 2. n. pl. goods, property. **arbitrium** 2. n. authority, decision, will. **mandō** 1. I entrust, commit. **ferē** almost, for the most part. **ubique** everywhere.

SECTION 8

See Grammar Notes №. 19,
Nouns of 2nd Declension in -er.

Exercise 52.

1. The boys loved wars and battles.
2. We laid waste the fields of the barbarians.
3. Our men will lay waste the fields of the Belgians.
4. Boys love horses.
5. The barbarians built towns.
6. The boys saved the town by their device.
7. They wounded the boy's horse with an arrow.
8. The boys were hastening.
9. He wounded the boy with an arrow.
10. I shall attack the camp of the barbarians.

boy puer, -ī 2. m. **I lay waste, ravage** vastō 1. **field** ager, agrī
2. m. **I build** aedificō 1.

Exercise 53.

1. The boys announced the victory of the Belgians.
2. We shall lay waste the field of the Belgians.
3. Boys do not love wisdom.
4. You did not lay waste the fields of the Gauls.
5. The boys avoided the dangers of the war.
6. We are preparing war, Romans.
7. The Gauls wounded the boy's horse with a weapon.
8. The boys will save the town by their device.
9. The weapons of the Gauls were wounding the boys.
10. You have laid waste the fields of the Romans.

Gauls Gallī, -ōrum 2. m. pl.

Exercise 54.

1. He had laid waste the fields of the Gauls.
2. The boys will avoid the danger.
3. The wisdom of the boys saved the town.
4. We attacked the camp of the Gauls.
5. The Gauls saved their camp by a stratagem.
6. Our men will lay waste the fields of the barbarians.
7. The Romans overcame the Gauls by a stratagem.
8. We assailed the Gauls with weapons.
9. The Gauls had built towns.
10. Boys love danger.

Exercise 55.

1. puerum tēlō vulnerāvistī.
2. barbarōrum tēla puerī vītābant.
3. agrōs Gallōrum vastāverātis.
4. puerī equum sagittā vulnerāverat.
5. agrōs Rōmānōrum Gallī vastābant.
6. Gallī bellī perīcula vītābunt.
7. Gallōs, Labiēne, nōn superābis.
8. nostrī oppida Gallōrum oppugnāverant.
9. Labiēnum puerī amābant.
10. puerī patriam amant.

puer 2. m. boy. **ager, agrī** 2. m. field, land, territory; pl. territories. **vastō** 1. I lay waste.

56. The Battle of the Lake Regillus

in Etrūriā habitābant Etruscī: inter Etruscōs Lars Porsena regnābat. ubi Rōmānī Tarquinium in Etrūriam fugāvērunt, Etruscī contrā Rōmānōs prō Tarquiniō coniūrāvērunt et sociōs ad bellum vocābant. cōpiās prope mūrōs Rōmae collocant et agrōs vastant: Rōmānōs trāns fluvium fugant. iam Rōmam prope expugnāverant, sed Horātius Coclēs cum Spuriō Lartiō et Titō Herminiō patriam servāvit.

posteā Tarquinius amīcitiam cum Latīnīs confirmāvit et bellum iterum parāvit. Rōmānī imperium Aulō Postumiō mandāvērunt. prope Regillum Lacum Etruscī cum Rōmānīs diū et ācriter pugnābant. tandem Aulus clāmat, "sī Etruscōs superāverō, templum deīs dēdicābō." tum geminī deī, Castor et Pollux, ex equīs contrā Etruscōs pugnant. Rōmānī victōriam reportant et templum deīs geminīs dēdicant.

Etrūria 1. f. Etruria. **Estruscus** 2. m. an Estruscan, inhabitant of Etruria. **socius** 2. m. ally. **fluvius** 2. m. river. **iam** now, already. **Regillus Lacus** the Lake Regillus. **ācriter** fiercely. **clāmō** 1. I cry out, cry, exclaim. **deus** 2. m. god. **dēdicō** 1. I dedicate. **tum** then. **ex equō, ex equīs** on horseback.

57. Greek Schools

ōlim in Graeciā, sīcut in Britanniā hodiē, puerī ad scholās commeābant. Spartānī vītam omnīnō patriae dēdicābant: itaque in Spartānōrum scholīs magistrī puerōrum animōs nōn sōlum librīs ad sapientiam informābant, sed per disciplīnam, etiam per lūdōs, ad mīlitiam confirmābant.

Athēnārum incolae nōn sōlum propter bella, sed etiam propter sapientiam et litterās, inter Graecōs fāmam comparāvērunt. ad historiam et philosophiam animōs applicābant: sī fīnitimōs bellō superāverant, victōriās litterīs mandābant. itaque in scholīs praecipuē ad litterās magistrī informābant. magistrī saepe servī erant: tamen puerōs verberābant, sī parum dīligenter labōrāverant. contrā puerī magistrōs saepe vexābant: Alcibiadēs ōlim magistrum verberāvit quod inter librōs Homērī scrīpta nōn erant.

sīcut just as. **Britannia** 1. f. Britain. **schola** 1. f. school. **commeō** 1. I go, go to and fro. **Spartānus** 2. m. Spartan. **omnīnō** altogether, wholly. **magister, magistrī** 2. m. master, schoolmaster. **liber, librī** 2. m. book. **lūdus** 2. m. game. **Athēnae** 1. f. pl. Athens. **historia** 1. f. history. **praecipuē** especially. **servus** 2. m. slave. **verberō** 1. I thrash. **parum** insufficiently, not enough. **dīligenter** diligently. **contrā** (adv.) on the other hand, in reply. **vexō** 1. I annoy, harass. **Homērus** 2. m. Homer, the first and greatest of the Greek epic poets. **scrīpta** 2. n. pl. writings.

58. The Roman Invasion of Britain

Rōmānī cum Gallīs saepe pugnāverant, sed ad Britanniam nōn nāvigāverant; Gallī tamen ā Galliā ad Britanniam commeāb-ant. tandem Iūlius Caesar, quod Britannī amīcī et sociī erant Gallōrum et in bellō saepe adiuvābant, ad Britanniam nāvig-āvit et incolās oppugnāvit, nōn tamen superāvit. posteā iterum ad insulam nāvigāvit; Rōmānī agrōs et oppida vastābant, cum Cassivellaunō prope Tamesim fluvium ācriter pugnāvērunt; victōriam reportāvērunt et ad Galliam nāvigāvērunt.

Caesar bella et victōriās litterīs mandāvit: hodiē in scho-līs per librōs Caesaris magistrī puerōrum animōs informant.

Iūlius, -iī 2. m. The nomen (family name) of Gaius Julius Caesar. **Caesar, -is** 3. m. The cognomen (family branch) of Gaius Julius Caesar. **adiuvō, adiūvī, adiūtum** 1. I help. **per** by means of.

SECTION 9

Present, Future, Imperfect, and Perfect
Indicative Active of *moneō* (Grammar Notes №. 83).
Adjectives in *-us* (Grammar Notes №. 43)

THE AGREEMENT OF
ADJECTIVES WITH NOUNS

English Adjectives have no terminations to mark the Gender or Number of Case. Hence we do not need to make them "agree" with the Noun to which they belong. In Latin the Adjective is declined as well as the noun.

An Adjective agrees with its Noun in Gender, Number, and Case.

e.g.	*A good field*	*A small arrow*	*A large town*
NOM. SING.	bonus ager	parva sagitta	magnum oppidum
GEN. SING.	bonī agrī	parvae sagittae	magnī oppidī
ACC. PLU.	bonōs agrōs	parvās sagittās	magna oppida

N.B. An Adjective can sometimes be used without a Noun. This is especially the case with the Masculine, when the word *man* or *men* is understood.

e.g.   *A good man loves a good man.*
bonus bonum amat.

Good men (or *the good*) *love good men.*
bonī bonōs amant.

Exercise 59.

1. Our men feared the great forces of the Gauls.
2. The Romans had small weapons.
3. The Gauls built small towns.
4. We overcame the great forces of the barbarians.
5. The Gauls had good horses.

6. By their great wisdom they avoided the dangers of war.
7. The arrows frightened the little boys.
8. We were attacking the great forces of the Belgians.
9. They reported a great victory.
10. The barbarians will not fear our men.

I fear timeō 2. **great, large** magnus, -a, -um. **I have** habeō 2. **small, little** parvus, -a, -um. **good** bonus, -a, -um. **I frighten, terrify** terreō 2.

Exercise 60.

1. We shall not have large forces.
2. You feared the small forces of the barbarians.
3. Good men do not fear danger.
4. The Belgians had small arrows.
5. The barbarians feared the small forces of the Romans.
6. Small dangers will not frighten the Gauls.
7. You have great wisdom.
8. He fears the great dangers of war.
9. The Belgians had good horses.
10. Small forces of Romans attacked the Gauls' camp.

good men bonī, -ōrum 2. m. pl.

Exercise 61.

1. Our men's great victory saved the town.
2. Cotta fears the large forces of the Belgians.
3. The barbarians had good fields.
4. He wounded the little boy with a large arrow.
5. Great dangers do not frighten good men.
6. You will not fear the great forces of the Gauls.
7. The barbarians have small horses.
8. Our men were frightening the Gauls with their large weapons.
9. They were wounding our men with small arrows.
10. We shall attack the great forces of the barbarians.

Exercise 62.

1. puerōs parvōs magna perīcula terrent.
2. magna perīcula puerī timent.
3. nōn magnam sapientiam Belgae habēbant.
4. puerī bonōs equōs amant.
5. magna bellī perīcula, Labiēne, vītāveris.
6. bonī pugnās nōn amant.
7. puerī parvī errābant.
8. nostrī magnās sagittās nōn habuērunt.
9. bellī perīcula timeō.
10. parva oppida Gallī habēbant.

parvus, -a, -um small. **magnus, -a, -um** great. **terreō** 2.
I frighten. **timeō** 2. I fear, am afraid of. **habeō** 2. I have,
hold. **bonus, -a, -um** good. **bonī** 2. m. pl. "good men". **nostrī**
2. m. pl. our men.

63. Mucius Scaevola

ubi Etruscī castra prope Rōmam collocāvērunt, C. Mūcius
cum multīs amīcīs contrā Porsenam coniūrāvit. "castra Etruscōrum," clāmat, "intrābō: tyrannum necābō." castra intrat, sed,
quoniam Porsenam ignōrābat, scrībam tyrannī prō tyrannō
necāvit. ubi fugam temptāvit, ministrī Mūcium reportāvērunt.
Porsena Mūcium magnā īrā multīs cum minīs dē cōnsiliō
interrogāvit. Mūcium nec īra nec minae terruērunt: nihil
dē amīcīs nūntiāvit. "sī dē amīcīs tacēbis," clāmat tyrannus,
"flammīs circumdābō." in ārā prope Porsenam flamma ardēbat:
Mūcius dextram in flammā diū tenēbat. "nec minās," respondet,
"nec supplicium timet Rōmānus." placuit tyrannō respōnsum.
"puerum tam intrepidum," clāmat, "nōn necābō, sed līberābō."
tum Mūcius, "minīs," clāmāvit, "animum nōn terruistī, beneficiō superāvistī. anteā nihil dē cōnsiliō nūntiāvī: iam nūntiābō.
cum multīs amīcīs coniūrāvī: sī Mūcium necābis, Mūciī amīcī
singulī tyrannum oppugnābunt, tandem necābunt." movet

Porsenam puerī Rōmānī audācia: statim līberat. Mūcium posteā amīcī "Scaevolam" vocābant.

multus, -a, -um much, many. **intrō** 1. I enter. **quoniam** since. **ignōrō** 1. I do not know. **scrība** 1. m. secretary. **fuga** 1. f. flight. **temptō** 1. I attempt, test. **minister, ministrī** 2. m. attendant. **īra** 1. f. anger. **minae** 1. f. pl. threats. **dē** (+abl.) concerning. **interrogō** 1. I ask. **nihil** nothing. **taceō** 2. I am silent, say nothing. **flamma** 1. f. flame. **circumdō** 1. I surround. **āra** 1. f. altar. **ardeō, ārsī, arsum** 2. I burn, (intransitive). **dextra** 1. f. right hand. **teneō, tenuī, tentum** 2. I hold, keep. **respondeō** 2. I answer. **supplicium** 2. n. punishment. **placeō** 2. I please (+dat.). **responsum** 2. n. the answer. **tam** so. **intrepidus, -a, -um** fearless. **līberō** 1. I set free. **beneficium** 2. n. kindness. **anteā** before. **singulī, -ae, -a** one by one, singly. **moveō, mōvī, mōtum** 2. I move, provoke, rouse. **Rōmānus, -a, -um** Roman. **audācia** 1. f. boldness. **statim** at once.

64. Hercules and Cacus

erat ōlim in Ītaliā monstrum horrendum Cācus: oculōs saevōs habēbat, flammās spīrābat: in spēluncā habitābat: per agrōs saepe errābat et fīnitimōs crūdēliter vexābat. incolae diū timēbant Cācum, nēmō tamen necāvit, nēmō etiam oppugnāverat. tandem Hercūlēs deus ad Ītaliam commeāvit: multōs taurōs habēbat. Cācus aliquot taurōs in spēluncam caudīs tractāvit; itaque, ubi Hercūlēs locum investīgāvit, vestīgia taurōrum latebrās nōn indicāvērunt. tum in spēluncā ūnus ē taurīs clāmāvit: statim Hercūlēs ad locum properāvit; īra animum movēbat. tum prīmum Cācus timēbat: frūstrā fugam temptāvit, frūstrā in spēluncā flammās spīrābat. Hercūlēs multīs tēlīs oppugnat, tandem superat et necat. itaque et taurōs reportāvit et incolās perīculō līberāvit.

monstrum 2. n. monster. **horrendus, -a, -um** horrible. **oculus** 2. m. eye. **saevus, -a, -um** fierce. **spīrō** 1. I breathe. **spēlunca** 1. f. cave. **taurus** 2. m. bull. **aliquot** some. **cauda** 1. f. tail. **tractō** 1. I drag. **locus** 2. m. place. **investīgō** 1. I search out. **vestīgium** 2. n. footprint. **latebrae** 1. f. pl. hiding-place. **indicō** 1. I show, reveal. **ūnus, -a, -um** one. **properō** 1. I hasten. **prīmum** for the first time. **frūstrā** in vain.

SECTION 10

Future Perfect and Pluperfect
Indicative Active of *moneō* (Grammar Notes №. 83).
Adjectives in *-er* (Grammar Notes №. 43).

───────────────

Exercise 65.

1. The wretched boys were working.
2. The Gauls have beautiful towns.
3. We had frightened the barbarians with our darts.
4. The barbarians had feared the dangers of war.
5. The Belgians had small shields.
6. You frightened the wretched prisoners.
7. He had frightened the wretched barbarians.
8. Unhappy men do not fear the dangers of war.
9. You have not frightened our men.
10. We shall not have feared the great forces of the Gauls.

wretched, unhappy miser, -era, -erum. **beautiful, splendid** pulcher, -chra, -chrum. **dart** iaculum, -ī 2. n. **shield** scūtum, -ī 2. n. **prisoner, captive** captīvus, -ī 2. m.

Exercise 66.

1. The Gauls had frightened the wretched prisoners.
2. Our men laid waste the beautiful towns of the Belgians.
3. By his plan he saved the wretched prisoners.
4. You will frighten the little boys.
5. The Gauls' weapons were wounding the wretched prisoners.
6. The barbarians have large shields.
7. Wars and dangers do not frighten good men.
8. We had frightened the great forces of the Gauls.
9. The wretched men did not avoid the barbarians' arrows.
10. By your plan you will save our men.

Exercise 67.

1. The wretched prisoners had not weapons.
2. The arrows of the Gauls will not have frightened our men.
3. By his great wisdom he will overcome a great danger.
4. The Gauls had good fields and beautiful towns.
5. The wretched prisoners have not shields.
6. He had frightened the wretched captive.
7. He announced to the unhappy man the victory of the Romans.
8. The wretched prisoner had not a horse.
9. The great victory of the Gauls had frightened our men.
10. We shall lay waste the Gauls' beautiful towns.

Exercise 68.

1. miserōs captīvōs terruērunt.
2. magna perīcula nōn timuerit.
3. puerōs miserōs barbarī terrent.
4. miserōrum Gallōrum agrōs vastābat.
5. nostrī barbarōs terruerant.
6. Gallī pulchra oppida habēbant.
7. nostrī scūta magna habēbant.
8. Belgae nostrōs sagittīs terruerant.
9. equī Gallōrum tēla timēbant.
10. miserī puerī labōrant.

miser, -era, -erum wretched, unhappy. **captīvus** 2. m. captive, prisoner. **Gallus** 2. m. a Gaul. **pulcher, -chra, -chrum** beautiful. **scūtum** 2. n. shield.

69. Patricians and Plebeians

nōn iam inter Rōmānōs, ubi Tarquinium fugāvērunt, regnābant tyrannī: nōndum tamen omnīnō līber erat populus. Rōmānōrum aliī patriciī, aliī plēbēiī erant: patriciī prīmī in oppidō
domicilium habuerant: plēbēiōrum multī propter mercātūram
eō commeāverant, multī ibi ex aliīs oppidīs exsulābant. patriciī
sōlī imperium administrābant: plēbēiī miserī prō patriciīs contrā
finitimōs populōs pugnābant, saepe superābant, victōriae tamen
ēmolumenta habēbant nūlla. ardēbant īrā animī plēbēiōrum
nec iam dē iniūriīs tacēbant. tandem turba miserōrum forum
intrāvit. "satis diū, patriciī," clāmāvērunt, "iniūriās sustinuimus:
nōs prō patriā pugnāmus, vōs patriae imperium administrātis,
vōs victōriae ēmolumenta habētis. sīcut servī, tyrannōrum arbitriō pārēmus: nōn iterum prō tyrannīs pugnābimus." movērunt
animōs patriciōrum nōn sōlum minae plēbēiōrum sed etiam
bellī perīculum, quoniam Volscī, finitimī Rōmānōrum, iam
mūrōs prope oppugnābant. "sī iam prō patriā contrā Volscōs
pugnābitis," clāmant, "nōn iterum tot iniūriās sustinēbitis." placuit plēbēiīs patriciōrum respōnsum. libenter contrā Volscōs
pugnāvērunt et ubique superāvērunt.

nōn iam no longer. **nōndum** not yet. **līber, -era, -erum** free.
alius, -a, -ud other; **aliī … aliī** some … others. **patricius, -a,
-um** patrician. **plēbēius, -a, -um** plebeian. **prīmus, -a, -um**
first. **domicilium** 2. n. home, dwelling. **mercātūra** 1. f. trade.
eō (adv.) to there. **exsulō** 1. I am an exile, I am in exile. **sōlus,
-a, -um** only, alone. **finitimus, -a, -um** neighbouring.
ēmolumentum 2. n. advantage. **nūllus, -a, -um** none, no.
iniūria 1. f. wrong, injury. **turba** 1. f. crowd. **forum** 2. n.
forum, market-place. **satis** enough, sufficiently. **sustineō** 2. I
endure. **pāreō** 2. (+dat.), I obey. **tot** (indecl.) so many.

70. The Minotaur

nōn procul ā Graeciā parva est insula Crēta: ōlim Crētae incolae magnam potentiam habēbant et magnam ubique fāmam
comparāvērunt: Mīnos tyrannus nōn sōlum in Crētā multā
sapientiā regnābat sed etiam per finitimās insulās imperium

administrābat: ā multīs tribūtum postulābat: pīrātae Crētae tyrannum timēbant nec iam inter insulās nāvigābant et agrōs vastābant. in labyrinthō monstrum horrendum Mīnōtaurum tenēbat. ab incolīs Athēnārum Mīnos quotannīs postulābat septem puerōs et septem puellās: quotannīs Mīnōtaurus septem puerōs et septem puellās vorābat. Graecī semper timuerant Crētae tyrannum, nēmō tamen oppugnāverat, nēmō contrā Crētam bellum parāverat. tandem Thēseus ad insulam nāvigāvit: virum intrepidum nec bellī perīcula nec fāma monstrī terruerat. tyrannum bellō superat: Mīnotaurum in latebrīs investīgat, tandem necat. itaque magnam fāmam comparāvit et patriam perīculō et exitiō līberāvit.

est is, there is. **insula** 1. f. island. **Crēta** 1. f. Crete. **potentia** 1. f. power. **tribūtum** 2. n. tribute. **postulō** 1. I demand. **pīrāta** 1. m. pirate. **labyrinthus** 2. m. labyrinth. **quotannīs** every year. **septem** seven. **puella** 1. f. girl. **vorō** 1. I devour. **vir** 2. m. man, hero. **exitium** 2. n. ruin, destruction.

71. St George and the Dragon

ōlim monstrum horrendum in Libyā prope Silenam oppidum habitābat et incolās terrae terrēbat; frūstrā tēlīs oppugnābant, semper monstrum incolās fugābat, saepe necābat. itaque filiōs et filiās singulās sortītās ad locum, ubi monstrum habitābat, addūcēbant: monstrum puerōs et puellās vorābat neque iam oppidī incolās vexābat. tandem sortīta erat tyrannī filia.

erat autem in Libyā vir intrepidus, Georgius nōmine. "perīculum nōn timeō," clāmāvit, "puellam līberābō." ubi monstrum appāruit, Georgius ex equō oppugnāvit et gladiō vulnerāvit, posteā necāvit.

sortītus chosen by lot. **addūcō, addūxī, adductum** 3. I bring. **fīlia** 1. f. daughter. **autem** (second word) but, however, now. **nōmine** by the name of, named. **appāreō** 2. I appear. **gladius** 2. m. sword.

SECTION 11

See Grammar Notes №. 84,
Present, Future, Imperfect, and Perfect
Indicative Active of *regō*.

Exercise 72.

1. We shall lead large forces of the Romans against the barbarians.
2. He neglected the good advice of Cotta.
3. The barbarians had not many arrows.
4. Cotta led large forces of Romans against the Belgians.
5. We rule the land of the barbarians.
6. You will rule your native country.
7. They wounded many Belgians with their arrows.
8. You will not neglect good advice.
9. We shall not fear the barbarians' arms.
10. We shall lead the Roman forces into the camp.

I lead, bring dūcō, dūxī, ductum 3. **against** contrā (+acc.).
I neglect neglegō, neglēxī, neglēctum 3. **much, many**
multus, -a, -um. **I rule, guide** regō, rēxī, rēctum 3. **land**
terra, -ae 1. f. **arms** arma, armōrum 2. n. pl. **Roman** *adj.*
Rōmānus, -a, -um. **into** in (+acc.).

Exercise 73.

1. The Belgians will lead their forces into the town.
2. Cotta led his forces into camp.
3. Many men do not fear danger.
4. We led the captives into the town.
5. He will lead his forces against the barbarians.
6. He rules his country with great wisdom.
7. You led the Roman forces against the Belgians.
8. The barbarians are leading their forces into the camp.
9. By his wisdom he avoided the many dangers of war.
10. The boys led the horses into the field.

Exercise 74.

1. They led the Roman captives into the barbarians' camp.
2. By his many victories he has saved his country.
3. We rule many lands by arms.
4. The barbarians' arms frightened the boys.
5. He is leading our men into the fields.
6. They will lead the Roman captives into the camp.
7. He did not neglect the advice of the Romans.
8. We do not fear the stratagems of the Belgians.
9. The Gauls have built many towns.
10. We shall rule the wretched barbarians.

mountain mōns, montis 3. m.

Exercise 75.

1. Labiēnus Rōmānōrum cōpiās dūcēbat.
2. multās et pulchrās terrās regēs.
3. Cottae cōnsilia neglēxit.
4. multa bellī perīcula vītāvit.
5. arma nōn habēbant miserī captīvī.
6. bonōrum cōnsilia nōn neglegit.
7. parvās cōpiās barbarōrum dūcet.
8. puerī parvī arma nōn habent.
9. magna perīcula magnā sapientiā superāvit.
10. multa Gallōrum oppida vastāverat.

dūcō, dūxī, ductum 3. I lead. **regō, rēxī, rēctum** 3. I rule. **neglegō, neglēxī, neglēctum** 3. I neglect. **arma** 2. n. pl. arms.

76. The Secession of the Plebs

quamquam plēbēiī prō patriā pugnāverant et Volscōs superāverant, nōn tamen prōmissa praestābant patriciī. itaque
domicilia relinquunt et Rōmā ad locum fīnitimum discēdunt. "nōn iam," clāmābant, "prō patriā pugnābimus nec agrōs
colēmus, nisi patriciī prōmissa praestābunt." terrēbant patriciōs plēbēiōrum minae: multa in cūriā disserunt: tandem
bona cōnsilia superant: lēgātōs ad plēbēiōs mittunt. ūnus ē
lēgātīs, Menēnius Agrippa, magnam fāmam propter sapientiam
habēbat. nōtam fābulam nārrāvit. tum "nōn iam," clāmāvit,
"patriciī sōlī imperium administrābunt: multa plēbēiīs concēd-
unt. quotannīs tribūnōs creābitis: tribūnī plēbēiōs ab iniūriīs
dēfendent. Agrippa plēbēiīs amīcus est: sī Agrippae cōnsiliō
pārēbitis, iterum iam prō patriā pugnābitis et agrōs colētis: sī
nōn pārēbitis, Volscī et patriciōs et plēbēiōs bellō superābunt."
placuit plēbēiīs Agrippae cōnsilium: ad domicilia revertērunt,
prō patriā pugnābant, agrōs colēbant. quotannīs plēbēiī tribūnōs creābant: tribūnōrum arbitriō etiam patriciī pārēbant.

quamquam although. **prōmissum** 2. n. promise. **praestō,
-itī, -ātum** 1. I keep (a promise), fulfil. **relinquō, relīquī,
relictum** 3. I leave. **discēdō, -cessī, -cessum** 3. I depart.
colō, coluī, cultum 3. I cultivate. **nisi** unless. **cūria** 1. f.
Senate-house. **disserō, disseruī** 3. I discuss. **lēgātus** 2. m.
ambassador, envoy, governor. **mittō, mīsī, missum** 3. I
send. **nōtus, -a, -um** known, well-known. **fābula** 1. f. fable,
story. **nārrō** 1. I narrate. **concēdō, -cessī, -cessum** 3. I
grant, concede. **tribūnus** 2. m. tribune. **creō** 1. I elect,
appoint. **dēfendō, -dī, -sum** 3. I defend. **revertī** (perfect
tense), 3. I returned.

77. The Wooden Horse

Graecī Trōiam obsidēbant: saepe mūrōs oppugnābant, saepe Trōianōrum cōpiās superāverant, nōn tamen oppidum expugnāvērunt. tandem Ulixēs clāmat "armīs oppidum nōn expugnāvimus: cōnsiliō expugnābimus." tum cōnsilium ostendit. Graecī libenter pārēbant. equum ligneum aedificāvērunt. magna turba Trōianōrum ex oppidō excēdit. ūnus ē Graecīs in silvā prope equum latēbat. Trōianī ē latebrīs trāxērunt et multa interrogābant. multa et falsa respondet. "Graecī ad ōram discēdunt: mox ad patriam nāvigābunt: equum Minervae dēdicāvērunt. vōs sī equum in oppidum trahētis, cōpiās in Graeciam dūcētis et Graecōs bellō superābitis." itaque Trōianī equum in oppidum trāxērunt: tōtus populus propter gaudium convīvium celebrāvit. tum repente ex equō excēdunt Graecī: portās oppidī reserant: reliquī Graecī intrant. oppidum incendunt et incolās necant.

obsideō, obsēdī, obsessum 2. I besiege. **Trōianus, -a, -um** Trojan. **Ulixēs** the hero Ulysses, known to the Greeks as Odysseus. **ostendō, -dī, -tum** 3. I show, set forth. **ligneus, -a, -um** wooden. **excēdō, excessī, excessum** 3. I go forth. **silva** 1. f. wood. **lateō** 2. I lie hid. **trahō, trāxī, tractum** 3. I drag. **falsus, -a, -um** false. **ōra** 1. f. shore. **mox** soon, later. **Minerva** 1. f. the goddess Minerva. **tōtus, -a, -um** whole. **gaudium** 2. n. joy. **convīvium** 2. n. feast. **celebrō** 1. I celebrate. **repente** suddenly. **porta** 1. f. gate. **reserō** 1. I unlock. **reliquus, -a, -um** the remaining, the other. **incendō, -dī, -sum** 3. I burn (transitive), set fire to.

SECTION 12

Future Perfect and Pluperfect
Indicative Active of *regō*. (Grammar Notes №. 84).
Nouns (Consonant stems) of 3rd Declension
(Grammar Notes №s. 22–27).

Exercise 78.

1. The general has led his forces into the town.
2. The soldiers are announcing the victory to the general.
3. He had led the wretched captives into the camp.
4. You will have ruled many towns, you will have saved your country.
5. The Gauls had led their forces into camp.
6. The Roman soldiers were wounding the Gauls with their darts.
7. He had neglected the advice of the guide.
8. The Roman soldiers had not good guides.
9. The cavalry attacked the camp with darts and arrows.
10. They had announced to the general the victory of the cavalry.

general imperātor, -ōris 3. m. **soldier** mīles, -itis 3. m. **leader, guide** dux, ducis 3. c. **horseman** eques, -itis 3. m. **cavalry** equitēs 3. m. pl.

Exercise 79.

1. You will have led your soldiers into great danger.
2. They announced to the general the soldiers' victory.
3. We did not neglect the general's advice.
4. They will lead the Roman cavalry against the barbarians.
5. I had led my forces into the Roman camp.
6. The soldier's device saved the town.
7. The victory of the Roman cavalry terrified the Belgians.

8. The barbarians had not good leaders.
9. Good soldiers love a good general.
10. He had led the cavalry against the Belgians.

Exercise 80.

1. The little boys frightened the soldiers' horses.
2. Our men announced the victory to their leaders.
3. The Belgians' weapons were wounding the Roman soldiers.
4. We had led our men into the fields.
5. He announced the general's plan to the Belgians.
6. You will not have neglected the general's advice.
7. They reported the victory to the Roman general.
8. The Roman cavalry had large horses.
9. You had led your soldiers into the fields of the barbarians.
10. Cotta will lead the Roman cavalry into the town.

Exercise 81.

1. cōpiās Rōmānās in castra imperātor dūxerat.
2. mīlitēs Rōmānōs in oppidum dūxerit.
3. Rōmānōrum victōriam imperātōrī nūntiāvērunt.
4. mīlitēs Rōmānī arma parābant.
5. patriam bonīs cōnsiliīs rēxerit.
6. imperātōris victōriam mīlitibus nūntiābimus.
7. equitēs Rōmānī barbarōs superāvērunt.
8. imperātōris cōnsilium nōn neglēxerat.
9. equitēs in castra dūcent.
10. dux cōnsiliō mīlitēs servāvit.

imperātor, -ōris 3. m. general, commander-in-chief. **mīles, -itis** 3. m. soldier. **eques, -itis** 3. m. horseman, knight; pl. cavalry. **dux, ducis** 3. c. leader.

82. Spurius Cassius

Rōmānī, sī finitimōs bellō superāverant, captum agrum pūblicum vocābant et inter patriciōs dīvidēbant; plēbēiī tamen agrum pūblicum habēbant nūllum. tandem Sp. Cassius, populī Rōmānī cōnsul, lēgem plēbēiōrum causā rogāvit. "nōn iam," clāmāvit, "patriciī sōlī pūblicum agrum colēmus: etiam plēbēiī victōriae ēmolumenta habēbunt." ardēbant īrā animī patriciōrum. "contrā populum Rōmānum," clāmābant, "Sp. Cassius coniūrat: regnum appetit: sī agrum pūblicum plēbēiīs concesserit et mūnere eiusmodī auctōritātem cōnfirmāverit, rēx inter Rōmānōs reget." itaque populus lēgem antīquāvit: lēgis lātōrem, quamquam Sabīnōs bellō superāverat, Latīnōs et Hernicōs Rōmānīs foedere adiūnxerat, patriciī falsīs crīminibus accūsāvērunt et iūdicēs damnāvērunt. sīc Sp. Cassius, pauperum amīcus, propter plēbēiōrum suspīciōnem et patriciōrum invidiam, nōn sōlum nōn plēbēiōs ab iniūriā dēfendit sed mortem oppetīvit inhonestam.

captus, -a, -um captured. **pūblicus, -a, -um** public. **dīvidō, dīvīsī, dīvīsum** 3. I divide. **cōnsul, -lis** 3. m. consul. **lēx, lēgis** 3. f. law. **causa** 1. f. cause; **causā** (+gen.) for the sake of. **rogō** 1. I ask; **lēgem rogō** I propose a law. **regnum** 2. n. royal power, kingdom. **appetō, -īvī, -ītum** 3. I aim at. **mūnus, -eris** 3. n. a gift. **eiusmodī** of that kind. **auctōritās, -ātis** 3. f. authority. **rēx, rēgis** 3. m. king. **antīquō** 1. I reject. **lātor, -ōris** 3. m. proposer. **foedus, -eris** 3. n. treaty. **adiungō, -iūnxī, -iūnctum** 3. I join. **crīmen, -inis** 3. n. charge, accusation. **accūsō** 1. I accuse; **falsīs crīminibus accūsō** I accuse on false charges. **iūdex, -icis** 3. c. judge. **damnō** 1. I condemn. **sīc** thus. **pauper, -eris** 3. poor, a poor man. **suspīciō, -ōnis** 3. f. suspicion. **mors, mortis** 3. f. death. **oppetō, -īvī, -ītum** 3. I meet. **inhonestus, -a, -um** shameful.

83. The Wrath of Achilles

ubi Graecī Trōiam obsidēbant, Achillēs magnā virtūte contrā Trōiānōs pugnāvit; agrōs lātē vastābat, multa oppida expugnāvit. Agamemnon rēx Graecārum erat cōpiārum imperātor. magna erat rixa inter rēgem et Achillem. ardēbat īrā animus Achillis propter minās et contumēliās Agamemnōnis: itaque

ad tabernāculum discessit nec iam prō Graecīs pugnābat. tum
ubique Trōianī superāvērunt: magnum erat perīculum Graecōrum. tandem rēx lēgātōs ad Achillem mīsit: mūnera portābant, multa frūstrā prōmīsērunt. Achillis animum nec mūneribus
nec prōmissīs movēbant. Patroclus tamen amīcus arma Achillis
sūmit et contrā Trōianōs pugnāvit. Hector, Priamī rēgis Trōianī
fīlius, Patroclum necāvit. magnus erat dolor, magna īra Achillis,
ubi Graecī mortem Patroclī nūntiāvērunt. iterum arma sūmit,
Trōianōs fugat, Hectōrem necat. tum Hectōris corpus ter cōtīdiē circum tumulum amīcī trāxit. tandem Priamus tabernāculum Achillis intrāvit. multīs cum lacrimīs corpus fīliī petīvit.
mōvērunt Achillem senis lacrimae et corpus Hectōris reddidit.

Achillēs, -is 3. m. the Greek hero Achilles. **virtūs, -ūtis** 3. f.
valour, courage. **rixa** 1. f. quarrel. **contumēlia** 1. f. insult.
tabernāculum 2. n. tent. **portō** 1. I carry. **prōmittō, -mīsī,
-missum** 3. I promise. **sūmō, sūmpsī, sūmptum** 3. I take,
take up. **dolor, -ōris** 3. m. grief. **corpus, -oris** 3. n. body. **ter**
three times, thrice. **cōtīdiē** daily, every day. **circum** (+acc.)
around. **tumulus** 2. m. tomb, mound. **lacrima** 1. f. tear.
petō, -īvī (-iī), -ītum 3. I seek, ask for. **senex, senis** 3. m.
old man. **reddō, -idī, -itum** 3. I give back, restore.

84. An Appeal to the Jury of Behalf of an Innocent Client

senī miserō et pauperī, iūdicēs, inimīcī exitium parant; virum ōlim
in bellō intrepidum falsīs crīminibus accūsant, minīs terrent, cōtīdiē contumēliīs vexant. vōs sī virtūtem amātis, sī lēgēs in honōre
habētis, reum nōn sōlum nōn damnābitis sed etiam suspīciōne
līberābitis: sīc enim bonōrum causam dēfendētis, aliīs iūstitiae
exemplum dabitis. magna est rēgis potentia, magna tamen lēgum
auctōritās; etiam sī rēgis amīcī contrā lēgēs bonum virum propter invidiam accūsāvērunt, nihil vōs ab officiō dēterrēbit nec vir
honestus mortem inhonestam in nostrā patriā oppetet.

inimīcus 2. m. enemy. **honor, -ōris** 3. m. honour; **in honōre
habeō** I hold in honour. **reus** 2. m. defendant. **enim** (second
word in sentence) for. **dō, dare, dedī, datum** 1. I give. **officium**
2. n. duty. **dēterreō** 2. I discourage, deter. **honestus, -a, -um**
respectable, honourable.

SECTION 13

Present, Future, Imperfect, and Perfect
Indicative Active of *audiō* (Grammar Notes №. 85).
Nouns (I stems) of 3rd Declension
(Grammar Notes №s. 28–31).

Exercise 85.

1. The soldiers hear the general's shout.
2. The Belgians fortified their towns with ramparts.
3. We shall hear the cries of the soldiers.
4. We shall attack the enemy's camp.
5. They led large forces of cavalry against the enemy.
6. The general heard the loud cries of the enemy.
7. Labienus fortified his camp with a large rampart.
8. The Belgians are fortifying their towns.
9. Cotta had attacked large forces of the enemy.
10. The shouts of the cavalry terrified the Belgians.

I hear audiō 4. **shout, cry** clāmor, -ōris 3. m. **rampart** agger,
-ris 3. m. **enemy** hostis, -is 3. c.; pl. hostēs, "the enemy." **loud**
magnus, -a, -um. **I fortify** mūniō 4.

Exercise 86.

1. The leaders of the enemy led their forces into camp.
2. We shall fortify the camp with a large rampart.
3. The cavalry hear the loud shouts of the barbarians.
4. Cotta had led his forces against the enemy.
5. The wretched soldiers heard the shouts of the enemy.
6. You will hear the shouts of the Roman citizens.
7. They announced to the Belgians the victory of the
   Roman general.
8. We shall not fear the small forces of the enemy.
9. The enemy had large forces of cavalry.
10. The Roman soldiers will fortify the town with ramparts.

citizen cīvis, cīvis 3. c.

Exercise 87.

1. The weapons of the enemy were wounding our men.
2. They will lead large forces of the enemy against the town.
3. We shall hear the shouts of the wretched captives.
4. The leaders of the cavalry had avoided danger.
5. We are fortifying the town with a large rampart.
6. Cotta led large forces of cavalry against the enemy.
7. The Belgians were fortifying their camp and their towns.
8. Labienus heard the loud shouts of the Gauls.
9. We shall not fear the arms of the enemy.
10. The barbarians are fortifying their towns with ramparts.

Exercise 88.

1. imperātor mīlitum clāmōrēs audīvit.
2. Rōmānī oppidum aggere mūniunt.
3. cīvium magnōs clāmōrēs audiet.
4. Labiēnus equitēs contrā aggerem dūxit.
5. Belgae castra aggeribus mūniēbant.
6. cīvium miserōrum clāmōrēs Rōmānī audīvērunt.
7. hostium castra tēlīs oppugnāvimus.
8. miserī puerī barbarōrum clāmōrēs audīvērunt.
9. hostēs oppida aggeribus mūnīvērunt.
10. barbarōrum ducēs castra Rōmāna oppugnābunt.

audiō 4. I hear. **clāmor, -ōris** 3. m. shout, cry. **agger, -ris** 3. m. rampart. **mūniō** 4. I fortify. **cīvis, cīvis** 3. c. citizen. **hostis, -is** 3. c. enemy.

89. Coriolanus

Rōmānī bellum cum Volscīs gerēbant: Volscī oppidum Corio-
lōs mūnīvērunt: diū frūstrā Rōmānī oppugnābant. tum Cn.
Marcius, iuvenis Rōmānus propter virtūtem nōtus, prope sōlus
oppidum intrāvit, incolās necāvit, mūrōs incendit: exinde
cīvēs Cn. Marcium Coriolānum vocābant. posteā tamen ubi
in urbem revertit et populī suffrāgia petēbat, per superbiam
plēbēiōrum īram mōvit; itaque Coriolānum cōnsulem nōn
creāvērunt. erat tum magna frūmentī inopia, quod plēbēiī, ubi
ex urbe in sacrum montem excessērunt, agrōs nōn coluerant.
Gelon rēx, populī Rōmānī amīcus, frūmentum ad Rōmānōs
mīsit. tum Coriolānus, "propter plēbēiōs," clāmāvit, "inopia in
urbe est: itaque frūmentum inter plēbēiōs nōn dīvidēmus, nisi
iūra patriciīs reddiderint: sī tribūnī auctōritātem servābunt,
frūmentum nōn habēbunt plēbēiī." Coriolānī minās magnā
cum īrā plēbēiī audīvērunt: frūstrā tamen tribūnī accūsāvērunt. "nec damnābitis Coriolānum," clāmat, "nec pūniētis: ex
urbe excēdam et inter Volscōs exsulābō." tum cum hostibus
populī Rōmānī bellum contrā patriam gessit, patriae agrōs
vastāvit. frūstrā Rōmānī lēgātōs mīsērunt: animum nōn mōvērunt. tandem māter Coriolānī et uxor cum lacrimīs petēbant: mātris lacrimīs concessit Coriolānus. "ō māter," clāmāvit,
"patriam servāvistī, filiō exitium parāvistī."

gerō, gessī, gestum 3. I carry on, wage, carry. **iuvenis, -is** 3.
m. young man. **exinde** from that time. **urbs, urbis** 3. f. city;
often "the city," (i.e. Rome). **suffrāgium** 2. n. vote. **superbia**
1. f. pride. **frūmentum** 2. n. corn. **inopia** 1. f. scarcity, want.
sacer, sacra, sacrum sacred. **mōns, montis** 3. m. mountain,
mount. **iūs, iūris** 3. n. right, privilege, law, justice. **pūniō** 4.
I punish. **māter, mātris** 3. f. mother. **uxor, uxōris** 3. f. wife.
ō oh!

90. Ulysses and the Winds

Ulixēs, ubi Graecī Trōiam expugnāvērunt et ad Graeciam
revertērunt, cum comitibus ad insulam Aeoliam nāvigāvit.
habitābat in insulā Aeolus rēx. deī Aeolō imperium ventōrum
mandāverant. diū cum rēge Ulixēs et comitēs manēbant.
tandem, ubi discēdēbant, Aeolus Zephyrum ēmīsit, reliquōs
autem ventōs in saccō vīnxit: saccum Ulixī dedit. "nisi saccum
aperiēs," inquit, "Zephyrus ad Ithacam insulam nāvem dūcet."
ubi iam ad patriam veniēbant et Ulixēs, labōre fessus, quod
sōlus diū nāvem rēxerat, dormiēbat, multa clam comitēs dis-
serēbant. "aurum et argentum," clāmābant, "in saccō Ulixēs
portat: rēgis mūnera inter comitēs nōn dīvīsit: saccum ape-
riēmus." itaque saccum aperuērunt et reliquōs ventōs ēmīsē-
runt. statim nāvis ad insulam Aeoliam revertit. frūstrā tum
Ulixēs et comitēs ā rēge auxilium petīvērunt. "inimīcus est
deōrum Ulixēs," inquit; "deōrum inimīcum nōn adiuvābimus."
itaque magnō dolōre ad ōram revertērunt. ventus autem nōn
iam ad patriam nāvem dūcēbat.

comes, -itis 3. c. companion. **ventus** 2. m. wind. **maneō,
mānsī, mānsum** 2. I remain, wait for. **Zephyrus** 2. m.
Zephyr (the god of the West Wind). **ēmittō, ēmīsī,
ēmissum** 3. I send forth. **saccus** 2. m. bag. **vinciō, vīnxī,
vīnctum** 4. I bind. **aperiō, -uī, -tum** 4. I open. **inquit**
(defective verb) he says, he said. **nāvis, -is** 3. f. ship. **veniō,
vēnī, ventum** 4. I come. **labor, -ōris** 3. m. work, toil. **fessus,
-a, -um** weary. **dormiō** 4. I sleep. **clam** secretly. **aurum** 2. n.
gold. **argentum** 2. n. silver. **auxilium** 2. n. help.

SECTION 14

Future Perfect and Pluperfect
Indicative Active of *audiō* (Grammar Notes №. 85).
Adjectives of 3rd Declension
(Grammar Notes №s. 44–47).

Exercise 91.

1. The Gauls had fortified their camp with a huge rampart.
2. He has avoided all the dangers of war.
3. We had heard the shouts of the wretched citizens.
4. The cavalry laid waste all the fields of the Gauls.
5. The barbarians had huge shields.
6. All the towns of the Belgians had ramparts.
7. Cotta had fortified the camp with a small rampart.
8. Huge forces of the enemy attacked our men.
9. He avoided all of the enemy's arrows.
10. The barbarians have fortified all their towns.

huge ingēns, ingentis. **all, every, whole** omnis, -is, -e.

Exercise 92.

1. Labienus led all the cavalry into camp.
2. We have fortified the city with a huge rampart.
3. He reported to the general all the enemy's plans.
4. Our men will attack the huge forces of cavalry.
5. All the barbarians were preparing war.
6. The Romans had large cities, the Gauls small towns.
7. They had fortified all their cities with ramparts.
8. By your wisdom you had avoided all the dangers of war.
9. Labienus will have heard the loud shouts of the enemy.
10. The cavalry have neglected the general's advice.

city urbs, urbis 3. f.

Exercise 93.

1. The Belgians had fortified the small city with a large rampart.
2. All heard the cries of the soldiers.
3. Huge weapons will not terrify the Roman forces.
4. The boys saved the city by their shouts.
5. Huge forces of the Belgians are attacking the Roman camp.
6. All the barbarians neglected the advice of their leaders.
7. We overcame all the forces of the enemy.
8. The Romans had beautiful cities.
9. Labienus will fortify his camp with a small rampart.
10. You have heard the cries of the wretched citizens.

Exercise 94.

1. barbarōrum ingentēs cōpiās nōn timēbimus.
2. Gallī omnia oppida mūnīverant.
3. omnēs hostium clāmōrēs audīverant.
4. oppida omnia aggeribus mūnīverint.
5. Gallī oppidum ingentī aggere mūnīvērunt.
6. miserōrum cīvium clāmōrēs audīveris.
7. equitēs ingentēs cōpiās Gallōrum oppugnābunt.
8. magnōs mīlitum clāmōrēs audīverās.
9. imperātor omnēs cōpiās in urbem dūcet.
10. omnēs barbarī ingentia arma habēbant.

ingēns, ingentis huge. **omnis, -is, -e** all.

95. An Heroic Family

est in Etrūriā urbs Veiī: Rōmānī ōlim cum Veientibus bellum
gerēbant. hostēs urbem mūrīs ingentibus mūnīverant et agrōs
finitimōs vastābant: ubi nostrī oppugnābant, intrā mūrōs mīlitēs dūcēbant; mox, ubi discessērunt, iterum agrōs vastābant.
tum Caesō Fabius, populī Rōmānī cōnsul, "vōs," inquit, "cīvēs
Rōmānī, aliīs bellīs animum iam applicābitis, Veiens bellum
gentī Fabiae mandābitis: Fabiī sōlī cum Veientibus pugnābunt:
nec pecūniam nec mīlitēs ā cīvitāte postulābimus." placuit cīvibus cōnsilium Fabiī: postrīdiē cōnsul cum omnī gente ex urbe
excessit. diū nōn sōlum agrōs Rōmānōs dēfendēbant sed etiam
omnem populum Veientem terruērunt. tandem dux hostium,
"armīs," inquit, "nōn superāvimus: cōnsiliō superābimus." itaque
pecora in agrīs relīquērunt, īnsidiās haud procul posuērunt.
Fabiī, quod propter multās victōriās nōn iam hostēs timēbant, praedam in agrīs incautē petēbant. tum repente magnōs
hostium clāmōrēs audīvērunt: undique Veientēs iaculīs et
sagittīs oppugnāvērunt. frūstrā Fabiī contrā ingentēs cōpiās
hostium pugnābant. gēns omnis Fabia, praeter ūnum puerum,
in pugnā cecidit: nam, ubi ex urbe excessērunt, ūnum puerum
propter aetātem domī relīquerant.

Veiens, Veientis of, or belonging to the city of Veii,
Veientian. **intrā** (+acc.) within. **gēns, gentis** 3. f. family,
race, nation. **gēns Fabia** the Fabii, one of the most ancient
patrician families. **pecūnia** 1. f. money. **cīvitās, -ātis** 3. f.
state. **postrīdiē** on the following day. **pecus, -oris** 3. n. herd,
cattle. **īnsidiae** 1. f. pl. ambush. **haud** not. **pōnō, posuī,
positum** 3. I place. **praeda** 1. f. booty. **incautē** incautiously.
undique on all sides. **iaculum** 2. n. dart. **praeter** (+acc.)
except, besides. **cadō, cecidī, cāsum** 3. I fall. **nam** for. **aetās,
-ātis** 3. f. age. **domī** at home.

96. The Ancient Egyptians

inter aliās fābulās Herodotus multa et mīra dē Aegyptiīs nārrāvit. canēs et faelēs praecipuē amābant: ubi incendium in urbe
erat, ubique in pūblicās viās veniēbant, alia omnia neglegēbant,
faelēs sōlās custōdiēbant; sī vel ūna faelis in flammās saltāverat,
magnus erat dolor Aegyptiōrum: sī domī faelis vīta excesserat,
incolae domiciliī propter dolōrem supercilia rādēbant: canis
autem propter mortem et caput et omne corpus radēbant.

in fluviō Nīlō multī erant crocodīlī: crocodīlōs sīc captāb-
ant Aegyptiī. carnem porcīnam hāmō infīgēbant et in fluvium
dēmittēbant: tum in rīpā vīvam porcum verberābant. crocodīlus ubi porcī clāmōrēs audīvit statim ad locum properābat,
carnem cum hāmō incautē vorābat. tum in ōram trahēbant
et necābant.

mīrus, -a, -um strange, wonderful. **Aegyptiī** 2. m. pl.
Egyptians. **canis, -is** 3. c. dog. **faelēs, -is** 3. f. cat. **incendium**
2. n. fire. **via** 1. f. street, road. **custōdiō** 4. I guard. **vel** even,
or. **supercilium** 2. n. eyebrow. **rādō, rāsī, rāsum** 3. I shave.
caput, -itis 3. n. head. **Nīlus** 2. m. the Nile. **crocodīlus** 2. m.
crocodile. **captō** 1. I catch, try to catch. **carō, carnis** 3. f.
flesh. **porcīnus, -a, -um** of or belonging to a pig. **hāmus** 2.
m. hook. **infīgō, infīxī, infīxum** 3. I fix to. **dēmittō, dēmīsī,
dēmissum** 3. I let down, throw down. **rīpa** 1. f. bank. **vīvus,
-a, -um** living, alive. **porcus** 2. m. pig.

SECTION 15

See Grammar Notes №. 86,
Present, Future, Perfect, and Imperfect
Indicative Passive of *amō*.

PASSIVE VOICE

When we use a Transitive Verb in the Active Voice the Subject is the doer of the action.

When we use it in the Passive Voice the Subject is the person or thing acted upon;

e.g.   Active: *The king built this house.*
       Passive: *This house was built by the king.*

Thus the Direct Object in the Active form of the sentence becomes the Subject in the Passive form. When the Verb is Transitive the same sense can always be expressed in either form.*

e.g.   *They are attacking the city.*
       urbem oppugnant.

       The city is being attacked.
       urbs oppugnātur.

*When the Verb is Intransitive there cannot be a Passive. Thus you cannot express *I tremble, the river flows,* or *they run* in a Passive shape. In Latin, however, there is a certain use of an Intransitive Verb in the Passive (3rd Person) which will be explained later on.

When the Verb is Passive the agent or doer of the action is expressed by using the Preposition *ā* or *ab* with the Ablative Case.

e.g. *The Gauls are attacking the Romans.*
Gallī Rōmānōs oppugnant.

The Romans are being attacked by Gauls.
Rōmānī ā Gallīs oppugnantur.

N.B. It is important to distinguish the *agent* and the *instrument*. The former is a *living being*. The rule for expressing instrument has already been given in Section 5 (Ablative).

Before doing the exercises notice also the following points:

1. The *Indirect* Object of the Active Verb (see Section 5, Dative) will remain unchanged in the Passive form of the sentence;

e.g. *The soldier will announce the victory to the general.*
mīles victōriam imperātōrī nūntiābit.

The victory will be announced to the general by the soldier.
victōria ā mīlite imperātōrī nūntiābitur.

2. It will be learnt from the Grammar that the Perfect, Pluperfect and Future Perfect Tenses of the Passive Voice are made up of the Past Participle of the Verb and forms of the Verb *sum,* I am. The Participle in these forms must be made to agree with the Subject just like an Adjective (see Section 9);

e.g. *We have been wounded.*
vulnerātī sumus.

The city was saved.
urbs servāta est.

Exercise 97.

1. The Gauls were wounded by our men's darts.
2. The barbarians were defeated by our men.
3. Many towns of the Gauls were laid waste.
4. The Roman soldiers were being wounded by the barbarians' arrows.
5. The horses will be wounded by the darts.
6. Many burdens were being carried by the captives.
7. The cities will be saved by the general's plan.
8. The cavalry were attacked by the barbarians.
9. You will be defeated by Labienus.
10. The victory is being announced to the Roman general.

by *(of living agent)* ā (+abl.); before vowel or h, ab (+abl.).
burden onus, oneris 3. n. **I carry** portō 1.

Exercise 98.

1. The fields of the Gauls will not be laid waste by our men.
2. A few barbarians were wounded by arrows.
3. The Belgians had fortified all their towns with ramparts.
4. Huge burdens were being carried by our men.
5. All the fields of the Gauls are being laid waste.
6. Few heard the loud shouts of the barbarians.
7. The camp of the enemy was attacked by our men.
8. All the dangers of war were avoided by the leader.
9. The huge forces of cavalry were attacked by the enemy.
10. We all fear the enemy's cavalry.

few paucus, -a, -um.

Exercise 99.

1. War is being prepared by the enemies of the city.
2. All the forces of the barbarians will be attacked.
3. The wretched citizens had few leaders.
4. Many towns are being built by the barbarians.
5. A few citizens heard the shouts of the enemy.
6. The huge burdens will be carried by the captives.
7. We are being defeated by small forces of the Belgians.
8. All the soldiers avoided the enemy's darts.
9. He is loved by all the citizens.
10. We shall be defeated by the cavalry of the Gauls.

Exercise 100.

1. imperātor ā mīlitibus Rōmānīs amātur.
2. oppidum ab equitibus oppugnātum est.
3. victōria dūcī ā puerīs nūntiāta est.
4. Gallī ā cōpiīs Rōmānīs superābuntur.
5. paucī clāmōrem captīvī audīvērunt.
6. omnēs barbarī imperātōrem Rōmānum timent.
7. victōriae multae Rōmānīs nūntiābuntur.
8. Gallōrum tēlīs vulnerāberis.
9. onera multa ā captīvīs portābantur.
10. paucōs equitēs in oppidum dūxerat.

onus, oneris 3. n. burden. **paucus, -a, -um** few.

101. Cincinnatus

L. Quinctius Cincinnātus, populī Rōmānī cōnsul, ubi imperium administrābat, fāmam inter omnēs propter virtūtem
comparāvit: posteā senex in parvō fundō haud procul ab urbe
habitābat et agrōs colēbat. mox in urbem revocātus est: nam
castra Rōmānōrum, ubi cum Aequīs bellum gerēbant, ab hostibus oppugnāta sunt. magnum erat perīculum, ingēns omnium
timor. statim Cincinnātus dictātor creātus est: senātōrēs ad
Cincinnātum nūntiōs mīsērunt. in parvō fundō, ubi agrōs
arābat, senem invēnērunt. statim togam ab uxōre sūmpsit,
nūntiōrum verba audiēbat. "dictātor, Cincinnāte," inquiēbant,
"creātus es: nisi statim ad urbem vēneris et cōpiās Rōmānās
contrā Aequōs dūxeris, nostrī ab hostibus superābuntur, cīvēs
omnēs necābuntur." postrīdiē prīmā lūce in forum vēnit, magnā
celeritāte cōpiās parāvit et ante mediam noctem ad montem
Algidum, ubi hostēs castra posuerant, dūxit. Aequī, quoniam
utrimque ā Rōmānīs oppugnābantur, arma dēposuērunt.
victor hostēs sub iugum mīsit, ducēs hostium captīvōs in
triumphō per urbem dūxit: posteā ad parvum fundum revertit.

fundus 2. m. farm. **timor, -ōris** 3. m. fear. **dictātor, -ōris** 3.
m. dictator. **senātor, -ōris** 3. m. senator. **nūntius** 2. m.
messenger. **arō** 1. I plough. **inveniō, invēnī, inventum** 4. I
find. **toga** 1. f. toga. **verbum** 2. n. word. **lūx, lūcis** 3. f. light;
prīmā lūce at daybreak. **celeritās, -ātis** 3. f. rapidity, speed.
ante (+acc.), before. **medius, -a, -um** middle. **nox, noctis** 3.
f. night; **media nox** midnight. **pōnō castra** I pitch camp.
utrimque on both sides. **dēpōnō, dēposuī, dēpositum** 3. I
lay down. **victor, -ōris** 3. m. victor. **sub** (+acc. or +abl.)
under. **iugum** 2. n. yoke. **captīvus, -a, -um** captive.
triumphus 2. m. triumphal procession.

102. The Fate of Two Beautiful Boys

Hyacinthus, rēgis Lacedaemoniī fīlius, nōtus inter omnēs propter pulchritūdinem erat: praecipuē ā deō Apolline amābātur.
ōlim cum deō discīs lūdēbat: tum Zephyrus propter invidiam,
quod puer Apollinem amābat, Zephyrum autem nōn amābat,
ventum ācrem ēmīsit et ingentem Apollinis discum in caput
Hyacinthī immīsit. statim mortuus humī cecidit. posteā ē terrā,
ubi puerī infēlīcis sanguine cruentābātur, flōs pulcher surgēbat:
flōris frondēs prīmā litterā nōminis notātae sunt. itaque flōs
ab omnibus hyacinthus vocābātur.

Narcissus quoque propter pulchritūdinem magnam
fāmam habēbat. propter superbiam īram omnium et invidiam
movēbat. itaque deī puerum infēlīcem pūnīvērunt. ōlim ōris
imāginem in fluviō spectābat: statim pulchritūdinis amōre
superātus est: diū frūstrā imāginem captābat, tandem propter dolōrem vīta excessit. ē locō, ubi ceciderat, flōs pulcher
surgēbat: flōs hodiē narcissus vocātur.

Lacedaemonius, -a, -um Lacedaemonian. **pulchritūdō,
-inis** 3. f. beauty. **Apollō, -inis** 3. m. Apollo. **discus** 2. m.
discus. **lūdō, lūsī, lūsum** 3. I play. **ācer, ācris, ācre** sharp,
fierce. **immittō, immīsī, immissum** 3. I hurl. **mortuus, -a,
-um** dead. **humī** on the ground. **infēlix, -īcis** unhappy,
unfortunate. **sanguis, -inis** 3. m. blood. **cruentō** 1. I stain
(with blood). **flōs, flōris** 3. m. flower. **surgō, surrēxī,
surrēctum** 3. I rise. **frōns, frondis** 3. f. leaf. **littera** 1. f. a
letter (of the alphabet). **nōmen, -inis** 3. n. name. **notō** 1. I
mark. **hyacinthus** 2. m. hyacinth. **quoque** also. **ōs, ōris** 3. n.
face, mouth. **imāgō, -inis** 3. f. refection, image. **spectō** 1. I
watch. **amor, amōris** 3. m. love.

SECTION 16

See Grammar Notes №. 86,
Future Perfect and Pluperfect
Indicative Passive of *amō*.

Exercise 103.

1. The city will have been saved by the citizens.
2. All the fields of the Gauls had been laid waste.
3. The victory had been reported by a boy.
4. A few towns will be laid waste by the soldiers.
5. The leaders of the enemy heard the shouts of the infantry.
6. The horses had been wounded with arrows.
7. The infantry are avoiding all dangers.
8. The camp is being attacked by the Belgians.
9. Few victories have been announced to the Romans.
10. The dangers of war will be avoided by our men.

foot-soldier pedes, -itis 3. m. **infantry** peditēs 3. m. pl.

Exercise 104.

1. The general had been wounded by the enemy's darts.
2. The Roman cavalry have laid waste all the fields.
3. The town had been built by the Gauls.
4. The Roman infantry were defeated by the Belgians.
5. The barbarians are frightening the citizens with their shouts.
6. He had fortified a few cities with ramparts.
7. You were wounded by an arrow.
8. Huge burdens had been carried by the captives.
9. Cotta led his infantry against the barbarians.
10. The cavalry of the enemy will have been defeated.

Exercise 105.

1. The camp has been attacked by large forces of cavalry.
2. The infantry neglected the advice of Labienus.
3. Our men will have been defeated by the barbarians.
4. The town is being laid waste by the Belgians.
5. Cotta is fortifying his camp with a huge rampart.
6. All the burdens were carried by the soldiers.
7. The city has been saved by the infantry.
8. All heard the loud cries of the barbarians.
9. He announced the victory to the leader of the Roman forces.
10. A few citizens were wounded with darts.

Exercise 106.

1. multī cīvēs barbarōrum tēlīs vulnerātī erunt.
2. omnia Gallōrum oppida vastāta erant.
3. victōria ab equitibus nūntiāta erit.
4. imperātōris cōnsiliō servātī erāmus.
5. onera ingentia miserī captīvī portābant.
6. puerōrum clāmōribus urbs servāta erat.
7. peditēs oppidum tēlīs oppugnāvērunt.
8. imperātor magnās peditum cōpiās in urbem dūcet.
9. omnia perīcula ab equitibus vītāta erant.
10. dux bonus clāmōrēs hostium nōn timet.

107. Unhappy Austria

magna ōlim Austrōrum cīvitās erat, magnam auctōritātem
in Eurōpā habēbant; omnibus propter virtūtem nōtī erant,
inter aliōs populōs imperium administrābant. tum repente
omnia mūtāta erant; bellum sociōrum causā contrā Gallōs et
Britannōs gessērunt; Gallī et Britannī superāvērunt.

    manet hodiē urbs antīqua Vindobona, manent templa et
domicilia, sed glōria et fāma discessērunt. rēx procul ā patriā
exsulat; domī misera est fortūna incolārum; cum dolōre
et lacrimīs auxilium ā finitimīs frūstrā petunt; nēmō audit,
nēmō adiuvat.

mūtō 1. I change, exchange. **antīquus, -a, -um** ancient.
Vindobona Vienna. **glōria** 1. f. glory. **fortūna** 1. f. chance,
fortune.

108. The Twelve Tables

praeter aliās causās īrae propter ūnam praecipuē causam plēbēiōrum animī īrā excitābantur. iūs administrābant sōlī patriciī,
lēgēs tamen omnīnō erant nūllae: itaque iūs omne ad arbitrium patriciōrum semper administrātum erat. tandem prō
cōnsulibus decemvirī ā populō creātī sunt: decemvirī prīmō
bene imperium administrāvērunt et lēgēs omnibus nōtās
condēbant. magnum erat gaudium plēbēiōrum: decemvirī
iterum creantur. iam tamen crūdēliter auctōritātem exercēb-
ant: praecipuē Appius Claudius per superbiam omnium īram
movēbat. "imperium," inquit, "decemvirīs populus concessit:
imperium nōn dēpōnēmus." tum iterum ad Montem Sacrum
plēbēiī discessērunt: statim decemvirī imperium dēposuērunt
nec iterum creātī sunt. manēbant tamen novae lēgēs in duodecim tabulīs scrīptae.

excitō 1. I rouse, arouse. **decem** ten; **decemvirī** 2. m. pl.
Decemvirs (commission of ten men). **condō, condidī,
conditum** 3. I put together, compile, found. **exerceō** 2. I
exercise. **novus, -a, -um** new. **duodecim** twelve. **tabula** 1. f.
tablet. **scrīptus, -a, -um** written.

109. A Horrible Banquet

dē Tantalō fābulae multae et mīrae nārrantur. saepe ad cēnam ā deīs immortālibus vocātus erat; semel deōs vōcāvit. magnam cēnam parāvit: simul "deōrum," inquit, "sapientiam temptābō: carnem hūmānam prō ferīnā carne appōnam: deī fraudem nōn sentient." itaque Pelopem fīlium necāvit, carnem et membra in multās partēs dīvīsit et in aēnō coxit. tum cibum mīrum et horrendum deīs apposuit. deī tamen fraudem statim sēnsērunt, nihil ēdērunt. Cerēs autem nūper fīliam āmīserat: propter dolōrem incautē Pelopis humerum ēdit. magna erat deōrum īra propter fraudem: membra Pelopis iterum in aēnum posuērunt, iterum coxērunt: sīc vītam puerō infēlīcī reddidērunt. prō humerō alter humerus eburneus datur: exinde semper Pelopidae omnēs alterum humerum candidum velut eburneum habēbant. Tantalum autem deī prō scelere magnīs suppliciīs pūnīvērunt.

cēna 1. f. dinner. **immortālis, -is, -e** immortal. **semel** once. **simul** at the same time. **hūmānus, -a, -um** human. **ferīnus, -a, -um** of animals. **appōnō, apposuī, appositum** 3. I serve up. **fraus, -dis** 3. f. deception. **sentiō, sēnsī, sēnsum** 4. I perceive. **Pelops, Pelopis** 3. m. Pelops. **membrum** 2. n. limb. **pars, -tis** 3. f. part. **aēnum** 2. n. bronze cauldron. **coquō, coxī, coctum** 3. I cook. **cibus** 2. m. food. **edō, ēdī, ēsum** 3. I eat. **Cerēs, -eris** Ceres. **nūper** lately. **āmittō, āmīsī, āmissum** 3. I lose. **humerus** 2. m. shoulder. **alter, -era, -erum** second, one or other (of two). **eburneus, -a, -um** of ivory. **Pelopidae** 1. m. pl. descendants of Pelops. **candidus, -a, -um** white. **velut** as if. **scelus, -eris** 3. n. crime.

110. A Frustrated Rising of Gauls

multī in Galliā contrā Caesarem coniūrābant: aliōs omnēs
audāciā et virtūte superābat. Indutiomarus, quī, ubi mīlitēs
ad ūnum locum vocāvit, "in agrōs Remōrum" inquit, "vōs
dūcam; quoniam pūblicam causam dēseruērunt nec patriam
contrā Rōmānōs dēfendērunt, contrā Remōs bellum gerēmus."
sed Labiēnus, dux Rōmānus, auxilium ā sociīs petīvit; intereā
cōpiās in castrīs tenēbat. cōtīdiē Gallī ad castra veniēbant, tēla
immittēbant, Rōmānōs contumēliīs vexābant: nihil respondēb-
ant Rōmānī, sed hostibus timōris suspīciōnem dabant. tandem
sociī auxilium mīsērunt; postrīdiē Gallī ā nostrīs oppugnātī
et fugātī sunt: Indutiomarus necātus est.

quī, quae, quod who, which. **dēserō, -uī, -tum 3.** I leave,
abandon. **intereā** meanwhile.

SECTION 17

See Grammar Notes №. 87,
Present, Future, Perfect, and Imperfect
Indicative Passive of *moneō.*

Exercise 111.

1. The Romans are not frightened by the shouts of the
   enemy.
2. A good general is not feared by his soldiers.
3. The cavalry were not frightened by the shouts of the
   barbarians.
4. Small dangers are not feared by our men.
5. We were not frightened by the enemy's darts.
6. We are feared by all the barbarians.
7. The leader of the enemy was feared by our men.

8. The town was built by the Gauls.
9. You will not be frightened by the small forces of the enemy.
10. The city is held by Cotta.

I hold, detain teneō 2.

Exercise 112.

1. The Roman people were feared by the Gauls.
2. A part of the cavalry was attacking the enemy's camp.
3. All the cities are held by the barbarians.
4. All the Belgians feared the Roman people.
5. We defeated a part of the infantry.
6. Huge forces of the enemy had seized the city.
7. We have already defeated a part of the Roman forces.
8. All cities fear the Romans.
9. The victory was announced to the Roman people.
10. The Belgians defeated a great part of our men.

people populus, -ī 2. m. **part** pars, -tis 3. f. **I seize** occupō 1. **now, already** iam.

Exercise 113.

1. The forces of Labienus seized a large city.
2. The cavalry will not be frightened by the shouts of the Gauls.
3. The dangers of war are not feared by the Roman people.
4. Roman soldiers are not frightened by barbarians.
5. The cities are not held by the enemy.
6. The Roman people ruled the Gauls.
7. The Gauls had already fortified the town with a rampart.
8. The general had already led a great part of his forces into camp.
9. A great part of the land had been seized by the enemy.
10. You will all hear the cries of the soldiers.

Exercise 114.

1. magnae barbarōrum cōpiae ā nostrīs nōn timentur.
2. hostium clāmōribus nostrī nōn terrēbuntur.
3. bellī perīculīs nōn terrēminī.
4. urbs ā Labiēnō tenēbātur.
5. pars mīlitum urbem iam occupāverat.
6. populus Rōmānus timētur.
7. hostium partem terruimus, partem superāvimus.
8. imperātor mīlitēs in castra iam dūxerat.
9. oppidum ā nostrīs tenēbitur.
10. barbarī nostrōrum tēlīs territī sunt.

115. Spurius Maelius

in urbe ōlim magna erat cibī inopia. tum Sp. Maelius, eques
plēbēius propter dīvitiās nōtus, frūmentum in Etrūriā emēbat
et cīvibus pauperibus aut parvō vendēbat aut grātīs dabat.
propter līberālitātem magnō in honōre ā plēbēiīs habēbātur,
patriciōrum autem īram movēbat. itaque falsus crīminibus
accūsātus est. "contrā populum Rōmānum," clāmābant patriciī, "Sp. Maelius coniūrat: regnum appetit: sī iam mūneribus
plēbēiōrum animīs placuerit auctōritātemque confirmāverit,
iterum mox sub rēgis imperiō cīvitās Rōmāna tenēbitur:
vōs, cīvēs, sī patriam amātis, Sp. Cassiī exemplō monēbiminī."
ingēns statim timor inter omnēs cīvēs movēbātur. Cincinnātus
dictātor, C. Servīlius Ahāla magister equitum creātus est. dictātōris imperiō Maelius nōn pārēbat: tum Ahāla cum turbā
iuvenum patriciōrum forum intrāvit; Maelium tēlīs oppugnāvērunt et necāvērunt. diū inter Rōmānōs Ahālae factum
laudābātur: hodiē tamen ā multīs Sp. Maelius vir bonus et
pauperum amīcus habētur: nam Ahāla posteā damnātus est
et ex urbe in exsilium discessit.

dīvitiae 1. f. pl. riches. **emō, ēmī, ēmptum** 3. I buy. **aut** or.
aut ... aut either ... or. **parvō** at a small price. **grātīs** for
nothing, gratuitously. **līberālitās, -ātis** 3. f. generosity.
moneō 2. I advise, warn. **magister equitum** Master of the
Horse. **factum** 2. n. deed. **exsilium** 2. n. exile.

116. Pride Punished

ōlim Minerva tībiā lūdēbat. repente ōris imāginem in aquā
videt. "tībia," inquit, "pulchram deam nōn decet." itaque magnā
īrā ā locō discessit, tībiam humī relīquit. posteā Marsyas
invēnit: tībia, quod nūper ōs deae tetigerat, ubi Marsyas
lūdēbat, sonōs mīrōs et dulcēs ēmīsit. magnum erat Marsyae
gaudium: etiam Apollinem ad certāmen prōvocāvit. "Mūsae,"
inquit, "inter nōs iūdicābunt; victor victō supplicium cōnstit-
uet." in spēluncā certāmen habēbātur: Apollō citharā, Marsyas tībiā lūdēbant. Mūsārum arbitriō penes Apollinem erat
victōria. tum deus hominem infēlīcem propter superbiam
crūdēliter pūnīvit: ad arborem vīnxit et cutem ā vīvō homine
dētrāxit. ē spēluncā, ubi sanguis humī ceciderat, fluvius fluēbat:
tībia fluviō ad aliam terram portābātur, ubi Apollinī in templō
dēdicāta est.

tībia 1. f. flute; tībiā lūdō I play on the flute.
aqua 1. f. water. videō, vīdī, vīsum 2. I see. dea 1. f. goddess.
decet 2. it suits, it befits. tangō, tetigī, tāctum 3. I touch.
sonus 2. m. sound. dulcis, -is, -e sweet. certāmen, -inis
3. n. contest. prōvocō 1. I challenge. Mūsa 1. f. Muse.
iūdicō 1. I judge. victus, -a, -um conquered. cōnstituō, -uī,
-ūtum 3. I decide, settle, draw up. cithara 1. f. lyre.
penes (+acc.) in the power of; penes nōs victōria est the
victory rests with us. homō, -inis 3. c. man, human being.
arbor, -oris 3. f. tree. cutis, -is 3. f. skin. dētrahō, dētrāxī,
dētractum 3. I drag off. fluō, flūxī 3. I flow.

SECTION 18

Future Perfect and Pluperfect
Indicative Passive of *moneō* (Grammar Notes №. 87).
Some exceptional Nouns of 2nd and 3rd
Declensions (Grammar Notes №s. 19 & 31).

Exercise 117.

1. You had already been warned by the general.
2. They had been terrified by the Roman people.
3. We had been warned by the guides.
4. The leader of the enemy will have been already warned.
5. You will be feared by all the barbarians.
6. They will have been terrified by the shouts of the enemy.
7. The Gauls have now been warned by the general.
8. The wretched citizens had been terrified by the cries of the enemy.
9. The boy had been warned by his father.
10. We shall not neglect the advice of a good general.

I advise, warn moneō 2. **father** pater, patris 3. m.

Exercise 118.

1. You were not warned by your father.
2. The city was saved by the gods.
3. The father led his sons into the city.
4. The barbarians were preparing war by land and sea.
5. The sons had heard the advice of their fathers.
6. The gods have fortified the land with the sea.
7. The wretched citizens were warned by the general.
8. The boys were frightened by the Belgians' arrows.
9. The citizens will be warned by the general.
10. A good father is not feared by his son.

god deus, -ī 2. m. **son** filius, -ī 2. m. **and** -que (joined to first word in clause). **sea** mare, -is 3. n. **by land and sea** terrā marīque.

Exercise 119.

1. The horses were carrying huge burdens.
2. The citizens have already fortified their city with a rampart.
3. The father was saved by his son's device.
4. We rule the barbarians by land and sea.
5. Good citizens fear the gods.
6. My son, you will not be wounded by your father's arrow.
7. Our men are feared by land and sea.
8. The city had been seized by our men.
9. A part of the cavalry will attack the camp.
10. Part of the city was saved by the general's stratagem.

Exercise 120.

1. puer ā patre monitus erit.
2. barbarōs terrā marīque superāvimus.
3. fīlius paterque in castra mātūrābant.
4. bellī perīculīs, fīlī, nōn territus eris.
5. Labiēnus ab imperātōre monitus erat.
6. terrā marīque Gallī superābantur.
7. urbem pars peditum tenēbat.
8. nostrī magna onera portābant.
9. perīculō peditēs nōn territī erant.
10. ā populō Rōmānō nōn territī erunt.

pater, patris 3. m. father. **-que** and. **mare, -is** 3. n. sea.

121. The Capture of Veii

Etruscī ōlim terrā marīque magnam potentiam habuerant:
tum ā Graecīs nāvēs dēlētae, ā Samnītibus agrī vastātī erant:
posteā simul ā Gallīs et ā Rōmānīs bellō vexābantur. urbs Veiī
diū ā Rōmānīs obsidēbātur: prīmō Etruscī nōn sōlum urbem
dēfendēbant sed etiam ingentem timōrem inter Rōmānōs
movērunt. itaque M. Furius Camillus dictātor creātus est:
Camillī cōnsiliō mīlitēs cunīculum sub terrā ad arcem urbis
ēgērunt. intereā rēx Veientium dīs immortālibus immolābat.
"sī dīs, ō rēx," inquit sacerdōs, "hostiam immolābis, dī victōriam in bellō dabunt." sacerdōtis verba Rōmānī audīvērunt:
aliquot mīlitēs ē cunīculō veniunt, hostiam ad dictātōrem
portant: Camillus dīs immolāvit. simul ex omnī parte urbis
mūrī ā Rōmānīs oppugnābantur: aliī arcem per cunīculum
intrāvērunt.

Camillus propter victōriam triumphum ēgit: posteā tamen,
quod plēbēiōrum īram mōverat, falsō crīmine ā tribūnīs accūsātus est. "nōn mē iūdicēs damnābunt," inquit; "ultrō in exsilium
discēdam; sī innocēns accūsor, cīvitās ingrāta mox dēsīderābit."

dēleō, -ēvī, -ētum 2. I destroy. **cunīculus** 2. m. mine. **arx,
arcis** 3. f. citadel. **agō, ēgī, āctum** 3. I drive, do, carry on;
cunīculum agō I construct a mine; **triumphum agō** I
celebrate a triumph. **immolō** 1. I sacrifice. **sacerdōs, -ōtis** 3.
m. priest. **hostia** 1. f. victim. **mē** me. **ultrō** of one's own
accord, voluntarily. **innocēns, innocentis** innocent.
ingrātus, -a, -um ungrateful. **dēsīderō** 1. I feel the want of,
I miss.

122. A Schoolmaster's Treachery

Rōmānī, ubi cum Etruscīs bellum gerēbant, urbem in Etrūriā
Falēriōs obsēdērunt. Faliscōrum fīliōs omnēs ūnus magister
docēbat, vir sapiēns sed improbus. cōtīdiē puerōs lūdī causā
ex urbe dūcēbat, tandem ad castra Rōmāna dūcit. tum ad

Camillum, imperātōrem Rōmānum, vēnit: "urbem," inquit,
"Rōmānīs trādō, nam prīncipum filiōs trādō: sī puerōs obsidēs
habēbitis, Faliscī statim urbem trādent." respondit Camillus,
"nōn ita bellum gerimus Rōmānī, nec contrā puerōs arma
sūmpsimus: sunt et bellī, sīcut pācis, iūra." tum magistrum
nūdāvit et puerīs trādidit: puerī prōditōrem verberāvērunt et
in urbem ēgērunt. mōvit animōs Faliscōrum Camillī līberālitās: lēgātōs statim ad castra Rōmāna, inde ad cūriam mīsērunt.
"beneficiō," clāmāvērunt, "sī nōn armīs, nōs superāvistis: ultrō
urbem trādimus: populī tam iūstī imperiō libenter pārēbimus."

Faleriī 2. m. pl. one of the chief cities of Etruria, Falerii.
Faliscus 2. m. inhabitant of Falerii, a Faliscan. **doceō, -uī,**
-tum 2. I teach. **sapiēns, sapientis** wise. **improbus, -a, -um**
wicked. **trādō, -didī, -ditum** 3. I hand over. **prīnceps, -ipis**
3. m. chief man. **obses, obsidis** 3. c. hostage. **ita** thus. **sunt**
are, there are. **pāx, pācis** 3. f. peace. **nūdō** 1. I strip.
prōditor, -ōris 3. m. betrayer, traitor. **inde** thence. **iūstus,**
-a, -um just.

123. Chivalry in War

diū Rōmānī cum Etruscīs bellum gerēbant. multa dē Por-
senā, rēge Etruscōrum, virō omnibus propter līberālitātem
nōtō, in historiā nārrantur. ubi pāx cōnfirmāta est, inter
aliōs obsidēs Cloelia, virī nōbilis filia, Porsenae data est. ubi
Etruscōrum castra haud procul ā rīpā Tiberis collocāta sunt,
Cloelia ē castrīs excessit, fluvium trānāvit, domum revertit.
Porsena prīmō īrā ardēbat; lēgātōs ad urbem mīsit et puellam
postulāvit; Rōmānī ex foedere reddidērunt. mox autem rēx
admīrātiōne mōtus est; nōn sōlum puellam līberāvit sed etiam
partem obsidum simul reddidit.

trānō I swim across. **domus** 4. f. house, home. **ex** (+abl.) in
accordance with. **admīrātiō, -ōnis** 3. f. admiration.

SECTION 19

Present, Future, Imperfect, and Perfect
Indicative Passive of *regō* (Grammar Notes №. 88).
Nouns in *-us* of 4th Declension
(Grammar Notes №. 34).

Exercise 124.

1. All armies are led by generals.
2. The Gauls were frightened by our men's fierce attack.
3. The land was ruled by the Romans.
4. We shall be led into many cities.
5. We shall not be ruled by the Roman people.
6. Roman soldiers are being led against their enemy.
7. They will not be guided by the advice of their fathers.
8. We were terrified by the enemy's fierce attack.
9. Part of the Roman army was attacked by the Gauls.
10. The general's advice was neglected by the soldiers.

army exercitus, -ūs 4. m. **fierce** ācer, ācris, ācre. **attack,
onset, charge** impetus, -ūs 4. m.

Exercise 125.

1. We overcame the huge forces of the enemy by a fierce charge.
2. A part of the army was attacking the Belgians' camp.
3. The city was neglected by the army.
4. The infantry are being led against the rampart.
5. The general is leading the army into the town.
6. The father's advice was often neglected by his sons.
7. We withstood the fierce charge of the cavalry.
8. The country is ruled by good leaders.
9. The general's advice will not be neglected by the
   Roman citizens.
10. The enemy will not withstand the onset of the Roman
    soldiers.

often saepe. **I withstand** sustineō 2.

Exercise 126.

1. Many armies were led against the Gauls by the Romans.
2. They announced the victory to the Roman army.
3. War is being prepared by every city.
4. The Gauls' onset was withstood by the whole army.
5. Barbarians often attacked Roman armies.
6. The army will be led into the fields of the Gauls.
7. The barbarians heard the loud cries of the Roman army.
8. The Gauls often fortified their towns with ramparts.
9. Large forces of infantry are being led against the Belgians.
10. You will not be neglected by your father.

Exercise 127.

1. exercitus Rōmānus hostium impetum sustinēbat.
2. terra deōrum cōnsiliīs regitur.
3. captīvī in oppidum dūcentur.
4. cīvēs hostium impetum sustinuērunt.
5. multae urbēs ā Rōmānīs reguntur.
6. exercitūs Rōmānī saepe contrā barbarōs dūcēbantur.
7. imperātor Rōmānus multōs Gallōrum impetūs sustinuit.
8. terrā marīque contrā Rōmānōs dūcēminī.
9. ab omnī exercitū dux amābātur.
10. filius patris cōnsiliō regitur.

exercitus 4. m. army. **impetus** 4. m. attack.

128. The Capture of Rome

ad Gallōs, quod in Etrūriam cōpiās dūxerant, lēgātī ā Rōmānīs
missī sunt: tum contrā iūs gentium lēgātī arma sūmpsērunt
et cum Etruscīs contrā Gallōs pugnāvērunt. itaque Gallī ab
Etrūriā in agrōs Rōmānōs vēnērunt. statim ab urbe exercitus contrā novum hostem missus est. prope Alliam fluvium
pugnābant. terrēbant Rōmānōs saeva ōra, magnī clāmōrēs,
ingentia corpora barbarōrum: nostrī vix prīmum impetum
sustinuērunt sed urbem fugā petīvērunt. omnium animī ingentī
timōre movēbantur. iuvenēs statim Capitōlium occupāvērunt,
relīquī, praeter senātōrēs, in Etrūriam discēdēbant. Gallī
urbem intrant, ad forum veniunt: mīrum ibi spectāculum
oculīs ostenditur: nam senātōrēs animīs ad mortem parātīs
adventum hostium exspectābant: magistrātūs in eburneīs sellīs
sēdērunt honōrumque insignia gerēbant. diū barbarī senēs
immōtōs, velut deum imāginēs, spectābant. tum ūnus ē Gallīs
M. Papīriī barbam manū permulsit: senex īrātus caput scīp-
iōne eburneō ferit statimque ā barbarō necātur. tum omnēs
īrā moventur reliquōsque senēs in sellīs trucīdant.

vix scarcely. **occupō** 1. I seize. **spectāculum** 2. n. sight,
show. **parātus, -a, -um** prepared. **adventus** 4. m. arrival.
exspectō 1. I await. **magistrātus** 4. m. magistrate. **sella** 1. f.
chair. **sedeō, sēdī, sessum** 2. I sit. **insigne, -is** 3. n. insignia,
indication of rank. **immōtus, -a, -um** motionless. **barba** 1.
f. beard. **manus** 4. f. hand, band of men. **permulceō, -sī,
-sum** 2. I stroke. **īrātus, -a, -um** angry, in anger. **scīpiō,
-ōnis** 3. m. staff. **feriō** 4. I strike. **trucīdō** 1. I massacre.

129. A Prophesy Independently Confirmed

erant in Etrūriā multī et sapientēs haruspicēs. ubi Rōmānī
urbem Veiōs obsidēbant, ūnus ex haruspicibus in sermōnem
cum mīlitibus Rōmānīs incīdit. "Rōmānī," inquit, "urbem Veiōs
nōn expugnābunt nisi aqua ē lacū Albānō ēmittētur." posteā ē
mūrīs in aggerēs Rōmānōs vēnit. tum ūnus ē Rōmānīs, iuvenis
fortis, senem infirmum superāvit et ad imperātōrem trāxit.
ab imperātōre ad urbem missus est. intereā Rōmānī lēgātōs
in Graeciam ad ōrāculum Apollinis mīserant et reditum
exspectābant. lēgātī ubi revertērunt deī responsum nūntiāvērunt: "sīc Apollō Rōmānōs monet: nisi aqua ē lacū Albānō
ēmittētur, Rōmānī Veiōs nōn expugnābunt." tum dēnique
senō crēdidērunt.

Lacus Albānus tum forte imbribus auctus erat. itaque
Rōmānī ōrāculō pārent, aquam per agrōs ēmittunt urbem
Veiōs expugnant.

haruspex, -icis 3. m. soothsayer. sermō, -ōnis 3. m.
conversation. incidō, incidī, incāsum 3. I fall into. lacus 4.
m. lake. fortis, -is, -e strong. infirmus, -a, -um weak.
ōrāculum 2. n. oracle. reditus 4. m. return. dēnique at last,
finally. crēdō, -didī, -ditum 3. (+dat.) I believe. forte by
chance. imber, imbris 3. m. rain. augeō, auxī, auctum 2. I
increase (transitive); in passive (of lakes, rivers, etc.), to be
flooded.

SECTION 20

Future Perfect and Pluperfect
Indicative Passive of *regō* (Grammar Notes №. 88).
Nouns in *-u* of 4th Declension
(Grammar Notes №. 34).

_____

Exercise 130.

1. The cavalry had been drawn up on the right wing.
2. The army will be led back into camp.
3. You will not have been neglected by the general.
4. Part of the army has been drawn up by Labienus.
5. The generals are drawing up their forces.
6. The left wing is held by the Roman infantry.
7. A part of the forces has already been led back into the camp.
8. He drew up the Roman cavalry on the right wing.
9. Part of the army has been drawn up opposite to the city.
10. They are announcing the victory to the army.

I draw up instruō, -xī, -ctum 3. **horn, wing (of an army)** cornū, -ūs 4. n. **right, right hand** dexter, -tra, -trum. **left, left hand** sinister, -tra, -trum. **on the right wing** dextrō cornū. **I lead back** redūcō, redūxī, reductum 3. **opposite to** contrā (+acc.).

Exercise 131.

1. The Roman soldiers had been drawn up opposite to the rampart.
2. The cavalry will be led back into the Roman camp.
3. The left wing of the army is held by the infantry.
4. A great part of the Roman army was defeated by the enemy.
5. The city had been ruled by the Romans.
6. The advice of the general will not have been neglected.
7. Romans will not be ruled by barbarians.

8. The city is being attacked by the whole army.
9. We shall be guided by the advice of our leaders.
10. Labienus had drawn up the cavalry on the right wing.

Exercise 132.

1. The Roman people were* feared by all the barbarians.
2. Part of the town had been seized by the army.
3. He is leading back his forces into camp.
4. The Roman army is being led against the forces of the Belgians.
5. The father's advice has not been neglected by his son.
6. Part of the army heard the cries of the citizens.
7. On the right wing our men were being wounded by arrows.
8. The soldiers were withstanding the fierce onsets of the enemy.
9. By a fierce charge we defeated the barbarians.
10. Soldiers, you will be led back into the camp.

*in English, "people" takes a plural verb, whereas in Latin it is singular.

Exercise 133.

1. imperātor peditēs dextrō cornū instruxit.
2. exercitūs iam instructī erant.
3. dextrum cornū ā Labiēnō tenēbātur.
4. pars equitum iam instructa est.
5. multae urbēs exercitūs Rōmānōs timēbant.
6. Labiēnus ab omnī exercitū timēbātur.
7. hostium impetū nōn terrēbimur.
8. equitēs in castra reductī erant.
9. exercitus ab imperātōre instructus erit.
10. pars peditum in urbem ducta erat.

instruō, -xī, -ctum 3. I draw up (soldiers).

134. The Return of Camillus

intereā arx Rōmae Capitōliumque in ingentī perīculō erat.
noctū aliquot Gallī per angustam viam genibus nīxī ascen-
dēbant: nōn sōlum mīlitēs, sed etiam canēs fallēbant, anserēs
tamen Iūnōnī sacrōs nōn fefellērunt. anserum clāmōribus
excitātus est M. Manlius: prīmum hostem manū dēturbat:
tum arma sūmpsit, reliquōs ad arma vocāvit; Gallōs singulōs
Rōmānī trucīdāvērunt.

magna iam cibī inopia in arce erat: diū tamen sustinēbant; etiam pānem inter hostēs iactābant. "nam sī cibī inopiam
sēnserint," dictātor inquit, "Gallōrum animī cōnfirmābuntur."
tandem lēgātōs ad hostem mīsērunt: salūtem mīlle lībrīs
aurī ēmērunt. aurum in forō ā Q. Sulpiciō tribūnō mīlitum
Brennō rēgī Gallicō datur: ubi tribūnus "inīqua pondera,"
inquit, "habētis, Gallī," Brennus ponderī gladium addidit:
simul "vae victīs" clāmāvit.

intereā tamen exercitus ā M. Furiō Camillō exsule in
Etrūriā collectus erat: verba insolentia ā rēge vix dicta erant
ubi Camillus cum novīs cōpiīs forum intrāvit. statim Gallōs
ācrī impetū oppugnant omnēsque mox trucīdant.

noctū by night. **angustus, -a, -um** narrow. **genū** 4. n. knee.
nīxus, -a, -um resting on (with abl.). **ascendō, -dī, -sum** 3.
I climb up, ascend. **fallō, fefellī, falsum** 3. I escape the
notice of, evade, deceive. **anser, -eris** 3. c. goose. **Iūnō,**
-ōnis 3. f. the goddess Juno. **dēturbō** 1. I throw down. **pānis,**
-is 3. m. bread. **iactō** 1. I throw. **salūs, -ūtis** 3. f. safety. **mīlle**
(pl. **mīlia**) thousand. **lībra** 1. f. a pound (in weight).
Gallicus, -a, -um of or belonging to the Gauls, Gallic.
inīquus, -a, -um unfair. **pondus, -eris** 3. n. weight. **addō,**
addidī, additum 3. I add. **vae** woe!, alas! **exsul, -lis** 3, c. an
exile. **colligō, -lēgī, -lectum** 3. I collect. **insolēns, insolentis**
insolent. **dīcō, dīxī, dictum** 3. I say.

135. The Quest of the Golden Fleece

ōlim cum Argonautīs, virīs multīs et intrepidīs, Iāson, quod
ā patruō missus erat, ē Graeciā in Asiam nāvigāvit: aureum
vellus ab Aeētā rēge petēbat. "vellus dabō," respondit rēx, "sī
sōlus taurōs arātrō iūnxeris, dentēs dracōnis in agrō sēveris."
Mēdēa autem, rēgis fīlia, Iāsonis amōre superāta est: ubi patris
verba audīvit magnō timōre movēbātur. tamen cōnsilium
Iāsonī dedit. "taurī," inquit, "ingentia cornua, aēneōs pedēs
habent; ex ōre flammās spīrant: ubi dentēs dracōnis sēveris,
virī armātī ē terrā surgent tēlīsque oppugnābunt: dēnique
aureum vellus dracō custōdit. Mēdēae tamen magicīs artibus
omnia perīcula superābis." sīc Iāson rēgis iussīs pāruit: aureum
vellus ad nāvem portāvit, cum Mēdēā et Argonautīs discessit. magna erat rēgis īra: nāvem parat, comitēs ad arma vocat.
Mēdēa tamen parvum frātrem in nāvem dūxerat: ubi ōram
relīquērunt, frātrem necāvit, corpus in multās partēs dīvīsit,
membra in mare iactāvit. rēx diū puerī īnfēlīcis membra
colligēbat: itaque Iāson et Mēdēa incolumēs ad Graeciam
nāvigāvērunt.

Argonautae 1. m. pl. Argonauts; sailors of the Argo.
patruus 2. m. uncle. **aureus, -a, -um** golden. **vellus, -eris** 3.
n. fleece. **arātrum** 2. n. plough. **iungō, iūnxī, iūnctum** 3. I
join; **arātrō iungō** I yoke (lit. I join to the plough). **dēns,
dentis** 3. m. tooth. **dracō, -ōnis** 3. m. dragon. **serō, sēvī,
satum** 3. I sow. **cornū, -ūs** 4. n. horn. **aēneus, -a, -um** of
bronze. **pēs, pedis** 3. m. foot. **armātus, -a, -um** armed.
magicus, -a, -um magic. **ars, artis** 3. f. art. **iussum** 2. n.
order. **incolumis, -is, -e** safe.

136. A Favourite of Fortune

Cyrus, rēx Persārum, vir propter virtūtem et imperiī glōriam omnibus nōtus, Lysandrum, exercitūs Lacedaemoniī ducem, ad cēnam invītāvit. rēx hortōs et lacūs, flōrēs arborēsque cum superbiā ostendit. Lysander nihil eiusmodī anteā vīderat. mox Cyrus, "meīs iussīs" inquit, "arborēs et flōrēs ita positī sunt; multae arborum etiam meā manū satae sunt." diū spectābat Lysander hortōs, spectābat, rēgis aurum et argentum. tandem "rectē" inquit, "ā cīvibus fēlix vocāris, Cyre; nam virtūtī tuae dīvitiae additae sunt."

Persae 1. m. pl. Persians. **invītō** 1. I invite. **hortus** 2. m. garden. **meus** my. **rectē** adv. rightly, properly. **fēlix, -īcis** adj. fortunate, happy, successful. **tuus** thy, your.

SECTION 21

Present, Future, Imperfect, and Perfect
Indicative Passive of *audiō* (Grammar Notes №. 89).

Exercise 137.

1. The Roman army was hindered by the wood.
2. The cries of the citizens were heard by the general.
3. A great part of the town is being fortified by the citizens.
4. We shall not be prevented by the Roman soldiers.
5. The city was being fortified with a rampart and towers.
6. The voice of the king will be heard by all the soldiers.
7. The citizens are fortifying their town with a huge rampart.
8. The victory of the cavalry will be announced to the king.
9. You will not be heard by the enemy's leaders.
10. All the towns of the Gauls are being fortified.

I hinder, prevent impediō 4. **wood** silva, -ae 1. f. **tower** turris, -is 3. f. **voice** vōx, vōcis 3. f. **king** rēx, rēgis 3. m.

Exercise 138.

1. We shall be hindered by the woods.
2. The Gauls had built many towers.
3. They were being prevented by the general of the Roman army.
4. The king will draw up the infantry on the left wing.
5. A great part of the city will be fortified by a rampart.
6. All the forces of the enemy were drawn up opposite to the tower.
7. The soldiers were being hindered by their burdens.
8. The enemy were withstanding the fierce attack of our men.
9. Huge forces of Gauls had seized a small wood.
10. The loud cries of the barbarians were heard by the Romans.

Exercise 139.

1. On the right wing the Belgians withstood our men's attack.
2. The voice of Labienus was heard by his soldiers.
3. The king has led back his cavalry into camp.
4. The land had many woods.
5. The Roman cavalry were drawn up opposite to the enemy's infantry.
6. The shouts of the barbarians will be heard by the whole army.
7. A great part of the city was saved by the Roman general.
8. All the towns will be laid waste by the king's forces.
9. The voice of the wretched is heard by the gods.
10. The cries of the captives are heard by the king.

Exercise 140.

1. cīvium clāmor ā rēge audītus est.
2. oppidum aggere mūniētur.
3. hostium clāmōrēs ā nostrīs audiuntur.
4. ā mīlitibus Rōmānīs nōn audiēris.
5. puerī clāmōrēs ā patre audiēbantur.
6. urbs multīs turribus mūniētur.
7. rēx equitēs dextrō cornū instrūxerat.
8. mīlitum vōcēs ā cīvibus audiēbantur.
9. multae turrēs ā barbarīs aedificatae sunt.
10. cīvium miserōrum vōcēs ā rēge nōn audientur.

turris, -is 3. f. tower. **vōx, vōcis** 3. f. voice.

141. The Fate of M. Manlius

M. Manlius, quod Capitōlium ē perīculō servāverat, Capitolīnus
ā cīvibus vocātus est. posteā pauperum causam contrā patriciōs
dēfendit. statim patriciī Manlium, sīcut anteā Sp. Cassium et Sp.
Maelium, accūsāvērunt. "regnum," clāmābant, "appetit." itaque
Cornēliī Cossī iussū vīnctus est et in carcerem ductus. tum plēbēiī sordidātī in viās pūblicās veniēbant, prope arma prō vindice
sūmēbant: patriciī propter timōrem līberāvērunt. statim Manliī
audācia augēbātur: apertē iam plēbēiōs ad vim et arma vocāvit.
tum etiam ā tribūnīs plēbis accūsātus est. frūstrā Manlius pectus
nūdāvit, vulnera ostendit, ā dīs immortālibus auxilium petīvit:
hominis īnfēlīcis verba sine misericordiā audiēbantur. ā iūdicibus damnātus est et mortī inhonestae trāditus. nam dē saxō
Tarpeiō, ubi Capitōlium servāverat, ā tribūnīs plēbis dēmissus
est. nēmō posteā ē Manliā gente Marcus vocātus est.

iussū by the order. **carcer, -eris** 3. m. prison. **plēbs, plēbis** 3.
f. the common people. **sordidātus, -a, -um** dressed in
mourning. **vindex, -icis** 3. c. champion. **apertē** openly. **vīs,
vīs (pl. vīrēs, -ium)** 3. f. force, violence. **pectus, -oris** 3. n.
breast. **vulnus, -eris** 3. n. wound. **sine** (+abl.), without.
misericordia 1. f. pity. **saxum** 2. n. rock, stone; **saxum
Tarpeium** the Tarpeian rock.

142. The First Aeronauts

Daedalus artifex erat per omnem Graeciam nōtus. templa aedificāvit, deum imāginēs mīrās et pulchrās fingēbat. tum, quod sorōris filium necāverat, ā iūdicibus damnātus est et ad Crētam insulam discessit. diū cum Īcarō filiō captīvus in insulā tenēbātur. tandem ālās finxit. "marī undique," inquit, "velut carcere impedimur: nāvēs nōn habēmus: arte tamen via aperiētur. sī patris cōnsiliō pārēbis, per āera salūtem petēs." tum ālās ad humerōs cērā dēligāvit. statim Īcarus in āera ascendit: mox, quoniam prope sōlem volābat, cēra liquescēbat, puer infēlix in mare cecidit et poenās audāciae morte persolvit. Daedalus autem incolumis in Ītaliam volāvit ubi templum aedificāvit ālāsque Apollinī dēdicāvit.

artifex, -icis 3. c. artist, craftsman. **fingō, finxī, fictum** 3. I fashion, make. **soror, -ōris** 3. f. sister. **āla** 1. f. wing. **impediō** 4. I hinder, shut in, surround. **āēr, āeris** 3. m. air. **cēra** 1. f. wax. **dēligō** 1. I fasten. **sōl, sōlis** the sun. **volō** 1. I fly. **liquescō** 3. I melt. **poena** 1. f. punishment. **persolvō, -vī, -ūtum** 3. I pay; **poenās persolvō** (+ gen.) I pay the penalty of.

SECTION 22

Pluperfect and Future Perfect
Indicative Passive of *audiō* (Grammar Notes №. 89)
Nouns of 5th Declension (Grammar Notes №. 35).

"THINGS"

The word "thing" if qualified by an Adjective or Adjectival
Pronoun, is usually expressed by the neuter of that Adjective
or Pronoun, when it is in the Nominative or Accusative
Case; in other Cases it is expressed by the word *rēs* with the
Adjective or Pronoun in agreement;

e.g. *Many things have been prepared.*
multa parāta sunt.

I am frightened by many things.
multīs rēbus terreor.

Exercise 143.

1. The loud cries of the enemy had already been heard by
   our men.
2. Huge forces of barbarians attacked the line of the
   Romans.
3. A great part of the city had been fortified with ramparts.
4. Roman soldiers will not be hindered by barbarians.
5. The leader of the army has drawn up his line.
6. Great men are not frightened by small things.
7. Many things hindered our men.
8. The voice of the king has been heard by all the citizens.
9. Caesar had drawn up his line of battle.
10. All the towns of the Gauls were fortified by walls.

line, line of battle aciēs, aciēī 5. f. **thing, affair, matter** rēs,
reī 5. f. **Caesar** Caesar, -is 3. m. **wall** mūrus, -ī 2. m.

Exercise 144.

1. The cries of the captives were heard by Caesar.
2. Our men attacked the line of the enemy with darts and arrows.
3. A great part of the city has already been fortified.
4. The line of the enemy was drawn up opposite the Roman camp.
5. The city had been fortified with a large rampart.
6. Already the voices of the soldiers had been heard.
7. The line of the Belgians had been drawn up by their king.
8. The cry of the citizens will have been heard by the whole army.
9. The king had neglected the advice of the citizens.
10. Huge burdens were carried by the king's soldiers.

Exercise 145.

1. Everything had been heard by the leader.
2. We were hindered by many things.
3. The shouts of the Roman army had not been heard by the barbarians.
4. The king's forces attacked the line of our men.
5. The camp has been fortified with a large rampart.
6. The cavalry was led back into camp by the king.
7. The city has been fortified with a large tower.
8. All things frighten boys and barbarians.
9. Caesar led back a great part of his forces into the wood.
10. The attack of our men was withstood by the enemy's line.

everything omnia, -ium 3. n. pl.

Exercise 146.

1. imperātor aciem contrā urbem instruxit.
2. multīs rēbus exercitus impediēbātur.
3. urbs mūrō et aggere mūnīta est.
4. hostium aciēs contrā nostrōs instructa est.
5. puerī clāmōrēs ab omnibus audītī erant.
6. multīs rēbus nostrī terrēbantur.
7. urbs magnīs mūrīs mūnīta erat.
8. vōx imperātōris ab omnibus audīta erit.
9. Belgae Rōmānōrum aciem tēlīs oppugnāvērunt.
10. pars urbis aggere mūnīta erit.

aciēs 5. f. line of battle. **rēs** 5. f. thing, affair, matter.

147. The Licinian Laws (368 BC)

quamquam multa pauperibus cīvibus concessa erant, nōndum tamen finītum erat inter patriciōs plēbēiōsque certāmen. lēgēs identidem ā tribūnīs plēbis Liciniō et Sextiō rogābantur, per patriciōrum auctōritātem antīquābantur. per multōs annōs multīs dē rēbus cīvitās dissensiōne perturbābātur. tandem Camillus dictātor rempūblicam iterum servāvit. "frūstrā iam," inquit, "tribūnōrum postulātiōnibus resistimus: multa patriciī concēdēmus; cōnsulum alter ē plēbēiīs semper creābitur; agrī pūblicī nēmō amplius quīngenta iūgera possidēbit: contrā rēs ūna concēdētur ā plēbēiīs; iūs ā praetōre administrābitur, praetor ē patriciīs creābitur. tum dēnique finīta erit dissensiō et pāx reīpūblicae reddētur." placuit omnibus Camillī cōnsilium: posteā nūllae erant inter patriciōs et plēbēiōs dissensiōnēs: dictātor templum Concordiae dēdicāvit.

fīniō 4. I finish. **identidem** again and again. **annus** 2. m. year. **dissensiō, -ōnis** 3. f. dissension, strife. **perturbō** 1. I throw into confusion, disturb. **rēspūblica, reīpūblicae** f. state, republic. **postulātiō, -ōnis** 3. f. demand. **resistō, restitī** 3. (+dat.) I resist. **amplius** more, more than. **quīngentī, -ae, -a** five hundred. **iūgerum** 2. n. acre. **possideō, -sēdī, -sessum** 2. I own. **praetor, -ōris** 3. m. praetor.

148. A Family Curse

deī Oenomaum rēgem per ōrāculum sīc monuerant: "ā generō necāberis." itaque Oenomaus "nēmō," inquit, "fīliam in mātrimōnium dūcet." multī tamen pulchram fīliam, Hippodamīam, amābant, multī petēbant. "fīliam in mātrimōnium nōn dūcēs," respondit omnibus, "nisi patrem in currūs certāmine vīceris: sī victus eris, morte poenās audāciae persolvēs." multī ad certāmen veniēbant, multī ā rēge superābantur. tandem Pelops Myrtilum, rēgis aurīgam, prōmissīs conciliāvit. "dīmidium regnī dabō," inquit, "sī in certāmine adiūveris." tum Myrtilus rēgiī currūs axem discidit: itaque rēx ē currū cecidit, Pelops victor cum Hippodamīā ad patriam revertit. sed quamquam ā Myrtilō via ad victōriam inventa erat, prōmissum Pelops nōn praestitit. nam ubi currum prope mare agēbat, aurīgam in aquam dēmīsit. Myrtilus autem, "ā dīs immortālibus," clāmāvit, "auxilium petō: rem tam foedam dī nōn neglegent: per omnēs annōs Pelopis perfidiae poenās Pelopidae persolvent."

gener 2. m. son-in-law. **mātrimōnium** 2. n. marriage; **in mātrimōnium dūcō** I marry. **currus** 4. m. chariot; **currūs certāmen** chariot-race. **vincō, vīcī, victum** 3. I conquer, defeat. **aurīga** 1. c. charioteer. **conciliō** 1. I win over. **dīmidium** 2. n. half. **rēgius, -a, -um** royal. **axis, axis** 3. m. axle. **discindō, discidī, discissum** 3. I cut asunder. **foedus, -a, -um** disgraceful.

149. An Unnatural Daughter

tum improba puella Tullia sine misericordiā currum ascendit; ubi in forum vēnērunt sine timōre in magnā turbā virōrum Lūcium ē cūriā vocāvit et "avē," inquit, "rēx Rōmāne." mox, ubi Lūciī iussū domum revertēbat, mortuī patris corpus in viā iacēbat; aurīga corpus ostendit: tum fīliae iussū trāns patris membra currus ab aurīgā āctus est et axis sanguine cruentābātur.

rēs tam foeda omnium īram mōvit et prīmō tōta urbs dissensiōne perturbāta est. fīlia tamen poenās nōn persolvit: Serviō rēgī Serviī gener L. Tarquinius successit.

avē hail! greetings! **iaceō** 2. I lie. **succēdō, -cessī, -cessum** 3. (+dat.) I succeed.

SECTION 23

See Grammar Notes №. 81,
Indicative of *sum*.

THE VERB *SUM*

In a sentence like *The world is* the word *is* means *exists,* and it makes sense without anything added. But this is not the commonest use of the Verb *to be.*

In sentences like *He is wise* or *He was king of Britain* the words *is, was* make no sense without the Adjective or Noun that follows them.

This Adjective or Noun that, so to speak, completes the sense of any form of the Verb *to be* or the corresponding Latin Verb *esse* is called its Complement and must always be in the same Case as the Subject; furthermore, if it is an Adjective, it must agree with the Subject in Number and Gender;

e.g. *Romulus was king of the Romans.*
   Romūlus rēx Rōmānōrum fuit.

   The boys will be happy.
   puerī fēlīcēs erunt.

Exercise 150.

1. There was a large number of captives in the camp.
2. We shall not be successful.
3. Cotta was the leader of the Roman forces.
4. The walls of the enemy were small.
5. There are many captives in the city.
6. Great was the wisdom of the Roman generals.
7. I am a Roman citizen.
8. The cities of Gaul were not beautiful.
9. The shouts of the barbarians never frightened our men.
10. The Romans were successful in every battle.

am (are, is, be) sum, esse, fuī (irreg.). **number** numerus, -ī
2. m. **in** in (+abl.). **fortunate, happy, successful** fēlix, -īcis.
Gaul Gallia, -ae 1. f. **never** numquam.

Exercise 151.

1. The general was fortunate, (but) not daring.
2. He had been the general of a Roman army.
3. You will never be Roman citizens.
4. The plan of the general was daring.
5. The Gauls had never feared an enemy.
6. The boy's father was a soldier.
7. The infantry had never attacked a city.
8. The gods never neglect good men.
9. There were large forces of cavalry in the woods.
10. A small number of citizens withstood the enemy's attack.

bold, daring audāx, -ācis.

Exercise 152.

1. The voice of the wretched will always be heard by the gods.
2. The fierce attacks of the enemy will never terrify our men.
3. A large number of the soldiers had been led back into camp.
4. Great plans are often hindered by small things.
5. The weapons of the enemy wounded a large number of our men.
6. Great dangers are never feared by bold men.
7. The cavalry had been drawn up in the wood.
8. Boys are often warned by their fathers.
9. There are many cities and large towers in Gaul.
10. Everything will be successful for the daring.

always semper. **bold** audāx, -ācis.

Exercise 153.

1. ingentēs erant Gallōrum cōpiae.
2. Rōmānī numquam hostēs timēbunt.
3. magna fuit sapientia imperātōris.
4. hostium turrēs parvae, mūrī magnī fuērunt.
5. magna erunt bellī perīcula.
6. numquam in Galliā exercitus Rōmānus fuerat.
7. magnus est numerus captīvōrum.
8. omnēs in castrīs erāmus.
9. barbarī nōn semper audācēs sunt.
10. magna fuerit nostrōrum victōria.

sum, esse, fuī I am. **numquam** adv. never. **numerus** 2. m. number. **audāx, -ācis** adj. bold.

154. M. Valerius Corvus (349 BC)

cōnsul Rōmānus cōpiās contrā Gallōs dūxerat et castra in locō
idōneō posuerat. tum Gallus, vir propter corporis magnitūd-
inem et pulchra arma insignis, ad nostrōrum statiōnēs vēnit:
scūtum hastā ferit, ūnum ē Rōmānīs ad certāmen prōvocat.
erat tum in exercitū Rōmānō tribūnus mīlitum, iuvenis posteā
propter multās victōriās nōtus, nōmine M. Valerius. "nisi cōns-
ulī," inquit, "ingrātum fuerit, sōlus contrā hominem insolentem
pugnābō." datur ā cōnsule venia: Valerius ad certāmen armātus
prōcessit. vix iam manum conseruerant, ubi corvus repente in
galeā Valeriī consēdit et identidem ōs oculōsque hostis rostrō
appetīvit. itaque mox Rōmānus barbarum superat. tum nec
Gallī in statiōnibus manēbant et Rōmānī ad victōrem cucurrērunt. nōn iam sōlum statiōnum mīlitēs sed legiōnēs utrimque pugnae interfuērunt. diū et ācriter pugnābant: tandem
Rōmānī barbarōs vīcērunt et ad maris ōram fugāvērunt.

idōneus, -a, -um suitable. **magnitūdō, -inis** 3. f. size, great
size. **statiō, -ōnis** 3. f. outpost. **hasta** 1. f. spear. **venia** 1. f.
permission. **prōcēdō, -cessī, -cessum** 3. I advance. **conserō,
-uī, -tum** 3. I join together; **manum conserō** I join battle
corvus 2. m. raven. **galea** 1. f. helmet. **consīdō, -sēdī,
-sessum** 3. I settle. **rostrum** 2. n. beak. **currō, cucurrī,
cursum** 3. I run. **legiō, -ōnis** 3. f. legion. **intersum, -esse,
-fuī** (+dat.) I take part in.

155. The Spirit of Ancient Rome

Rōmānī cum Latīnīs bellum gerēbant. deī cōnsulēs per somnium sīc monuerant: "sī exercitus vīcerit, occīdētur imperātor: sī imperātor superfuerit, vincētur exercitus." utrimque ad pugnam prope Vesuvium montem prōcessērunt: T. Manlius Torquātus dextrō, P. Decius Mus sinistrō cornū praeerat: mox hostēs sinistrum cornū ācrī impetū oppugnāvērunt; nostrī paulātim locō cēdēbant. tum Decius, "prō rēpūblicā Rōmānā," inquit, "prō populī Rōmānī exercitū, legiōnibus, sociīs, Deciī vītam cum legiōnibus sociīsque hostium dīs mānibus dēvoveō." tum armātus in equum insiluit, sōlus in Latīnōrum aciem invāsit, ingentem numerum hostium occīdit, tandem mortem oppetīvit. mōvit virī intrepidī exemplum reliquōrum animōs: statim pugnam redintegrāvērunt, simul dextrō cornū Manlius novās cōpiās contrā fessum hostem dūxit. ubique Rōmānī vīcērunt: Latīnōrum paucī pugnae superfuērunt.

Latīnī 2. m. pl. the Latin people. **somnium** 2. n. dream. **occīdō, -dī, -sum** 3. I kill. **supersum, -esse, -fuī** (+dat.) I survive. **dexter, -tra, -trum** right, on the right hand; **dextrum cornū** the right wing (of an army); **dextrō cornū** on the right wing. **sinister, -tra, -trum** left, on the left hand; **sinistrum cornū** the left wing (of an army); **sinistrō cornū** on the left wing. **praesum, -esse, -fuī** (+dat.) I command. **paulātim** gradually. **cēdō, cessī, cessum** 3. I yield; **locō cēdō** I yield from my position, give ground. **mānēs** 3. m. pl. ghosts; **dī mānēs** the gods of the world below. **dēvoveō, dēvōvī, dēvōtum** 2. I devote, consecrate. **insiliō, -uī** 4. I leap. **invādō, -sī, -sum** 3. I make an attack. **redintegrō** 1. I renew.

SECTION 24

See Grammar Notes №s. 48–50,
Regular Comparison of Adjectives.

TO EXPRESS COMPARISON

A Comparative Adjective may be followed by the Ablative
Case to express the thing with which another is compared.
This is called the Ablative of Comparison;

> e.g. *The general was not braver than the king.*
> imperātor rēge nōn fortior erat.

Instead of this Ablative of Comparison we can always use
quam, than. The two things compared are then always in
the same Case:

> e.g. imperātor fortior erat quam rēx.

The construction with *quam* must always be used except
where the two things compared are expressed by two Nouns
and the first of these is in the Nominative or Accusative Case.

Exercise 156.

1. The danger will be more serious for our men.
2. The cavalry will be hindered by a very broad river.
3. The city was very beautiful.
4. The bravest soldiers held the right wing.
5. I have avoided the most serious dangers.
6. The infantry were more successful than the cavalry.
7. The attack of the enemy was very fierce.
8. The general drew up the boldest soldiers opposite the town.
9. Many burdens hinder a soldier.
10. Large cities are not always very beautiful.

heavy, serious gravis, -is, -e. **broad** lātus, -a, -um. **river**
flūmen, -inis 3. n. **brave** fortis, -is, -e. **than** quam.

Exercise 157.

1. Our men have overcome the Gauls by a very fierce attack.
2. The infantry will be braver than the cavalry in the battle.
3. The towers of the Gauls were higher than their walls.
4. We were hindered by a very broad river.
5. The burdens of the Roman citizens were very heavy.
6. The Belgians fortified their towns by very high walls.
7. The plan of the general is bolder.
8. The wall (is) very high, the river is very broad.
9. Nothing is more beautiful than wisdom.
10. The Romans are not more daring than the Belgians.

deep, high altus, -a, -um. **wall** mūrus, -ī 2. m. **nothing** nihil.

Exercise 158.

1. The bravest leader is not always the most successful.
2. The Gauls' arms were heavier than (those) of our men.
3. We fiercely attacked the cavalry of the Belgians.
4. The line was drawn up opposite a very deep river.
5. The boldest generals are always loved by their soldiers.
6. You will not be more daring than your father.
7. The town was fortified by a high rampart and a broad river.
8. We shall avoid the more serious dangers of war.
9. The camp was attacked by the brave general.
10. The broadest rivers are not always the deepest.

fiercely ācriter.

Exercise 159.

1. altior erat turris quam mūrus.
2. Galliae flūmina lātissima sunt.
3. ācerrimō impetū barbarōs superābant.
4. fortiōrēs erant equitēs quam peditēs.
5. nihil gravius est bellī perīculō.
6. cīvium onera gravissima sunt.
7. barbarī Rōmānīs nōn fortiōrēs erant.
8. ducis cōnsilia audācissima fuērunt.
9. hostium cōpiae ingentiōrēs quam Rōmānōrum erunt.
10. altissimō mūrō urbs mūnīta erat.

altus, -a, -um high. **lātus, -a, -um** adj. wide. **gravis, -is, -e** heavy, serious.

160. The Caudine Forks (321 BC)

est in Ītaliā locus propter clādem Rōmānam nōtissimus. exercitus Rōmānus, ubi cum Samnitibus bellum gerēbat, per saltum angustum in campum intrāvit: campō utrimque montēs altissimī impendēbant: mox ad alterum saltum etiam angustiōrem vēnērunt. intereā hostēs utrimque saltūs arboribus saepserant exercitumque Rōmānum velut in carcere tenēbant. frūstrā aliam viam petēbant nostrī: tandem arma hostibus trādidērunt. tum C. Pontius, Samnitium imperātor, ad patrem, virum sapientissimum, nūntiōs mīsit cōnsiliumque petīvit. "sī patris cōnsiliō pārēbis," respondit senex, "Rōmānōs omnēs aut incolumēs līberābis aut occīdēs." fīlius tamen patris cōnsilium neglēxit: Rōmānōs sub iugum mīsit, tum līberāvit. anteā tamen C. Pontiī iussū Rōmānī pācem et amīcitiam cum Samnitibus iūsiūrandō cōnfirmāvērunt et obsidēs dedērunt. "nōn sīc," pater fīlium monuit, "aut amīcōs conciliābis aut hostēs dēlēbis."

clādēs, -is 3. f. disaster. **saltus** 4. m. pass. **campus** 2. m. plain. **impendeō, -ndī, -nsum** 2. (+dat.) I overhang. **saepiō, -psī, -ptum** 4. I block up. **iūsiūrandum** 2. n. oath.

161. A Roman Father

T. Manlius Torquātus cōnsul exercitum Rōmānum ad disciplīnam sevērissimam instituit. "nēmō" (sīc mīlitibus ēdīxerat)
"sōlus extrā ōrdinēs cum hostibus pugnābit." praeerat tum
hostium equitibus vir propter virtūtem nōtissimus Geminus
Mettius: Manliī fīlium Mettius ad certāmen prōvocāvit. mōvit
iuvenis animum intrepidum vel īra vel pudor: patris iussa
nēglexit hostemque superāvit et occīdit. tum corpus Mettiī
spoliāvit, spolia magnō cum gaudiō ad patrem portāvit. pater
autem "quoniam, T. Manlī," inquit, "nec cōnsulis imperium
nec patris auctōritātem timēs contrāque imperātōris iussa
extrā ōrdinēs sōlus hodiē cum hoste pugnāvistī mīlitāremque
disciplīnam neglēxistī, poenās audāciae morte persolvēs. trīste
exemplum erimus, sed reliquīs iuvenibus ūtile." statim patris
iussī fīlius ad supplicium dūcitur.

sevērus, -a, -um severe. **instituō, -uī, -ūtum** 3. I train.
ēdīcō, ēdīxī, ēdictum 3. I proclaim. **extrā** (+acc.) outside.
ōrdō, -inis 3. m. rank. **vel ... vel** either ... or. **pudor, -ōris** 3.
m. shame. **spoliō** 1. I despoil. **spolium** 2. n. spoil (usually pl.
spoils). **mīlitāris, -is, -e** military. **trīstis, -is, -e** sad. **ūtilis,
-is, -e** useful.

162. A Great Man's Contempt For Riches

Phocion Athēniensis, quamquam saepe exercitibus praefuit et ab omnibus vir fortissimus habēbātur, tamen nōtior
est propter virtūtem vītae quam propter bellī victōriās. fuit
semper pauper, quamquam virō tam praeclārō mūnera pulcherrima ā populō saepe dabantur. ōlim magnam pecūniam ā
rēge Philippō datam repudiāvit; tum lēgātī "sī pecūniam nōn
amās," clāmāvērunt, "tamen fīliōs, crēdō, amās; sī bonus pater
es, fīliōrum causā rēgis mūnera nōn repudiābis." respondit
Phocion, "sī fīliī patrī similēs erunt, dīvitiās nōn dēsiderābunt."

quam than. **praeclārus, -a, -um** eminent. **datus, -a, -um**
given, offered. **repudiō** 1. I reject. **similis, -is, -e** like.

SECTION 25

See Grammar Notes №s. 24 & 25,
Comparison of Adjectives in -ilis,
and Irregular Comparison.

Exercise 163.

1. He had easily avoided the greatest dangers.
2. The towns of the barbarians were very small.
3. The Gauls had larger weapons than our men.
4. War is a very easy matter to a Roman.
5. The greatest dangers never terrify a brave man.
6. The camp of the Belgians is smaller than (that) of the Romans.
7. The plan of the general is better than (that) of the citizens.
8. Our men had better arms than the enemy.
9. The Gauls had very good horses.
10. It was an easy matter for the Roman army.

easily *adv.* facile. **greatest** maximus, -a, -um. **smallest, very small** minimus, -a, -um. **larger** māior, -or, -us. **smaller** minor, -or, -us. **easy** facilis, -is, -e. **better** melior, -or, -us.

Exercise 164.

1. He drew up the best soldiers opposite the rampart.
2. The largest cities are not always the most beautiful.
3. The best citizens will not neglect the king's advice.
4. The town was fortified by very large towers.
5. The line of the Romans was smaller than (that) of the barbarians.
6. The plan of the general will be very useful for the army.
7. The shields of the enemy were very small.
8. We had never attacked a larger camp.
9. Labienus was liked by the best soldiers.
10. With the greatest courage you have overcome all dangers.

best optimus, -a, -um. **largest** māior, -or, -us. **useful** ūtilis, -is, -e. **valour, courage** virtūs, -ūtis 3. f.

Exercise 165.

1. The most fierce attacks are not always the most successful.
2. The best soldiers have been led back into camp.
3. Our men seized the town with great valour.
4. The cavalry easily overcame the enemy's forces.
5. A small number of infantry was attacked by our men.
6. The soldiers had fought well against the barbarians.
7. Our men withstood the attack with great courage.
8. The Gauls fiercely attacked the Roman infantry.
9. We shall easily overcome the forces of Belgians.
10. The boy had been well advised by his father.

valour virtūs, -ūtis 3. f. **well** *adv.* bene.

Exercise 166.

1. Cottae cōnsilium melius quam imperātōris erat.
2. rēs facillima erit equitibus.
3. Gallīs scūta ūtilissima ērant.
4. barbarōrum quam Rōmānōrum castra minōra erant.
5. nihil melius est sapientiā.
6. plūrimī barbarōrum equōs nōn habēbant.
7. minimīs rēbus maxima saepe cōnsilia impediuntur.
8. nostrī minōre virtūte pugnābant.
9. arma in bellō ūtilissima sunt.
10. puerī rēs facillimās amant.

facilis, -is, -e easy. **minor, -or, -us** compar. adj. smaller. **plūrimus, -a, -um** superl. adj. most. **minimus, -a, -um** superl. adj. smallest. **maximus, -a, -um** superl. adj. greatest.

167. A Pyrrhic Victory (280 BC)

Tarentī incolae, ubi bellum cum Rōmānīs gerēbant, auxilium ā Pyrrhō, Ēpīrī rēge, petiērunt. Pyrrhus cum maximō exercitū Graecōrum ad Ītaliam vēnit et cum Rōmānīs prope Hēraclēam pugnāvit. tum prīmum in proelium contrā Rōmānōs elephantī ductī sunt. Rōmānī partim propter animālium ingentium timōrem, partim propter optimam disciplīnam Graecōrum victī sunt. plūrimī tamen utrimque cecidērunt. Pyrrhus, ubi tot mortuōrum corpora vīdit, "sī eiusmodī victōriam iterum reportāverō," clāmāvit, "sōlus ad Ēpīrum nāvigābō." ūtilissima fuit Pyrrhō Cīneae lēgātī sapientia, nam plūra oppida per ēloquentiam conciliāvit Cīneās quam rēx bellō superāvit: frūstrā tamen cum Rōmānīs in urbe dē pāce disseruit: "numquam cum hostibus, dum in Ītaliā sunt," Appius Claudius senātor respondit, "dē pāce Rōmānī disserunt." Cīneās, ubi ad Pyrrhum revertit, "Rōmānōrum," inquit, "urbs deōrum templum, senātus deōrum concilium est." tandem Pyrrhus prope Beneventum victus est; posteā ad Graeciam revertit.

proelium 2. n. battle. **elephantus** 2. m. elephant. **partim** partly. **animal, -ālis** 3. n. animal. **optimus, -a, -um** superl. adj. best. **plūrēs, -ēs, -a** pl. adj. more. **ēloquentia** 1. f. eloquence. **dum** (+indicative) while. **senātus** 4. m. senate. **concilium** 2. n. assembly.

168. The Judgment of Paris

deī ōlim, quod Pēleus Thetin deam in mātrimōnium dūcēbat, magnum convīvium celebrābant. dī deaeque omnēs ad
cēnam vocantur, praeter Discordiam: itaque īrāta dea pōmum
in mediam turbam iactāvit; in pōmō inscripta erant verba
"pulcherrimae deae mūnus pōmum mittitur." statim maxima
fuit inter Iūnōnem, Minervam, Venerem rixa: rēs Paridis
arbitriō mandāta est. Paris, rēgis Trōiānī Priamī fīlius, ovēs
tum in monte Idaeō pāscēbat. ad montem veniunt deae: puerī
animum prōmissīs conciliant. Iūnō magnās dīvitiās, Minerva
bellī fāmam, Venus pulcherrimam omnium uxōrem prōmittit.
Venerī dat Paris pōmum: Veneris auxiliō ad Graeciam nāvigāvit, mox cum Helenā, rēgis Menelāī uxōre, omnium tum
fēminārum pulcherrima, ad patriam revertit. tum Menelāus
cum Agamemnōne frātre plūrimus nāvēs parāvit, ad Asiam
nāvigāvit, urbem Trōiam obsidēbat decemque post annōs
expugnāvit.

Thetis, (acc. Thetin), Thetidis 3. f. Thetis. pōmum 2. n.
apple. media turba the middle of the crowd. inscrībō,
inscrīpsī, inscriptum 3. I inscribe. ovis, ovis 3. f. sheep.
Idaeus, -a, -um of Ida; mōns Idaeus Mount Ida. pāscō,
pāvī, pāstum 3. I feed. fēmina 1. f. woman. frāter, -tris 3.
m. brother.

SECTION 26

See Grammar Notes Nºs. 61 & 63,
1st and 2nd Persons; 3rd Person, *is, ea, id.*

PERSONAL PRONOUNS

Latin has no 3rd Person Pronoun like *he, she, it.* It uses Demonstratives instead, most frequently *is, ea, id.*

> e.g. *I love my country: I will save it.*
> patriam amō: eam servābō.

Remember that the Personal Pronoun is not usually expressed when it is the subject of a Verb. It should be expressed where there is emphasis or a contrast.

> e.g. *You love your country: we saved it.*
> vōs patriam amātis, nōs servāvimus.

REFLEXIVE PRONOUNS

A Reflexive is a Pronoun used in an Oblique Case, and standing for the same person as the subject of its sentence.

In the 1st and 2nd Persons the Personal Pronouns are used as Reflexives;

> e.g. tē cēlās.
> *You are hiding yourself.*

In the 3rd Person there is a special Reflexive, that is *sē* (both Singular and Plural);

> e.g. mīlitēs sē cēlant
> *The soldiers are hiding themselves.*

See Grammar Notes №. 62,
1st Person, *meus, noster;* 2nd Person, *tuus, vester;*
3rd Person, *suus* [Reflexive only].

POSSESSIVE ADJECTIVES

The words called Possessive Pronouns are all *Adjectives,* and must agree with the Noun to which they belong;

> e.g.   *Your father saved our city.*
> tuus pater nostram urbem servāvit.

It is not usually necessary to express the Possessive Adjective in Latin when it is of the same person as the subject of the sentence;

> e.g.   *I love my father.*   patrem amō.
> *I love your father.* tuum patrem amō.

For the 3rd Person the Adjective suus is only to be used Reflexively, i.e. referring to the subject of its sentence;

> e.g. *The Gauls laid waste their own fields.*
> Gallī suōs agrōs vastāvērunt.

When *his, their,* etc., are not Reflexive, we must use the Genitives of *is, ea, id;* e.g.

> Gallī Germānōs oppugnant et tecta eōrum incendunt.
> *The Gauls attack the Germans and set fire to their homes.*
> (i.e. the houses of the Germans)

N.B.—It will be obvious from the above rule that *his, their,* etc., cannot be Reflexive which they qualify the subject of the sentence;

> e.g.   *His father heard him.*
> Eius pater eum audivit.

Exercise 169.

1. My plan was better than yours.
2. Your victory was announced to me.
3. Our soldiers attacked their town.
4. We have announced the victory to him.
5. I shall not hide myself in the city.
6. The citizens have saved their own city.
7. The cavalry hid themselves in the wood.
8. The barbarians have laid waste our fields.
9. We shall not be terrified by the attack of your infantry.
10. His plan was very useful to the citizens.

I hide cēlō 1.

Exercise 170.

1. We announced the battle to you.
2. The Gauls bravely withstood our attack.
3. Their city was well fortified by a high rampart.
4. Our country will never be ruled by barbarians.
5. The enemy were overcome by me.
6. We shall not neglect the advice of your general.
7. The enemies' soldiers are hiding themselves in the woods.
8. Your army will be hindered by the river.
9. His son was not wounded by the arrow.
10. Our cavalry had been drawn up on the right wing.

bravely *adv.* fortiter.

Exercise 171.

1. The heaviest burdens will very easily be carried by us.
2. The king will hear you and save the city.
3. The advice of my son was very useful to me.
4. The affair will be very difficult for you and your citizens.
5. Nothing is more beautiful than our city.
6. It will be easier for you than for us.
7. He saved himself by his own stratagem.
8. Their cavalry are braver than their infantry.
9. The rivers of our country are very broad and deep.
10. Their camp was smaller than ours.

difficult difficilis, -is, -e.

Exercise 172.

1. urbs nostra ab equitibus servāta est.
2. clāmōrēs tuī ā rēge audiēbantur.
3. omnēs imperātōrem nostrum amāmus.
4. equitēs in silvīs sē cēlābant.
5. victōriam mihi mīlitēs nūntiāvērunt.
6. hostium dux mē sagittā vulnerāvit.
7. eius pater saepe eum monuerat.
8. urbem nostram aggere et mūrō mūniēmus.
9. pater meus tē impediet.
10. equitum victōriam vōbīs nūntiābunt.

cēlō 1. I hide.

173. Chivalry in War

Rōmānīs, ubi cum Pyrrhō bellum gerēbant, praeerat Fabricius. multa in historiā dē Fabriciō, multa dē Pyrrhō nārrantur. ōlim transfuga ē Graecōrum exercitū ad castra Rōmāna vēnit: statim ad imperātōrem ductus est. "via ad victōriam facillima Rōmānīs aperitur," inquit; "sī pecūniam mihi dabis, castra petam, rēgem venēnō necābō." respondit Fabricius, "ingrātior

erit nōbīs eiusmodī victōria quam miserrima clādēs: virtūte,
nōn perfidiā, hostēs vincīmus." tum imperātōris iussū eum
ad Graecōrum castra mīlitēs redūcunt tōtamque rem Pyrrhō
nārrant. mōvit rēgis animum Fabriciī līberālitās: statim omnēs
captīvōs Rōmānīs sine pretiō reddidit. contrā Rōmānī lēgātōs
ad Pyrrhum mīsērunt. "dē pāce," inquiunt, "Rōmānī cum
hostibus, dum in Ītaliā sunt, nōn disserunt: tibi tamen, virō
omnium generōsissimō, libenter concēdimus indūtiās."

transfuga 1. c. deserter. **venēnum** 2. n. poison. **perfidia** 1. f.
treachery. **redūcō, redūxī, reductum** 3. I lead back.
pretium 2. n. price, ransom. **generōsus, -a, -um** generous.
indūtiae 1. f. pl. truce.

174. Ancient Robbers

Thēseus, praeter alia facta insignissima, maximam sibi fāmam
comparāvit quod latrōnēs propter crūdēlitātem nōtōs Procru-
stem, Scirōnem, Sinōnem occīderat.

Procrustēs, sī forte advenam vī superāverat, eum nōn
sōlum spoliābat sed ad lectum dēligābat: tum sī hominis
infēlīcis corpus brevius erat quam lectus, membra eius ad
idōneam longitūdinem tendēbat; contrā sī brevior lectus erat
quam corpus, pedēs vel partem membrōrum gladiō abscīdēbat.

Sciron in saxō altissimō sedēbat. eius iussū viātōrēs pedēs
latrōnis lavābant; dum lavant, Sciron ictū pedis in mare dēmit-
tēbat.

Sinon verticem arboris ad terram flectēbat: captīvī caput
ad verticem, pedēs ad truncum dēligābat: tum repente verticem remittēbat.

insignis, -is, -e distinguished, remarkable. **sē** himself
(reflexive). **latrō, -ōnis** 3. m. robber. **crūdēlitās, -ātis** 3. f.
cruelty. **lectus** 2. m, bed. **brevis, -is, -e** short. **longitūdō,
-inis** 3. f. length. **tendō, tetendī, tentum** 3. I stretch.
abscīdō, -dī, -sum 3. I cut off. **viātor, -ōris** 3. m. traveller.
lavō, lāvī, lautum 1. I wash. **ictus** 4. m. blow. **flectō, flexī,
flexum** 3. I bend. **vertex, -icis** 3. m. top. **truncus** 2. m.
trunk. **remittō, -īsī, -issum** 3. I send back, let go.

175. An Appeal to Resist the Invader

hostēs nostrī propter invidiam contrā nōs coniūrāvērunt et
cōpiās parant; ad terram nostram hodiē nāvigant, crās fortasse
nōs oppugnābunt; perīculum nōbīs maximum impendet. sī
patriam amāmus, sī prō eā in aciē cadēmus, maximam fāmam
inter omnēs gentēs comparābimus; sī hostibus iam resistēmus,
sī eōs ad mare fugābimus, nēmō nōs iterum oppugnābit. nihil,
crēdō, cārius vōbīs est quam patria, nihil fortī virō foedius
quam patriae exitium; prō eā optimī cīvēs libenter vītam
dēvovent. egō vōs ad arma vocō, egō in proelium dūcam; vōs
sī mihi pārēbitis, penes nōs victōria erit.

cārus, -a, -um dear.

SECTION 27

See Grammar Notes №. 63,
hic and *ille*

DEMONSTRATIVE PRONOUNS

N.B.—*hic* is used like the English *this* for what is near to the speaker in place or time;

e.g.   *This city (where I am).*
       haec urbs.

ille is used like *that* for what is further away;

e.g.   *This tower is not higher than that (one over there).*
       haec turris nōn altior est illā.

Exercise 176.

1. Nothing will be more useful to our citizens than your plan.
2. This part of the city had not been fortified.
3. We shall lead our soldiers into that town.
4. The dangers of this war will be very serious.
5. Your soldiers assailed this tower.
6. Their cavalry were hidden in this wood.
7. That danger will be overcome by our leaders.
8. The greatest wars are not feared by those barbarians.
9. That horse has been wounded by an arrow.
10. This battle was very fortunate for our troops.

this hic, haec, hoc. **that** ille, illa, illud.

Exercise 177.

1. This city was built by the Gauls.
2. This sea is very deep.
3. This general saved himself, but not his country.
4. These attacks are easily withstood by the brave soldiers.
5. Their weapons were wounding our horses.
6. You will not frighten the brave citizens by this device.
7. This part of the city was held by Labienus.
8. These soldiers were drawn up on the left wing.
9. The barbarians will never overcome this army.
10. You will not save yourself by this plan.

Exercise 178.

1. This victory was announced to us by the captives.
2. That advice will never be neglected by me.
3. These arms were carried by my father.
4. The dangers of war will never terrify these citizens.
5. This thing will be easy to me and to you.
6. This most beautiful city was attacked by the enemy.
7. These fields were laid waste by the Belgians.
8. The victory was announced to me by this boy.
9. These shields are very broad and very heavy.
10. These cities were fortified by high ramparts and towers.

Exercise 179.

1. hoc onus gravius quam illud est.
2. hanc urbem virtūte suā servābant.
3. nihil illā urbe pulchrius est.
4. tē nōn timēbimus, Labiēne.
5. haec onera facile ā mīlitibus portābantur.
6. illud cōnsilium ūtilissimum fuerit.
7. haec terra numquam ā barbarīs regētur.
8. hōs in castra redūxerat imperātor.
9. hoc illī nōn neglegent.
10. huius urbis mūrī altissimī sunt.

hic, haec, hoc this. **ille, illa, illud** that. **suus, -a, -um** his, her, their (reflexive). **facile** adv. easily.

180. The First Punic War (264–241 BC)

Tyriī ōlim in Āfricā haud procul ab Hispāniā colōniam collocāverant magnamque urbem, Carthāginem nōmine, aedificāverant: huius urbis incolae Poenī vocābantur. hī per mercātūram magnās dīvitiās comparāvērunt finitimōsque populōs imperiō suō adiūnxērunt: urbem ingentibus mūrīs mūnīverant templīsque pulcherrimīs ornāverant. multa in historiā dē illīus gentis crūdēlitāte nārrantur: ducēs, sī in bellō victī erant, sine misericordiā occīdēbant; īnfantēs suōs dīs immolābant.

omnium iam populōrum Rōmānī et Poenī potentissimī erant: inter aemulās gentēs causa bellī mox invenītur.

in Siciliā Hierō, rēx Syracusārum, Māmertīnōs obsidēbat: Rōmānī ad Māmertīnōs, Poenī ad Hierōnem auxilium mīsērunt. tum Hierō pācem amīcitiamque cum Rōmānīs confirmāvit, Poenī sōlī cum Rōmānīs bellum gerēbant ōramque Ītaliae nāvibus vastābant.

Hispānia 1. f. Spain. **Carthāgō, -inis** 3. f. Carthage. **Poenī** 2. m. pl. the Carthaginians (descended from the Phoenicians). **ornō** 1. I adorn. **īnfāns, īnfantis** 3. c. infant, child. **potēns, potentis** powerful. **aemulus, -a, -um** rival. **Syracusae** 1. f. pl. Syracuse.

181. An Ancient Sorceress

Ulixēs cum comitibus ōlim ad insulam Aeaeam nāvigāvit:
habitābat in eā insulā Circē, dea propter artem magicam
nōtissima. Ulixēs prīmō in ōrā manēbat, comitum nōnnullōs
in interiōrem partem insulae mīsit. ex hīs Eurylochus sōlus
ad ducem revertit. "magnum nōs perīculum manet in hāc
insulā," inquit; "vix ā tē discesserāmus ubi magnam domum
in mediā silvā vīdimus: prope portās errābant multa animālia,
neque tamen nōs oppugnābant. tum domō excessit fēmina, vel
dea, pulcherrima: verbīs nōs dulcibus compellāvit et cibum
dedit: tum comitēs meōs repente virgā ferit et in suēs vertit.
egō sōlus domum nōn intrāveram, sōlus ad tē revertī." tum
Ulixēs ad locum statim properāvit: occurrit in itinere Mercurius. "frūstrā tū," inquit, "homō contrā deam pugnābis: meō
tamen auxiliō incolumis eris." tum herbam magicam dedit et
multa monēbat. itaque nōn sōlum sibi sed comitibus salūtem
comparāvit: nam Circē frūstrā contrā Ulixem artēs exercuit
et comitibus formam hūmānam reddidit.

nōnnullus, -a, -um some. interior, -or, -us inner. compellō
1. I address. virga 1. f. wand. sūs, suis 3. c. pig. vertō, -tī,
-sum 3. I turn. occurrō, -rrī, -rsum 3. I run to meet. iter,
itineris 3. n. journey. Mercurius 2. m. the messenger of
the gods, Mercury. herba 1. f. herb. forma 1. f. shape, form.

SECTION 28

See Grammar Notes № 64,
ipse and *īdem*

SELF AND SAME

Self in the Nominative always, and in the Oblique Cases
when not Reflexive, is expressed by *ipse;*

> e.g.   *I myself heard it.*
> ipse audīvī.
>
> *He was praised by Caesar himself.*
> ā Caesare ipsō laudātus est.

Exercise 182.

1. The soldiers themselves were terrified by the enemy.
2. The soldiers saved themselves by the same plan.
3. They will attack our city themselves.
4. The same things are not easy to all men.
5. The burden itself was not very heavy.
6. The same part of the city was being attacked by the infantry.
7. The Belgians themselves do not fear our soldiers.
8. The wisdom of the same general saved the town.
9. We announced the victory to the general himself.
10. Both cavalry and infantry were overcome by the same attack.

same īdem, eadem, idem. **both...and** et...et.

Exercise 183.

1. You praise yourself; you do not praise your soldiers.
2. His army was defeated by the same enemy.
3. The son himself is more daring than his father.
4. This camp was attacked by the same troops.
5. The general had drawn up all the cavalry on the same wing.
6. We were fighting bravely opposite the same rampart.
7. These serious dangers are feared by all the citizens.
8. Both the cavalry and the infantry were praised by the same general.
9. Their leaders bravely withstood our attacks.
10. War itself is not a serious danger.

praise laudō 1.

Exercise 184.

1. The wretched captives were saved by their own device.
2. We hid ourselves in the same wood.
3. This land is loved by me, that (one) by you.
4. The king himself was not terrified by fear of war.
5. In the same part of the city the shouts of the enemy were heard.
6. That (thing) itself will not be feared by a brave man.
7. His horse was wounded by the same arrow.
8. The general himself avoided all the dangers of war.
9. The same river was both very broad and very deep.
10. The general will draw up his cavalry on the left wing.

Exercise 185.

1. in eādem urbe et equitēs et peditēs fuērunt.
2. ab ipsō imperātōre bellum timēbātur.
3. ipse numquam māiōrem exercitum oppugnāverat.
4. urbs ipsa ā mīlitibus neglēcta erat.
5. in eōdem virtūs erat et sapientia.
6. haec mihi ab eōdem nūntiābantur.
7. īdem dux patriam servāvit.
8. ipsum bellum ā nostrīs nōn timētur.
9. īdem tibi ā mīlitibus nūntiābitur.
10. imperātor ipse mīlitēs laudāvit.

īdem, eadem, idem the same. **ipse, -a, -um** himself, herself, itself.

186. The First Roman Naval Victory (261 BC)

Rōmānī terrā, Poenī marī omnium tum populōrum potentissimī erant. itaque in hōc bellō Rōmānī maxima difficultāte tenēbantur quod Poenī plūrimās nāvēs, ipsī nūllās omnīnō habēbant. hāc dē rē mīra fābula in historiā nārrātur. ūna ē nāvibus Pūnicīs in ōram Ītaliae ventō repulsa erat: statim Rōmānī aliam nāvem eiusdem formae, mox aliās nāvēs aedificābant: tandem magnam classem habēbant. tum marī quoque cum Poenīs bellum gessērunt: C. Duilius maximam sibi fāmam comparāvit quod prīmus omnium ducum Rōmānōrum victōriam marī prope Mylas reportāvit. nāvium captārum rostrīs forum ornāvērunt: haec rostra Columnam Rostrātam vocābant. Duiliō ipsī maximus honor ā cīvibus datus est. nam quotiēns noctū ad suum domicilium commeābat tībīcinēs eum cum taedīs dēdūcēbant.

difficultās, -ātis 3. f. difficulty. **Pūnicus, -a, -um** Punic, Carthaginian. **repellō, reppulī, repulsum** 3. I drive back. **classis, -is** 3. f. fleet. **columna** 1. f. column. **rostrātus, -a, -um** beaked. **quotiēns** as often as, whenever. **tībīcen, -inis** 3. m. flute-player. **taeda** 1. f. torch. **dēdūcō, dēdūxī, dēductum** 3. I lead back, escort.

187. Orpheus

omnium ōlim poētārum nōtissimus erat Orpheus: multae dē
illō fābulae nārrantur. quotiēns citharā lūdēbat, post sē nōn
sōlum animālia sed etiam arborēs et saxa trahēbat. eiusdem
citharae dulcī sonō Argonautae nāvem in mare dēdūxērunt, et
dracō, aureī velleris custōs, sōpītus est. uxōrem ille Eurydicen
ante omnia amābat: haec ubi vītā excessit, et ipse ad mānēs dēscendit uxōremque ā Plūtōne petīvit. respondit deus, "uxōrem
post tē ad terram dūcēs, in terrā iterum faciem eius spectābis:
tū prīmus ascendēs: sī semel oculōs retrō verteris, uxor tua ad
mānēs dēscendet nec iterum, ascendet." maximō tum gaudiō
discessērunt; prope iam ad terram vēnerant ubi poēta propter
ingentem amōrem oculōs retrō vertit: statim Eurydice ad mānēs
revertit. posteā semper Orpheus propter dolōrem aliās fēminās
contemnēbat: illae īrātae hominis īnfēlīcis corpus dīlaniāvērunt,
caput in Hebrum fluvium dēmīsērunt.

poēta 1. m. poet. **custōs, -ōdis** 3. c. guardian, guard. **sōpiō**
4. I put to sleep. **dēscendō, -dī, -sum** 3. I descend. **Plūtō,**
-ōnis 3. m. Pluto (the god of the lower world). **faciēs** 5. f.
face. **retrō** back, backwards. **contemnō, -mpsī, -mptum** 3.
I despise. **dīlaniō** 1. I tear to pieces.

188. The Good Old Times

ōlim pūblicīs rēbus multum interfuī, sed tempora iam mūtāta
sunt, egō cum temporibus mūtātus sum. senex nōn saepe in
cūriā videor. multī tamen ad mē cōtīdiē veniunt, multī cōnsilium ā mē petunt: nam in hāc urbe, crēdō, quamquam senex
sum, nōnnullam tamen auctōritātem habeō. nōn semper
eadem cum illīs dē rēpūblicā sentiō: nam haec nostrī temporis
mala plūra sunt quam priōra. tē autem amīcōsque tuōs bonōs
cīvēs nōn vocō sī hīs malīs nōn resistitis. annōs illōs priōrēs
trīstissimō animō dēsīderō ubi filiī patribus, filiae mātribus
pārēbant, et virtūs in māiōre honōre erat quam pecūnia.

tempus, -oris 3. n. time. **malum** 2. n. evil. **prior, -or, -us**
compar. adj. former.

SECTION 29

See Grammar Notes №. 65,
Relative Pronoun, *quī*

RELATIVE PRONOUNS

In *I saw the gate: this was open,* we have two separate sentences. In the second *this* is a Demonstrative Pronoun standing for *the gate* in the first, and it would be parsed as having the same Gender and Number as *gate*. But its Case has nothing to do with *gate*; it is the Subject of *was*, and is therefore in the Nominative Case.

In *I saw the gate, which was open,* we say the same thing, but in place of the Demonstrative *this* we use the Relative *which,* because it serves to connect the sentences. Here *which* stands for *gate* just as *this* did, and for the same reasons it must have the same Gender and Number as *gate,* but gets its Case from its own clause. The word *gate* is called the Antecedent.

Therefore in Latin as in English we have the rule:

A Relative Pronoun agrees with its Antecedent in Gender, Number, and Person, but its Case depends on its relation to its own clause.

> e.g. *I praised the soldier, who had fought bravely.*
> mīlitem laudāvī quī bene pugnāverat.
>
> *The wall, which we built, was very high.*
> mūrus, quem aedificāmus, altissimus erat.
>
> *This is Gaius, whose son I was praising.*
> hic   est Gaius cuius fīlium laudābam.

If you are ever in doubt as to the Case of the Relative, turn the clause into one with a Demonstrative or Personal Pronoun. The above could only be "I praised the soldier. *He* had fought bravely." "This is Gaius. I was praising *his* (Lat. eius) son." Remember that the Relative stands for these

Demonstratives or Personal Pronouns, and must have the same Case that they would have.

N.B.—The Relative can never be omitted in Latin as it often is in English. The second of the above sentences could in English be "The wall we built was very high." This is impossible in Latin.

Exercise 189.

1. The ship which we built was very large.
2. The camp which they attacked was smaller than their own.
3. The man who announced the victory was praised by the general.
4. The part of the city which we neglected was attacked by the enemy.
5. The men whom you rule do not like you.
6. The soldiers were terrified of the shouts which they heard.
7. We were attacked by the enemy, who had always feared us.
8. The wall which we built was higher than (that) of the Gauls.
9. Citizens do not like a general who is always defeated.
10. The ships which we are building will avoid all dangers.

ship nāvis, -is 3. f. **who, what, which** quī, quae, quod.

Exercise 190.

1. The soldiers whom we had praised were defeated.
2. I, who have never avoided danger, shall be your leader.
3. The gods, whom we fear, will hear us.
4. In this city, which we were attacking, there were many captives.
5. The general himself, whom all loved, was wounded.
6. We seized the city, which had been fortified with a high rampart.
7. They will never defeat us who defeated their fathers.

8. Many things which frighten barbarians do not frighten us.
9. The soldiers who were holding the town fought fiercely.
10. Cotta led his troops into the fields which had been ravaged by the enemy.

Exercise 191.

1. This victory was announced by a soldier who had avoided the battle.
2. The town we were attacking had been fortified with towers and ramparts.
3. We shall not neglect the advice of the general who defeated the enemy.
4. The ships we had built were larger than (those) of the Gauls.
5. The burden, which you are carrying, is very heavy.
6. The general we loved was defeated by the Gauls.
7. Wisdom is very useful to men.
8. The same army has defeated Labienus.
9. We shall fortify the city which we are building.
10. This camp is larger than (that) which you were attacking.

Exercise 192.

1. patria, quam omnēs amāmus, ā barbarīs numquam regētur.
2. equitēs, quōs in silvā cēlāvit, superātī sunt.
3. onera, quae mīlitēs portābant, gravissima erant.
4. mīles, quī victōriam nūntiāvit, laudātus est.
5. perīcula, quae vītāvimus, gravissima erant.
6. ea quae monuistī ūtilissima fuērunt.
7. rēgem vestrum, quī barbarōs superāvit, amātis.
8. quod tū timēs, id nōs nōn terret.
9. castra, quae oppugnābāmus, māiōra erant quam nostra.
10. quae vōs neglēxistis, ea nōs nōn neglegēmus.

193. The Romans Invade Africa (256 BC)

Rōmānōrum iam animī victōria cōnfirmātī erant. "nōn sōlum nōs contrā Poenōs dēfendēmus," clāmābant; "ipsō ultrō in Āfricā bellum gerēmus." itaque classem Pūnicam iterum superāvērunt, mox ingentem exercitum in hostium agrō exposuērunt. Poenī prīmō dēspērābant: erat autem inter mīlitēs mercēnāriōs, quōrum auxiliō bella gerēbant, vir quīdam Lacedaemonius, Xanthippus nōmine, mīlitiae perītissimus. is cōpiās Pūnicās ad summam disciplīnam īnstituit, locum idōneum dēlēgit, Rōmānōs in magnō proeliō superāvit. Rēgulus, quī exercituī Rōmānō praefuit, cum plūrimus aliīs in hostium manūs vēnit. hic posteā ad urbem lēgātus missus est, Poenōrum tamen iussīs nōn pāruit. "sī sapientēs estis, cīvēs Rōmānī," inquit, "captīvōs nōn mūtābitis nec pecūniā redimētis eōs quī hostibus sē trādidērunt. ipse senex sum nec iam reīpūblicae ūtilis: Poenōrum ducēs, quōs habētis captīvōs, arma iterum, sī līberābitis, contrā vōs sūment." tum ad Poenōs, quod sīc prōmīserat, revertit, quamquam illīus gentis crūdēlitātem haud ignōrābat. trīstis dē virō intrepidō fābula posteā nārrābātur; nam Poenī crūdēlissimis eum suppliciīs occīdērunt.

expōnō, exposuī, expositum 3. I put forth; (of troops) I land (trans.). **dēspērō** 1. I despair. **mercēnārius, -a, -um** mercenary. **quīdam, quaedam, quoddam** a certain. **perītus, -a, -um** skilled; (+gen.) skilled in. **summus, -a, -um** highest, utmost. **dēligō, dēlēgī, dēlectum** 3. I choose. **redimō, -ēmī, -emptum** 3. I buy back, ransom.

Exercise 194.

1. The general, by whose arrival the city was saved, was wounded himself.
2. The man to whom you announced the victory announced it to me.
3. This custom, which you praise, I blame.
4. The cavalry, by whose valour the city was saved, were praised by the general.
5. All whose fathers fought against the Gauls will fight bravely now.
6. This was the king whose troops we overcame.
7. The army which you led back into camp had never been defeated.
8. The wood in which we hid our men was very large.
9. Nothing will be more useful to us than this plan.
10. The country which we love we will save by our valour.

arrival adventus 4. m. **custom** mōs, mōris 3. m. **blame** culpō 1.

Exercise 195.

1. You will not be terrified by the arrival of larger forces.
2. The soldiers' hearts were emboldened by the victory.
3. We withstood the attack of the enemy who assailed us.
4. The bravest men had been placed on the right wing.
5. The same city was held by smaller forces of Romans.
6. The gods rule the plans of men.
7. The general by his arrival emboldened the hearts of the soldiers.
8. The shouts of the barbarians were heard in our camp.
9. The arrival of these troops emboldened the hearts of our men.
10. To a soldier nothing is more useful than his arms.

embolden confirmō 1. **heart, mind** animus 2. m. **place** (*verb*) collocō 1.

Exercise 196.

1. The enemy were terrified by the arrival of the general who had often defeated them.
2. We all praised the general by whose valour the town has been saved.
3. The Romans, whose customs all praise, were not often defeated.
4. Labienus, who had been warned by us, was wounded by the enemy.
5. The river by which we were hindered was very deep.
6. That part of the city which the enemy attacked had been neglected by us.
7. Your sons will rule the land in which you are now fighting.
8. All blamed the general by whose advice we had fortified the city.
9. The town in which we hid the captives is now held by the enemy.
10. The Gauls built the town, the walls of which we are attacking.

Exercise 197.

1. urbs, in quā captīvī erant, bene mūnīta erat.
2. Gallī, quōrum virtūtem laudāvistī, nōs superāvērunt.
3. imperātor, cuius equus vulnerātus est, suōs redūxit.
4. Rōmānōrum mōrēs omnēs laudābant.
5. mīlitum animōs adventū suō cōnfirmāvit.
6. peditēs, quōrum tēla nōs vulnerābant, dextrō cornū collocātī sunt.
7. hostēs, ā quibus superātī sumus, agrōs nostrōs vastant.
8. perīcula, quibus tū terrēbāris, nōs nōn timēmus.
9. Belgae, quōrum impetum sustinēbāmus, ab omnibus timēbantur.
10. hominum mōrēs nōn semper sapientiā reguntur.

mōs, mōris 3. m. custom.

198. A Faithless King

urbs Trōia, quam per tot annōs Graecī obsidēbant, ā dīs Nep-
tūnō et Apolline aedificāta est. hīs rēx urbis magna mūnera
prōmīsit, prōmissum tamen nōn praestitit. īrātus tum Neptūnus monstrum horrendum ad terram mīsit, quod agrōs diū
vastābat: Trōianī quotannīs ōrāculī iussū puellam immolābant. hīs hostiās populus sorte dēligēbat: tandem rēgis ipsīus
filiam dēligēbant. magnō tum dolōre Laomedon movēbātur:
forte tamen Hercūlēs nūper eō vēnerat. "Iuppiter ōlim," inquit,
"equum tibi dedit: hunc sī tū equum mihi dederis, filiam tuam
ē morte servābō." quod petierat, rēx prōmīsit. tum Hercūlēs
monstrum occīdit filiamque patrī reddidit: ille autem iterum
prōmissum nōn praestitit. itaque Hercūlēs magnam classem
parāvit, magnum exercitum collēgit. tum urbem obsēdit tan-
demque expugnāvit: rēgem ipsum cum filiīs omnibus praeter
Priamum occīdit.

Neptūnus 2. m. god of the sea, Neptune. **sors, sortis** 3. f.
lot. **Iuppiter, Iovis** 3. m. Jupiter.

SECTION 30

See Grammar Notes №s. 58 & 59,
Cardinal Numbers, 1–20

TO EXPRESS *PLACE*

Place is generally expressed by phrases with Prepositions:

1. Place to which motion is directed by *ad* or *in* with the Accusative.
2. Place from which motion proceeds by *ab* or *ex** with the Ablative.
3. Place at which anything happens by *in* with the Ablative.

> e.g. *He marches out of Italy into the territories of the Gauls.*
> ex Ītaliā in agrōs Gallōrum contendit.
>
> *He was sent to me and remained in the city.*
> ad mē missus est in urbe mansit.

The important exceptions to this will be given in the next rule (Section 31).

　　*Where *from* is equal to *out of,* use *ex.*

Exercise 199.

1. He sent seven cohorts out of the camp.
2. Caesar marched from Italy into the territories of the Gauls.
3. The legions which we sent were defeated.
4. The soldiers of this legion do not fear the enemy.
5. One cohort was hindered by the river.
6. This legion was attacked by the enemy's cavalry.
7. Caesar will send five cohorts into the town.
8. We shall march out of the camp into Italy.
9. The soldiers of that legion will remain in the camp.

10. Two armies of the enemy were marching to the town.

send mittō, mīsī, missum 3. **seven** septem. **cohort** cohors, -rtis 3. f. **march** contendō, -dī, -tum 3. **from, out of** ē, ex (+abl.). **Italy** Ītalia 1. f. **legion** legiō, -ōnis 3. f. **five** quīnque. **remain, stay** maneō, mānsī, mānsum 2. **two** duo, duae, duo. **to** ad (+acc.).

Exercise 200.

1. The soldiers brought twenty captives to Caesar.
2. The cavalry of two legions will remain in the wood.
3. Larger forces were sent by the general to Gaul.
4. There were in Gaul eight towns which we had not attacked.
5. The three legions which you sent have been defeated.
6. Two cohorts will be drawn up opposite the rampart.
7. Caesar praised the soldiers of that legion.
8. We shall place four cohorts on the left wing.
9. The enemy were defeated by the valour of this legion.
10. Eight cohorts have been sent into the town.

twenty vīgintī. **eight** octō. **three** trēs, trēs, tria. **four** quattuor.

Exercise 201.

1. The soldiers of one cohort avoided all risks.
2. A Roman army has been sent into the territories of the Gauls.
3. Two boys announced the victory to us.
4. The barbarians withstood the attack of the three cohorts.
5. One legion which they have sent has been defeated.
6. Wise men will not neglect the advice of the gods.
7. The camp was fortified by three ramparts.
8. There were fifteen captives in the town.
9. They have sent to us a large number of soldiers.
10. Five legions were marching from Italy to Gaul.

one ūnus, -a, -um. **wise** sapiēns, sapientis. **fifteen** quīndecim.

Exercise 202.

1. trēs legiōnēs in Galliam missae sunt.
2. quīnque cohortēs in castrīs manēbant.
3. quattuor cohortēs dextrō cornū instruxerat.
4. adventū legiōnem cīvēs terrēbantur.
5. ūna legiō Gallōrum agrōs vastāverat.
6. urbs, quam oppugnābāmus, trēs turrēs habēbat.
7. sex cohortēs in oppidō collocatae sunt.
8. ex Galliā in Ītaliam contendērunt.
9. omnēs equitēs in silvīs mānsērunt.
10. duās legiōnēs Caesar in Belgās mīsit.

duo, duae, duo two. **quīnque** five. **cohors, -rtis** 3. f. division of soldiers. **quattuor** four. **sex** six. **trēs, trēs, tria** three.

203. End of the First Punic War (241 BC)

magnam victōriam in illō bellō Rōmānī ā Poenīs prope Panormum reportāvērunt. hoc proelium ob eam rem insigne est, quod Rōmānī elephantōs, quōs anteā semper timuerant, reppulērunt. tum urbem Lilybaeum, quam Pyrrhus ōlim frūstrā oppugnāverat, classe per decem annōs obsidēbant.

erant semper cum exercitū Rōmānō in omnibus bellīs haruspicēs quī pullōs dīs sacrōs custōdiēbant: quī pullī sī cibum nōn edēbant, īra deōrum ostendēbātur. ōlim P. Claudius, quī nūper ad classem imperātor vēnerat, impetum in hostium classem parābat. monēbant eum haruspicēs, "hodiē pullī cibum nōn edunt." "bibent tamen," respondit īrātus imperātor, manūque pullōs in mare dēmīsit. tum classem oppugnāvit: dī autem hominis insolentis superbiam pūnīvērunt: ipse enim superātus est nāviumque maximam partem āmīsit: nec multō posteā nāvēs longae centum et vīgintī, onerāriae octingentae dēlētae sunt.

tandem autem Rōmānī in magnō proeliō prope Aegātēs insulās Poenōs vīcērunt. tum dēnique pāx inter duōs populōs confirmātur: Poenī Siciliam Rōmānīs trādunt, captīvōs sine pretiō reddunt, amplius tria mīlia talentum persolvunt.

ob (+acc.) on account of. **pullus** 2. m. chicken. **bibō, bibī** 3. I drink. **longus, -a, -um** long; **nāvis longa** man-of-war. **centum** a hundred. **vīgintī** twenty. **onerārius, -a, -um** of burden; **nāvis onerāria** transport ship. **octingentī, -ae, -a** eight hundred. **talentum** 2. n. a talent (a unit of weight around 30 kg, or that amount of silver, worth about $15,000 in today's money).

SECTION 31

See Grammar Notes №. 181,
Locative Case

TO EXPRESS *PLACE (continued)*

With the proper names of towns and small islands and also with the two words *domus* and *rūs*—

1. **Place to which** is expressed by the Accusative, and **Place from which** by the Ablative, but without a Preposition;

   e.g.   He sailed from Rhodes to Athens.
   Rhodō Athēnās nāvigāvit.

2. **Place at which** is expressed by the Locative Case.
   The Locative was a Case meant to express "place where" but was only partly preserved in Latin. Its forms are the same as those of the Ablative except in the Singular of the 1st and 2nd Declensions, where they are the same as those of the Genitive; e.g.

Rōmae	*at Rome*	(Nom. Rōma)
Rhodī	*at Rhodes*	(Nom. Rhodus)
Athēnīs	*at Athens*	(Nom. pl. Athēnae)

| Gādibus | *at Cádiz* | (Nom. pl. Gādēs) |
| Carthāgine (or Carthāginī) | *at Carthage* | (Nom. Carthāgō) |

So domī, *at home,* rūrī or rūre *in the country.*

Exercise 204.

1. We marched from Rome to the territories of the Gauls.
2. At Athens all feared the arrival of the enemy.
3. Many ships will sail to Athens.
4. The soldiers whom we defeated at Cádiz will not fight again.
5. The general brought all the captives to Rome.
6. At Rome the advice of Caesar had been neglected.
7. The men whom we saw at Rome are marching to Athens.
8. The boy who remained in the camp announced the victory of the enemy.
9. The barbarians were defeated by the Romans at Carthage.
10. His father had been wounded by an arrow at Cádiz.

Rome Rōma 1. f. **Athens** Athēnae 1. f. pl. **Cádiz** Gādēs, -ium 3. f. pl. **again** iterum. **see** videō, vīdī, vīsum 2. **Carthage** Carthāgō, -inis 3. f.

Exercise 205.

1. He marched with three legions to Carthage.
2. The citizens who remained at Athens were blamed by the General.
3. The danger will be more serious at Rome than at Carthage.
4. The barbarians wounded the king himself with an arrow.
5. In Athens all men praise wisdom.
6. Two cohorts are remaining at Cádiz.
7. Three towns had been seized by the enemy.
8. Caesar marched into the territories of the Gauls with all his forces.

9. There is a large number of citizens at Rome.
10. By your valour you have again saved your country.

with cum (+abl.).

Exercise 206.

1. There are in Cádiz two legions who have never been defeated.
2. The soldiers whom Labienus sent announced the victory to us.
3. There are at Rome the best soldiers and the bravest generals.
4. We shall never see a more beautiful city.
5. My father sailed with three ships from Athens to Rhodes.
6. The shouts of the barbarians were heard in Rome by all the citizens.
7. The city which we saw has been fortified with a rampart.
8. We shall march with one legion to Carthage.
9. Larger forces of the enemy are marching to Rome.
10. The river which you saw is very broad and very deep.

Rhodes Rhodus 2. f.

Exercise 207.

1. Rhodō Rōmam cum decem nāvibus nāvigāvit.
2. Athēnās omnēs legiōnēs contendēbant.
3. nihil Athēnīs ūtilius est sapientia.
4. Rōmae ab omnibus virtūs laudātur.
5. omnēs captīvī Carthāginem missī sunt.
6. trēs legiōnēs Athēnās mittēmus.
7. cīvēs suam ipsī urbem servāvērunt.
8. illī cum quattuor nāvibus Athēnās nāvigābunt.
9. Rōmae omnēs hostium adventū terrēbantur.
10. Gādibus nostrī fortiter cum hostibus pugnābant.

Rhodus 2. f. the island of Rhodes. **Gādēs, -ium** 3. f. pl. the town of Cádiz.

208. The Gorgon's Head

erant ōlim trēs sorōrēs Gorgonēs, ē quibus ūna, Medūsa
nōmine, pulchra puella fuerat: quoniam autem Minervae
displicuerat, crīnēs eius ā deā in serpentēs versī sunt. posteā
omnēs quī Medūsae caput spectāverant in lapidem vertēb-
antur. Perseus tamen deōrum auxiliō eam occīdit. nam speculum eī Minerva, Mercurius falcem dedit. itaque Medūsam,
dum dormit, per speculum spectam, caput falce abscindit et
in saccō āvehit.

erat tum pulchra puella, rēgis Aethiopum fīlia, Andro-
meda nōmine, cuius māter deōrum īram mōverat quod fīliae
pulchritūdinem nimis laudāverat. itaque Neptūnus monstrum
ingēns in terram mīsit: incolae ōrāculō sīc monēbantur: "perīculō līberābiminī sī monstrō Andromedam trādētis." itaque
puella ad saxum dēligāta est. ibi eam invēnit Perseus, quī dracōnem Medūsae capite in lapidem vertit puellamque līberāvit.
tum Andromedam in mātrimōnium dūxit caputque Medūsae
dedit Minervae quae in mediō scūtō posuit.

displiceō 2. I displease (+dat.). **crīnis, -is** 3. m. hair.
serpēns, serpentis 3. f. serpent. **lapis, -dis** 3. m. stone.
speculum 2. n. mirror. **falx, falcis** 3. f. sickle. **abscindō, -idī,
-īssum** 3. I tear off. **āvehō, -xī, -ctum** 3. I carry off.
Aethiops, -is 3. m. Ethiopian. **nimis** too much.

209. A Great Ruler

Rōmānī ōlim contrā tyrannōs, quī imperium crūdēliter admi-
nistrāverant, coniūrāvērunt eōsque in exsilium pepulērunt;
etiam fīnitimās gentēs, quae eōs adiūverant, bellō vīcērunt.
posteā cōnsulēs quotannīs creāvērunt quī reīpūblicae praeerant.

hodiē in Ītaliā imperium administrātur ab ūnō virō quī
ab inimīcīs tyrannus vocātur; sed contrā eiusmodī tyrannum
nēmō coniūrāte, nēmō bellum parat; hunc incolae nōn sōlum
laudant sed etiam amant, quod populī amīcus est et patriam
servāvit. cīvēs suōs ad disciplīnam informat et contrā fīnitimōs
dēfendit, ipse omnibus sapientiae et iūstitiae exemplum est.

SECTION 32

See Grammar Notes №. 59,
Ordinal Numbers, 1–20

TO EXPRESS *TIME*

1. The length of time during which an action last is
   expressed by the Accusative Case with a Preposition;

   > e.g. *They were fortifying the city twenty years.*
   > (for, during, throughout twenty years)
   > vīgintī annōs urbem mūniēbant.

2. The time at which a thing happens or the limit of time
   within which it happens is expressed by the Ablative
   Case without a Preposition;

   > e.g. *On the fifth day he was set free.*
   > quīntō diē līberātus est.
   >
   > *Within five days he was set free.*
   > quīnque diēbus līberātus est.

N.B.—This last is sometimes confused with the "length of
time" expressed by the Accusative. But remember that when
the Accusative is used the action is represented as going on
throughout the whole time, when the Ablative is used it
is represented as happening at a certain point within the
period.

> *He was sailing for five days* = quīnque diēs nāvigābat.
> *Within five days he set sail* = quīnque diēbus nāvigāvit.

Exercise 210.

1. The captives will be set free in three days.
2. On that day the sixth legion marched to Rome.
3. One cohort fought with the enemy for five hours.
4. In the same year the city was seized by the Gauls.
5. His father remained at Carthage for three years.
6. In a few years the city will have been fortified with walls.
7. For many hours we were attacking the line of the enemy.
8. The men whom we saw at Carthage remained for a few days.
9. On the same day the tenth legion was led into the territories of the Gauls.
10. In the third year the Gauls were defeated by their enemies.

free, set free līberō 1. **day** diēs 5. m/f. **sixth** sextus, -a, -um. **hour** hōra 1. f. **year** annus 2. m. **tenth** decimus, -a, -um. **third** tertius, -a, -um

Exercise 211.

1. On that day the cries of the barbarians were heard in the city.
2. The captives whom we saw will be set free in a few days.
3. For very many days there was a serious danger of war.
4. On the sixth day we saw the same men again.
5. At the sixth hour the army was led back into camp.
6. For three hours the tenth legion fought with the enemy.
7. The soldier by whose valour the town was saved has been set free.
8. On the tenth day we sailed from Athens to Italy.
9. The soldiers of the fifth legion were laying waste the fields.
10. The general to whom we reported the victory has been sent to Rome.

fifth quīntus, -a, -um.

Exercise 212.

1. In the tenth year the enemy were defeated.
2. For a few days we shall remain at Athens with our father.
3. The barbarians are marching to Rome with huge forces.
4. On the fourth day the king led his forces into the city.
5. The fifth legion, which was marching to Carthage, was hindered by a river.
6. For two hours our men fought bravely with the enemy.
7. The boy whom we have sent will report the battle in five days.
8. On the third day the town was seized by the Belgians.
9. The tenth legion, by whose valour the enemy were defeated, was praised by Caesar.
10. We ourselves saw the man on the same day.

fourth quartus, -a, -um.

Exercise 213.

1. quīntō diē urbs ab hostibus oppugnāta est.
2. decima legiō ā Caesare laudābātur.
3. hōc annō Rōmānī cōpiās in Galliam mīsērunt.
4. trēs hōrās nostrī cum barbarīs fortiter pugnāvērunt.
5. eōdem diē rēx cīvibus victōriam nūntiāvit.
6. multōs annōs Rōmae fuit pater meus.
7. Carthāgine quattuor annōs mānsimus.
8. omnēs captīvī illō diē līberātī sunt.
9. nostrī sex hōrās hostium impetum sustinēbant.
10. multās hōrās gravissima onera portābant.

quīntus, -a, -um fifth. **decimus, -a, -um** tenth. **hōra** 1. f. hour. **diēs** 5. m/f. day.

214. Hannibal (Born 246 BC)

Poenī post hunc clādem magnīs difficultātibus tenēbantur,
nam multae gentēs, quās anteā rēxerant, ab imperiō Pūnicō
iam dēsciscēbant. hās bellō longō et crūdēlī Hamilcar, quī
Poenōrum cōpiīs praefuit, superāvit. movēbat semper virī
fortissimī animum clādis, quam nūper patriā sustinuerat,
memoriā: mox bellum contrā Hispānōs parāvit. ōlim dīs
hostiam immolābat: aderat fīlius eius Hannibal, puer tum
novem annōs nātus, quī multīs cum lacrimīs patrem implōrāvit. "sī mē amās, pater," clāmāvit, "mē quoque cum exercitū
ad bellum dūcēs." tum patris iussū puer manum in ārā posuit
et hīs verbīs iūreiūrandō sē obligāvit: "semper egō Rōmānīs
hostis erō, semper cum illā gente bellum geram." nōnō illīus
bellī annō Hamilcar in proeliō cecidit: Hannibal autem patris
verba semper memoriā tenēbat nec multō post sociōs Rōmānōrum Saguntiōs oppugnāvit.

dēsciscō, dēscīvī, dēscītum 3. I revolt. **crūdēlis, -is, -e**
cruel. **memoria** 1. f. memory; **memoriā teneō** I hold in
memory, remember. **Hispānī** 2. m. pl. inhabitants of Spain.
adsum, adesse, adfuī I am present. **novem** nine. **nātus, -a,
-um** born; **novem annōs nātus** nine years old. **implōrō** 1. I
implore. **obligō** 1. I bind. **nōnus, -a, -um** ninth. **multō** by
much; **nec multō post** and not long afterwards.

215. How to Evade Destiny

Mycerīnī, rēgis Aegyptiī, pater Cheops deōs neglēxerat, crūdēliter imperium administrāverat, multōs tamen annōs rēxerat: ipsum autem Mycerīnum omnēs propter hūmānitātem
amābant. tum deī eum per ōrāculum hīs verbīs monuērunt:
"sex annōs in hāc terrā regnābis: septimō annō vītā excēdēs."
rēx īrātus ad ōrāculum nūntiōs mīsit, inīquōs deōs multīs
verbīs accūsāvit. respondit illī, "ob eam ipsam rem vīta tibi
tam brevis concēditur: quod deīs placuerat, id tū neglēxistī.
poena in Aegyptiōs per centum et quīnquāgintā annōs ā dīs
cōnstitūta erat: id pater tuus et patruus intellēxērunt, tū nōn
intellēxistī." quod ubi audīvit, Mycerīnus per reliquam vītam
voluptātī sē trādidit: diē per silvās et loca iūcundissima errābat;
per tōtam noctem rēgiam taedīs illūminābat et convīvia cum
comitibus celebrābat. "sīc enim," inquit, "annōs nōn sex, sed
duodecim vīvam."

hūmānitās, hūmānitātis 3. f. kindness. **septimus, -a, -um**
seventh. **quīnquāgintā** fifty. **intellegō, intellēxī,**
intellēctum 3. I understand. **voluptās, -ātis** 3. f. pleasure.
iūcundus, -a, -um pleasant. **rēgia** 1. f. palace. **illūminō** 1. I
light up, illuminate. **vīvō, vīxī, vīctum** 3. I live.

SECTION 33

See Grammar Notes Nºs. 81–85,
Imperative Active of Regular Verbs and of *sum*

THE IMPERATIVE MOOD

N.B.—The longer forms given in the Grammar are not to be used in the following exercises. The only forms wanted are

Active   2nd Sing.   amā   2nd Plu.   amāte
Passive   2nd Sing.   amāre   2nd Plu.   amāminī

and the corresponding forms in the other Conjugations.

Exercise 216.

1. Hide yourselves, citizens: the enemy have seized the town.
2. Free the captives, Commius: they have saved the state.
3. You remain at Carthage: I shall march to Rome.
4. Be brave soldiers: we have always defeated these men.
5. Praise the valour of your father, citizens.
6. Hold the city with a few cavalry.
7. Fortify the walls with three ramparts and a high tower.
8. Rule yourself: men who rule themselves are praised by all.
9. Fight bravely: the tenth legion is marching to us.
10. Lay waste your fields, citizens: the Romans will not have corn.

state cīvitās, -ātis 3. f. **corn** frūmentum 2. n.

Exercise 217.

1. Set free the hostages: the Gauls are not preparing war.
2. Love your country and your king, boys.
3. Avoid all dangers: the rivers of this land are very deep.
4. Send the fifth legion to Gaul, (and) the sixth to Carthage.
5. Withstand the fiercest attacks of the enemy bravely.
6. Remain in the city for three days: the danger is serious.

7. Defeat the enemy whom we was already defeated.
8. Send five cohorts to Cádiz.
9. Fortify the camp with a high rampart.
10. Hold the city with five cohorts: send more men to us.

hostage obses, obsidis 3. c.

Exercise 218.

1. Sail to Rhodes with four ships: carry corn to our soldiers.
2. Draw up the cavalry on the left wing.
3. The hostages which were sent by the Belgians were set free by Caesar.
4. The state which our fathers saved will never be ruled by barbarians.
5. The battle, in which the fourth legion had fought, was reported at Rome.
6. On the same day twenty hostages were set free.
7. Many states had not sent corn to Caesar.
8. We shall not again see that most beautiful city.
9. The general himself remained in the town with a few cohorts.
10. The citizens of this state had never seen a Roman army.

Exercise 219.

1. pugnāte fortiter, mīlitēs: hostium cōpiās superāte.
2. nāvigāte ad Ītaliam cum omnibus nāvibus.
3. hoc proelium imperātōrī nūntiā.
4. parāte bellum, cīvēs: magnum est perīculum.
5. monē fīlium tuum: cōnsilium meum neglēgit.
6. instrue decimam legiōnem contrā oppidum.
7. audī patris vōcem: semper tē monet.
8. cēlāte arma: rēx in urbe est.
9. laudāte deōs, cīvēs: hostēs superātī sunt.
10. vōs Rōmae manēte: nōs in Galliam contendēmus.

220. The Fall of Saguntum (218 BC)

Saguntīnī, quī urbem mūrīs et turribus mūnīverant, octō
mensēs Poenōrum impetum sustinēbant: frūstrā ā Rōmānīs
auxilium, ab Hannibale pācem petīvērunt. tandem prīmī cīv-
itātis aurum argentumque omne in forum colligunt, in ignem
iactant, ipsī in flammās saltant: reliquōrum plūrimī cum uxōr-
ibus līberīsque domōs super sē ipsōs incendunt. intereā, quoniam mūrī custōdibus nūdātī erant, hostēs urbem intrāvērunt.

tum Q. Fabius cum aliīs lēgātīs Rōmā Carthāginem missus
est. "nisi pūblicō cōnsiliō," inquit, "sociōs nostrōs oppugnāv-
istis et ducis vestrī factum ipsī probātis, Hannibalem Rōmānīs trādite." ad quae ubi multā et insolentiā respondērunt
Poenī, togae sinum manū tenuit, tum "hīc," inquit, "bellum
et pācem portāmus: utrum placet, sūmite." illī, nōn minōre
cum superbiā, "utrum placet, dā" clāmāvērunt. "bellum dō,"
respondit lēgātus. illī "sīc estō: bellum eōdem nōs animō, quō
sūmpsimus, gerēmus."

octō eight. **mēnsis, -is** 3. m. month. **ignis, -is** 3. m. fire.
līberī 2. m. pl. children. **super** (+acc. or +abl.) above, over.
vester, -tra, -trum you (pl.). **probō** 1. I approve of.
insolentia 1. f. insolence. **sinus** 4. m. fold. **hīc** (adv.) here.
uter, utra, utrum which of two.

221. A Tragic End

omnium ōlim āthlētārum nōtissimus fuit Milō, quī identidem
in lūdīs aemulōs superābat. ā cīvibus suīs in magnō honōre
habēbātur etiamque populī exercituī in bellō praefuit. fābulae
multae et mīrae dē Milōne trāduntur, nam propter ingentēs
vīrēs maximam sibi fāmam comparāvit. ōlim iuvencam quattuor annōs natam in humerīs per stadium portāvit: eandem
posteā iuvencam ūnō diē ēdit. senex tandem infirmō iam
corpore aliquandō per silvam errābat, ubi arborem quandam
vīdit quae rīmīs mediā parte hiābat. tum ille manūs in rīmās
immīsit truncumque discindēbat: et mediam quidem partem
discidit, tum infirmās iam manūs remīsit. statim arbor ad nāt-
ūram revertit. itaque, quoniam manūs eius truncō tenēbantur,
in locō mānsit et ā leōnibus vorātus est.

āthlēta 1. m. athlete. **iuvenca** 1. f. heifer. **stadium** 2. n.
stadium. **aliquandō** once. **rīma** 1. f. cleft. **hiō** 1. I gape open.
quidem indeed. **nātūra** 1. f. nature, natural condition. **leō,
leōnis** 3. m. lion.

222. The Battle of Hastings

hostēs ad Britanniam nāvigāverant et cōpiās haud procul ā
marī exposuerant. rēgis nostrī Haraldī, quī prō patriā nihil nōn
temptāvit, nōmen semper in honōre habēbitur. quoniam multī
illō tempore contrā eum coniūrābant, diū in aliā parte insulae
tenēbātur. ubi tandem ad ōram vēnit et hostēs oppugnāvit, diū
nec hī neque illī vincēbant. tandem ūnus ex hostibus Haraldī
oculum sagittā forte vulnerāvit et virum intrepidum occīdit:
tum frūstrā Britannī, quī sine rēge dē salūte dēspērābant,
hostium impetum sustinuērunt. in locō ubi pugnāverant dux
hostium templum Deō dēdicāvit.

SECTION 34

Comparison of Adverbs (Grammar Notes №. 55)
Imperative Passive of Regular Verbs
(Grammar Notes №s. 86–89)

Exercise 223.

1. Be advised by your father: he will advise you better than this man.
2. We shall fight more bravely than the Gauls.
3. Fear the gods: be feared by men.
4. The Gauls were building larger ships.
5. The fifth legion fought most bravely on that day.
6. For a few hours the enemy withstood our attack more bravely.
7. Be feared by the barbarians, Romans.
8. We shall defeat the soldiers of this state more easily.
9. The same part of the city was held by the fifth legion.
10. The town itself was not known to our general.

known *adj.* nōtus, -a, -um.

Exercise 224.

1. All the nations of Gaul feared Caesar.
2. Be advised by me: avoid the risk.
3. Our men fought very fiercely for three hours.
4. Your father has advised you very well.
5. Never had the cavalry fought more bravely than on that day.
6. We defeated the forces of the Gauls very easily.
7. Be praised by all men: praise is always welcome.
8. Withstand their attacks more bravely.
9. That part of the land was known to few men.
10. The eighth legion marched on the same day to Gaul.

nation gēns, gentis 3. f. **pleasant, welcome** grātus, -a, -um.
eighth octāvus, -a, -um.

Exercise 225.

1. The citizens, who had been warned by us, very easily withstood the enemy's attack.
2. The cavalry fought more bravely than the infantry.
3. Be ruled by the advice of your general: fortify the city.
4. The king of this state had not sent corn to Caesar.
5. We shall send hostages to the enemy.
6. The Romans fought most bravely by land and by sea.
7. The enemy's weapons were more heavy than our shields.
8. Nothing is more welcome to us than your advice.
9. The voice of the king himself was heard in the city.
10. Two legions fought most bravely on behalf of their country.

for, on behalf of prō (+abl.).

Exercise 226.

1. monēre ā mē: vītā bellum.
2. fortissimē nostrī cum hostibus pugnāvērunt.
3. cōnsiliō meō regere: magnus est hostium numerus.
4. ācrius nostrī quam Gallī pugnābant.
5. cum decem mīlitibus hostium impetum sustinuit.
6. hostium cōpiās tertia legiō facillimē superavit.
7. laudāre ab omnibus: nihil laude grātius est.
8. haec gēns numquam ā Rōmānīs superāta est.
9. amā omnēs: ab omnibus amāre.
10. rēs nāta fuit paucīs mīlitibus.

tertius, -a, -um third. **laus, -dis** 3. f. praise. **grātē** agreeably, gratefully.

227. Crossing the Alps

cum quīnquāgintā mīlibus peditum, equitum novem mīlibus,
magnōque numerō elephantōrum Hannibal ex Hispāniā
excessit: mīrā celeritāte trāns montēs Pyrēnaeōs per Galliam
contendit: tum ingentibus cum cōpiīs, quārum dīmidium in
itinere āmīsit, Alpēs superāvit, quā rē nihil magis memorāb-
ile ab ūllō imperātōre gestum est. magnīs ille difficultatibus
impediēbātur, nam flūmina nive et imbribus aucta erant, simul
ā barbarīs, quī saxa ingentia in agmen dēmīsērunt, oppugnāb-
ātur. tandem decimō diē ad summōs montēs vēnērunt, unde
campōs Ītaliae oculīs spectābant. eō tamen vel difficilius dēs-
cendēbant quam nūper ascenderant: nam in nive nec hominēs
nec animālia vestīgia firmē pōnēbant: aliquandō (sīc enim in
historiā trāditur), quod saxa ardēbant, acētum infūdērunt:
statim liquescēbant saxa et via tandem aperiēbantur. octāvō
diē eī quī supererant in campōs Ītaliae dēscendērunt.

pedes, -itis 3. m. foot-soldier; (pl.) infantry. **contendō, -dī,
-tum** 3. I march, hasten. **Alpēs, Alpium** 3. f. pl. the Alps.
magis (comparative of adverb magnopere) more.
memorābilis, -is, -e memorable. **ūllus, -a, -um** any. **flūmen,
-inis** 3. n. river. **nix, nivis** 3. f. snow. **agmen, -inis** 3. n.
marching column (of soldiers). **summus mōns** the top of
the mountain. **unde** whence. **difficilius** (comparative of
adverb difficulter) with more difficulty. **firmē** firmly.
acētum 2. n. vinegar. **infundō, infūdī, infūsum** 3. I pour
on. **octāvus, -a, -um** eighth.

228. The Jealousy of a Goddess

Arachne arte lānificā aliīs omnibus praestābat, quam ob causam magnam ubique fāmam comparāvit et multae undique puellae domum eius veniēbant tēlāsque quās texuerat spectābant. hīs rēbus animus ad superbiam movēbātur: "tēlās," clāmat, "perītius quam Minerva ipsa texō: deam etiam ad certāmen prōvocō." haud multō posteā anus infirmō corpore ad eam vēnit. "multī," inquit, "deōs ad certāmen prōvocāvērunt: omnēs poenās audāciae persolvērunt: hōrum tū exemplō monēre." illa tamen cōnsilium contempsit; iterum prōvocat. tum repente rēs mīra oculīs ostenditur: nōn iam anus infirma, sed dea ipsa adest. "Minervam," inquit, "ad certāmen prōvocāvistī: venīs." statim ad rem sē applicant. texit Arachne tēlam pulcherrimam, in quā deōrum imāginēs fingēbat. operis pulchritūdine etiam Minervae animus movētur: tum īrāta propter invidiam manū discidit. tantam iniūriam Arachne nōn sustinuit: multīs cum lacrimīs mortem sibi laqueō parābat: dea autem puellam in arāneae formam vertit.

lānificus, -a, -um of wool-work, of weaving. tēla 1. f. web. texō, -uī, -tum 3. I weave. perītē skillfully. anus 4. f. old woman. opus, operis 3. n. work. tantus, -a, -um so great. laqueus 2. m. halter, snare. arānea 1. f. spider.

SECTION 35

See Grammar Notes Nºs. 81–85,
Infinitive Active of Regular Verbs and of *sum*

THE INFINITIVE

In the sentence *Seeing is believing* we have instances of what we call Verbal Nouns, i.e. Nouns which express the action of the Verb. We should parse *seeing* as a Noun, the Subject of *is,* and believing as a Noun, the Complement of *is* (see Section 23).

From every English Verb we can form a Verbal Noun ending in *-ing.* But we can always use the Infinitive instead, e.g. the above sentence might be *To see is to believe.* This shows that the Infinitive is a Verbal Noun as much as the Noun in *-ing.*

The Latin Infinitive has precisely the same use. The Infinitive is a Verbal Noun and as such it can be the subject or Complement of a Verb, most frequently of *est.*

e.g.   *To work is to pray (working is praying).*
        labōrāre est ōrāre.

[*Labōrāre* is the Subject, *ōrāre* the Complement of *est.*]

        It is an evil to err.
        errāre malum est.

[The Latin literally means *To err is an evil,* and *errāre* is the Subject of *est.*]

Exercise 229.

1. It was easier to conquer the Gauls than the Romans.
2. It will be difficult to carry on war for three years.
3. Fighting will be more welcome to the soldiers than to the citizens.

4. It will be most useful to our state to have conquered these enemies.
5. It was a splendid thing to have defeated so large a number of Gauls.
6. In three years it will be more easy to carry on war.
7. It is pleasant to fight on behalf of our country and citizens.
8. It was the custom of the Roman to carry on war by land and sea.
9. It will be very easy to hear the general's voice.
10. It will be better to hide the cavalry in the woods.

conquer vincō, vīcī, victum 3. **so large** tantus, -a, -um.

Exercise 230.

1. It will be most useful to us to have laid waste the enemy's fields.
2. It is better to conquer by courage than by stratagem.
3. It was the custom of this nation to fortify their towns with high walls.
4. To send forces to Gaul will be easier than to fight in Italy.
5. It is better to withstand the attack than to have avoided danger.
6. The ninth legion will be sent this year to Carthage.
7. It will be very difficult to fortify that part of the city.
8. It is a splendid thing to have withstood the attack of the enemy.
9. The Romans have carried on war by land and see for many years.
10. A campaign was conducted by Caesar against the Gauls.

ninth nōnus, -a, -um. **carry on, conduct, wage (war)** gerō, gestī, gestum 3.

Exercise 231.

1. The Gauls, against whom we had conducted a campaign, conquered us.
2. The fifth legion, which was sent to Gaul, has been conquered.
3. It is often more easy to praise than to blame.
4. It is most pleasing to me to see so large a number of citizens.
5. The soldiers whom we sent to Gaul carried on war for many years.
6. In a few years it will be easy to carry corn to the city.
7. It was most difficult to avoid so great a danger.
8. It is a bad (thing) to have neglected a good general's advice.
9. It will be very easy to have conquered the enemy.
10. It was the custom of the Romans to fortify all their camps with ramparts.

bad, evil malum 2. n.

Exercise 232.

1. Caesaris cōnsilium ūtilissimum erit cīvitātī.
2. nihil grātius erit nōbīs quam bellum gerere.
3. ūtile erit nōbīs Rōmae fuisse.
4. facile est parvum numerum hostium vincere.
5. pulcherrimum est prō patriā pugnāre.
6. malum est omnēs laudāre.
7. ūtile erit urbem mūrīs et aggeribus mūnīvisse.
8. pulchrum est hostēs saepe vīcisse.
9. mōs fuit Rōmānōrum numquam perīcula vītāre.
10. adventū tuō mīlitum animī cōnfirmātī erunt.

233. Hannibal's Victories (218–217 BC)

intereā P. Cornelius Scipiō cum exercitū Rōmānō Poenōrum adventum exspectābat: inter equitēs utrimque prope Tīcīnum flumen pugnātum est, quō in proeliō Rōmānī locō cēdere cōgēbantur, imperātor ipse graviter vulnerātus est. mox T. Semprōnius cum alterō exercitū advēnit: is, dum incautius hostium equitēs trāns Trebium fluvium fugat, repente māiōribus cōpiīs occurrit, simul ab aliīs quōs Hannibal cum Magōne frātre in īnsidiīs collocāverat oppugnātur. iterum Rōmānī vincuntur. proximō autem annō vel māiōrem clādem sustinuērunt.

est prope Cortōnam via angusta inter montēs altissimōs et lacum Trasumenum, per quam C. Flāminius Nepos, vir audācissimus, cui turpe fuit tardē et cautē rem gerere, exercitum dūxit. Hannibal autem iam anteā peditēs expedītōs in montibus, equitēs ad faucēs saltus collocāverat; ipse cum reliquō exercitū ad alterum exitum manēbat. Rōmānī, ubi saltum intrāvērunt, statim undique oppugnābantur: trēs hōrās ācriter ubique, circum cōnsulem autem ācrius pugnātum est, quem armīs insignem hostēs petēbant, dēfendēbant cīvēs. tandem ab equite quōdam Gallicō occīsus est. reliquī statim fugā salūtem petere coepērunt.

cōgō, coēgī, coactum 3. I compel. **graviter** seriously. **adveniō, advēnī, adventum** 4. I arrive. **incautius** (comparative of adverb incautē) more incautiously, too incautiously. **proximus, -a, -um** next. **turpis, -is, -e** disgraceful. **tardē** slowly. **cautē** cautiously. **expedītus, -a, -um** light-armed. **faucēs** 3. f. pl. throat, entrance. **exitus** 4. m. exit. **pugnātum est** (impersonal) it was fought, a battle was fought. **coepī** I began.

234. The Labours of Hercules

inter deōs antīquōs nēmō magis hodiē nōtus est quam Iovis
fīlius Hercūlēs, dē quō fābulae multae et mīrae trāditae sunt.
vī corporis et hominibus et deīs omnibus praestābat. paucōs
iam mēnsēs nātus, dum in cūnīs iacet, in maximum perīculum vēnit: nam Iūnō, quae semper eī inimīcissima erat, duōs
serpentēs contrā eum mīsit: suīs autem manibus deus īnfāns
faucēs eōrum ēlīsit. posteā, quod Iūnō mentem eius aliēnāverat,
suōs ipse līberōs occīdit. magnō tum dolōre ultrō in exsilium
discessit: mox ad Apollinis ōrāculum vēnit ibique auxilium ā
deō petīvit. ab eō iussus est rēgī cuidam Eurystheō duodecim
annōs pārēre: "tum dēnique," inquit deus, "immortālis eris."
ab hōc rēge Iūnōnis iussū coāctus est Hercūlēs duodecim
labōrēs peragere.

cūnae 1. f. pl. cradle. **ēlīdō, -sī, -sum** 3. I strangle, smash,
dash to pieces. **mēns, mentis** 3. f. mind. **aliēnō** 1. I
estrange; **mentem aliēnō** (+gen. of person) I drive mad.
iubeō, iussī, iussum 2. I order. **peragō, -ēgī, -actum** 3. I
accomplish.

235. Britain deserted by the Romans

Rōmānī, ubi Britanniam bellō superāvērunt, lēgātōs ad īnsu-
lam mīsērunt et imperium multōs annōs optimē administrābant; incolās enim contrā iniūriam fīnitimōrum dēfendēbant,
agrōs coluērunt, oppida et domicilia aedificāvērunt. mox
tamen propter barbarōs quī Rōmam obsēderant et tribūtum
postulābant Britanniam relinquere et ad Ītaliam nāvigāre
coāctī sunt. misera tum fortūna erat Britannōrum; "Rōmānī"
clāmābant, "nōs relīquērunt; pīrātae exitium nōbīs parant;
nēmō nōs dēfendit; barbarī ad mare nōs pellunt, repellit mare
ad barbarōs."

optimē adv. best.

SECTION 36

See Grammar Notes №s. 86–89,
Infinitive Passive of Regular Verbs

Exercise 236.

1. It is easier to be blamed than to be praised.
2. It will be a good thing for these men to be conquered by the Romans.
3. It is an evil to be ruled by bad kings.
4. It will be a serious thing to be attacked by so great a number of barbarians.
5. It is most disgraceful to be terrified by the arrival of the enemy.
6. It will be pleasant to be led back into camp.
7. It was difficult to be heard by all the citizens.
8. Be advised by us: it is better to be advised than to be conquered.
9. It will be very difficult for our men to avoid the arrows of the enemy.
10. It is more disgraceful to be praised by this man than to be blamed by that one.

disgraceful, base turpis, -is, -e.

Exercise 237.

1. Our men were confused by the arrival of the Gauls.
2. Praise those who have conquered the enemies of the state.
3. You have fought most bravely: you have never been conquered.
4. It is most easy to be praised by the base.
5. The camp, which we had fortified, was attacked for three hours.
6. In a few days you will be in a city which I have never seen.
7. The soldiers marched through the territories of the Gauls.
8. It is not disgraceful to be conquered by so large a number of enemies.
9. It is easier to carry on war by land than by sea.
10. It will be more disgraceful to remain in the city than to be defeated.

confuse, disturb perturbō 1. **through** per (+acc.).

Exercise 238.

1. Send larger forces to us in a few days.
2. In ten days we shall see the general who conquered the Gauls.
3. The Gauls will carry on the war more bravely this year.
4. The plan of the general was to attack the enemy's camp.
5. It is easier to prepare war than to defeat the enemy.
6. The ninth legion, which was sent to Gaul, had never been defeated.
7. It will be very difficult to march through these fields.
8. The leader of the barbarians was defeated by a stratagem.
9. In the same year the citizens of this town built a wall.
10. For five hours we remained in the smaller camp.

ten decem.

Exercise 239.

1. bonum est ā bonīs laudārī et amārī.
2. mōs fuit semper noster ab hostibus nōn terrērī.
3. ūtile est cīvitātī ā bonō rēge regī.
4. difficile erit ā tantō numerō cīvium audīrī.
5. facile est ā malīs laudārī.
6. obsidēs, quōs mīserāmus, dux līberāvit.
7. haec rēs, quae iam paucīs nōta est, mīlitum animōs confirmābit.
8. turpe erit nōbīs ā paucīs peditibus vincī.
9. magnum est numquam ab hostibus perturbātum esse.
10. ūtilissimum fuit mīlitibus cum tantō hoste pugnāvisse.

difficilis, -is, -e difficult.

240. Cannae (216 BC)

maximam autem omnium clādem in illō bellō prope Cannās Rōmānī sustinuērunt, quod oppidum Hannibal cum cōpiīs occupāverat. hostium equitēs nostrōs prīmum dextrō cornū, mox sinistrō cornū vīcērunt: intereā Rōmānī mediam aciem Poenōrum repellēbant: tum repente ab utrōque latere peditēs, ā tergō equitēs oppugnāvērunt. Rōmānōrum nōn amplius decem mīlia superfuērunt. "sī iam ad urbem, Hannibal, mē cum equitibus miserīs," clāmāvit Maharbal, dux equitum Poenōrum, "quīntō diē in Capitōliō cēnābis." ille autem virī sapientis cōnsilium neglēxit: Capuam exercitum dūxit, ubi mīlitēs multōs diēs voluptātī sē trādidērunt. hāc morā vidētur urbs servāta esse.

Rōmae, ubi trīstis clādēs nūntiāta est, omnium animī maximō timōre movēbantur: crēdēbātur prīmō tōtus exercitus dēlētus esse, tōta Ītalia ab Hannibalis cōpiīs tenērī. urbem tamen contrā hostium impetum mūniēbant, puerōs servōsque ad arma vocābant. Terentius, cuius propter audāciam tantam clādem sustinuerant, ā senātū laudātus est quod dē rēpūblicā nōn dēspērāverat.

uterque, utraque, utrumque each (of two). **latus, -eris** 3. n. side; **ā latere** on the flank. **tergum** 2. n. back; **ā tergō** in the rear. **cēnō** 1. I dine. **mora** 1. f. delay. **videor** (passive of videō) I seem.

241. The Labours of Hercules (continued)

in valle quādam, Nemea nōmine, habitābat illō tempore ingēns leō quem maximē eius terrae incolae timēbant. hunc Hercūlēs occīdere et ad rēgem portāre iussus est. diū frūstrā cum monstrō clāvā et sagittīs pugnābat: tandem faucēs eius suīs manibus ēlīsit. tum mortuum leōnem in humerīs ad rēgiam reportāvit. quem ubi vīdit rēx ipse dīcitur virī fortissimī vīribus territus esse Herculēmque iussisse exinde extrā oppidī mūrōs victōriās nūntiāre.

posteā taurum ingentem, quī Crētae agrōs vastābat, occīdere iussus est. hoc quoque opus dīcitur perēgisse vīvumque animal in humerīs domum reportāvisse, mox līberāvisse.

vallis, -is 3. f. valley. **clāva** 1. f. club.

SECTION 37

See Grammar Notes №s. 82–85,
Active Participles of Regular Verbs

PARTICIPLES

A Participle is a Verbal Adjective, and always agrees, like an Adjective, with some Substantive expressed or understood.

In the sentence I saw a brown horse we parse brown as an Adjective qualifying horse.

In I saw a galloping horse (or I saw a horse galloping) and I saw a tethered horse we parse galloping and tethered as Participles, i.e. forms of Verbs. Yet it is obvious that galloping and tethered qualify horse just as brown did in the first sentence—in other words, they are Adjectives in character.

That Participles are also Verbs is clear from the fact that they always express the action of some Verb, and (when Active) can govern an object; e.g. I saw a horse drawing a cart.

Hence we speak of them as Verbal Adjectives.

Latin has the following Participles:

1. The Present Participle Active, which represents an action as still going on at any time. It corresponds to the English -ing;

    e.g.   *I saw a horse running.*
            equum vīdī currentum.

2. The Future Participle Active, which represents an action as about to take place at any time.

    e.g.   *He was about to sail to Athens.*
            Athēnās nāvigātūrus erat.

    Note that English has no Future Participle, and is obliged to render the Latin by such phrases as "about to sail."

3. The Perfect Participle Passive, which represents an action as already completed at any time.

    e.g.   *Having been wounded he is carried out of the battle.*
            vulnerātus ē proeliō portātur.

    N.B.—It is important to notice that Latin has no Perfect Participle Active like the English "having freed his slave," "having lost his money." The form of the sentence must be changed to express these in Latin. This will be explained later.

The Latin Participle can often be used to express a longer English phrase or clause. It is necessary to recognise these sentences:

> *He was killed*
> pugnāns necātus est.

> *He attacked the enemy*
> iam perturbātōs hostēs oppugnāvit.

N.B.—In the following exercises the words (like while and when in the above sentences) which do not need separate expression in Latin are printed in italics.

Exercise 242.

1. Our men, *while** fortifying their camp, were fiercely attacked by the Gauls.
2. The Romans, *while* hastening to the city, were hindered by a broad river.
3. *While* sailing to Athens we saw the enemy's ships.
4. We saw the boys working in the fields.
5. I fear the general *when he is* blaming me.
6. The Romans were about to lay waste the fields of the Gauls.
7. *While* fighting at Carthage he was wounded by an arrow.
8. We saw a boy running to the wood.
9. The Gauls, *while* attacking our camp, were themselves attacked.
10. *While* freeing the captives he praised their courage.

run currō, cucurrī, cursum 3.

Exercise 243.

1. The tenth legion was about to attack the enemy's camp.
2. *While* setting free the hostages he was killed by his own soldiers.
3. We saw the barbarians hiding arms in the woods.
4. At the fifth hour of the day he marched against the enemy.
5. The enemy, *while* fighting most bravely, were attacked by our cavalry.
6. We were about to carry on war in Gaul.
7. Our men, *while* attacking the camp, were wounded by the enemy's darts.
8. It is disgraceful to kill the men by whom we were saved.
9. Run to the city: announce the victory to the citizens.
10. The men whom we saw in the wood ran to the city.

kill necō 1.

Exercise 244.

1. *While* drawing up his line of battle he was killed by an arrow.
2. There are in this state twenty men who have never seen the king.
3. We attacked the enemy *while they were* carrying corn to the city.
4. The Gauls attacked Labienus *when he was* leading his men into camp.
5. The enemy were about to draw up their line of battle.
6. He was wounded by an arrow *while* leading his men out of the battle.
7. He was about to send larger forces to the city.
8. It is better to be killed than to be conquered.
9. We announced the victory to him *while he was* hastening out of the city.
10. *While* marching through the territories of the Gauls we saw a very broad river.

Exercise 245.

1. legiōnem ad urbem contendentem hostēs oppugnāvērunt.
2. miserōs captīvōs līberātūrus erat.
3. Rōmānōs Carthāginem nāvigantēs vīcērunt.
4. barbarōs bellum parantēs impedīvimus.
5. puerum victōriam nūntiantem audīvistī.
6. hostēs bellum parantēs nōn timēbimus.
7. fortissimē pugnāns ā Gallīs necātus est.
8. mīlitēs castra mūnientēs ab hostibus oppugnātī sunt.
9. multōs diēs Rōmae mānsūrus erat.
10. barbarōs bellum gerentēs nostrī nōn timēbunt.

246. Rome's Recovery (215–207 BC)

proximō annō cōnsul creātus est Q. Fabius Maximus, quī dictātor anteā tardē et cautē rem gesserat proeliumque cum hostibus quam maximē vītāverat, quam ob rem Cūnctātor vocābātur. eiusmodī tamen cōnsilia māiōrī partī cīvium minimē placēbant; itaque per M. Terentiī Varrōnis audāciam clādemque quam exercitus Cannis sustinuit tōta cīvitās prope dēlēta erat. exinde autem ſpem omnem salūtis in Q. Fabiō posuērunt. saepissimē pugnābātur, numquam tamen cum tōtis cōpiīs hostium: Hannibal, quod multārum urbium cīvēs ā Rōmānīs dēscīverant et Poenīs sē trādiderant hās omnēs dēfendere cōpiāsque in plūrimās partēs dīvidere cōgēbātur. tandem frāter eius, Hasdrubal, quī cum alterō exercitū in Ītaliam vēnerat, ad Metaurum flumen victus est: diē ille suōs pugnantēs exemplō cōnfirmat, locō cēdentēs in proelium revocat, tandem fortissimē pugnāns cecidit.

quam maximē as much as possible. **ſpēs, ſpeī** 5. f. hope. **fortiter** bravely.

247. The Labours of Hercules (continued)

erat ōlim monstrum horrendum, Hydra nōmine, quod in palūde prope lacum Lernaeum habitābat agrōsque finitimōs vastābat. huic novem erant capita quōrum medium immortāle fuit. Hercūlēs, quī ab Eurystheō monstrum occīdere iussus erat, ingentī clāvā oppugnāvit: quotiēns autem ūnum caput abscīderat, statim duo capita eōdem locō crēscēbant: etiam pugnantō ingēns subvēnit cancer, ā quō Hercūlēs vulnerātus est. erat autem Hercūlī minister quīdam fīdus, Iolāus nōmine, cuius auxiliō reliqua capita incendit, medium illud, quod immortāle esse dīcēbātur, sub magnō saxō sepelīvit. tum sanguine eius sagittās cruentāvit, cuius venēnō omnēs posteā, quī Hercūlis sagittīs vulnerātī erant, necābantur.

palūs, -ūdis 3. f. marsh. **crēscō, crēvī, crētum** 3. I grow. **subveniō, -vēnī, -ventum** 4. (+dat.) I come to the help of. **cancer, cancrī** 2. m. crab. **fīdus, -a, -um** faithful. **sepeliō, -elīvī, -ultum** 4. I bury.

248. King Alfred

rēgem tam bonum, tam intrepidum cīvēs iūre Magnum vocābant. barbarōs procul ā regnō pepulit; mox, ubi revertērunt, amīcitiam cum eīs per foedus confirmāvit. magnās nāvēs aedificāvit et tum prīmum barbarōrum nāvēs Britannī marī superāvērunt. nōn sōlum propter bellī victōriās nōtus est, sed pauperum causam contrā eōrum inimīcōs dēfendēbat (quoniam nēmō tum nisi rēx pauperibus amīcus erat); optimae lēgēs ab eō cōnstitūtae, virī multī et sapientēs ad regnum invītātī, scholae et templa condita esse dīcuntur.

SECTION 38

See Grammar Notes №s. 86–89,
Passive Participles of Regular Verbs

Exercise 249.

1. We attacked the Gauls *when* hindered by the river.
2. We conquered the enemy *when they had been* terrified by the arrival of Caesar.
3. They killed the captives *when they had been* condemned.
4. We attacked a city fortified by a high wall.
5. For three days Labienus held the city with a few troops.
6. We set free the prisoners *who had been* neglected by the soldiers.
7. The cavalry, hidden in the woods, were defeated by our men.
8. This city, preserved by our fathers, we all love.
9. The wounded general was carried into the camp by the soldiers.
10. In a few years it will not be easy to send corn.

condemn damnō 1.

Exercise 250.

1. The prisoners, *when* condemned, were killed by the soldiers.
2. Those whom we praise we do not always like.
3. The wall, built by the Gauls, was seen by our fathers.
4. Wounded by an arrow, he ran into the camp.
5. Attacked by the enemy, we fought most bravely for three hours.
6. It will be more easy to attack this city than to conquer the citizens.

7. Blamed by all, he hastened to Rome.
8. Kill the men whom we have condemned.
9. Attack the enemy *while* hindered by this river.
10. It is better to have saved our country than to have avoided danger.

Exercise 251.

1. *While* fighting on behalf of their country they were conquered.
2. *While* hindered by the river they were attacked by the Roman cavalry.
3. By the valour of the citizens our city has been set free.
4. The best plan will be to send larger forces to the war.
5. Neglected by his own father, he remained in the city.
6. The cohorts which we sent were led by Labienus.
7. They are holding that part of the city which we have often attacked.
8. It is very easy to fight, very difficult to conquer.
9. It is not disgraceful to be condemned by a bad man.
10. We were about to send a large army into Gaul.

Exercise 252.

1. hostium aciem, equitum adventū perturbātam, superāvimus.
2. hominēs damnātōs necābimus.
3. urbem mūrīs mūnītam oppugnāvimus.
4. mīlitēs ā sē laudātōs in castra redūxit.
5. equum tēlō vulnerātum ē proeliō dūcit.
6. per agrōs ab hostibus vastātōs cucurrērunt.
7. turrem ā mīlitibus vīsam oppugnātūrus erat.
8. hostēs gravissimīs oneribus impedītōs oppugnāvimus.
9. mīlitēs ad bellum missōs nōn iterum vidēbis.
10. hōrum adventū nōn maximē terrēbimur.

253. Zama (202 BC)

exinde bellum in Āfricā gerēbātur, quō Hannibal ā cīvibus suīs ex
Ītaliā revocātus est. ibi ā Scipiōne prope Zāmam victus est: Poenī
Rōmānīs Hispāniam colōniāsque omnēs quās extrā Āfricam
possidēbant cum nāvibus longīs praeter decem trādere, decem
mīlia talentum quīnquāgintā annīs persolvere coāctī sunt. Hannibal tamen, nōn minus quam anteā odiō Rōmānōrum mōtus,
bellum redintegrāre summīs vīribus parābat: ab inimīcīs tamen
Carthāgine excēdere coactus ad Antiochum, Syriae rēgem, quī
tum bellum cum Rōmānīs gestūrus erat, discessit. posteā apud
Bithyniae rēgem multōs annōs exsulābat: tum, quod rēx ā Rōmānīs eum trādere iussus erat, venēnum, quod in ānulō semper portāre solēbat, sūmpsit vītaque, sexāgintā iam annōs nātus, excessit.

quō whither. **odium** 2. n. hatred. **apud** (+acc.) with, at the
court of. **ānulus** 2. m. ring. **soleō, solitus sum** 2. I am
accustomed. **sexāgintā** sixty.

254. The Labours of Hercules (continued)

nympha quaedam Dianae, quod illīus auxiliō ē magnō perīculō
servāta erat, cervum, quī aurea cornua pedēsque aēneōs habēbat,
dēdicāverat. hunc Hercūlēs vīvum Mycēnās portāre iussus per
tōtum annum frūstrā petēbat: tandem sagittā vulnerātum in
humerīs portantī repente occurrit Diana quae magna est īra
permōta quod animal ipsī sacrum ille vulnerāverat. Hercūlēs
tamen deae īram permulsit praedamque Mycēnās āvexit.

    erant prope lacum Stymphālum mīrae quaedam avēs quae
ālās et rostra aēnea habēbant carnemque hūmānam vorābant. hās
quoque expellere iussus prīmum sistrō, quod eī Minerva dederat,
terruit, tum per āera volantēs sagittīs occīdit. qua tamen dē rē nōn
eādem ab omnibus nārrantur: nam, ut aliī trādidērunt, avēs ad
insulam quandam pepulit, ubi posteā ab Argonautis inventae sunt.

nympha 1. f. nymph. **cervus** 2. m. stag. **permoveō, -mōvī,
-mōtum** 2. I move, stir. **avis** 3. f. bird. **expellō, expulī,
expulsum** 3. I drive out, expel. **sistrum** 2. n. rattle. **ut** (with
indicative) as. **pellō, pepulī, pulsum** 3. I drive.

SECTION 39

See Grammar Notes №s. 81–83,
Subjunctive Active of Regular Verbs
(1st and 2nd Conjugations) and *sum*

THE SUBJUNCTIVE MOOD

1. An Exhortation (1st or 3rd Person), or a Wish for the
    Future, is expressed by the Present Subjunctive. If
    negative, nē is used with it.

    e.g.   Let all fear my words.
           omnēs verba mea timeant.

           Let us not praise evil men.
           nē malōs laudēmus.

           May the citizens be brave.
           sint cīvēs fortēs.

2. Translate the Conjunction *since* by cum with a
    Subjunctive Tense.*
         If the English has a
                 Present Tense use the Present Subjunctive.
                 Past   "   "   Imperfect Subjunctive.
                 Perfect   "   "   Perfect Subjunctive.
                 Pluperfect "   "   Pluperfect Subjunctive.

*The introduction of this construction here is anticipating
future work. But as practice is required in the formation of
all the Subjunctive tenses, this construction has been chosen
for the purpose as involving least difficulty to the learner at
this stage.
         e.g.   Since they *are* allies we will summon all.
                cum sociī *sint* omnēs convocābimus.

179

Since they *were* allies we summoned all.
cum sociī *essent* omnēs convocāvimus.

Since Caesar *has remained* we are safe.
cum Caesar *mānserit* tūtī sumus.

Since Caesar *had remained* we were safe.
cum Caesar *mānsisset* tūtī erāmus.

Exercise 255.

1. Let us avoid all dangers, citizens.
2. Let us not sail to Athens.
3. Build larger ships, Romans.
4. May they be more fortunate than their fathers.
5. Since he fears the enemy, he will remain in the camp.
6. May we not see the enemy in this land.
7. Since he had laid waste the fields of allies, he was blamed by all.
8. Since he was at Rome, he was not condemned.
9. Since you have soldiers, send forces to your allies.
10. Let us withstand their attack and free our country.

since cum (+subjunctive). **ally** socius 2. m.

Exercise 256.

1. May the Romans defeat the Gauls this year.
2. Let us not attack the larger camp.
3. Let me not remain in the camp with the wounded.
4. Since you have freed your country, you will be praised by all.
5. Let us summon all the forces of the allies.
6. Let us build a greater number of ships this year.
7. Let us defeat the enemy whom we never feared.
8. May he not remain in that city.
9. Let us kill the condemned prisoners.
10. Let us defeat the enemy by our valour.

summon convocō 1. **greater** māior, -or, -us.

Exercise 257.

1. Let us not blame the good customs of our fathers.
2. May we free the country which we all love.
3. May you fight bravely and defeat the Gauls.
4. Let us not fear a conquered enemy.
5. Let us seize that part of the city.
6. Since he is preparing war, let us attack his camp.
7. May we never see the Roman legions in this city.
8. Since he has remained at Rome he will not fight for his country.
9. Let us carry the wounded men to the camp.
10. Since he was not in the city he did not see the king.

Exercise 258.

1. hostēs oppugnēmus, agrōs vastēmus.
2. mīlitēs quī urbem servāvērunt laudēmus.
3. cum Gallī bellum parent, ipsī bellum parēmus.
4. cum sociī sint, exercitum mittēmus.
5. cum fortiter pugnāvissent, ab omnibus laudābantur.
6. cum mīlitēs nōn habeāmus, bellum nōn gerēmus.
7. nē magnum hostium numerum timeāmus.
8. omnēs patrum nostrōrum virtūtem laudent.
9. hostium impetum fortiter sustineāmus.
10. nāvēs māiōrēs aedificēmus.

259. Rome and Greece (200–146 BC)

vix iam Rōmānī Poenōs superāverant, ubi Macedoniīs bellum indīxērunt. huius gentis rēx Philippus in Thessaliā prope collēs quī Cynoscephalae vocābantur castra posuerat: ibi gaudiō permōtus, cum parvam manum Rōmānōrum fugāvisset, contrā tōtum exercitum prōcessit. tum ā Flāminīnō, quī nostrīs praeerat, victus terrās omnēs quās extrā Macedoniam regēbat trādere coactus est. nec multō posteā Antiochus, quī socius fuerat Philippī nec tamen in bellō eī subvēnerat, cum auxilium ab eō plūrimae in Graeciā cīvitātēs implōrāvissent, arma contrā Rōmānōs sūmpsit. is quoque, prīmum Thermopylīs, mox Magnēsiae superātus magnum numerum nāvium longārum trādere decemque mīlia talentum persolvere cōgitur. vigintī post annīs iterum cum Macedoniīs pugnātum est: quō in bellō L. Aemilius Paulus ā rēge Perseō magnam victōriam reportāvit. tandem omnis Graecia in Rōmānōrum potestātem vēnit.

indīcō, indīxī, indictum 3. I proclaim; **bellum indīcō** (+dat.) I declare war on. **collis, -is** 3. m. hill. **cum** (+subjunctive) since, when. **potestās, -ātis** 3. f. power.

260. The Labours of Hercules (continued)

ingēns ōlim aper ā monte Erymanthō in campōs dēscenderat. hunc, cum agrōs ubique vastāret, vivum ad rēgem portāre iussus Hercūlēs per altam nivem diē petēbat: tum labōre fessum rēte impedīvit Mycenāsque āvexit. aprum dum petit, Centaurō Pholō occurrit, cui Bacchus ōlim cadum optimī vīnī dederat. hunc cadum Hercūlēs aperuit: tum reliquī Centaurī, vīnī odōre dulcissimō ductī, spēluncam in quā Pholus habitābat obsēdērunt: ab Hercūle pulsī Chīrōnis domum fuga petīvērunt. quōs ille cum fugāret incautē amīcum suum Chīrōnem sagittā venēnātā vulnerāvit: Pholus quoque sagittā, quae in pedem eius forte ceciderat, vulnerātus est.

Chīron, cum immortalis esset, sagittā nōn necātus erat: ultrō tamen vīta excessit.

aper, aprī 2. m. boar. **rēte, -is** 3. n. net. **cadus** 2. m. cask. **vīnum** 2. n. wine. **odor, odōris** 3. m. smell. **venēnātus, -a, -um** poisoned.

261. Military Discipline

imperātor quīdam ōlim urbem obsidēns ūnum ē mīlitibus, virum fortissimum, ad sē vocāvit. "scālam," inquit, "ad mūrōs crās pōnam; tū prīmus scālam ascendēs." "fiet," respondit mīles. "custōs mūrī clāmābit, 'quis venit?' nihil respondēbis." "fiet." "custōs tēlum immittet; tē nōn vulnerābit." "fiet." "tū custōdem occīdēs." "fiet." "egō tibi subveniam et hostēs oppugnābō." "fiet." mīles imperātōrī pāruit et scālam ascendit; custōs tēlum immīsit; mīlitem nōn vulnerāvit; mīles custōdem occīdit; imperātor cum aliīs mīlitibus urbem intrāvit et incolae superātī sunt.

scāla 1. f. ladder. **fiet** "yes, sir" (lit., it will be done). **quis, quis, quid** who? what?

SECTION 40

See Grammar Notes №s. 84 and 85,
Subjunctive Active of Regular Verbs
(3rd and 4th Conjugations).

SUBJUNCTIVE AND PROHIBITIONS

A command in the negative (i.e. a prohibition) may be expressed by nē with the 2nd Person of the Perfect Subjunctive.

> e.g.   Do not be afraid.
>   nē timuerīs.

N.B.—For a more usual way of expressing a prohibition, see Section 46.

Exercise 262.

1. Let us not neglect the advice of our generals.
2. Do not send the boy to the city.
3. May we conquer the enemy who are terrifying our allies.
4. Let us carry on the war in the territories of the Gauls.
5. Let us send corn to the Roman army.
6. Let us not fear the men whom our fathers conquered.
7. Since the citizens have neglected our advice they will be conquered.
8. Since he had sent troops to the town, he remained in the camp himself.
9. Let us fortify this city with walls and towers.
10. Let us not hear the words of this evil man.

man vir 2. m. **word** verbum 2. n.

Exercise 263.

1. At that time the customs of the Romans were praised by all.
2. Praise the valour of these men who have fought bravely for their country.
3. Let us on this day conquer the enemy who have killed our general.
4. Since we have conquered this nation we shall hasten to Rome.
5. Since they had not sent hostages Caesar summoned their leaders.
6. Let us not hinder the victory of our men.
7. Let us send an army to that state.
8. Let us not neglect those by whose valour we were saved.
9. Since he is carrying on war in Gaul, he will not be sent to Carthage.
10. Let us draw up our line of battle opposite the city.

time tempus, -oris 3. n.

Exercise 264.

1. Since he was attacking the camp, he did not see our men.
2. It was the custom of the Romans to carry the wounded out of battle.
3. At that time the enemy were holding our city.
4. The Gauls have withstood our attacks most bravely.
5. It is most disgraceful to condemn a man whom all praise.
6. Let us lead back our conquered soldiers into the camp.
7. Let all the states send corn to Caesar.
8. Since the tenth legion is afraid, all are afraid.
9. Let us hinder the Romans *while* fortifying their camp.
10. At that time we had both ships and soldiers.

Exercise 265.

1. hostēs vincāmus quī bellum contrā nōs gerunt.
2. nē hōs timueritis quōs saepe vīcistis.
3. imperātōris nostrī verba audiāmus.
4. nē patris cōnsilium neglēxeris.
5. cum frūmentum mīserint, eōrum agrōs nōn vastābimus.
6. cum multās hōrās pugnāverint, in castra redūcentur.
7. cīvēs, cum barbarōrum clāmōrēs audīrent, timēbant.
8. nostrī, cum hostēs vīcissent, ab imperātōre laudābantur.
9. Gallī, cum urbem mūrō mūnīvissent, impetus nostrōs nōn timuērunt.
10. nē vulnerātōs mīlitēs neglegāmus.

266. The End of Carthage (146 BC)

eōdem annō, quō omnis Graecia in potestātem Rōmānōrum vēnit, Carthāgō quoque dēlēta est. Poenī, cum iam per mercātūram dīvitiās augērent et ex clāde illā quam sustinuerant sē colligere coepissent, Rōmānōrum invidiam mōvērunt. quī saepissimē ā M. Porciō Catōne monitī tandem bellum indīxērunt. Poenī statim ultrō sē suaque omnia Rōmānīs trādidērunt: prīmum obsidēs, mox arma et nāvēs postulantibus libenter dedērunt. cum autem victor superbus urbem dēlēre iussisset trīgintā diērum indūtiās petiērunt summīsque vīribus bellum parābant. maxima est pertinācia utrimque pugnātum. tandem Poenī magnā clāde superātī, urbs ipsa omnīnō dēlēta est.

sīc urbs Rōma, cum reliquās Ītaliae gentēs, mox populōs fīnitimōs bellō superāvisset, in magnum iam imperium crēverat.

superbus, -a, -um proud, haughty. **trīgintā** thirty. **pertinācia** 1. f. obstinacy.

267. The Labours of Hercules (continued)

rēx quīdam, Diomēdēs nōmine, equās suās carne hūmānā
pāscēbat. hās Mycenās portāre iussus Hercūlēs cum paucīs
comitibus ad ōram dūxit. quō cum cīvēs rēgis vēnissent, diū
et ācriter pugnātum est. equās, dum proeliō interest, Hercūlēs amīcō suō Abdērō mandat, quem illae statim vorant.
Hercūlēs, cum hostēs vīcisset, rēgem occīdit corpusque equīs
iactāvit: tum urbem in eō locō condidit, quam urbem Abdēra
vocāvit. Equās, quae cum dominī carnem ēdissent mansuēv-
erant, Mycenās āvexit: mox līberātae et ipsae ā ferīs in Monte
Olympō vorābantur.

posteā Amazōnum rēgīnae zōnam, quam eī Mars dederat,
petere iussus, cum multa perīcula superāvisset, rēgīnam ipsam
occīdit zōnamque reportāvit.

equa 1. f. mare. **dominus** 2. m. master. **mansuescō, -suēvī,
-suētum** 3. I become tame. **fera** 1. f. wild beast. **rēgīna** 1. f.
queen. **zōna** 1. f. girdle.

SECTION 41

See Grammar Notes №s. 86 and 87,
Subjunctive Passive of Regular Verbs
(1st and 2nd Conjugations).

Exercise 268.

1. Let us not be terrified by a conquered enemy.
2. May we always be loved by our allies.
3. Since he has been wounded, he will not fight again.
4. Since the city had been preserved, the citizens were not afraid.
5. Let the heaviest burdens be carried by the soldiers.
6. Since the victory had been announced, they ran to the city.
7. We are all in the city, since the enemy are laying waste our fields.
8. Since all things have been prepared, let us hasten to the city.
9. Let a meeting be held in three days.
10. May the enemy be defeated by our cavalry.

meeting concilium 2. m.

Exercise 269.

1. May the city be preserved by the valour of our men.
2. Let meetings be held at the same time in Rome.
3. Let us not be frightened by an enemy whom our fathers defeated.
4. Since the wall has now been built, we do not fear the enemy.
5. Let us not be thrown into confusion by the arrival of Caesar.
6. Since they had withstood our attack, we summoned a meeting.
7. Let the wounded be carried out of the battle.
8. Since our leaders have been killed, we shall not remain.

9. Let us praise those who rule us well.
10. Do not remain: the enemy have drawn up their line.

Exercise 270.

1. They have set free the hostages whom we sent.
2. For many years this state carried on war with the Romans.
3. Since the tenth legion had been defeated, we summoned a meeting.
4. Since part of the Roman army had been seen by the enemy, the barbarians were terrified.
5. Let him be condemned himself, since he has set free the prisoners.
6. He was afraid, since he had never seen a Roman army.
7. Let us attack the enemy at the fourth hour.
8. Hold meetings, citizens: free your country.
9. Let the captives, whom we sent, be killed.
10. He had conducted a campaign in Gaul most successfully for many years.

successfully fēlīcissimē.

Exercise 271.

1. nē ab iīsdem iam hostibus superēmur.
2. Gallī, cum Caesaris adventū territī essent, bellum nōn parābant.
3. cum urbs nōn oppugnāta esset, cīvēs tūtī erant.
4. cuius adventū cum mīlitum animī cōnfirmātī essent, vīcimus.
5. patria nostra cīvium virtūte servētur.
6. nē bellī perīculō terreāmur.
7. cum dux eum laudāverit, nōs nōn culpābimus.
8. mīlitēs, cum hostium adventū perturbārentur, redūxit.
9. cum agrī nostrī vastārentur, frūmentum nōn habēbāmus.
10. nē concilium sociōrum convocēmus.

tūtus, -a, -um safe. **culpō** 1. I blame. **convocō** 1. I call together, summon.

272. Rome After the Great Wars

amplius centum iam annōs Rōmānī bella prope perpetua cum
externīs populīs gerēbant: domī intereā senātus auctōritās,
pauperum inopia adeō crēverant ut maxima esset in cīvitāte
dissensiō: mediī inter hōs equitēs magnās dīvitiās per mercātūram sibi comparāverant. plēbēiī quidem iūra paria cum
patriciīs habēbant: magistrātus autem semper ex eīsdem ferē
gentibus, quae nōbilēs vocābantur, creātī sunt. cum agrī ubique
bellō vastātī essent, per tōtam Ītaliam maxima omnium rērum
inopia fuit: mercātōrēs quoque frūmentum ex Siciliā et Āfricā
importātum tam parvō in Ītaliā vendēbant ut nōn iam agricolās
prōdesset parvōs fundōs colere. ager pūblicus ā paucīs et dīvit-
ibus possidēbātur in quō servī dominōrum pecora custōdiēbant.

perpetuus, -a, -um perpetual, continuous. **externus, -a,
-um** foreign. **adeō** to such an extent, so. **ut** (with
subjunctive) that, so that (as a consequence). **pār, paris**
equal. **nōbilis, -is, -e** noble. **mercātor, -ōris** 3. m. merchant.
importō 1. I import. **vendō, -didī, -ditum** 3. I sell. **agricola**
1. m. farmer. **prōsum, -desse, -fuī** (+dat.) I benefit;
(impersonally) **prōdest** it is profitable.

273. The Labours of Hercules (continued)

ōlim in insulā quādam, quae prope Hispāniam esse crēdēbātur,
habitābat monstrum horrendum, Gēryon nōmine, quī tria
corpora habēbat: huius pecora gigās et canis, cui duo erant
capita, custōdiēbant. haec cum reportāre iussus esset Herculis
Columnās posuit; quō in itinere, cum magnopere sōlis ardōre
vexārētur, sagittam in ipsum sōlem ēmīsit. quā audāciā adeō
deō placuit ut auream eī lintrem daret, in quā ad illam insulam nāvigāvit. ibi et giganta et canem ūnā cum ipsō dominō
occīdit, tum praedam āvexit: auream autem lintrem sōlī
reddidit. pecora, cum plūrimā perīculā superāvisset, tandem
reportāvit ad rēgem, ā quō Iūnōnī immolāta sunt.

gigās (acc. **giganta**), **gigantis** 3. m. giant. **magnopere** greatly.
ardor, -ōris 3. m. heat. **linter, -tris** 3. f. boat. **ūnā** together.

274. An Attack on Foragers Repulsed

inde Caesar suōs redūxit et castra in locō idōneō posuit. postrīdiē haud procul ab oppidō hostium cōpiae in collibus vidēbantur; nōn tamen ad campum dēscendērunt. intereā, cum in castrīs Rōmānīs magna esset frūmentī inopia, tertiā hōrā Caesar aliquot mīlitēs et paucōs equitēs cum C. Trebonio lēgātō in agrōs mīsit. repente ex omnibus partibus hostēs ad locum veniunt. nostrī contrā plūrēs numerō sē dēfendere coactī, cum nihil eiusmodī exspectāvissent, tamen aliōs occīdērunt, aliōs ad collēs reppulērunt, neque posteā frūmentum in agrīs petentēs ā Gallīs oppugnātī sunt.

SECTION 42

See Grammar Notes №s. 88 and 89,
Subjunctive Passive of Regular Verbs
(3rd and 4th Conjugations).

Exercise 275.

1. May the words of our fathers be heard by all.
2. Since the city has now been fortified, the citizens are preparing war.
3. Let us not send help to the enemies of our state.
4. Let part of the city be fortified by the citizens themselves.
5. Since we have been prevented by the general, we shall not fight.
6. Since the army is being sent into Gaul, there will be danger in Italy.
7. The help of the Romans was most useful to us in the war.
8. Do not be prevented by the words of the enemy.
9. Let not his advice be neglected by our citizens.
10. It is better to send help to our allies than to carry corn to Caesar.

help, aid auxilium 2. n.

Exercise 276.

1. Let the words of the wounded general be heard by all.
2. Let us hear the words of Caesar himself.
3. Since the line has now been drawn up, let us fight bravely.
4. Let all the infantry be hidden in this part of the town.
5. Since the Gauls had now been conquered, he led his men back into camp.
6. Let war be carried on by land and sea.
7. May the enemy be conquered by the valour of the soldiers, not by stratagem.
8. Since the allies had been placed on the left wing, we were conquered.
9. The king of this nation has not sent help to Caesar.
10. It will be more useful to summon a meeting of all the Gauls.

Exercise 277.

1. Let two cohorts be sent to Carthage.
2. This thing was quickly announced to the Gauls.
3. Let not the advice of the gods be neglected by men.
4. Since the campaign was being conducted by Caesar, the barbarians were afraid.
5. Let us not be ruled by men whom our fathers conquered.
6. Help will be sent to the allies in three days.
7. Advised by you, he quickly led his men back.
8. May this beautiful city not be seized by the enemy.
9. This nation has always sent help to the Gauls in all the wars.
10. Since the corn has been sent, the hostages will be set free.

quickly celeriter.

Exercise 278.

1. auxilium ad sociōs nostrōs celeriter mittātur.
2. cum urbs mūrīs mūnīta sit, perīculum nōn timēmus.
3. imperātor, cum iam barbarōrum clāmōrēs audīrentur, suōs ē castrīs dūxit.
4. nōna legiō celerrimē ad urbem contendit.
5. equitēs dextrō cornū instruantur.
6. ego, cum cōnsilium meum neglēctum sit, nōn iterum vōs monēbō.
7. Gallī, cum flūmine impedītī essent, ā Rōmānīs superābantur.
8. urbs aggeribus et turribus mūniātur.
9. quīnque hōrās sociī nostrī hostium impetum sustinēbant.
10. nē imperātor cīvium verbīs impediātur.

279. The Gracchi (133–121 BC)

Tī. Semprōnius Gracchus, pauperum misericordia permōtus, lēgem rogāvit ut ager pūblicus ita inter cīvēs dīviderētur, ut anteā ā Sextiō et Liciniō cōnstitūtum erat. lēgī resistēbant senātōrēs, intercessit M. Octavius tribūnus plēbis. tum ille populī suffrāgiō confirmātus Octavium tribūnātum dēpōnere iussit et proximō annō contrā lēgēs iterum ipse tribūnātum petīit. tum senātōrēs cum turbā cīvium īrātōrum eum in forō oppugnātum occīdērunt.

decem post annīs frāter eius frāter eius C. Semprōnius Gracchus multās lēgēs rogāvit, ut pauperibus licēret frūmentum parvō emere, iūdicēs nōn iam ē senātōribus sed ex equitibus dēligerentur; posteā ut iūs suffrāgiī Latīnīs darētur. hāc autem lēge cum omnibus displicuisset, is quoque ā suīs ipse cīvibus occīsus est.

ut (with subjunctive) that, in order that (expressing a purpose). **intercēdō, -cessī, -cessum** (+dat.) 3. I veto. **tribūnātus** 4. m. tribunate, office of tribune. **licet** 2. (impersonal), it is allowed.

280. The Labours of Hercules (concluded)

in hortō quōdam haud procul ā Monte Atlante trēs erant
sorōrēs pulcherrimae, Hesperidēs nōmine: hae ūna cum ingentī
dracōne aurea illa pōma custōdiēbant quae Iūnōnī, cum ā
Iove in mātrimōnium ducerētur, ā Terrā data erant. haec
pōma petere iussus Hercūlēs, cum situm hortī ignōrāret, per
multās terrās diē frūstrā errābat. monitus autem ā Prometheō
Atlantem, quī humerīs caelī onus sustinēbat, mīsit ut pōma
invenīret: ipse intereā onus sustinet. tum ad rēgem reportāvit
pōma quae posteā, cum sibi ab illō data essent, Minervae dēdicāvit: haec autem in eundem hortum restituit.

   ultimus labōrum etiam omnium difficillimus fuit: nam
ā rēge iussus est Cerberum canem ā mānibus ad terram suīs
ipsīus vīribus, sine armīs reportāre. hoc monstrum, quod
tria capita habēbat, vī superātum āvexit, rēgī ostendit, tum
ad mānēs redūxit.

situs 4. m. position, situation. **caelum** 2. n. heaven, the
heavens. **restituō, -uī, -ūtum** 3. I restore.

SECTION 43

See Grammar Notes №. 90,
The Verb *ūtor*

DEPONENT VERBS

A Deponent Verb is one which is Passive in form but Active
in meaning. But note especially that

1. It has *all* the Participles (ūtēns, ūsūrus, ūsus), and the
   Perfect Participle has usually an Active meaning like
   the rest of the Verb; e.g. ūsus, *having used.*
2. The Future Infinitive is of the Active form; e.g. ūsūrus
   esse.

Exercise 281.

1. We encouraged the soldiers with a few words before the battle.
2. We delayed a few days at Athens.
3. The words of our allies encourage us.
4. We do not use arrows in war.
5. We shall encourage our men *when they are* drawn up in line of battle.
6. Our fathers employed the same device.
7. Since there is danger in the city, we shall not delay.
8. *While* exhorting his men he was wounded by an arrow.
9. The leaders of the Gauls are employing our devices.
10. Having exhorted his men with a few words, he will hasten to Carthage.

encourage, exhort hortor, hortātus 1. deponent. **before** ante (+acc.). **delay** moror (deponent). **use, employ** ūtor, ūtī, ūsus 3. deponent (+abl.).

Exercise 282.

1. Having encouraged his men, he drew them up in line of battle.
2. We had never used these shields in war.
3. Let us encourage the defeated soldiers.
4. It is better to stay in the camp than to be conquered.
5. Hindered by the river, they stayed in this land for many days.
6. Let us use our victory well.
7. The gods employ the plans of men.
8. I have never seen the arms which they used.
9. Having delayed a few days in Gaul, they laid waste the fields.
10. Let us employ the help of our allies.

Exercise 283.

1. He will not stay many days in Athens.
2. He emboldened the hearts of the soldiers by his valour.
3. All our plans will be known to the enemy in a few hours.
4. We heard the general encouraging his men.
5. It is better to employ wisdom than courage.
6. Since the enemy had seized the town, we stayed in the fields.
7. This nation does not employ ships in war.
8. It will be most disgraceful now to stay in the camp.
9. The general was about to exhort his soldiers.
10. I have never seen the city in which you are staying.

Exercise 284.

1. mīlitēs hortātus, ad urbem contendit.
2. Gallī hīs tēlīs in bellō nōn ūtuntur.
3. cīvēs in multīs conciliīs hortābātur.
4. in hāc urbe paucōs diēs morātī sumus.
5. Caesar, mīlitēs hortātus, animōs ad proelium confirmāvit.
6. cum trēs diēs in hāc terrā morātī sīmus, iam in Ītaliam contendāmus.
7. hīs tēlīs in omnibus bellīs ūtēmur.
8. nē multās hōrās Rōmae morēmur.
9. mōs erat imperātōris mīlitēs ante proelium hortārī.
10. in hāc terrā quīnque diēs morātī multōs hominēs, multās urbēs vīdimus.

hortor, hortātus 1. deponent. I encourage.
ūtor, ūtī, ūsus 3. deponent (+abl.) I use.
morior, mortuus 3. deponent. I die.

285. Jugurtha (116–105 BC)

Micipsa, rēx Numidiae, populī Rōmānī socius regnum inter duōs fīliōs, Hiempsalem Adherbalemque, et frātris fīlium Iugurtham dīvīserat. Iugurtha Hiempsalem occīdit, bellō superāvit Adherbalem, quī ā Rōmānīs auxilium petīvit. hī regnum per lēgātōs inter duōs dīvīsērunt: Iugurtha autem, quamquam lēgātōrum animōs magnīs pecūniīs adeō sibi conciliāverat ut melior pars regnī eī darētur, iterum Adherbalem oppugnāvit bellōque victum occīdit. tum dēnique bellum eī Rōmānī indīxērunt: is autem eīsdem artibus ūsus pācem pecūniā ēmit. posteā ob eam rem in urbem arcessītus, cum consōbrīnum suum Massīvam ibi occīdisset, tantam inter omnēs īram mōvit ut ex Ītaliā excēdere iubērētur. bellum tum redintegrātum est; quō in bellō Jugurtha Aulum cōnsulem superāvit, exercitus partem trucīdāvit, partem sub iugum mīsit. posteā ā Q. Metellō quem pecūnia sibi conciliāre frūstrā cōnātus est, identidem superābātur: tandem ā C. Mariō victus et in urbem ductus diū in carcere tenēbātur ibique fame necātus est.

arcessō, -īvī, ītum 3. I summon. **consōbrīnus** 2. m. cousin.
cōnor 1. dep. I try. **famēs, -is** 3. f. hunger, starvation.

286. The Story of Cadmus

Cadmus, ā patre iussus sorōrem āmissam domum reportāre, cum diē frūstrā petīvisset, ab ōrāculō sīc monitus est: "vaccam quam mox vidēbis sequere: haec ubi fessa humī dēcumbet, oppidum in eō locō conde." vaccam haud multō posteā inventam secūtus ubi dēcubuerat ibi condidit Cadmeam quae posteā urbis Thēbārum arx fuit. hanc vaccam cum Minervae immolātūrus esset, quōsdam mīsit ut aquam peterent: aquam autem custōdiēbat dracō quī hominēs ā Cadmō missōs occīdit. tum ille dracōnem occīdit et ā Minervā monitus dentēs monstrī in terrā sēvit: ex eō locō surrēxērunt virī armātī quī statim inter sē pugnantēs cecidērunt: supererant quīnque ā quibus Thēbānī orīginem dūxērunt. Cadmus posteā in serpentem versus ā Iove ad Elysium missus est.

vacca 1. f. cow. **sequor, secūtus sum** 3. dep. I follow.
dēcumbō, dēcubuī 3. I lie down. **orīgō, -inis** 3. f. origin.

287. The Last Days of a Great General

Hannibal, dux Carthāginiensium, iam ā Rōmānīs victus pācem ab hostibus petīvit: pāx Carthāginiensibus concessa est, timor autem Hannibalis ipsīus diū inter Rōmānōs manēbat. itaque, cum spēs esset nūlla relicta, omnia ad fugam parāvit et noctū ex urbe excessit: nōnnullī comitēs, cōnsiliōrum ignārī, eum sequēbantur. iam anteā equī haud procul ā portā parātī erant: postrīdiē ad mare inter Achollam et Thapsum incolumis advēnit, ubi amīcī eum cum nāve expectābant. ita Hannibal ex Āfricā excessit nec posteā cum Rōmānīs bellum gessit. virī intrepidī misericordiā nēmō nōn hodiē movētur, quamquam gēns Carthāginiensis propter crūdēlitātem in odiō est.

ignārus ignorant.

SECTION 44

See Grammar Notes №. 98,
Verbs in *-io* of the 3rd Conjugation.

CAPIŌ AND *FACIŌ*

Note—The Verbs conjugated like capiō lose the i of their stem before another i, final e, and the syllable er.

    e.g. cap-it, cape, capere.

Exercise 288.

1. They are making a journey through the territories of the Gauls.
2. Let us take the city which we are attacking.
3. Corn was carried to them on the march by the allies.
4. He does everything by his father's advice.
5. Hasten, soldiers: our city is being taken by the enemy.
6. We captured the ships which the Gauls had sent.
7. The enemy are adopting a bold plan.
8. The Romans were marching to the territories of their allies.
9. The city, which our fathers saved, will now be taken by the Gauls.
10. Adopt a bolder plan, Labienus: make an attack on the enemy.

do, make faciō, fēcī, factum 3. **journey, route** iter, itineris 3. n. **take, capture, adopt, form (a plan)** capiō, cēpī, captum.

Exercise 289.

1. Let us not delay: let us march against the enemy.
2. Our camp was being taken by the Gauls.
3. Since he has adopted this plan, we shall stay in the camp.
4. It will be more useful to do this than to capture the city.
5. Since the camp was being taken, the soldiers ran into the city.
6. We shall not employ the plan which Caesar adopted.
7. The camp of the Gauls has been taken by our men.
8. The citizens were doing everything that the general had advised.
9. It will be very difficult for us to make a journey through your territories.
10. Since a plan is being formed by the general, we shall summon a meeting.

Exercise 290.

1. All will praise the plan you are adopting.
2. Since the city has been very well fortified, let us stay in it.
3. The plan which I had adopted was blamed by all.
4. On the march we saw the forces which our allies had sent.
5. A conquered army will not adopt this plan.
6. The Gauls are now marching through our territories.
7. In a few days they will take the city which we built.
8. The citizens are doing what you advised.
9. Since they are adopting a very bad plan, let us not fear them.
10. *When* preparing war they did the same thing themselves.

capiō and faciō

Exercise 291.

1. urbem altō aggere mūnītam cēpit.
2. faciāmus id quod imperātor monet.
3. impetum in nostrōs ācriter fēcērunt.
4. equitēs nostrī ab hostibus captī sunt.
5. bellum in nostrīs agrīs gerēbant.
6. id quod facitis omnēs laudābunt.
7. in Ītaliam celeriter iter faciāmus.
8. Gallī in Rōmānōrum aciem impetum fēcērunt.
9. cum ab omnibus culpātus sit, īdem nōn iterum faciet.
10. oppidum nostrā virtūte capiēmus.

capiō, cēpī, captum 3. I take, capture. **faciō, fēcī, factum** 3. I do, make.

292. Marius (157–86 BC)

C. Marius, homō obscūrō locō nātus, in bellō contrā Iugurtham gestō magnam sibi fāmam comparāvit. mox cōnsul creātus Teutonōs, quī arma contrā Rōmānōs sumpserant, prope Aquās Sextiās vīcit. domī populārium causam contrā senātum dēfendit, quōrum suffrāgiīs exercituī, quem tum L. Cornelius Sulla contrā Mithridatem, Pontī rēgem, dūcēbat, praefectus est. quod cum audīvisset Sulla cum exercitū Rōmam contendit: Marius fugere coāctus diū in summā inopiā exsulābat. posteā cum Cinnā, dux populārium, Rōma pulsus exercitum in Ītaliā colligeret, cum eō Rōmam revertit, mox victor intrāvit. maxima tum caedēs secūta est: omnēs quōs Marius nōn salūtāverat ā mīlitibus eius trucīdābantur. proximō annō morbō mortuus est.

obscūrus, -a, -um obscure. **populāris, -is, -e** of the people; **populārēs** 3. m. pl. the democrats. **praeficiō, -fēcī, -fectum** (+dat.) 2. I appoint to the command of. **fugiō, fūgī** 3. I flee. **caedēs, -is** 3. f. slaughter, murder. **salūtō** 1. I greet. **morbus** 2. m. illness.

293. Ulysses and the Cyclops

erant ōlim in Siciliā gigantēs quīdam quī Cyclōpēs vocābantur, ē quibus ūnus, Polyphēmus nōmine, in magnā spēluncā cum ovibus suīs habitābat. eō Ulixēs cum comitibus vēnit: Polyphēmus tum forte ovēs in monte pāscēbat. quī cum domum revertisset ovēs in spēluncam dūxit magnumque saxum ad ōs spēluncae posuit. Ulixem cum vīdisset, multa rogāvit: respondit ille, "Graecī sumus, quī trāns mare ad hanc insulam nāvigāvimus: sī deōs timēs, nōs adiuvā: nam dī eōs quī advenās auxilium petentēs neglegunt maximīs suppliciīs pūnīre solent." "deōs," respondit Polyphēmus, "Cyclōpēs nōn timēmus: ipsī enim fortiōrēs eīs sumus." tum duōs ē comitibus Ulixēs manū corripuit: quōrum cum capita saxō ēlīsisset membra dīlaniāta vorāvit.

corripiō, -ripuī, -reptum 3. I seize.

SECTION 45

See Grammar Notes №s. 100 and 104,
The Verbs *possum, volō*

PROLATIVE INFINITIVE

In English Grammar we learn the meaning of an Auxiliary Verb. It is one that is used to help form the tense of another Verb; e.g. *shall* or *will* in *I shall go, He will go.* The words *I shall, He will* would make no sense unless we either express or understand the Verb which completes them.

There is a large class of Verbs in English which are not thus used to form tenses, but which are like those Auxiliary Verbs in making no complete sense without another verb following. Such Verbs are *I wish, I intend, I dare, I try, I can, I am able.* The completing Verb which follows them is put

in the Infinitive; e.g. *I wish to speak, He will be able to return.*
Sometimes the *to* of the Infinitive is omitted; e.g. *I can come,*
I dare say; but nevertheless *come* and *say* in these sentences
are Infinitives.

The corresponding Verbs in Latin for the most part take
the same construction, and the Infinitive following them
is called the Prolative Infinitive, but as they do not *all* take
the Infinitive only practice can lead to absolute correctness.

Verbs which require another action of the same subject
are usually followed by the Infinitive.

> e.g.   We can fight.
>
>   pugnāre possumus

Notice especially the following as taking this construction
in Latin:

1. Verbs meaning **wish** or **determine**; e.g. *volō, nōlō, mālō,*
   constituō.
2. Verbs meaning **begin, cease, be accustomed**; e.g. *incipiō,*
   dēsinō, soleō.
3. Verbs meaning **be able, dare, ought**; e.g. *possum, audeō,*
   dēbeō.

Exercise 294.

1. We wished to do the same ourselves.
2. All were able to see the king *when* exhorting the
   citizens.
3. The boys could not carry the heavy burden.
4. Warned by his father, he wished to stay in the city.
5. The general cannot send larger forces to the allies.
6. The citizens could not save the city which they loved.
7. We can all fight on behalf of our country.
8. The cavalry will not be able to use their horses.
9. He could not lead his men back before night.
10. We wish to praise the courage of the soldiers.

wish volō, velle, voluī. **can, am able (to)** possum, posse,
potuī (+inf.). **night** nox, noctis 3. f.

Exercise 295.

1. We could not stay many days in Athens.
2. He cannot set free the hostages, since the Gauls are laying waste our fields.
3. We cannot take the city which we are attacking.
4. They wished to see the general himself.
5. We shall not be able to make a journey through this land.
6. The barbarians had wished to attack our camp.
7. Hindered by the river, they could not withstand our attack.
8. They will not be able to use these weapons in war.
9. The fifth legion could not defeat the cavalry of the Gauls.
10. He is not able to do all that he wishes.

Exercise 296.

1. Frightened by Caesar's arrival, the barbarians could not take arms.
2. We are not able to adopt the plan which you advised.
3. We cannot fortify this town with a high rampart.
4. He wishes to conduct the campaign himself.
5. They could not neglect the advice of their own general.
6. He wished to encourage the soldiers before the battle.
7. We all wish to be ruled by the Romans.
8. That part of the city could not be taken by the enemy.
9. Since they could not fight, they stayed in the camp.
10. Since he wished to see the king, he hid himself.

Exercise 297.

1. mīlitēs imperātōris vōcem audīre nōn poterant.
2. flūmine impedītī iter facere nōn poterunt.
3. vult in castrīs paucōs diēs morārī.
4. volumus id, quod monēs, facere.
5. id quod vīs omnēs facient.
6. voluimus frūmentum ad castra mittere.
7. cīvēs volent urbem mūrīs mūnīre.
8. patrum mōribus ūtī volumus.
9. cōnsilium quod cēpistī laudāre nōn possumus.
10. eī quī in urbe erant perīculum vītāre nōn potuērunt.

possum, posse, potuī I am able. **volō, velle, voluī** I wish.
moror 1. (dep.) I delay.

298. Sulla (138–78 BC)

intereā Sulla, cum Mithridatem vīcisset, ad Ītaliam cōpiās
redūcere voluit. itaque, cum Marius mortuus esset et Cinna
ā mīlitibus esset occīsus, ex Asiā profectus Brundusium nāvigāvit. eī sē adiūnxērunt virī posteā in cīvitāte nōtissimī Cn.
Pompeius et M. Crassus, quōrum auxiliō populārium exercitum superāvit. tum Samnitēs, quī ad urbem cum ingentibus
cōpiīs contendēbant, magnā cum caede vīcit. posteā dictātor
creātus (quō ūsus imperiō velut rēgiam potentiam exercēbat)
prīmum inimīcōs suōs trucīdāvit, quoad potuit, tum per plūrimus lēgēs senātus auctōritātem cōnfirmāvit. nam tribūnōrum
potestātem minuēbat, senātōribus ea iūra, quae Gracchus
equitibus dederat, reddidit. tum imperium dēposuit, mox
Puteolōs sē recēpit, ubi duōbus post annīs mortuus est.

profīcīscor, profectus sum 3. (dep.) I set out. **quoad** as far
as. **minuō, -uī, -ūtum** 3. I diminish. **recipiō, recēpī,
receptum** 3. I take back; **mē recipiō** I betake myself, go,
retreat.

299. Ulysses and the Cyclops (continued)

hoc Ulixēs multō dolōre spectābat: voluit ille quidem Poly-
phēmum occīdere sed ipse infirmior erat nec magnum illud
saxum ad ōs spēluncae positum movēre potuit. postrīdiē
Cyclops, cum duōs ē comitibus Ulixēs ēdisset, cum ovibus ad
montem discessit; anteā autem saxum in eōdem locō posuit.
intereā Ulixēs ingentem stīpitem, quem Cyclops in spēluncā
relīquerat, in ignem posuit: mox cum gigās revertisset ite-
rumque duōs ēdisset, Ulixēs vīnum illī dulcissimum dat quod
ē nāve in saccō portāverat. is magnō gaudiō bibit; tum plus
vīnī postulāvit iussitque Ulixem nōmen sibi dīcere. respondit
"nēmō vocor." tum ille, "nēminem," inquit, "ultimum omnium
edam; hoc tibi mūnus prō vinō dabō." tum humī cecidit dor-
miēbatque.

stīpes, -itis 3. m. stake. **ultimus, -a, -um** last.

300. Better Death than Surrender

multae et fortēs gentēs trāns Rhēnum fluvium habitābant,
quārum gentium prīnceps cum finitimīs diē bellum gerēbat.
magnam arcem aedificāverat, ē quā mīlitēs eius in agrōs profectī omnia lātē vastābant. miserī incolae, quoniam tot iniūriās
nōn iam sustinēre poterant, magnō exercitū mūrōs arcis oppugnāvērunt et hostēs diē obsidēbant: iī, quod iam nec tēla nec
frūmentum habēbant, lēgātōs dē pāce mīsērunt. responsum
est, "pācem exercituī concēdere volumus, dux autem ad supplicium trādētur." is autem, "in manūs hostium," inquit, "nōn
veniam; arcem flammīs circumdābō, ipse in flammīs moriar."

Rhēnus Rhine.

SECTION 46

See Grammar Notes №. 104,
The Verbs *nōlō, mālō*

NEGATIVE COMMANDS

The commonest way of expressing a negative command is by the use of the Imperative of nōlō followed by the Infinitive.

> e.g.   Do not be afraid.
> nōlī timēre.

Exercise 301.

1. We would rather be wounded than conquered.
2. He refused to kill the wounded soldier.
3. He does not wish to march to Rome.
4. They prefer to defeat the enemy by their valour.
5. He was unwilling to be advised by a bad man.
6. They wished to be feared by all men.
7. He prefers to conduct the campaign in our territories.
8. They refused to withstand the enemy's fierce attack.
9. They could not fight more bravely than the enemy.
10. We can adopt a better plan than yours.

prefer, rather (be) mālō, mālle, māluī. **refuse, am unwilling** nōlō, nōlle, nōluī.

Exercise 302.

1. We refused to hear the words of the king.
2. They will not be able to stay many days at Carthage.
3. Caesar was unwilling to lead his men back before night.
4. All men would rather be praised than blamed.
5. The boy could not run very quickly, since he had been wounded.
6. Since war is being carried on by land and sea, the danger cannot be avoided.
7. Do not be disturbed by the words of this man.
8. They will be unwilling to attack a Roman legion.
9. We could not see the enemy marching to the city.
10. This state refused to send corn to Caesar.

Exercise 303.

1. We cannot withstand so large a number of cavalry.
2. The city could not be fortified in three days.
3. The soldiers would rather be led by you than by me.
4. He was unwilling to stay many days in the same city.
5. Having encouraged the soldiers we summoned a meeting of the citizens.
6. Hidden in the wood they could not see the enemy.
7. Do not praise a man who praises himself.
8. Since he preferred to fight he was sent to the army.
9. It was very easy to form a safer plan.
10. Do not neglect the words of the god himself.

safe tūtus, -a, -um.

Exercise 304.

1. nōluērunt damnātōs necāre.
2. mālō pugnāre quam in urbe morārī.
3. māluērunt suīs tēlīs quam tuīs ūtī.
4. oppidum altīs mūrīs mūnītum oppugnāre nōlēbant.
5. mālent virtūte quam cōnsiliō vincere.
6. obsidēs, cum necāre nōllent, līberāvērunt.
7. nōlī auxilium ad nostrōs hostēs mittere.
8. cum māllent Rōmae morārī quam bellum gerere ab omnibus culpātī sunt.
9. māvīs ab hōc culparī quam ab illō laudārī.
10. nostrī perturbātōs hostēs oppugnāre volēbant.

nōlō, nōlle, nōluī I am unwilling. **mālō, mālle, māluī** I prefer.

305. Pompey and Crassus Consuls (70 BC)

iūcundissima erant Rōmānīs spectācula in quibus servī quīdam, quī gladiātōrēs vocābantur, in lūdīs ā magistrīs doctī, inter sē pugnābant. sī pugnāre nōlēbant, virgīs cōgēbantur: plūrimī tamen morī quam ignāvī habērī mālēbant. hōrum iam magna multitūdō, ā Spartacō quōdam ducta, arma contrā rempūblicam sūmpserat legiōnēsque Rōmānās superāverat: cum autem Spartacus ad disciplīnam eōs instituere nōn posset, posteā ā M. Crassō victī sunt. in illō bellō M. Crassō subvēnit Cn. Pompeius, quī nūper ex Hispāniā reverterat, ubi bellum ā Sertōriō, populārium duce, gestum cōnfēcerat.

ad id tempus Cn. Pompeius causam senātūs dēfenderat: mox cum magnopere vellet exercituī, quem Lūcullus contrā Mithridatem dūcēbat, praeficī, senātus autem Lūcullum revocāre nōllet, populāribus sē adiūnxit, quōrum suffrāgiīs cum M. Crassō cōnsul creātus est.

gladiātor, -ōris 3. m. gladiator. **ignāvus, -a, -um** cowardly, lazy. **multitūdō, -inis** 3. f. multitude. **cōnficiō, -fēcī, -fectum** 3. I finish, put an end to.

306. Ulysses and the Cyclops (continued)

tum dormientis gigantis in oculum, quem ūnum habēbat in
mediā fronte positum, ardentem stīpitem immittit. magnō ille
cum clāmōre surgit et ā reliquīs Cyclopibus auxilium implōrat:
quibus interrogantibus respondit "nēmō mē fraude occīdit." illī
autem "sī nēmō tē occīdit," clāmāvērunt "nōlī nōs clāmōribus
perturbāre." tum Polyphēmus, cum saxum ē locō mōvisset, ad
exitum spēluncae sēdit manusque tetendit et Ulixem comitēs-
que ēgredientēs corriperet. is autem singulōs comitēs ovī, hanc
ovem mediam inter duās aliās, tandem sē ipsum arietis ingentis
ad ventrem dēligāvit. ovium ēgredientum terga Polyphēmus
manū permulsit, cum autem proximam sibi sōlam permulceret
hominēs nōn tetigit; arietis quoque tergum sōlum, nōn ventrem,
manū permulsit; Ulixēs autem incolumis sub ventre eius latēbat.

frōns, frontis 3. f. forehead. **ēgredior, ēgressus** (deponent)
3. I go out. **ariēs, -etis** 3. m. ram. **venter, -tris** 3. m. belly.

SECTION 47

See Grammar Notes №s. 101 and 102,
The Verbs *ferō, eō*

Exercise 307.

1. We did not wish to go with you* to the city.
2. A few soldiers had gone out of the town.
3. He bears everything most bravely.
4. Caesar determined to send help to our allies.
5. We shall go to Rome in five days.
6. Since he had determined to remain, he refused to go.
7. For many days the citizens endured the dangers of war.
8. All good men would rather be conquered than adopt
   this plan.

9. He went with Caesar to Gaul.
10. Let us go, since the enemy are attacking our allies.

go eō, īre, īvī (iī), itum (irregular). **bear, endure** ferō, ferre, tulī, lātum. **decide, determine** cōnstituō, -uī, -ūtum 3.

*The preposition **cum** is placed *after* Personal and Relative Pronouns, the two being written as one word, thus: **mēcum, tēcum, sēcum, nōbīscum, vōbīscum, quōcum, quibuscum.**

Exercise 308.

1. You will go with me in two hours to the camp.
2. Since they were unwilling to go, we determined to remain.
3. Do not summon a meeting in the city.
4. We saw the general *when he was* going to the war.
5. Having exhorted his soldiers he went to Rome.
6. Since they cannot free their country, they will go to Gaul.
7. The soldiers had endured worse things in war.
8. They are going to the city which they have always wished to see.
9. Let them go: they will not be able to prevent our plan.
10. Since he had not gone with us, he was not captured.

worse pēior, pēior, pēius.

Exercise 309.

1. All dangers are borne bravely by good men.
2. The wounded general was borne to the camp.
3. This state had determined to send help to our enemies.
4. It is better to endure danger than to neglect our allies.
5. Since he was going with us, we could not sail.
6. They have decided to kill the king.
7. We cannot endure the praise of this man.
8. Since they have decided to fight, they are going to the camp.
9. Do not place the cavalry on the right wing.
10. I had never seen the town to which we were going.

Exercise 310.

1. omnia bellī perīcula ferre volumus.
2. nōn potuit mēcum* ad urbem īre.
3. volet Athēnis Rōmam celerrimē īre.
4. per agrōs Gallōrum cum magnō exercitū ībat.
5. cum omniā ferre vellet, ab ipsō imperātōre laudātus est.
6. cōnstituit cum paucīs equitibus iter in agrōs eōrum facere.
7. poterunt māiōra perīcula quam haec ferre.
8. cum bellum gereret, ad urbem īre nōn potuit.
9. cum in Ītaliā essem, mīlitēs ad bellum euntēs vīdī.
10. nihil gravius quam hoc tulimus.

ferō, ferre, tulī, lātum (irregular) I bear. **eō, īre, īvī (iī), itum** (irregular) I go.

*The preposition **cum** is placed *after* Personal and Relative Pronouns, the two being written as one word, thus: **mēcum, tēcum, sēcum, nōbīscum, vōbīscum, quōcum, quibuscum.**

311. Pompey in the East (67–61 BC)

cōnsulēs creātī Pompeius et Crassus tribūnīs antīqua iūra red-didērunt, senātuī auctōritātem ā Sullā concessam abstulērunt. posteā lēge ab Aulō Gabīniō lata imperium Pompeiō datum est contrā pīrātās, quī tum ōrās ubique vastābant nāvēsque Rōmānās oppugnābant, ita ut nēmō sine magnō perīculō mare transīre posset; quam ob rem in urbe maxima erat frūmentī inopia. tribus mensibus pīrātās omnēs marī pepulerat. mox lēge ā C. Māniliō lāta exercituī quī tum contrā Mithridatem bellum gerēbat praefectus hostem vīcit: tum ad Syriam iit urbemque Hierosolyma magna cum caede cepit. tum dēnique, cum multam sibi fāmam comparavisset et magnam partem Asiae imperiō Rōmānō adiūnxisset. Rōmam rediit.

auferō, auferre, abstulī, ablātum (compound of ferō) I take away; (+dat.) I take away from. **lēgem ferō** I propose a law. **transeō, -īre, -īvī (-iī), -itum** (compound of eō) I cross. **Hierosolyma** 2. n. pl. Jerusalem. **redeō, -īre, -iī, -itum** (compound of eō) I return.

312. Ulysses and the Cyclops (concluded)

ē spēluncā incolumis ēgressus Ulixēs prīmum sē ipsum, mox
comitēs suōs līberāvit. tum ovēs ad ōram ēgērunt nāvemque
conscendērunt. cum iam paulum ā terrā nāvigāvissent, Poly-
phēmum verbīs insolentibus compellāvit; quam ob rem ille
īrā permōtus montis verticem manū correptum contrā nāvem
cōniēcit: quī cum haud procul ante nāvem in mare cecidisset,
prope ad ōram reppulit. iterum tamen Ulixēs eum compellat:
"egō Ulixēs sum," inquit; "Ulixēs tibi hanc iniūriam fēcit." ille
autem, cum frūstrā implōrāvisset ut ad insulam redīret sēc-
umque cēnāret, iterum ingēns saxum in mare cōniēcit, quod
tamen post nāvem cecidit: tum deum Neptūnum hīs verbīs
implōrat: "nē ad patriam redeat Ulixēs; sī autem dī placuit ut
redeat, sōlus sine comitibus redeat."

conscendō, -dī, -sum 3. I embark upon. **paulum** a little
(adverb). **cōniciō, -iēcī, -iectum** 3. I throw. **nē** (with
subjunctive), let … not, may … not, lest.

313. A Successful Appeal to Patriotism

lēgātī ad urbem rediērunt. "cōnsulēs," nūntiant, "occīsī sunt;
exercitus prope dēlētus est." cīvēs, quī verba lēgātōrum trīstī
animō audierant, maximō in timōre erant: tamen mōrem
antīquum secūtī dictātōrem creāvērunt. Servilius dictātor
creātus cīvēs ad forum vocāvit. "patria nostra" inquit, "in
maximō perīculō est; nēmō vestrum, crēdō, hodiē reīpūblicae
dēesse volet. omnēs mōrī quam victōrīs contumēliās ferre
mālumus; paucī contrā plūrēs numerō libenter pugnābimus;
sī in aciē victī cadēmus, honestē moriēmur." dictātōris ēloquentia omnēs mōtī sunt; postrīdiē ingēns numerus cīvium ad
proelium parātōrum urbe ēgressus est.

dēsum I fail. **honestē** adv. honourably.

SECTION 48

See Grammar Notes №. 105,
The Verb *fiō*

VERBS REQUIRING A COMPLEMENT

It has been explained (see Section 23) that the Verb *to be* does not usually take a complete predicate by itself without a Noun or Adjective for *complement*.

There are other Verbs like this. Without the words in brackets, the following sentences would make no complete sense:—He seems [afraid]. He is thought [a great man]. The magistrates are named [consuls]. He is becoming [wiser].

Intransitive or Passive Verbs meaning (1) *to seem* or *to be thought*, (2) *to become* or *to be made*, (3) *to be named*, require a Complement like the Verb esse, *to be,* and this Complement is always in the same Case as the Subject; e.g.

1. *He seems brave.*
   fortis vidētur.

   Caesar is considered a remarkable man.
   Caesar vir ēgregius habētur.

2. *My brother has been elected consul.*
   frāter meus consul creātus est.

   My son is becoming wiser.
   filius meus sapientior fit.

3. *The magistrates are called consuls.*
   magistrātus cōnsulēs nōminantur.

Exercise 314.

1. The boy is now becoming wiser.
2. Since he had never been conquered, he was considered a remarkable man.
3. He seems a bolder man than his brother.
4. Their camp seemed smaller than ours.
5. The captives seemed very wretched.
6. We wished to be guided by the advice of the wise.
7. The city seemed to us most beautiful.
8. We did not wish to become allies of this nation.
9. May you become wiser than your father.
10. All praised the remarkable valour of the tenth legion.

consider a person as having a quality habeō 2.
remarkable ēgregius, -a, -um. **seem** videor (passive of
videō). **brother** frāter, -tris 3. m.

Exercise 315.

1. The customs of our fathers seem to have been very good.
2. You cannot become wiser than your brother.
3. He would rather be considered brave than good.
4. Having been made general, he advised us very well.
5. Nothing can hinder the enemy *when* marching against us.
6. He seems a better man than his father.
7. Since he could not become general, he remained at Rome.
8. Their territories seem broader than ours.
9. He seems to have determined to go with us.
10. Since he had fought well in Gaul, he was considered useful to the state.

Exercise 316.

1. The gods seem to have prevented our plans.
2. The ships seemed very large to the barbarians.
3. Since he could not be general, he preferred to remain at Carthage.
4. They seem to use these weapons in all their battles.
5. You are considered by all the bravest general.
6. Having stayed a few years in Athens, he became a wiser man.
7. Since he has conquered the Gauls, he is considered a great man.
8. He who neglects the advice of wise men never becomes wise himself.
9. Since he was considered useful to the state, he was not condemned.
10. Your father was considered very wise by all the students.

student discipulus 2. m.

Exercise 317.

1. Caesar dux fortissimus habēbātur.
2. cīvēs iam sapientiōrēs fiunt.
3. omnibus cōnsilium tūtum vidēbātur.
4. mihi vir ēgregius vidēris.
5. nihil peius hōc cōnsiliō vidētur.
6. maximus imperātor paucīs annīs fīēs.
7. tū, cum Gallōs vīceris, fēlīcissimus haberis.
8. eō diē nihil ab hostibus factum est.
9. nōn omnēs ēgregiī fierī possumus.
10. vir fortior quam ipse imperātor vīsus est.

fīō, fierī, factus sum (passive of faciō) (irregular) I am made; happen, take place. **ēgregius, -a, -um** remarkable, distinguished.

318. The Conspiracy of Catiline (63 BC)

multa intereā Rōmae fiēbant, dum Pompeius cum Mithridate
bellum gerit. ōrātōrum Rōmānōrum maximus fuit M. Tullius Cicerō: is, cōnsul creātus, eōdem annō cīvēs suōs servāvit.
nam L. Sergius Catilina, vir nōbilī locō nātus, cum sibi pes-
simis cīvium adiūnxisset, contrā rempūblicam coniūrāverat
cōnsiliumque cēperat cōnsulēs et bonōs cīvēs omnēs occīdere. haec Cicerōnī per lēgātōs quōsdam Gallōrum, quī tum
forte Rōmae erant, nūntiāta sunt. ab eō accūsātus, Catilina,
cum urbe paucīs cum comitibus excessisset, bellum contrā
rempūblicam in Etrūriā parāvit: reliquī in urbe manēbant
cōnsulisque iussū in carcerem cōniectī sunt. dē quibus multā
in cūriā disseruntur: tandem, cum ita senātōribus placuisset,
necātī sunt. mox Catilina, quem contrā exercitus missus erat,
in aciē fortiter pugnāns cecidit. posteā Cicerō, quod cīvēs
Rōmānōs sine iūdiciō morte pūnīverat, in exsilium pulsus,
proximō annō revocātus est.

ōrātor, -ōris 3. m. orator. **iūdicium** 2. n. judgment.

SECTION 49

When the Verbs described in the last rule are Transitive and used in the Active Voice, the Complement is in agreement with the Object;

> e.g. *The people made him consul.*
> populus eum cōnsulem creāvit.
>
> *They call the magistrate a consul.*
> magistrātum cōnsulem nōminant.
>
> *They thought him a distinguished man.*
> hunc ēgregium virum putābant.

Exercise 319.

1. This year the people will elect Cotta consul.
2. In that city the magistrates are not elected by the people.
3. Those who free their country I call good men.
4. Since he was considered useful to the state, they elected him consul.
5. We cannot call a general who has been conquered successful.
6. I would rather be the consul of the Roman people than the leader of an army.
7. Since he has always advised us well, we call him wise.
8. The people will not elect you magistrate.
9. He is called wise by all who have seen him.
10. Since he had been elected consul, he decided to go to the city.

elect, appoint creō 1. **consul** cōnsul, -lis 3. m. **magistrate** magistrātus 4. m. **call, name** nōminō 1.

Exercise 320.

1. The Roman citizens were unwilling to call Caesar king.
2. He seemed wiser than his father.
3. Having been condemned by the magistrate, he could not remain at Rome.
4. He wishes to be elected consul by the citizens.
5. The Roman people has decided to name you general.
6. The citizens dare not elect him consul.
7. Since we have appointed Caesar general, the state will be safe.
8. Since we had endured many dangers, he was thought a brave man.
9. We cannot condemn a man whom the Roman people has appointed magistrate.
10. Let them not dare to call me base.

dare audeō, ausus sum 2. (semi-deponent). **think** putō 1.

Exercise 321.

1. Since he endures everything on behalf of his country, we call him a good man.
2. We dared not send corn to the Roman army.
3. Since he could do everything, he seemed a remarkable man.
4. He has never dared to summon a meeting of citizens.
5. Since he refused to be elected consul, he was praised by all.
6. Terrified by their shouts, he ran to the magistrates.
7. Since we were hindered by the river, we dared not go.
8. Since he seemed useful to the state, he was elected consul.
9. The prisoners whom we condemned will be set free by the magistrate.
10. The enemy dared not attack a Roman legion.

Exercise 322.

1. populus Rōmānus Caesarem cōnsulem creāvit.
2. nōs eum virum ēgregium semper putābimus.
3. ausus bellum in Galliā gerere multās gentēs vīcit.
4. nōluērunt cīvēs eum rēgem nōmināre.
5. ā populō Rōmānō cōnsul creātus est.
6. cum cīvitatem virtūte suā servāverit, eum damnāre nōn audēbunt.
7. omnibus vīsus est optimus magistrātus.
8. eōs quī patriam liberāverant populus cōnsulēs creāvit.
9. cum grave sit perīculum, omnia audeāmus.
10. nōlī omnēs hominēs turpissimōs putāre.

putō 1. I think. **audeō, ausus sum** 2. semi-deponent. I am bold.

323. Sisyphus

Sīsyphus rēx per mercātūram et ipse dīves fīēbat et cīvium suōrum dīvitiās magnopere auxit: erat autem omnium hominum pessimus. multā dē perfidiā eius ab antīquīs nārrantur. ab uxōre suā petīverat nē sē mortuum sepelīret: mortuus autem apud Plūtōnem illam accūsāvit quod ita neglēxerat et ab eō petīvit ut sibi licēret ad terram redīre. cum autem redisset, "nōn iterum," inquit, "ad mānēs dēscendam: sīc immortālis fīam." ā Mercuriō tamen vī ablātus gravissimō est suppliciō pūnītus. nam saxum ingēns semper ad summum collem portāre cōgēbātur: quotiēns autem ad summum vēnerat, saxum ad īmum collem volvēbātur isque ad summum iterum portāre coactus est.

dīves, -itis rich. **pessimus, -a, -um** (superlative of malus) worst, very bad. **īmus, īma, īmum** lowest; **īmus collis** the bottom of the hill. **volvō, -vī, -ūtum** 3. I roll (transitive); (in passive) I roll (intransitive).

SECTION 50

See Grammar Notes №. 66,
Interrogative Pronoun.

QUESTIONS

Questions can be asked in Latin as in English by Interrogative Pronouns or Adverbs.

> e.g. *Who is he?*
> quis est?
>
> *Why are you afraid?*
> cur timēs?

When there is no such word English makes the questions clear by the order of the words, e.g. *Is he a friend?* But Latin has no such fixed order, and either *amīcus est* or *est amīcus* could mean *He is a friend.* Therefore it uses Interrogative Particles which mark the sentence as a question but do not need to be translated by a separate word in English. The usual ones are

1. -ne, which has to be appended to a principal word;
   > e.g. *Is he a friend?*
   > amīcusne est?
   When the sentence has the negative *nōn* the *-ne* is appended to this word, making nōnne. A sentence in this form shows that the answer yes is expected;
   > e.g. *Is he not a friend?*
   > nōnne amīcus est?

2. num, which puts the question in such a way that the answer no is expected;
   > e.g. *Is he (really) a friend?*
   > num amīcus est?

Exercise 324.

1. Who has dared to adopt this plan?
2. What shall we be able to do at Rome?
3. Why do they set free the hostages which we sent?
4. Who will be elected consul this year?
5. What did you see in that part of the city?
6. Why was this cohort led back into the camp?
7. Who is unwilling to endure dangers on behalf of his country?
8. Why were consuls not elected that year at Rome?
9. By whom have the fields of our allies been laid waste?
10. To whom did your leader announce this victory?

why? cūr.

Exercise 325.

1. What are you doing? The city is being taken by the enemy.
2. Why did you place the cavalry on the right wing?
3. Did you not see the Roman soldiers building ships?
4. Do you really consider our general a brave man?
5. Have you done what your father advised?
6. Did not the general exhort his soldiers?
7. You will always be considered the friend of the Roman people.
8. Cannot this nation send corn to our army?
9. Does he really wish to set free the men whom we condemned?
10. Shall you stay many days at Rome?

friend amīcus 2. m.

Exercise 326.

1. Is it really useful to the state to have a large number of ships?
2. Is not praise welcome to all men?
3. Have they really dared to attack a Roman legion?
4. Will the cries of the citizens be heard by the king?
5. Will you really adopt a plan which is blamed by all?
6. Did you not hear the words of your father?
7. Why have you neglected the advice of the wisest men?
8. Who will be willing to remain at Carthage?
9. What did you send to your father?
10. Why are the men whom we conquered fighting again?

Exercise 327.

1. nōnne bellum in Galliā multōs annōs gessit?
2. potesne oppidum quattuor diēbus capere?
3. num turpe est omnia prō patriā audēre?
4. hic rēx populī Rōmānī amīcus semper habitus est.
5. nōnne grāta erit cīvibus exercitus victōria?
6. num puer grave onus portāre poterit?
7. nōnne hoc flūmen lātius quam illud est?
8. quis hoc concilium convocāvit?
9. cūr hostium numerō perturbāminī, mīlitēs?
10. ā quibus agrī nostrī vastātī sunt?

-ne a particle showing that the sentence is interrogative; often joined with **nōn** making **nōnne** which introduces a question to which the answer "yes" is expected: e.g. **nōnne monet?** does he not advise? **num** a particle introducing a question to which the answer "no" is expected: e.g. **num monet** does he really advise? **grātus, -a, -um** pleasant, welcome. **cūr** why?

328. Caesar (Born 100 BC)

C. Iūlius Caesar, vir nōbilī locō nātus, cuius patris soror Mariī
uxor fuerat, per tōtam vītam populārium causam contrā
senātum dēfendit: ipse Corneliam, Cinnae fīliam, in mātrimōnium dūxerat, iussusque ā Sullā uxōrī nūntium mittere
pārēre nōluit: quam ob rem urbe ēgressus ad Asiam sē recēpit.
posteā, cum Rōmam redisset, causam eōrum, quī cum Catilina
coniūrāverant, contrā Cicerōnem in cūriā dēfendit. "multā,"
inquit, "dē sceleribus hōrum Cicerō dīxit; sed quō cōnsiliō
ea dīxit? nōnne omnibus haec scelera nōta sunt? morte hōs
pūnīre vult. cūr nōn etiam verberāre vōs iubet? num gravius
est verberārī quam necārī? id autem iubēre nōn vult, quod
eī vidētur indignum esse vōbīs eiusmodī suppliciō hominēs
pūnīre. mihi autem vidētur vōbīs indignum esse hōs sine iūdiciō necāre." hīs verbīs omnium animōs magnopere permōvit;
cum tamen etiam magis permovēret ōrātiō Catōnis, quī post
Caesarem verba fēcit, Cicerōnis cōnsilium sequēbantur.

uxōrī nūntium mittere (+dat.) to send a message (i.e. of
divorce) to a wife, i.e. to divorce a wife. **indignus, -a, -um**
unworthy; (+abl.) unworthy of. **ōrātiō, -ōnis** 3. f. speech.

SECTION 51

See Grammar Notes №s. 129,
Apposition and Composite Subject.

APPOSITION

A Noun, added directly to another Noun in order to describe
it further, is said to be in Apposition with it.

A Noun in Apposition with another Noun agrees with
is in Case;

    e.g.   *Caesar, a very brave man, conquered the Gauls.*
           Caesar, vir fortissimus, Gallōs vīcit.

           I have often seen Caesar, our great general.
           saepe Caesarem vīdī, magnum nostrum imperātōrem.

           We have the Roman legions, a great protection.
           legiōnēs Rōmānās habēmus, magnum praesidium.

Notice especially

           The City of Rome.
           urbs Rōma.

           The town of Verona.
           oppidum Vērōna.

In such expressions, Latin puts the name in Apposition "the
city Rome," "the town Verona," and does not say "the city *of*".

COMPOSITE SUBJECT

If a Verb has more than one Subject, the rules for Number and Person will be the same as in English, viz:—

1. The Verb will be in the Plural.

2. If the Subjects differ in Person the Verb will be in the 1st rather than the 2nd, and in the 2nd rather than in the 3rd.
   e.g.   Both my son and I shall come.*
          et ego et filius meus veniēmus.
   Note the order of the Latin in this sentence. The First Person Subject comes first in Latin, last in English.

The rule for the Gender of a Participle or Adjective Complement when there are two Subjects is as follows:—

1. If the Subjects are of the same Gender the Participle or Adjective agrees with them.

2. If the Subjects differ in gender—
   (a)   When the Subjects are persons the Participle or Adjective is in the Masculine rather than the Feminine.
   Both my father and mother remained at Rome.
   et pater meus et māter Rōmae morātī sunt.
   (b)   When the Subjects are lifeless things it is most usual to make both Verb and Complement agree with the nearest Subject only, but often the Complement is put in the Neuter Plural. As this rule is difficult, no instances will occur in the present exercises.

*Do not confuse with these those sentences in which the Subjects are connected by [Either] ... or ... ; e.g. [Either] my brother or my sister is coming. This is not a double Subject— the two Subjects are alternative—and in Latin as in English the Verb will agree with the nearest Subject.

ADJECTIVES AGREEING
WITH TWO NOUNS

If an Adjective qualifies as an Attribute more than one Noun, make it agree with the nearest; e.g.

He maintained his kingship by his great influence and wealth.
magnā et auctōritāte et opibus regnum obtinēbat.

Exercise 329.

1. You and I will go with the army to Gaul.
2. The city of Rome was taken by the Gauls.
3. Caesar, the consul, will come to our city.
4. You will have the Roman legions, a great protection.
5. You and your son were blamed by all the citizens.
6. Rome, the largest city of Italy, will be taken by the enemy.
7. You and I cannot bear aid to the wounded soldiers.
8. Will they not go to the city of Athens?
9. Who can withstand the fierce attack of our troops?
10. By his great wisdom and wealth he will maintain his kingship for many years.

come veniō, vēnī, ventum 4. **garrison, protection** praesidium 2. n. **wealth** opēs, -um 3. f. **maintain** obtineō 2. **kingdom, kingship** regnum 2. n.

Exercise 330.

1. You and he were unwilling to come with us.
2. What will Cotta, a Roman citizen, be able to do on behalf of us?
3. His father and mother dared not stay in Rome.
4. The town of Verona is being attacked by the Gauls.
5. He and I were coming from Athens to Rome.
6. Cotta and I will bear aid to the conquered allies.
7. Why did you not consider me a friend of the Roman people?
8. Shall you really use all the weapons which you are carrying?
9. You and your friend have neglected the advice of your father.
10. Since he had come to us, we dared not go with you.

mother māter, mātris 3. f. **Verona** Vērōna 1. f.

Exercise 331.

1. Did you see your friend coming to the city?
2. Since you and I have been condemned, we shall be killed.
3. Having stayed three days in the town of Verona, he came to us.
4. You and Caesar have carried on many wars.
5. His son had obtained the kingship by his great valour and wealth.
6. Your father and mother have dared to set free a condemned prisoner.
7. Having been elected consul, he exhorted the citizens with a few words.
8. Has this state really dared to send corn to the town of Verona?
9. You and I will call a meeting of all the citizens.
10. Why have you, a Roman consul, come against us who are considered your allies?

obtain potior 3. (deponent).

Exercise 332.

1. Cotta, vir fortissimus, legiōnēs Rōmānās contrā Belgās dūxit.
2. cum clāmōrēs cīvium audītī essent opem tūlimus.
3. magnā et virtūte et opibus regnum occupāvit.
4. pater et māter filium suum hortātī sunt.
5. Cotta, populī Rōmānī cōnsul, ad urbem veniet.
6. Caesar et Cotta multa bella gessērunt.
7. ego et tū hoc cōnsilium capiēmus.
8. Caesar, vir sapientissimus, nōluit regnum occupāre.
9. tū et Labiēnus facile poteritis hostem superāre.
10. mōs erat Rōmānōrum sociīs suīs opem ferre.

ops, opis 3. f. help; pl. wealth.

333. Croesus

Croesus, rēx Lydiae, finitimōs populōs bellō superāvit maximamque fāmam propter dīvitiās et potentiam comparāvit. itaque multī ad eum ex omnibus partibus Graeciae vēnērunt, inter reliquōs Sōlon, omnium tum Athēniensium sapientissimus. cui cum magnās suās dīvitiās ostendisset, "quem tū, Sōlon," interrogāvit, "omnium hominum beātissimum putās?" respondit ille, "Tellus Athēniensis mihi omnium beātissimus fuisse vidētur; huic enim erant līberī et pulchrī et bonī, quōrum nēmō ante patrem mortuus est: ipse cum cīvibus suīs contrā finitimōs pugnantibus subvēnisset hostēsque fugāvisset in aciē fortissimē pugnāns cecidit eodemque locō ab Athēniensibus magnō cum honōre sepultus est." "quis tibi post eum," inquit Croesus, "beātissimus videntur?" "Cleobis et Biton," respondit, "quī mātrem suam ipsī in currū trāxērunt. illā ā dīs implōrāvit ut rem omnium optimam filiīs concēderent: eādem nocte uterque mortuus est."

Athēniensis, -is, -e Athenian. **beātus, -a, -um** happy.

SECTION 52

See Grammar Notes №s. 133–138 and 164–177,
Accusative and Genitive Cases.

DOUBLE ACCUSATIVE

Some Verbs of *teaching* (especially doceō) and *asking* may take two Accusatives, one of the person, the other of the thing;

> e.g.   *He taught me letters.*
>   litterās mē docuit.
>
>   *I ask you your opinion.*
>   rogō tē sententiam.*

PARTITIVE GENITIVE

Any word that signifies a *part* can be followed by a Genitive signifying that of which it is a part.

This is called the Partitive Genitive. In English we express it by the Preposition of;

> e.g.   *A portion of the Britons.*
>   pars Britannōrum.
>
>   *The bravest of the Britons.*
>   fortissimī Britannōrum.

*Except in the phrase *rogāre sententiam* use *rogō* with two Accusatives only when the second object is a Neuter Pronoun. With a Neuter Pronoun for one object the Verb *cēlō* (conceal) can also take two Accusatives;

> e.g.   *I hide this from Caesar.*
>   hoc Caesarem cēlō.

Exercise 334.

1. Having been elected magistrate, he asked me my opinion.
2. Since he wished to stay in the city, he went to the consul.
3. Let us teach them everything ourselves.
4. Why did you not ask your father his opinion?
5. Who sent so great a number of cavalry to the town of Verona?
6. Did not your father, the wisest of all men, teach you this?
7. *When he was* going to the city I asked him his opinion.
8. Do not come with us: it will be safer to remain at Rome.
9. The Britons used these weapons in all battles.
10. For five days the hostages which we had sent were detained in the camp.

ask rogō 1. **opinion** sententia 1. f. **teach** doceō, -uī, -tum 2. **Britons** Britannī 2. m. pl.

Exercise 335.

1. The general whose army conquered us has been elected consul.
2. Having been sent to Rome, he announced the victory to the magistrate.
3. You will not be able to teach me many things: I have been taught by my father.
4. The boldest of the soldiers were terrified by the arrival of the general himself.
5. It is easier to teach boys letters than to conduct a campaign.
6. Are not the bravest of the Gauls fighting against our legions?
7. War has been waged for many years against the Britons.
8. This was the most difficult route of all.
9. Since I have been elected consul, I shall not be able to go with you.
10. We have borne aid to the Romans *when* conquered.

letters, literature litterae 1. f. pl.

Exercise 336.

1. They were going from Rome to the city in which were the captives.
2. You and I will teach the boy letters.
3. The greatest part of this city has been fortified with a high rampart.
4. It is better to have conquered the enemy than to have taught boys letters.
5. Were not wounded men borne to the camp by us?
6. The bravest of the soldiers refused to use shields.
7. For many years he held the kingship of the Britons.
8. My father and mother were killed by this king.
9. The citizens did not dare to elect this man magistrate.
10. Do not blame the general: he could not hold that part of the town.

Exercise 337.

1. Gallī mē multā dē suīs rēbus docuērunt.
2. cum amīcus sit populī Rōmānī, sententiam eum rogābimus.
3. cum omnium sapientissimus esset, rēgis fīlium docēbat.
4. nōlī mē sententiam rogāre.
5. haec tibi omnium pulcherrima urbs vidēbitur.
6. maxima pars cīvium nōlēbat bellum gerere.
7. fac tū quod rogō: melius cōnsilium capere nōn potes.
8. suōs hortātus contrā Britannōs dūxit.
9. quis tē illud docuit?
10. mōs erat puerī multa patrem rogāre.

sententia 1. f. opinion. **melior, -or, -us** compar. adj. better.

338. An Unsuspected Witness

poēta quīdam, Ibicus nōmine, ā latrōnibus ōlim oppugnātus
et graviter vulnerātus, ubi iam morītūrus erat, forte aliquot
gruēs in caelō volantēs vīdit. "nēmō mihi iam subvenīre potest,"
inquit, "vōs autem, gruēs, testēs caedis eritis contrā latrōnēs."
illī diū posteā, ubi in oppidō quōdam fuērunt, iterum gruēs
nōnnullās in caelō volantēs vīdērunt. ē quibus ūnus "vidētisne,"
inquit, "poētae Ibicī testēs?" verba hominis ab amīcō Ibicī
audīta sunt. is statim rem magistrātibus nārrāvit. latrōnēs
apud iūdicēs accūsātī et damnātī poenās sceleris persolvērunt.

grūs, gruis 3. f. crane (bird). **testis, -is** 3. c. witness.

SECTION 53

See Grammar Notes №s. 139–147,
Dative Case.

DATIVE CASE

1. The Dative after Intransitive Verbs.

The Dative of the Indirect Object following a Transitive Verb
has been explained in Section 5.

An Intransitive Verb, though it has no Direct Object, can
take an Indirect Object whenever its sense permits;

> e.g. *To be subject to kings.*
> servīre rēgibus.
>
> *To yield to the enemy.*
> hostī cēdere.

Many of the commonest of these Intransitive Verbs correspond to Verbs that are Transitive in English;

e.g.   *To obey*   pārēre (= *to be obedient to*).

Those required in the following exercises are given in the vocabulary.

2. The Dative of the Possessor.

A Dative can be used with the Verb *esse* to express the Possessor;

e.g.   *I have three brothers.*
sunt mihi trēs frātrēs.
(literally, *There are to me three brothers*).

Exercise 339.

1. The allies were unwilling to obey our general.
2. A small number of the Gauls was at that time subject to the Romans.
3. Did not my mother teach your sister letters?
4. Since you and I have obeyed the consul, we shall be set free.
5. Between the camp and the river was the town of Verona.
6. It will be better to obey our leader than to seize a kingdom.
7. Your brother and sister dared not come to Rome.
8. Let us yield to the advice of those who are exhorting us.
9. This boy has a brother and a sister.
10. Is it not better to be subject to the Romans than to do this?

obey pāreō (+dat.) 2. **subject to (be)** serviō (+dative).
sister soror, -ōris 3. f. **between** inter (+acc.). **yield** cēdō, cessī, cessum 3.

Exercise 340.

1. Having been elected magistrate, he refused to obey his father.
2. Who will bear aid to the wounded soldiers?
3. By his remarkable valour he defeated the boldest nation of all Gaul.
4. Do not yield to an enemy whom our fathers conquered.
5. Since they were subject to us, they could not bear aid to the Gauls.
6. You and I cannot use the weapons which the Britons use.
7. War was being waged between the Romans and Gauls.
8. Is your brother really considered very wise?
9. Since he obeys his father, he is considered a good boy.
10. These men to whom you wish to yield, have often been conquered.

Exercise 341.

1. Let us not yield to a conquered enemy.
2. Did you see him taking arms to the camp?
3. The king does not use his wealth well.
4. The citizens of this state were subject to the Romans.
5. Those who obey the gods we consider the friends of their country.
6. We, who have conducted many campaigns, will not yield to you.
7. The worst of the citizens wished to be subject to kings.
8. What shall you do at Rome? Shall you be able to see the consul?
9. He has a brother who will be elected consul.
10. Between your country and ours there is broad sea.

worst pessimus, -a, -um.

Exercise 342.

1. et frāter eius et soror in urbe morātī sunt.
2. nē rēgibus serviāmus, cīvēs.
3. erat inter urbem et castra nostra flūmen lātissimum.
4. mīlitēs semper imperātōrī pārēbant.
5. cum numquam hostī cesserimus, nōn vōbīs cēdēmus.
6. pārē patrī: nōlī nōbīscum venīre.
7. erant illī hominī frāter et soror.
8. Rōmānī rēgī numquam serviēmus.
9. melius erit necārī quam Rōmānīs pārēre.
10. multa nōs dē rēbus Rōmānīs frāter tuus docuit.

serviō 4. I serve; (+dat) I serve for.

343. Caesar's First Consulship (59 BC)

Cn. Pompeius, cum ex Asiā redisset, ā senātū petīverat ut agrōs
mīlitibus suīs bellō confectō darent. id illī facere nōluērunt. M.
Crassō quoque et reliquīs equitibus multā postulantibus nihil
concēdere volēbant. frūstrā Cicerō concordiam inter senātum
et equitēs confirmāre cōnābātur. intereā Caesar in Hispāniā
bellum gerēbat: is ubi Rōmam revertit Pompeiō et Crassō sē
adiūnxit: simul Pompeius Iūliam, Caesaris fīliam, in mātrimōnium dūxit. mox cōnsul creātus altera lēge agrōs Pompeī
mīlitibus dedit, altera equitibus ea quae postulābant concessit.

    mōs fuit Rōmānōrum terrās quās bellō superāverant
prōvinciāsque vocābant per cōnsulārēs regere. hī ūnum annum
imperium administrāre solēbant. eō tempore pars Galliae
prōvincia Rōmāna erat. huius prōvinciae imperium, per lēgēs
ā Vatīniānō tribūnō et Pompeiō rogātās, in quīnque annōs
Caesarī datum est.

concordia -ae 1. f. harmony. **prōvincia** 1. f. province.
cōnsulāris, -is, -e consular; (as noun) ex-consul.

SECTION 54

See Grammar Notes №s. 148–163,
Ablative Case.

ABLATIVE CASE

We have had (Section 5) the Ablative used to express the *instrument*. It can also be used to express the *cause*.

> e.g.   *He perished of hunger.*
> fame periit.

A few Deponent Verbs take an Ablative where the corresponding English has a Direct Object. The commonest are ūtor and potior.

> e.g.   *Let us use these books*
> hīs librīs ūtāmur.
>
> *He obtains (possession of) the kingdom.*
> regnō potitor.

Exercise 344.

1. His father holds the kingship which he obtained through his wealth.
2. The citizens whom we conquered are perishing of hunger.
3. Let us use the book which your father sent.
4. Do not ask me my opinion.
5. Who can rule a people well without wisdom?
6. Those who now obey us will not dare to fight.
7. Let us teach our sons to use weapons.
8. It is better to perish of hunger than to be subject to a king.
9. You and I will return to the city in a few days.
10. Who would rather stay at Carthage than see Italy?

perish pereō, -iī, itum 4. **hunger** famēs, -is 3. f. **book** liber, librī 2. m. **without** sine (+abl.). **return** redeō, -īre, -iī, -itum (compound of eō).

237

Exercise 345.

1. Let us return to the town through these fields.
2. You will not be able to conquer the barbarians without the help of the allies.
3. Having stayed ten days at Rome, they are now returning to Gaul.
4. We shall take the city and obtain possession of the kingdom.
5. It is more disgraceful to yield than to be conquered.
6. He could not teach his brother without his father's help.
7. Did you see the army returning to the camp?
8. They will come in a few days and set free the prisoners.
9. Take this book: use it well.
10. The boldest of the soldiers would rather perish than yield.

Exercise 346.

1. Why are the citizens perishing of hunger? Let us summon a meeting.
2. The king whom we obey is considered the worst of all men.
3. You and your father will return on the tenth day.
4. The fifth legion was returning with him to the camp.
5. We dared not return to the father without his son.
6. This nation had never yielded to a Roman army.
7. They have obtained possession of the city which they were attacking.
8. It is not disgraceful to obey a magistrate whom we ourselves elected.
9. He always seemed to himself the wisest of men.
10. Since the cohort has not returned, we shall perish of hunger.

Exercise 347.

1. cīvēs miserī fame perībant.
2. puer libris ūtitur quōs pater ad eum mīsit.
3. cum ā legiōnibus victī sint, urbe nostrā nōn potientur.
4. hostēs sine virtūte vincere nostrī nōn potērunt.
5. puer, quem litterās docēbam, hōc librō ūtēbātur.
6. omnēs quī nōbīscum vēnērunt fame periērunt.
7. ā Gallīs victī ad castra redibant.
8. Gallōrum regnō sine virtūte potīrī nōn poteris.
9. cīvēs, fame victī, hostibus cēdere voluērunt.
10. omnēs puerōs, quī patribus pārent, laudāmus.

pereō, -iī, -itum 4. I perish. **potior** 4. dep. I obtain, gain possession of.

348. Croesus (continued)

tum, magna īra permōtus, Croesus "num tū hōs," clāmāvit, "beātiōrēs quam mē putās?" "nunc quidem, Croese," respondit, "dīvitiās maximās habēs, gentēs plūrimās rēgis: nēminem autem beātum vocō priusquam mortuus sit: nam dī saepe hominibus plūrima dant, mox eōsdem maximīs malīs opprimunt."

mox, Persārum potentia territus, cōnstituit bellum Cyrō, Persārum rēgī, indīcere: anteā tamen nūntiōs Delphōs ad ōrāculum Apollinis mīsit, ut hoc deum interrogārent: "Croesumne monēs ut bellum contrā Persās gerat?" respondit deus "Croesus cōpiās contrā Persās dūcet et magnum imperium dēlēbit." quod cum responsum eī nūntiātum esset, multō gaudiō Croesus bellum parāre coepit.

nunc adv. now. **priusquam** before, until. **opprimō, -ressī, -ressum** 3. I overwhelm.

SECTION 55

See Grammar Notes №s. 109 and 110,
Parts of Verbs.

Exercise 349.

1. The book which you sent I gave to my sister.
2. Do not help the men who have destroyed our city.
3. Since he had stood under the wall for three hours, he saw everything.
4. May the number of soldiers and ships be increased!
5. Give me the book: you cannot use it.
6. The forces which you sent have been destroyed by the enemy.
7. We have increased the number of our ships this year.
8. Who gave you the books that you use now?
9. Did you help your brother with your advice?
10. Has that part of the city been destroyed?

give dō, dare, dedī, datum. **destroy** dēleō, -ēvī, -ētum 2.
stand stō, stetī, statum 1. **under, beneath** sub (+abl.).
increase augeō, auxī, auctum 2.

Exercise 350.

1. Did not the barbarians fight very fiercely?
2. You and I have given advice to Caesar.
3. Has not your brother conducted the campaign very well?
4. Do not bear aid to men who obey the Romans.
5. Do you not think him a very wise man?
6. What did you give to the soldier who announced the victory?
7. The gods help those who dare everything.
8. What I have not seen I cannot praise.
9. He would rather be conquered than increase the number of ships.
10. Help us, Romans: our citizens are perishing of hunger.

Exercise 351.

1. The men to whom you gave this advice are returning.
2. Since he had destroyed the citizens, he obtained the sovereignty.
3. Cotta, the leader of the Roman army, will come in a few days.
4. Since their city had been destroyed, they could not help us.
5. On the march they were attacked by large forces of Gauls.
6. Having encouraged the soldiers, he returned to the city.
7. Nothing is more pleasant than to help our friends.
8. What you have taught me will be most useful.
9. The number of Roman citizens has now been increased.
10. We gave corn to the soldiers who were perishing of hunger.

Exercise 352.

1. hunc tibi librum, quem vidēs dabō.
2. imperātor sub altā turre stābat.
3. cīvēs victōs adiuvēmus: nē morēmur.
4. haec urbs decimō annō ab hostibus dēlēta est.
5. Caesaris adventus hostium timōrem maximē auxit.
6. exercitus sub mūrum urbis īvit.
7. Gallī hanc urbem dēlēvērunt.
8. nē cīvium timōrem hīs verbīs augeāmus.
9. tibi, quī patrēs nostrōs iūvistī, omnēs pārēbimus.
10. hic rēx numerum equitum auxit.

stō, stetī, statum 1. I stand. **iuvō, iūvī, iūtum** 1. I help.

353. Caesar in Gaul (59–56 BC)

ad Galliam profectus prīmō annō Helvētiōs, quī ā Germānīs
saepissimē oppugnātī ex angustīs fīnibus ēgredī in aliā parte
Galliae consīdere volēbant, per prōvinciam Rōmānam iter
facere cōnantēs, reppulit. eōdem annō Ariovistum, quī Germānōs trāns Rhēnum dūxerat et Gallōrum agrōs occupāverat,
proeliō superāvit. annō secundō Belgās (quī contrā Rōmānōs
coniūrāverant) vīcit. proximō annō, cum inter Cn. Pompeium
et M. Crassum dissensiō fieret, cum utrōque apud Lūcam
cōnsilium habuit; ibi cōnstitūtum est ut Pompeius et Crassus
populārium suffrāgiīs cōnsulēs creārentur, Caesarī imperium
in Galliā in quīnque annōs prōrogārētur. eō annō ipse Venetōs,
Q. Titūrius Sabīnus Unellōs, P. Crassus Aquitānōs vīcit.

Germānī, -ōrum 2. m. pl. Germans. **fīnis, -is** 3. m. end;
(plural) boundaries. **secundus, -a, -um** second. **prōrogō** 1.
I extend.

SECTION 56

See Grammar Notes №. 111,
Parts of Verbs.

Exercise 354.

1. The soldiers who had come with Labienus told us this.
2. Caesar has departed with all his army.
3. They have not received the corn which you sent.
4. Since they have told us nothing, let us go to the consul.
5. We ascertained this from spies which we sent into the
fields.

6. We shall not retreat into a city which is held by the Romans.
7. Have you received the hostages which we sent?
8. Let us join our forces with the army of Labienus.
9. You and I will depart to Italy.
10. This was ascertained through spies sent by Caesar.

say, tell dīcō, dīxī, dictum 3. **depart** discēdō, -cessī, -cessum 3. **accept, receive, sustain** accipiō, accēpī, acceptum 3. **join** coniungāmus, -nxī, -nctum 3. **ascertain** cognoscō, -nōvī, -nitum 3. **spy** explōrātor, -ōris 3. m. **retreat** recipiō, recēpī, receptum 3. (reflexive).

Exercise 355.

1. Do not retreat into our country: we are friends of the Roman people.
2. We have ascertained much about the Gauls through spies.
3. Since he had conducted many campaigns successfully, he was unwilling to retreat.
4. They retreated into the city, which they had freed from the enemy.
5. Caesar had not received hostages from this state.
6. The Romans who were attacking us have departed.
7. Labienus held this place with a small garrison.
8. Since they had given us corn, we were unwilling to destroy their city.
9. Who told your father this? Did he blame you?
10. From this place we marched to the sea.

place *(noun)* locus 2. m.

Exercise 356.

1. You and I will retreat to this place.
2. We were returning to this place by the same route.
3. Having stayed many days in Rome, he wished to depart.
4. We announced the victory to him *when he was* retreating into the camp.
5. Since they are adopting this plan, let us depart.
6. You and I will be able to hold this place with a small garrison.
7. They have given much to the citizens, who are perishing of hunger.
8. Since the allies have not come, Caesar has moved to his camp.
9. We cannot accept advice from the man who destroyed the city.
10. Let us retreat to the river, which is between the city and the camp.

move moveō, mōvī, mōtum 2.

Exercise 357.

1. mīlitēs hortātus Caesar in Ītaliam discessit.
2. quid dīxit? nōn audīvī.
3. Caesar hās cohortēs cum exercitū coniunxerat.
4. haec Caesar per explōrātōrēs cognōverat.
5. post sextam hōram nostrī hostium impetum sustinēre nōn poterant.
6. obsidēs quōs missūrī erant nōn accēpimus.
7. victōria potīrī potest, ūtī nōn potest.
8. ab hostibus victus in castra sē recēpit.
9. hic locus ā Labiēnō cum praesidiō tenēbātur.
10. Caesar castra ex locō mōvit.

coniungō, -nxī, -nctum 3. I join. **explōrātor, -ōris** 3. m. spy, scout. **sextus, -a, -um** adj. sixth. **praesidium** 2. n. garrison, fort.

358. Croesus (continued)

hoc in bellō Croesus cum tōtō exercitū victus est. ipse ā Cyrō vīvus igne concremārī iubētur. cum autem in rogum impositus esset rēgisque ministrī iam rogum succendērunt, magnō ille dolōre permōtus, "ō Sōlon, Sōlon!" clāmāvit. "quem tū nōmine vocās?" Cyrus interrogāvit. tum ille rem tōtam nārrāvit. victor autem, misericordia permōtus, captīvum līberārī iussit. rogus tamen iam succensus ardēbat. tum Croesus magnā vōce ā dīs petīvit ut ignem restinguerent. quod cum ille multīs lacrimīs implōrāvisset, magnus repente imber dē caelō dēscendit ignemque restinxit.

posteā nūntiōs mīsit deumque, cuius ōrāculō falsus erat, multīs verbīs accūsāvit. hīs autem responsum est "sīc ā deō monitus est Croesus, 'cōpiās contrā Persās dūcet et magnum imperium dēlēbit.' dūxit cōpiās magnumque imperium dēlēvit, nam suum dēlēvit. cūr igitur deum accūsat?"

concremō 1. I burn. **rogus** 2. m. pyre. **impōnō, imposuī, impositum** 3. I place upon. **succendō, -dī, -sum** 3. I set fire to, kindle. **restinguō, -nxī, -nctum** 3. I extinguish. **igitur** (second word in clause) therefore.

SECTION 57

See Grammar Notes №. 111,
Parts of Verbs.

Exercise 359.

1. We will spare the citizens, since they have given us corn.
2. We routed the enemy whom we had attacked.
3. Do not fly to the camp: the allies are coming.
4. Let us leave the captives in the city.
5. The citizens defended the town which the Gauls attacked.
6. All kinds of weapons were known to the Roman soldiers.
7. It was the custom of the Romans to spare a conquered enemy.
8. They have routed the army which we sent.
9. These places are known to us through spies.
10. We believe the allies who have always helped us.

spare parcō, pepercī, parsum 3. **fly** *verb* fugiō, fūgī 3. **leave** relinquō, relīquī, relictum 3. **defend** dēfendō, -dī, -sum 3. **kind (type)** genus, -eris 3. n. **believe** crēdō, -didī, -ditum 3. (+dat.).

Exercise 360.

1. Have not the forces which we sent been routed?
2. Do not return to the city from which you have departed.
3. Why are they flying? The camp has not been taken.
4. You and I have always spared the conquered.
5. This was ascertained by the general through spies.
6. He believed me: why does he not believe you?
7. The captives who were left in the city seem very wretched.
8. We received the flying soldiers into the camp.
9. They cannot defend the town which we are attacking.
10. Since the general had returned, we dared not fly.

Exercise 361.

1. Let us return before night: it is a very difficult journey.
2. They have left their heaviest weapons in the camp.
3. Since he had come from the consul, we believed him.
4. These places are known to the enemy whom we are attacking.
5. Since we could hear the general's voice, we dared not fly.
6. Caesar will move his camp before the fifth hour of the day.
7. The city has been taken: the enemy are flying.
8. Having been left in the city, he could not bear arms.
9. It is disgraceful not to spare a flying enemy.
10. Since you say this, we are willing to return.

Exercise 362.

1. Caesar castra prope hoc flūmen posuit.
2. victīs hostibus parcāmus.
3. nostrōs ab hōc locō in urbem pepulērunt.
4. patriam ā patribus servātam virtūte nostrā defendēmus.
5. obsidēs et captīvōs in castrīs relīquērunt.
6. hoc genere tēlōrum Britannī semper ūtuntur.
7. post trēs hōrās castra in hōc locō posuimus.
8. ā Gallīs pulsī ad castra fūgimus.
9. hoc ā mīlitibus ad urbem redeuntibus cognōvērunt.
10. Rōmānōs in castra fugientēs vīdimus.

genus, -eris 3. n. kind, sort.

363. The Death of Marcellus

tōta rēs brevī confecta est: Marcellus hastā vulnerātus statim moritur: filius eius et Crispinus gravissima vulnera accēperant. equitēs Etruscī, quī rem diūtius gerere nōluērunt, prīmī fūgērunt; reliquī, ex eō locō sē recipere coāctī, ad castra quam celerrimē rediērunt. legiōnēs in castrīs relictae, quae certāmen inde spectāverant, suīs tempore subvenīre nōn potuērunt. Crispinus filiusque Marcellī sanguine cruentātī advēnērunt: sequēbātur reliqua multitūdō. ipse autem Marcellus, vir fortissimus, quī sexiēs cōnsul fuerat et rēgis Gallicī, suā manū occīsī, spolia Iovī Feretriō dēdicāverat, mortuus in colle ignōtō iacēbat; arme eius corpusque penes Hannibalem erant.

diūtius adv. compar. for longer, for a longer time. **sexiēs** adv. six times. **ignōtus, -a, -um** adj. unknown, obscure.

SECTION 58

See Grammar Notes Nᵒs. 112–116,
Parts of Verbs.

Exercise 364.

1. The enemy were following the Roman army.
2. We shall start in a few hours.
3. Having followed up our column for several days, they returned to their city.
4. Having set out with him, we could not leave him.
5. The Romans were praised by all on account of their courage.
6. It is better to die than be taken by the enemy.
7. Men are dying of hunger in this city.
8. The enemy are following by an easier route.
9. Do not tell them this: they know it already.

10. On the march we saw their cavalry returning.

follow sequor, secūtus sum 3. deponent. **start, set out** proficīscor, profectus sum 3. deponent. **follow up, pursue** īnsequor, -cūtus 3. deponent. **column (of soldiers)** agmen, -inis 3. n. **several** complūrēs, -ēs, -a (pl. adj.). **on account of** propter (+acc.). **die** morior, mortuus 3. deponent. **know** sciō, scīvī, scītum 4.

Exercise 365.

1. Many things were done by the citizens on that day.
2. His brother and sister died at Rome.
3. Several of the soldiers were left in the camp.
4. You and I will start in three days for Rome.
5. The legion which was sent to us has departed.
6. After the battle Caesar moved his camp.
7. Having followed for several days, we came to a river.
8. The army has set out with a general whom we appointed.
9. The Gauls will follow our column for several days.
10. Since he has been wounded by an arrow, he will die in a few hours.

after post (+acc.).

Exercise 366.

1. Having been left in the town, the prisoners died of hunger.
2. Our men made an attack on the enemy *when they were* retreating.
3. Nothing can be more base than to wound a dying man.
4. We shall not spare the soldiers who are following us.
5. You and your brother did not follow the flying enemy.
6. Do you really believe the man who said this?
7. We drove several of the Gauls into their camp.
8. Do not we Romans always spare a conquered enemy?
9. It will be very easy to pursue them *when they are* retreating.
10. We shall follow the soldiers who are now setting out.

drive, rout pellō, pepulī, pulsum 3.

Exercise 367.

1. hic propter sapientiam magistrātus creātus est.
2. cum hōc scīrēmus, nōn ausī sumus nōs recipere.
3. ab urbe profectī per sociōrum agrōs iter fēcimus.
4. hostēs agmen nostrum īnsecūtī sunt.
5. melius est prō patriā morī quam vincī.
6. ego dux erō: vōs mē sequiminī.
7. nōlumus sine imperātōre proficīscī.
8. nōn poteris eōdem itinere redīre.
9. pater meus et māter Carthāgine mortuī sunt.
10. omnia deōrum cōnsiliō fiunt.

īnsequor, -cūtus 3. dep. I follow up, pursue. **sciō, scīvī, scītum** 4. I know.

368. Caesar's Remaining Years in Gaul (56–49 BC)

Caesar, cum in Galliam redisset, Usīpetēs et Tenctheros, quī Rhēnum transierant, magnā cum caede superāvit. tum ipse, ut Germānōs terreret, mīrā celeritāte pontem fēcit Rhēnumque cum exercitū transiit. ibi breve tempus morātus cum in Galliam redisset pontem rescidit, nē Germānī, illō ponte ūsī, in Galliam iterum transīrent. eōdem annō cum paucīs nāvibus ad Britanniam nāvigāvit, cuius insulae incolae in omnibus ferē bellīs auxilium ad Gallōs contrā Rōmānōs mīserant. haud diū in insulā morātus proximō annō cum quattuor legiōnibus iterum eō nāvigāvit: Cassivellaunum, quī Britannōrum cōpiīs praeerat, superāvit obsidēsque ab eō accēpit. tum in Galliam rediit, ubi Belgās, quī iterum coniūrāverant, vīcit. tandem Vercingetorix, omnium Gallōrum dux mīlitiae perītissimus, quī cum omnibus ferē gentibus Galliae coniūrāverat, ā Caesare victus est. haec omnia Caesar in septem librīs dē bellō Gallicō scrīptīs nārrāvit.

pōns, pontis 3. m. bridge. **rescindō, -cidī, -cissum** 3. I break down. **Britannus** 2. m. a Briton. **accipiō, accēpī, acceptum** 3. I receive.

SECTION 59

See Rules on pp. 260–262,
Gender of Nouns. 1st and 2nd Declensions,
and 3rd Declension (Masculine
Terminations with exceptions).

Exercise 369.

1. The Roman sailors refused to leave their ships.
2. By this talk the fear of the citizens was increased.
3. There were many trees and most beautiful flowers in this place.
4. We saw the bones of the soldiers who had been killed in that war.
5. The bold faces of the enemy terrified our men.
6. These boats are smaller than (those) of the Gauls.
7. You will not dare to pursue so great a multitude.
8. Let us make an attack on the confused ranks of the Romans.
9. Rest was given to the soldiers by the general.
10. Caesar encouraged the soldiers by this speech.

sailor nauta 1. m. **conversation, talk** sermō, -ōnis 3. m.
tree arbor, -oris 3. f. **flower** flōs, flōris 3. m. **bone** os, ossis 3.
n. **face** ōs, ōris 3. n. **boat** linter, -tris 3. f. **multitude**
multitūdō, -inis 3. f. **rank** ōrdō, -inis 3. m. **rest** quiēs, -ētis 3.
f. **speech** ōrātiō, -ōnis 3. f.

Exercise 370.

1. The soldiers will receive this reward from the state.
2. Many boats were following our ships.
3. The horse's foot had been wounded by an arrow.
4. Your conversation had been heard by the general.
5. Rest was welcome to the soldiers who had started at night.
6. After this speech they were unwilling to spare him.
7. His face had been wounded by a dart.
8. A reward has been given to the men who defended the town.
9. These sailors gave us a few boats.
10. Did you not see this tree and these flowers.

reward mercēs, -ēdis 3. f. **foot** pēs, pedis 3. m.

Exercise 371.

1. To whom did you give the reward?
2. Do not follow this multitude of citizens.
3. This tree was left in the field by my father.
4. The confused ranks of the enemy could not withstand our attack.
5. My speech was heard very easily by everybody.
6. Let us not give them a reward which they will not dare to accept.
7. By much labour we can all obtain wealth.
8. We could not see the faces of the sailors.
9. What did you say to the man who has increased our work?
10. All who heard your speech praised it.

labour labor, labōris 3. m.

Exercise 372.

1. nautae ad nāvēs tribus hōrīs redībunt.
2. hīs ōrātiōnibus duōrum exercituum ducēs mīlitum animōs confirmāvērunt.
3. arborēs et flōrēs in hāc terrā nōn vīdimus.
4. hostium multitūdinem virtūte suā superāvērunt.
5. mīlitēs nostrī labōrem nōn vītābant.
6. hostium ōrdinēs nostrī oppugnābant.
7. dux mīlitibus quiētem dedit.
8. nauta ad lintrem redīre nōluit.
9. hīs sermōnibus omnēs maximē perturbābantur.
10. complūrēs mīlitum sub arboribus sē cēlāverant.

nauta 1. m. sailor. **quiēs, -ētis** 3. f. rest. **maximē** adv. very greatly, chiefly. **complūrēs, -ēs, -a** pl. adj. several.

373. Phaethon

Phaethon, Sōlis fīlius, ā patre ōlim petīvit ut sibi licēret ūnum diem sōlis currum per caelum agere. quod cum ab illō concessum esset, magnō cum gaudiō puer currum ascendit. gravissimās tamen poenās audāciae persolvere coactus est. nam propter corporis īnfirmitātem equōs fortissimōs coercēre nōn potuit: illī igitur ē cursū ēgressī tam prope terram dēscendērunt ut eam ferē incendērunt. itaque Iuppiter, īrā permōtus, puerum īnfēlīcem fulmine necāvit mortuumque in Ēridanum flūmen coniēcit. sorōrēs eius, quae equōs curruī dolōre propter frātris mortem movēbantur ut deōrum misericordiam excitārent, ā quibus ipsae in arborēs, lacrimaeque eārum in ēlectrum versae sunt.

īnfirmitās, -tātis 3. f. weakness. **coerceō** 2. I check. **cursus** 4. m. course. **fulmen, fulminis** 3. n. lightning. **ēlectrum** 2. n. amber.

SECTION 60

See Rules on pp. 260–262,
Gender of Nouns. 3rd Declension (Feminine
Terminations with exceptions).

Exercise 374.

1. That summer we sustained a great disaster in Italy.
2. We dared not neglect your safety.
3. A few boats were following our fleet.
4. This mountain has been seized by our infantry.
5. This law has always been neglected in our state.
6. We shall lead a large army into your boundaries.
7. This winter many will die of hunger in the city.
8. Having followed our fleet for three days, they sailed to Athens.
9. In this valley there are very many trees and most beautiful flowers.
10. The bridge was made by the soldiers with much labour.

summer aestās, -ātis 3. f. **disaster** clādēs, -is 3. f. **safety** salūs, -ūtis 3. f. **fleet** classis, -is 3. f. **law** lēx, lēgis 3. f. **boundaries** fīnēs, -ium 3. m. pl. **winter** hiems, -mis 3. f. **valley** vallis, -s 3. f. **bridge** pōns, pontis 3. m.

Exercise 375.

1. Let us not accept this peace, citizens.
2. There are many flocks in this valley.
3. Who will dare to announce this disaster to the king?
4. Do not neglect our safety: we are dying of hunger.
5. By this fraud he has obtained much wealth.
6. Our army has sustained a great disaster: let us defend the city.
7. Having started that summer from Rome, he marched into our boundaries.
8. This reward was given to those who had saved our fleet.
9. Your flocks were praised by all who had seen them.

10. On this hill we saw the enemy's line drawn up.

peace pāx, pācis 3. f. **flock** grex, -gis 3. m./f. **fraud** fraus, -dis 3. f. **hill** collis, -is 3. m.

Exercise 376.

1. That winter the citizens were perishing of hunger.
2. By this peace the city was saved.
3. We dared not depart from the mountain near which we had pitched the camp.
4. By this fraud he obtained a large reward.
5. Since we have sustained this disaster, let us not return to Rome.
6. Having set out from the camp, we came to this mountain.
7. On this hill there are many trees, beneath which we shall be able to hide ourselves.
8. These laws will be most useful to our state.
9. It will be very easy to obtain wealth by this fraud.
10. This mountain had been seized by the soldiers whom we had sent.

near prope (+acc.). **pitch (camp)** pōnō, posuī, positum 3.

Exercise 377.

1. aestāte cum exercitū Rōmam redībō.
2. bellum in Gallōrum fīnibus multōs annōs gessimus.
3. haec gēns hieme bellum gerere nōlēbat.
4. collis ā Labiēnō cum praesidiō tenēbātur.
5. omnēs cīvēs lēgibus pārēre voluērunt.
6. in hīs vallibus et arborēs et flōrēs vīdimus.
7. cūr nōn mīlitēs in monte relīquistī?
8. Caesar ad montem cum exercitū profectus est.
9. castra in colle pōnere omnēs voluērunt.
10. aestāte quam hieme pugnāre mālō.

aestās, -ātis 3. f. summer. **hiems, -mis** 3. f. winter.

378. Caesar crosses the Rubicon (49 BC)

intereā M. Crassus contrā Parthōs pugnāns cecitiderat, Cn. Pompeius, invidiā permōtus propter tot victōriās ā Caesare reportātās, senātuī sē adiūnxerat. Caesar ā senātū iussus est legiōnēs dīmittere Rōmamque redīre. "egō meās legiōnēs," respondit, "dēmittam, sī suās quoque legiōnēs dēmīserit Pompeius." id autem ille facere nōluit. tandem, bellum cīvīle vītāre quam maximē cōnātus, cum senātus plānē eum hostem reīpūblicae habitūrus esset, ē Galliā in Ītaliam profectus, ad parvum flūmen Rubicōnem vēnit. multās ibi hōrās morātus esse dicitur: nam hoc flumen nōn licuit imperātōrī Rōmānō cum armātis legiōnibus transīre: tandem "iacta est ālea," clāmāvit, flūmenque cum cōpiīs transiit: qua rē bellum reīpūblicae indixit.

dīmittō, dīmīsī, dīmissum 3. I dismiss, disband. **cīvīlis, -is, -e** civil. **plānē** clearly. **Rubicō, Rubicōnis** the Rubicon. **iaciō, iēcī, iactum** 3. I throw, cast. **ālea** 1. f. die (in gambling game).

SECTION 61

See Rules on pp. 260–262,
Gender of Nouns. 3rd Declension
(Neuter Terminations with exceptions),
4th and 5th Declensions.

Exercise 379.

1. We did not see many animals in this land.
2. These nets will be most useful to the sailors.
3. We have determined to leave a small fleet in this harbour.
4. Your poem will be praised by all your friends.
5. The knees of these animals are very small.

6. A small band of soldiers set out for this hill.
7. Your name is feared by the enemies of our state.
8. The flashes of lightning terrified the barbarians with whom we were fighting.
9. These spurs were left in the camp by the cavalry.
10. We received corn and milk from these barbarians.

animal animal, -ālis 3. n. **net** rēte, -is 3. n. **harbour** portus, -ūs 4. m. **poem** poēma, -atis 3. n. **knee** genū 4. n. **band (of men)** manus 4. f. **name** *(noun)* nōmen, -inis 3. n. **flash of lightning** fulgur, -uris 3. n. **spur** calcar, -āris 3. n. **milk** lac, lactis 3. n.

Exercise 380.

1. Let us not leave on the ships the bodies of men who died for their country.
2. This house was built by the Romans who conquered our fathers.
3. His head was wounded by an arrow.
4. Beneath this oak stands the house in which you taught me letters.
5. In these woods we saw many animals.
6. From whom did you ascertain the general's name?
7. In this valley stood a little house and a few trees.
8. Caesar determined to seize this mountain before night.
9. A little band of Romans was fighting against a large multitude of Gauls.
10. We decided to pitch our camp between the river and this hill.

body corpus, -oris 3. n. **house** domus 4. f. **head** caput, -itis 3. n. **oak** quercus, -ūs 4. f.

Exercise 381.

1. Did not a small band of our men rout a large multitude of the enemy?
2. This house stands near the mountain to which we are coming.
3. This reward was given to the consul who defended our city.
4. We have conquered the enemy: the ships are returning to the harbour.
5. Beneath this hill there is a valley in which we saw many flowers and trees.
6. His face is known to me: his name I could not ascertain.
7. These animals have small feet, large heads.
8. Having been routed by the enemy, they dared not return to Rome.
9. Caesar dared not pitch his camp in this valley.
10. That harbour will not take many ships.

Exercise 382.

1. in portū plūrimās nāvēs vīdimus.
2. puer manibus ūtī nōn potest.
3. quercus quam domus altior est.
4. animal pedēs habet, manus nōn habet.
5. nē calcāribus ūtāmur: equīs parcāmus.
6. num quercum, puer, numquam vīdistī?
7. cīvēs imperātōrī domum, labōrum mercēdem, dedērunt.
8. omnium arborum quercus maximē laudātur.
9. nāvēs in portū relictae sunt.
10. castra prope collem pōnere cōnstituit.

portus -ūs 4. m. harbour. **quercus,** -ūs 4. f. oak. **calcar,** -āris 3. n. spur. **mercēs,** -ēdis 3. f. reward.

383. The Death of Caesar (44 BC)

Caesar cum in Ītaliam vēnisset senātōrum cōpiās ubique vīcit. Pompeius, quī ad Aegyptum nāvigāverat, Ptolemaeī rēgis iussū occīsus est. eō secūtus Caesar in magnum perīculum vēnit: nam ab exercitū, quem Ptolomaeus collēgerat, repente oppugnātus nandō vītam servāvit, manū intereā tenēns librōs illōs quōs dē bellō scrīpserat. posteā tamen mīrā celeritāte hostēs omnēs superāvit: quās victōriās hīs verbīs nūntiāvit, "vēnī, vīdī, vīcī."

dictātor creātus maximā cum clēmentiā inimīcīs omnibus parcēbat optimāsque lēgēs tulit. priusquam tamen omnia quae in animō habēbat peragere posset ab inimīcīs in cūriā occīsus est. ē quibus ūnus, M. Brūtus nōmine, ōlim inimīcus, posteā in amīcitiam ab illō acceptus erat. hunc ubi vīdit, "et tū, Brūte!" clāmāvit, nec diūtius resistēbat: multīs vulneribus trānsfīxus prope statuam Pompeiī cecidit.

nō 1. I swim; **nandō** (gerund) by swimming. **scrībō, -ipsī, -iptum** 3. I write. **clēmentia** 1. f. mercy, clemency. **parcō, pepercī, parsum** 3. I spare. **trānsfīgō, -fīxī, -fīxum** 3. I pierce. **statua** 1. f, statue.

384. A Father's Last Advice

pater ubi rediit fīliōs omnēs ad sē venīre iussit. "per multās terrās," inquit, "iter fēcī, praeter multās ōrās nāvigāvī; nihil ferē est quod nōn oculīs spectāvī. tandem dī mē sinunt iterum vōs vidēre. audīte ea quae iam vōbīs dīcō; haec ultima verba semper in memoriā tenēte. nōn iterum vōs compellāre poterō, nam mors, crēdō, brevī tempore vīta mē prīvābit. conāminī iuvenēs dē officiō saepe meditārī et ea facere quae senibus vōbīs nōn turpia fuisse vidēbuntur. inter sē contrāria sunt virtūs et vitium: quae cum ita sint, hoc fugite, illam sequiminī."

sinō, sīvī, situm 3. I allow. **prīvō** 1. (+abl.) I deprive. **contrārium, -ī** 2. n. the opposite. **vitium, -ī** 2. n. vice.

GENDER AS SHOWN BY MEANING

Gender is properly the Grammatical distinction that indicates sex. Therefore:

(1) A Noun that stands for a male or a nation is **Masculine**: e.g. cōnsul, *a consul*; Persae, *Persians*.

(2) A Noun that stands for a female is **Feminine**, e.g. mulier, *a woman*.

(3) Many Nouns can stand for male or female persons or animals. These are called **Common** in Gender, and they can be Masculine or Feminine according to the sense: e.g. cīvis, *citizen*; testis, *witness*; sacerdōs, *priest* or *priestess*; canis, *dog*.

In English the names of *things*, which cannot be male or female, are called **Neuter**, and this is a natural distinction. But this does not hold in Latin. The names of things that have no natural Gender may in Latin be Masculine, Feminine, or Neuter, and their Genders must be learnt by practice.

But as particular *terminations* in the different Declensions for the most part belong to particular Genders, it is possible to lay down certain rules. The following are the most important ones with the commonest exceptions. There are many other exceptions in less common Nouns.

GENDER AS SHOWN BY TERMINATION

DECLENSION I

RULES.	EXCEPTIONS.
-A Fem.	Masc. are some denoting males; e.g. **nauta**, *sailor*; **poēta**, *poet*.
-AS, -ES Masc.	—

DECLENSION II

RULES.	EXCEPTIONS.
-US, -ER Masc.	Fem. **humus**.
-UM Neut.	—

DECLENSION III

RULES.

(a) Masculine in

EXCEPTIONS.

-O	Fem in -io, -go, and -do (except **ōrdō**).	
-OR	Fem. **arbor**.	Neut. **cor**.
-OS	—	Neut. **ōs**, **ŏs**.
-ER	Fem. **linter**.	Neut. **iter**, **vēr**.
-ES (with Genitive increasing)	Fem. **mercēs**, **quiēs**.	

DECLENSION III (CONTINUED)

RULES.	EXCEPTIONS.
(b) Feminine in	
-IS	Besides many that are Common from their meaning (e.g. **cīvis**, *citizen*), the following are regularly Masculine: **amnis, cinis, collis, crīnis, ēnsis, fīnis, ignis, lapis, mēnsis, orbis, pānis, piscis, pulvis, sanguis.**
-AS	—
-AUS	—
-ES (Genitive not increasing)	—
-ŪS	— Neut. **crūs, iūs, rūs.**
-X	Masc. all in -ex, except **lēx.**
-S preceded by a consonant	Masc. **dēns, fōns, mōns, pōns.**
(c) Neuter in	
-AR	—
-UR	Masc. **fūr.**
-ŬS	Masc. **pecŭs (pecudis).**
-L,-A,-N,-C,-E,-T	Masc. **sōl, cōnsul.**

DECLENSION IV

RULES.	EXCEPTIONS.
-US Masc.	Fem. are names of trees and **domus, tribus, manus.**
-U Neut.	—

DECLENSION V

RULES.	EXCEPTIONS.
-ES Fem.	Masc. is **diēs** in its ordinary sense of *day.* It can be Fem. in the sense of *time* or *date.*

ABBREVIATIONS OF NAMES

C. = Gaius.*
Cn. = Gnaeus.*
L = Lūcius.
M. = Marcus.
P. = Publius.
Q. = Quintus.
Sp. = Spurius.
T. = Titus.
Ti. = Tiberius.

*The Letter C originally represented the G sound; when G was introduced into the Latin alphabet, C still denoted the G sound when standing for the names Gaius and Gnaeus.

ENGLISH-TO-LATIN VOCABULARY

Figures in brackets indicate the exercise where the word is first defined.

able (to), am *see* can, am able to.

accept, receive, sustain accipiō, accēpī, acceptum 3. (354).

account (on account of) propter (+acc.) (364).

adopt *see* take, capture, adopt.

advice cōnsilium, -ī 2. n. (46).

advise moneō 2. (117).

affair rēs, reī 5. f. (143).

afraid (of), am *see* fear, am afraid of.

after post (+acc.) (365).

again iterum (204).

against contrā (+acc.) (72).

aid *see* help, aid.

all omnis, -is, -e (91).

ally socius 2. m. (255).

already iam (112).

always semper (152).

am (are, is, be) sum, esse, fuī (irreg.) (150).

and et (40); -que (118).

animal animal, -ālis 3. n. (379).

announce nūntiō 1. (21).

appoint *see* elect, appoint.

arms arma, armōrum 2. n. pl. (72).

army exercitus, -ūs 4. m. (124).

arrival adventus 4. m. (194).

arrow sagitta, -ae 1. f. (27).

ascertain cognoscō, -nōvī, -nitum 3. (354).

ask rogō 1. (334).

assail oppugnō 1. (21).

Athens Athēnae 1. f. pl. (204).

attack (*noun*) impetus, -ūs 4. m. (124). (*verb*) oppugnō 1. (21).

avoid vītō 1. (46).

bad, evil malum 2. n. (231).

band (of men) manus 4. f. (379).

barbarian barbarus, -ī 2. m. (39).

base *see* disgraceful, base.

battle pugna, -ae 1. f. (21).

bear, endure ferō, ferre, tulī, lātum (307).

beautiful pulcher, -chra, -chrum (65).

before ante (+acc.) (281).

behalf (on behalf of) *see* for, on behalf of.

Belgians Belgae, -ārum 1. m. pl. (21).

believe crēdō, -didī, -ditum 3. (+dat.) (359).

beneath *see* under, beneath.

best optimus, -a, -um (164).

better melior, -or, -us (163).

between inter (+acc.) (339).

blame culpō 1. (194).

boat linter, -tris 3. f. (369).

body corpus, -oris 3. n. (380).

bold audāx, -ācis (152).

bone os, ossis 3. n. (369).

book liber, librī 2. m. (344).

both...and et...et (182).

boundaries fīnēs, -ium 3. m. pl. (374).

boy puer, -ī 2. m. (52).

brave fortis, -is, -e (156).

bravely *adv.* fortiter (170).

bridge pōns, pontis 3. m. (374).

bring dūcō, dūxī, ductum 3. (72).

Britons Britannī 2. m. pl. (334).

broad lātus, -a, -um (156).

brother frāter, -tris 3. m. (314).

build aedificō 1. (52).

burden onus, oneris 3. n. (97).

by (*of living agent*) ā (+abl.); *before vowel or h*, ab (+abl.) (97).

Cádiz Gādēs, -ium 3. f. pl. (204).
Caesar Caesar, -is 3. m. (143).
call, name nōminō 1. (319).
call a meeting *see* summon.
camp castra, -ōrum 2. n. pl. (47).
campaign *see* war, campaign.
can, am able (to) possum, posse, potuī
  (+inf.) (294).
captive captīvus, -ī 2. m. (65).
capture *see* take, capture, adopt.
carry portō 1. (97).
Carthage Carthāgō, -inis 3. f. (204).
cavalry equitēs 3. m. pl. (78).
charge impetus, -ūs 4. m. (124).
citizen cīvis, cīvis 3. c. (86).
city urbs, urbis 3. f. (92).
cohort cohors, -rtis 3. f. (199).
column (of soldiers) agmen, -inis 3. n.
  (364).
come veniō, vēnī, ventum 4. (329).
condemn damnō 1. (249).
conduct, wage (war) gerō, gestī,
  gestum 3. (230).
confuse, disturb perturbō 1. (237).
confusion (throw into) *see* confuse,
  disturb.
conquer vincō, vīcī, victum 3. (229).
consider a person as having a quality
  habeō 2. (314).
consul cōnsul, -lis 3. m. (319).
conversation, talk sermō, -ōnis 3. m.
  (369).
corn frūmentum 2. n. (216).
Cotta Cotta, -ae 1. m. (21).
country patria, -ae 1. f. (21).
courage virtūs, -ūtis 3. f. (164).
cry clāmor, -ōris 3. m. (85).
custom mōs, mōris 3. m. (194).

danger perīculum, -ī 2. n. (46).
dare audeō, ausus sum 2. (semi-
  deponent) (320).
daring audāx, -ācis (151).
dart iaculum, -ī 2. n. (65).
day diēs 5. m/f. (210).
decide, determine cōnstituō, -uī,
  -ūtum 3. (307).
deep altus, -a, -um (157).
defeat superō 1. (39).

defend dēfendō, -dī, -sum 3. (359).
delay moror (deponent) (281).
depart discēdō, -cessī, -cessum 3.
  (354).
destroy dēleō, -ēvī, -ētum 2. (349).
detain *see* hold, detain.
determine *see* decide, determine.
device cōnsilium, -ī 2. n. (46).
die morior, mortuus 3. deponent
  (364).
difficult difficilis, -is, -e (171).
disaster clādēs, -is 3. f. (374).
disgraceful, base turpis, -is, -e (236).
disturb *see* confuse, disturb.
do, make faciō, fēcī, factum 3. (288).
draw up instruō, -xī, -ctum 3. (130).
drive, rout pellō, pepulī, pulsum 3.
  (366).

easily *adv.* facile (163).
easy facilis, -is, -e (163).
eight octō (200).
eighth octāvus, -a, -um (224).
elect, appoint creō 1. (319).
embolden cōnfirmō 1. (195).
employ *see* use, employ.
encourage, exhort hortor, hortātus 1.
  deponent (281).
endure *see* bear, endure.
enemy hostis, -is 3. c.; pl. hostēs "the
  enemy" (85).
every, everybody omnis, -is, -e (91).
everything omnia, -ium 3. n. pl. (145).
evil *see* bad, evil.
exhort *see* encourage, exhort.

face ōs, ōris 3. n. (369).
father pater, patris 3. m. (117).
fear, am afraid of timeō 2. (59).
few paucus, -a, -um (98).
field, territory ager, agrī 2. m. (52).
fierce ācer, ācris, ācre (124).
fiercely ācriter (158).
fifteen quīndecim (201).
fifth quīntus, -a, -um (211).
fight *verb* pugnō 1. (2).
five quīnque (199).
flash of lightning fulgur, -uris 3. n.
  (379).

fleet classis, -is 3. f. (374).
flock grex, -gis 3. m./f. (375).
flower flōs, flōris 3. m. (369).
fly *verb* fugiō, fūgī 3. (359).
follow sequor, secūtus sum 3.
  deponent (364).
follow up, pursue īnsequor, -cūtus 3.
  deponent (364)
foot pēs, pedis 3. m. (370).
for, on behalf of prō (+abl.) (225).
forces cōpiae, -ārum 1. f. pl. (21).
form *see* take, capture, adopt, form.
fortify mūniō 4. (85).
fortunate fēlix, -īcis (150).
four quattuor (200).
fourth quartus, -a, -um (212).
fraud fraus, -dis 3. f. (375).
free, set free līberō 1. (210).
friend amīcus 2. m. (325).
frighten terreō 2. (59).
from, out of ē, ex (+abl.) (199).

garrison, protection praesidium 2. n.
  (329).
Gaul Gallia, -ae 1. f. (150).
Gauls Gallī, -ōrum 2. m. pl. (53).
general imperātor, -ōris 3. m. (78).
give dō, dare, dedī, datum (349).
go eō, īre, īvī (iī), itum (irregular)
  (307).
god deus, -ī 2. m. (118).
good bonus, -a, -um (59).
great magnus, -a, -um (59).
greater māior, -or, -us (256).
greatest maximus, -a, -um (163).
guide *(noun)* dux, ducis 3. c. (78).
  (verb) regō, rēxī, rēctum 3. (72).

harbour portus, -ūs 4. m. (379).
hasten mātūrō 1. (1).
have habeō 2. (59).
head caput, -itis 3. n. (380).
hear audiō 4. (85).
heart, mind animus 2. m. (195).
heavy gravis, -is, -e (156).
help, aid auxilium 2. n. (275).
hide cēlō 1. (169).
high altus, -a, -um (157).
hill collis, -is 3. m. (375).

hinder impediō 4. (137).
hold, detain teneō 2. (111).
horse equus, -ī 2. m. (39).
hostage obses, obsidis 3. c. (217).
hour hōra 1. f. (210).
house domus 4. f. (380).
huge ingēns, ingentis (91).
hunger famēs, -is 3. f. (344).

in in (+abl.) (150).
increase augeō, auxī, auctum 2. (349).
infantry peditēs 3. m. pl. (103).
into in (+acc.) (72).
Italy Ītalia 1. f. (199).

join coniungāmus, -nxī, -nctum 3.
  (354).
journey, route iter, itineris 3. n. (288).

kill necō 1. (243).
kind (type) genus, -eris 3. n. (359).
king rēx, rēgis 3. m. (137).
kingdom, kingship regnum 2. n.
  (329).
knee genū 4. n. (379).
know sciō, scīvī, scītum 4. (364).
known *adj.* nōtus, -a, -um (223).

Labienus Labiēnus 2. m. (39).
labour labor, labōris 3. m. (371).
land terra, -ae 1. f. (72).
large magnus, -a, -um (59).
larger māior, -or, -us (163).
largest māior, -or, -us (164).
law lēx, lēgis 3. f. (374).
lay waste vastō 1. (52).
lead dūcō, dūxī, ductum 3. (72).
lead back redūcō, redūxī, reductum 3.
  (130).
leader dux, ducis 3. c. (78).
leave relinquō, relīquī, relictum 3.
  (359).
left, left hand sinister, -stra, -strum
  (130).
legion legiō, -ōnis 3. f. (199).
letters, literature litterae 1. f. pl. (335).
lightning (flash of) *see* flash of
  lightning.
like amō 1. (39).

line, line of battle aciēs, aciēī 5. f. (143).
little parvus, -a, -um (59).
loud magnus, -a, -um (85).
love amō 1. (1).

magistrate magistrātus 4. m. (319).
maintain obtineō 2. (329).
make *see* do, make.
man vir 2. m. (262). good men bonī, -ōrum 2. m. pl. (60). our men nostrī, -ōrum 2. m. pl. (40).
many multus, -a, -um (72).
march contendō, -dī, -tum 3. (199).
matter rēs, reī 5. f. (143).
meeting concilium 2. m. (268).
milk lac, lactis 3. n. (379).
mother māter, mātris 3. f. (330).
mountain mōns, montis 3. m. (374).
move moveō, mōvī, mōtum 2. (356).
much multus, -a, -um (72).
multitude multitūdō, -inis 3. f. (369).

name *(noun)* nōmen, -inis 3. n. (379) *(verb)* nōminō 1. (319).
nation gēns, gentis 3. f. (224).
native country patria, -ae 1. f. (21).
near prope (+acc.) (376).
neglect neglegō, neglēxī, neglēctum 3. (72).
net rēte, -is 3. n. (379).
never numquam (150).
night nox, noctis 3. f. (294).
ninth nōnus, -a, -um (230).
not nōn (39).
nothing nihil (157).
now iam (112).
number numerus, -ī 2. m. (150).

oak quercus, -ūs 4. f. (380).
obey pāreō (+dat.) 2. (339).
obtain potior 3. (deponent) (331).
often saepe (125).
one ūnus, -a, -um (201).
onset impetus -ūs 4. m. (124).
opinion sententia 1. f. (334).
opposite to contrā (+acc.) (130).
out of *see* from, out of.
overcome superō 1. (39).

part pars, partis 3. f. (112).
peace pāx, pācis 3. f. (375).
people populus, -ī 2. m. (112).
perish pereō, -iī, itum 4. (344).
pitch (camp) pōnō, posuī, positum 3. (376).
place *(noun)* locus 2. m. (355). *(verb)* collocō 1. (195).
plan cōnsilium, -ī 2. n. (46).
pleasant, welcome grātus, -a, -um (224).
poem poēma, -atis 3. n. (379).
possession (obtain) *see* obtain.
praise laudō 1. (183).
prefer mālō, mālle, māluī (301).
prepare parō 1. (46).
preserve servō 1. (28).
prevent impediō 4. (137).
prisoner captīvus, -ī 2. m. (65).
protection *see* garrison, protection.
pursue *see* follow up, pursue.

quickly celeriter (277).

rampart agger, -ris 3. m. (85).
rank ōrdō, -inis 3. m. (369).
rather (would) *see* prefer.
ravage vastō 1. (52).
receive *see* accept, receive, sustain.
refuse, am unwilling nōlō, nōlle, nōluī (301).
remain, stay maneō, mānsī, mānsum 2. (199).
remarkable ēgregius, -a, -um (314).
report nūntiō 1. (21).
rest quiēs, -ētis 3. f. (369).
retreat recipiō, recēpī, receptum 3. (reflexive) (354).
return redeō, -īre, -iī, -itum (compound of eō) (344).
reward mercēs, -ēdis 3. f. (370).
Rhodes Rhodus 2. f. (206).
right, right hand dexter, -tra, -trum (130).
risk perīculum, -ī 2. n. (46).
river flūmen, -inis 3. n. (156).
Roman *adj.* Rōmānus, -a, -um (72). *noun.* Rōmānus, -ī 2. m. (39).
Rome Rōma 1. f. (204).

rout *see* drive, rout.
route *see* journey, route.
rule regō, rēxī, rēctum 3. (72).
run currō, cucurrī, cursum 3. (242).

safe tūtus, -a, -um (303).
safety salūs, -ūtis 3. f. (374).
sail nāvigō 1. (13).
sailor nauta 1. m. (369).
same īdem, eadem, idem (182).
save servō 1. (28).
say, tell dīcō, dīxī, dictum 3. (354).
sea mare, -is 3. n. (118).
see videō, vīdī, vīsum 2. (204).
seem videor (passive of videō) (314).
seize occupō 1. (112).
send mittō, mīsī, missum 3. (199).
serious gravis, -is, -e (156).
set free *see* free, set free.
set out *see* start, set out.
seven septem (199).
several complūrēs, -ēs, -a (pl. adj.)
    (364).
shield scūtum, -ī 2. n. (65).
ship nāvis, -is 3. f. (189).
shout clāmor, -ōris 3. m. (85).
since cum (+subjunctive) (255).
sister soror, -ōris 3. f. (339).
sixth sextus, -a, -um (210).
small parvus, -a, -um (59).
smaller minor, -or, -us (163).
smallest, very small minimus, -a, -um
    (163).
so large tantus, -a, -um (229).
soldier mīles, -itis 3. m. (78).
son fīlius, -ī 2. m. (118).
sovereignty *see* kingdom, kingship.
spare parcō, pepercī, parsum 3. (359).
speech ōrātiō, -ōnis 3. f. (369).
splendid pulcher, -chra, -chrum (65).
spur calcar, -āris 3. n. (379).
spy explōrātor, -ōris 3. m. (354).
stand stō, stetī, statum 1. (349).
start, set out proficīscor, profectus
    sum 3. deponent (364).
state cīvitās, -ātis 3. f. (216).
stay *see* remain, stay.
stratagem cōnsilium, -ī 2. n. (46).

student discipulus 2. m. (316).
subject to (be) serviō (+dative) (339).
successful fēlīx, -īcis (150).
successfully fēlīcissimē (270).
summer aestās, -ātis 3. f. (374).
summon convocō 1. (256).
sustain *see* accept, receive, sustain.

take, capture, adopt, form (a plan)
    capiō, cēpī, captum (288).
talk *see* conversation, talk.
teach doceō, -uī, -tum 2. (334).
tell *see* say, tell.
ten decem (238).
tenth decimus, -a, -um (210).
terrify terreō 2. (59).
territory *see* field, territory.
than quam (156).
that ille, illa, illud (176).
thing rēs, reī 5. f. (143).
think putō 1. (320).
third tertius, -a, -um (210).
this hic, haec, hoc (176).
three trēs, trēs, tria (200).
through per (+acc.) (237).
throw into confusion *see* confuse,
    disturb.
time tempus, -oris 3. n. (263).
to ad (+acc.) (199).
tower turris, -is 3. f. (137).
town oppidum, -ī 2. n. (46).
tree arbor, -oris 3. f. (369).
troops cōpiae, -ārum 1. f. pl. (21).
twenty vīgintī (200).
two duo, duae, duo (199).

under, beneath sub (+abl.) (349).
unhappy miser, -era, -erum (65).
unwilling *see* refuse, am unwilling.
use, employ ūtor, ūtī, ūsus 3.
    deponent (+abl.) (281).
useful ūtilis, -is, -e (164).

valley vallis, -s 3. f. (374).
valour virtūs, -ūtis 3. f. (165).
Verona Vērōna 1. f. (330).
victory victōria, -ae 1. f. (21).
voice vōx, vōcis 3. f. (137).

wage (war) *see* conduct, wage (war).

wall mūrus, -ī 2. m. (157).

wander errō 1 (5).

war, campaign bellum, -ī. n. (46).

warn moneō 2. (117).

wealth opēs, -um 3. f. (329).

weapon tēlum, -ī 2. n. (46).

welcome *see* pleasant, welcome.

well adv. bene (165).

who, what, which quī, quae, quod (189).

whole omnis, -is, -e (91).

why? cūr (324).

willing (be) *see* wish.

wing *(of an army)* cornū, -ūs 4. n. (130). on the right wing dextrō cornū (130)

winter hiems, -mis 3. f. (374).

wisdom sapientia, -ae 1. f. (28).

wise sapiēns, sapientis (201).

wish volō, velle, voluī (294).

with cum (+abl.) (205).

without sine (+abl.) (344).

withstand sustineō 2. (125).

wood silva, -ae 1. f. (137).

word verbum 2. n. (262).

work labōrō 1. (1).

worse pēior, pēior, pēius (308).

worst pessimus, -a, -um (341).

wound vulnerō 1. (27).

wretched miser, -era, -erum (65).

year annus 2. m. (210).

yield cēdō, cessī, cessum 3. (339).

LATIN-TO-ENGLISH VOCABULARY

(Figures in brackets indicate the exercise where the word is first defined.)

ā, ab (+abl.) from, by (35).

abscīdō, -dī, -sum 3. I cut off (174).

abscindō, -idī, -īssum 3. I tear off (208).

accipiō, accēpī, acceptum 3. I receive (368).

accūsō 1. I accuse; falsīs crīminibus accūsō I accuse on false charges (82).

ācer, ācris, ācre sharp, fierce (102).

acētum 2. n. vinegar (227).

aciēs 5. f. line of battle (146).

ācriter fiercely (56).

ad (+acc.) to, towards (25).

addō, addidī, additum 3. I add (134).

addūcō, addūxī, adductum 3. I bring (71).

adeō to such an extent, so (272).

adiungō, -iūnxī, -iūnctum 3. I join (82).

adiuvō, adiūvī, adiūtum 1. I help (58).

administrō 1. I administer (50).

admīrātiō, -ōnis 3. f. admiration (123).

adsum, adesse, adfuī I am present (214).

advena 1. c. stranger (33).

adveniō, advēnī, adventum 4. I arrive (233).

adventus 4. m. arrival (128).

aedificō 1. I build (32).

Aegyptiī 2. m. pl. Egyptians (96).

aemulus, -a, -um rival (180).

Aenēadae 1. m. pl. the descendants of Aeneas (32).

Aenēās (nom.) Aeneas, the Trojan hero (37).

aēneus, -a, -um of bronze (135).

aēnum 2. n. bronze cauldron (109).

āēr, āeris 3. m. air (142).

aestās, -ātis 3. f. summer (377).

aetās, -ātis 3. f. age (95).

Aethiops, -is 3. m. Ethiopian (208).

ager, agrī 2. m. field, land, territory; pl. territories (55).

agger, -ris 3. m. rampart (88).

agmen, -inis 3. n. marching column (of soldiers) (227).

agō, ēgī, āctum 3. I drive, do, carry on; cunīculum agō I construct a mine; triumphum agō I celebrate a triumph (121).

agricola 1. m. farmer (272).

āla 1. f. wing (142).

ālea 1. f. die (in gambling game) (378).

aliēnō 1. I estrange; mentem aliēnō (+gen. of person) I drive mad (234).

aliquandō once (221).

aliquot some (64).

alius, -a, -ud other; alius ... alius one ... another; aliī ... aliī some ... others (69).

Alpēs, Alpium 3. f. pl. the Alps (227).

alter, -era, -erum second, one or other (of two) (109).

altus, -a, -um high (159).

amīcitia 1. f. friendship (43).

amīcus 2. m. friend (50).

āmittō, āmīsī, āmissum 3. I lose (109).

amō 1. I love (4).

amor, amōris 3. m. love (102).

amplius more, more than (147).

angustus, -a, -um narrow (134).

animal, -ālis 3. n. animal (167).

animus 2. m. mind (44).

annus 2. m. year (147).

anser, -eris 3. c. goose (134).

ante (+acc.), before (101).

anteā before (63).

antīquō 1. I reject (82).

antīquus, -a, -um ancient (107).

ānulus 2. m. ring (253).

anus 4. f. old woman (228).

aper, aprī 2. m. boar (260).

aperiō, -uī, -tum 4. I open (90).

apertē openly (141).

Apollō, -inis 3. m. Apollo (102).

appāreō 2. I appear (71).

appetō, -īvī, -ītum 3. I aim at (82).

applicō 1. I apply (44).

appōnō, apposuī, appositum 3. I serve up (109).

apud (+acc.) with, at the court of (253).

aqua 1. f. water (116).

āra 1. f. altar (63).

arānea 1. f. spider (228).

arātrum 2. n. plough (135).

arbitrium 2. n. authority, decision, will (51); ad arbitrium according to the caprice or will.

arbor, -oris 3. f. tree (116).

arcessō, -īvī, ītum 3. I summon (285).

ardeō, ārsī, arsum 2. I burn, (intransitive) (63).

ardor, -ōris 3. m. heat (273).

argentum 2. n. silver (90).

Argonautae 1. m. pl. Argonauts; sailors of the Argo (135).

ariēs, -etis 3. m. ram (306).

arma 2. n. pl. arms (75).

armātus, -a, -um armed (135).

arō 1. I plough (101).

ars, artis 3. f. art (135).

artifex, -icis 3. c. artist, craftsman (142).

arx, arcis 3. f. citadel (121).

ascendō, -dī, -sum 3. I climb up, ascend (134).

Athēnae 1. f. pl. Athens (57).

Athēniensis, -is, -e Athenian (333).

āthlēta 1. m. athlete (221).

auctōritās, -ātis 3. f. authority (82).

audācia 1. f. boldness (63).

audāx, -ācis adj. bold (153).

audeō, ausus sum 2. semi-deponent. I am bold (322).

audiō 4. I hear (88).

auferō, auferre, abstulī, ablātum (compound of ferō) I take away; (+dat.) I take away from (311).

augeō, auxī, auctum 2. I increase (transitive); in passive (of lakes, rivers, etc.), to be flooded (129).

aureus, -a, -um golden (135).

aurīga 1. c. charioteer (148).

aurum 2. n. gold (90).

aut or (115).

aut ... aut either ... or (115).

autem (second word) but, however, now (71).

auxilium 2. n. help (90).

avē hail! greetings! (149)

āvehō, -xī, -ctum 3. I carry off (208).

avis 3. f. bird (254).

axis, axis 3. m. axle (148).

barba 1. f. beard (128).

barbarus 2. m. barbarian, foreigner (42).

beātus, -a, -um happy (333).

Belgae, -ārum 1. m. pl. Belgians (24).

bellum 2. n. war (49).

bene well (51).

beneficium 2. n. kindness (63).

bibō, bibī 3. I drink (203).

bona 2. n. pl. goods, property (51).

bonī 2. m. pl. "good men" (62).

bonus, -a, -um good (62).

brevis, -is, -e short (174).

Britannia 1. f. Britain (57).

Britannus 2. m. a Briton (368).

cadō, cecidī, cāsum 3. I fall (95).

cadus 2. m. cask (260).

caedēs, -is 3. f. slaughter, murder (292).

caelum 2. n. heaven, the heavens (280).

Caesar, -is 3. m. The cognomen (family branch) of Gaius Julius Caesar (58).

calcar, -āris 3. n. spur (382).

campus 2. m. plain (160).

cancer, cancrī 2. m. crab (247).

candidus, -a, -um white (109).

canis, -is 3. c. dog (96).

capiō, cēpī, captum 3. I take, capture (291).

Capitōlium 2. n. the Capitol (the citadel of Rome) (50).

captīvus 2. n. captive, prisoner (68).

captīvus, -a, -um captive (101).

captō 1. I catch, try to catch (96).

captus, -a, -um captured (82).

caput, -itis 3. n. head (96).

carcer, -eris 3. m. prison (141).

carō, carnis 3. f. flesh (96).

Carthāgō, -inis 3. f. Carthage (180).

cārus, -a, -um dear (175).

castra 2. n. pl. camp (49).

cauda 1. f. tail (64).

causa 1. f. cause; causā (+gen.) for the sake of (82).

cautē cautiously (233).

cēdō, cessī, cessum 3. I yield; locō cēdō I yield from my position, give ground (155).

celebrō 1. I celebrate (77).

celeritās, -ātis 3. f. rapidity, speed (101).

cēlō 1. I hide (172).

cēna 1. f. dinner (109).

cēnō 1. I dine (240).

centum a hundred (203).

cēra 1. f. wax (142).

Cerēs, -eris Ceres (109).

certāmen, -inis 3. n. contest (116).

cervus 2. m. stag (254).

cibus 2. m. food (109).

circum (+acc.) around (83).

circumdō 1. I surround (63).

circus 2. m. circus, racecourse (43).

cithara 1. f. lyre (116).

cīvīlis, -is, -e civil (378).

cīvis, cīvis 3. c. citizen (88).

cīvitās, -ātis 3. f. state (95).

clādēs, -is 3. f. disaster (160).

clam secretly (90).

clāmō 1. I cry out, cry, exclaim (56).

clāmor, -ōris 3. m. shout, cry (88).

classis, -is 3. f. fleet (186).

clāva 1. f. club (241).

clēmentia 1. f. mercy, clemency (383).

coepī (defective) I began (233).

coerceō 2. I check (373).

cōgō, coēgī, coactum 3. I compel (233).

cohors, -rtis 3. f. division of soldiers (202).

colligō, -lēgī, -lectum 3. I collect (134).

collis, -is 3. m. hill (259).

collocō 1. I place (44).

colō, coluī, cultum 3. I cultivate (76).

colōnia 1. f. colony; colōniam collocō I plant a colony (44).

columna 1. f. column (186).

comes, -itis 3. c. companion (90).

commeō 1. I go, go to and fro (57).

comparō 1. I gain, win (25).

compellō 1. I address (181).

complūrēs, -ēs, -a pl. adj. several (372).

concēdō, -cessī, -cessum 3. I grant, concede (76).

conciliō 1. I win over (148).

concilium 2. n. assembly (167).

concordia -ae 1. f. harmony (343).

concremō 1. I burn (358).

condō, condidī, conditum 3. I put together, compile, found (108).

conficiō, -fēcī, -fectum 3. I finish, put an end to (305).

confirmō 1. I establish, strengthen (43); confirmō animōs I embolden the hearts.

cōniciō, -iēcī, -iectum 3. I throw (312).

coniungō, -nxī, -nctum 3. I join (357).

coniūrō 1. I conspire (36).

cōnor 1. dep. I try (285).

conscendō, -dī, -sum 3. I embark upon (312).

cōnserō, -uī, -tum 3. I join together; manum cōnserō I join battle (154).

cōnsīdō, -sēdī, -sessum 3. I settle (154).

cōnsilium 2. n. plan, stratagem, advice (49).

cōnsōbrīnus 2. m. cousin (285).

cōnstituō, -uī, -ūtum 3. I decide, settle, draw up (116).

cōnsul, -lis 3. m. consul (82).

cōnsulāris, -is, -e consular; (as noun) ex-consul (343).

contemnō, -mpsī, -mptum 3. I despise (187).

contendō, -dī, -tum 3. I march, hasten (227).

contrā (+acc.) against (35).

contrā (adv.) on the other hand, in reply (57).

contumēlia 1. f. insult (83).

convīvium 2. n. feast (77).

convocō 1. I call together, summon (271).

cōpiae 1. f. pl. troops, forces (25).

coquō, coxī, coctum 3. I cook (109).

cornū, -ūs 4. n. horn (135).

corpus, -oris 3. n. body (83).

corripiō, -ripuī, -reptum 3. I seize (293).

corvus 2. m. raven (154).

cōtīdiē daily, every day (83).

Cotta 1. m. Cotta, an officer in the Roman army (24).

crās tomorrow (36).

crēdō, -didī, -ditum 3. (+dat.) I believe (129).

creō 1. I elect, appoint (76).

crēscō, crēvī, crētum 3. I grow (247).

Crēta 1. f. Crete (70).

crīmen, -inis 3. n. charge, accusation (82).

crīnis, -is 3. m. hair (208).

crocodīlus 2. m. crocodile (96).

crūdēlis, -is, -e cruel (214).

crūdēlitās, -ātis 3. f. cruelty (174).

crūdēliter cruelly (51).

cruentō 1. I stain (with blood) (102).

culpō 1. I blame (271).

cum (+abl.) with (33).

cum (+subjunctive) since, when (259).

cūnae 1. f. pl. cradle (234).

cunīculus 2. m. mine (121).

cūr why? (327)

cūria 1. f. Senate-house (76).

currō, cucurrī, cursum 3. I run (154).

currus 4. m. chariot; currūs certāmen chariot-race (148).

cursus 4. m. course (373).

custōdiō 4. I guard (96).

custōs, -ōdis 3. c. guardian, guard (187).

cutis, -is 3. f. skin (116).

damnō 1. I condemn (82).

datus, -a, -um given, offered (162).

dē (+abl.) concerning (63).

dea 1. f. goddess (116).

decem ten; decemvirī Decemvirs (commission of ten men) (108).

decet 2. it suits, it befits (116).

decimus, -a, -um tenth (213).

dēcumbō, dēcubuī 3. I lie down (286).

dēdicō 1. I dedicate (56).

dēdūcō, dēdūxī, dēductum 3. I lead back, escort (186).

dēfendō, -dī, -sum 3. I defend (76).

dēleō, -ēvī, -ētum 2. I destroy (121).

dēligō 1. I fasten (142).

dēligō, dēlēgī, dēlectum 3. I choose (193).

dēmittō, dēmīsī, dēmissum 3. I let down, throw down (96).

dēnique at last, finally (129).

dēns, dentis 3. m. tooth (135).

dēpōnō, dēposuī, dēpositum 3. I lay down (101).

dēscendō, -dī, -sum 3. I descend (187).

dēscīscō, dēscīvī, dēscītum 3. I revolt (214).

dēserō, -uī, -tum 3. I leave, abandon (110).

dēsīderō 1. I feel the want of, I miss (121).

dēspērō 1. I despair (193).

dēsum I fail (313).

dēterreō 2. I discourage, deter (84).

dētrahō, dētrāxī, dētractum 3. I drag off (116).

dēturbō 1. I throw down (134).

deus 2. m. god (56).

dēvoveō, dēvōvī, dēvōtum 2. I devote, consecrate (155).

dexter, -tra, -trum right, on the right hand; dextrum cornū the right wing (of an army); dextrō cornū on the right wing (155).

dextra 1. f. right hand (63).

dīcō, dīxī, dictum 3. I say (134).

dictātor, -ōris 3. m. dictator (101).

diēs 5. m/f. day (213).

difficilis, -is, -e difficult (239).

difficilius (comparative of adverb difficulter) with more difficulty (227).

difficultās, -ātis 3. f. difficulty (186).

dīlaniō 1. I tear to pieces (187).

dīligenter diligently (57).

dīmidium 2. n. half (148).

dīmittō, dīmīsī, dīmissum 3. I dismiss, disband (378).

discēdō, -cessī, -cessum 3. I depart (76).

discindō, discidī, discissum 3. I cut asunder (148).

disciplīna 1. f. discipline (44).

discus 2. m. discus (102).

displiceō 2. I displease (+dat.) (208).

dissensiō, -ōnis 3. f. dissension, strife (147).

disserō, disseruī 3. I discuss (76).

diū for a long time (25).

diūtius adv. compar. for longer, for a longer time (363).

dīves, -itis rich (323).

dīvidō, dīvīsī, dīvīsum 3. I divide (82).

dīvitiae 1. f. pl. riches (115).

dō, dare, dedī, datum 1. I give (84).

doceō, -uī, -tum 2. I teach (122).

dolor, -ōris 3. m. grief (83).

domicilium 2. n. home, dwelling (69).

dominus 2. m. master (267).

domus 4. f. house, home (123); domī at home (95).

dormiō 4. I sleep (90).

dracō, -ōnis 3. m. dragon (135).

dūcō, dūxī, ductum 3. I lead (75).

dulcis, -is, -e sweet (116).

dum (+indicative) while (167).

duo, duae, duo two (202).

duodecim twelve (108).

dūrō 1. I remain, last (31).

dux, ducis 3. c. leader (81).

ē, ex (+abl.) from, out of (36); see also ex.

eburneus, -a, -um of ivory (109).

ēdīcō, ēdīxī, ēdictum 3. I proclaim (161).

edō, ēdī, ēsum 3. I eat (109).

ēgredior, ēgressus (deponent) 3. I go out (306).

ēgregius, -a, -um remarkable, distinguished (317).

eiusmodī of that kind (82).

ēlectrum 2. n. amber (373).

elephantus 2. m. elephant (167).

ēlīdō, -sī, -sum 3. I strangle, smash, dash to pieces (234).

ēloquentia 1. f. eloquence (167).

ēmittō, ēmīsī, ēmissum 3. I send forth (90).

emō, ēmī, ēmptum 3. I buy (115).

ēmolumentum 2. n. advantage (69).

enim (second word in sentence) for (84).

eō (adv.) to there (69).

eō, īre, īvī (iī), itum (irregular) I go (310).

equa 1. f. mare (267).

eques, -itis 3. m. horseman, knight; pl. cavalry (81).

equus 2. m. horse (42); ex equō, ex equīs on horseback (56).

erant were, there were (43).

erat was, there was (50).

errō 1. I wander (26).

est is, there is (70).

et and (34).

et ... et both ... and (45).

etiam also, even (44).

Etruscus 2. m. an Etruscan, inhabitant of Etruria (56).

Etrūria 1. f. Etruria (56).

ex (+abl.) in accordance with (123); see also ē, ex.

excēdō, excessī, excessum 3. I go forth (77).

excitō 1. I rouse, arouse (108).

exemplum 2. n. example (51).

exerceō 2. I exercise (108).

exercitus 4. m. army (127).

exinde from that time (89).

exitium 2. n. ruin, destruction (70).

exitus 4. m. exit (233).

expedītus, -a, -um light-armed (233).

expellō, expulī, expulsum 3. I drive out, expel (254).

explōrō 1. I seek to find (38).

explōrātor, -ōris 3. m. spy, scout (357).

expōnō, exposuī, expositum 3. I put forth; (of troops) I land (trans.) (193).

expugnō 1. I take by storm (25).

exsilium 2. n. exile (115).

exsp̄ectō 1. I await (128).

exsul, -lis 3, c. an exile (113).

exsulō 1. I am an exile, I am in exile (69).

externus, -a, -um foreign (272).

extrā (+acc.) outside (161).

Fabius, -a, -um Fabian (95).

fābula 1. f. fable, story (76).

faciēs 5. f. face (187).

facile adv. easily (179).

facilis, -is, -e easy (166).

faciō, fēcī, factum 3. I do, make (291).

factum 2. n. deed (115).

faelēs, -is 3. f. cat (95).

Faleriī 2. m. pl. one of the chief cities of Etruria, Falerii. (122).

Faliscus 2. m. inhabitant of Faleriī, a Faliscan (122).

fallō, fefellī, falsum 3. I escape the notice of, evade, deceive (134).

falsus, -a, -um false (77).

falx, falcis 3. f. sickle (208).

fāma 1. f. fame, glory (25).

famēs, -is 3. f. hunger, starvation (285).

faucēs 3. f. pl. throat, entrance (233).

fēlix, -īcis adj. fortunate, happy, successful (136).

fēmina 1. f. woman (168).

fera 1. f. wild beast (267).

ferē almost, for the most part (51).

ferīnus, -a, -um of animals (109).

feriō 4. I strike (128).

ferō, ferre, tulī, lātum (irregular) I bear; lēgem ferō I propose a law (310).

fessus, -a, -um weary (90).

fīdus, -a, -um faithful (247).

fīet "yes, sir" (lit., it will be done) (261).

fīlia 1. f. daughter (71).

fīlius 2. m. son (50).

fingō, finxī, fictum 3. I fashion, make (142).

fīniō 4. I finish (147).

fīnis, -is 3. m. end; (plural) boundaries (353).

fīnitimus 2. m. neighbour (43).

fīnitimus, -a, -um neighbouring (69).

fīō, fierī, factus sum (passive of faciō) (irregular) I am made; happen, take place (317).

firmē firmly (227).

flamma 1. f. flame (63).

flectō, flexī, flexum 3. I bend (174).

flōs, flōris 3. m. flower (102).

flūmen, -inis 3. n. river (227).

fluō, flūxī 3. I flow (116).

fluvius 2. m. river (56).

foedus, -a, -um disgraceful (148).

foedus, -eris 3. n. treaty (82).

forma 1. f. shape, form (181).

fortasse perhaps (38).

forte by chance (129).

fortis, -is, -e strong (129).

fortiter bravely (246).

fortūna 1. f. chance, fortune (107).

forum 2. n. forum, market-place (69).

frāter, -tris 3. m. brother (168).

fraus, -dis 3. f. deception (109).

frōns, frondis 3. f. leaf (102).

frōns, frontis 3. f. forehead (306).

frūmentum 2. n. corn (89).

frūstrā in vain (64).

fuga 1. f. flight (63).

fugiō, fūgī 3. I flee (292).

fugō 1. I put to flight, drive (36).

fulmen, fulminis 3. n. lightning (373).

fundus 2. m. farm (101).

Gādēs, -ium 3. f. pl. the town of Cádiz (207).

galea 1. f. helmet (154).
Gallia 1. f. Gaul (44).
Gallicus, -a, -um of or belonging to the Gauls, Gallic (134).
Gallus 2. m. a Gaul (68).
gaudium 2. n. joy (77).
geminus 2. m. twin-brother (43).
gener 2. m. son-in-law (148).
generōsus, -a, -um generous (173).
gēns, gentis 3. f. family, race, nation (95).
genū 4. n. knee (134).
genus, -eris 3. n. kind, sort (362).
Germānī, -ōrum 2. m. pl. Germans (353).
gerō, gessī, gestum 3. I carry on, wage, carry (89).
gigās, (acc. giganta), gigantis 3. m. giant (273).
gladiātor, -ōris 3. m. gladiator (305).
gladius 2. m. sword (71).
glōria 1. f. glory (107).
Graecia 1. f. Greece (26).
Graecus 2. m. a Greek (44).
grātīs for nothing, gratuitously (115).
grātus, -a, -um pleasant, welcome (327).
gravis, -is, -e heavy, serious (159).
graviter seriously (233).
grūs, gruis 3. f. crane (bird) (338).

habeō 2. I have, hold (62).
habitō 1. I dwell (35).
hāmus 2. m. hook (96).
haruspex, -icis 3. m. soothsayer (129).
hasta 1. f. spear (154).
haud not (95).
herba 1. f. herb (181).
hīc (adv.) here (220).
hic, haec, hoc this (179).
hiems, -mis 3. f. winter (377).
Hierosolyma 2. n. pl. Jerusalem (311).
hiō 1. I gape open (221).
Hispānia 1. f. Spain (180).
Hispānī 2. m. pl. inhabitants of Spain (214).
historia 1. f. history (57).
hodiē today (26).
Homērus 2. m. Homer (57).

homō, -inis 3. c. man, human being (116).
honestē adv. honourably.
honor, -ōris 3. m. honour; **in honōre habeō** I hold in honour (84).
hōra 1. f. hour (213).
horrendus, -a, -um horrible (64).
hortor, hortātus 1. deponent. I encourage (284).
hortus 2. m. garden (136).
hostia 1. f. victim (121).
hostis, -is 3. c. enemy (88).
hūmānitās, hūmānitātis 3. f. kindness (215).
hūmānus, -a, -um human (109).
humerus 2. m. shoulder (109).
humī on the ground (102).
hyacinthus 2. m. hyacinth (102).

iaceō 2. I lie (149).
iaciō, iēcī, iactum 3. I throw, cast (378).
iactō 1. I throw (134).
iaculum 2. n. dart (95).
iam now, already (56); **nōn iam** no longer (69).
ibi there (33).
ictus 4. m. blow (174).
Idaeus, -a, -um of Ida; **mōns Idaeus** Mount Ida (168).
īdem, eadem, idem the same (185).
identidem again and again (147).
idōneus, -a, -um suitable (154).
igitur (second word in clause) therefore (358).
ignārus ignorant (287).
ignāvus, -a, -um cowardly, lazy (305).
ignis, -is 3. m. fire (220).
ignōrō 1. I do not know (63).
ignōtus, -a, -um adj. unknown, obscure (363).
ille, illa, illud that (179).
illūminō 1. I light up, illuminate (215).
imāgō, -inis 3. f. refection, image (102).
imber, imbris 3. m. rain (129).
immittō, immīsī, immissum 3. I hurl (102).

immolō 1. I sacrifice (121).

immortālis, -is, -e immortal (109).

immōtus, -a, -um motionless (128).

impediō 4. I hinder, shut in, surround (142).

impendeō, -ndī, -nsum 2. (+dat.) I overhang (160).

imperātor, -ōris 3. m. general, commander-in-chief (81).

imperium 2. n. supreme power, rule (50).

impetus 4. m. attack (127).

implōrō 1. I implore (214).

impōnō, imposuī, impositum 3. I place upon (358).

importō 1. I import (272).

improbus, -a, -um wicked (122).

īmus, īma, īmum lowest; īmus collis the bottom of the hill (323).

in (+abl.) in, on (31).

in (+acc.) into, against (34).

incautē incautiously (95).

incautius (comparative of adverb incautē) more incautiously, too incautiously (233).

incendium 2. n. fire (96).

incendō, -dī, -sum 3. I burn (transitive), set fire to (77).

incidō, incidī, incāsum 3. I fall into (129).

incola 1. c. inhabitant (26).

incolumis, -is, -e safe (135).

inde thence (122).

indicō 1. I show, reveal (64).

indīcō, indīxī, indictum 3. I proclaim; bellum indīcō (+dat.) I declare war on (259).

indignus, -a, -um unworthy; (+abl.) unworthy of (328).

indūtiae 1. f. pl. truce (173).

īnfāns, īnfantis 3. c. infant, child (180).

īnfēlix, -īcis unhappy, unfortunate (102).

īnfīgō, īnfīxī, īnfīxum 3. I fix to (96).

īnfirmitās, -tātis 3. f. weakness (373).

īnfirmus, -a, -um weak (129).

īnformō 1. I train (44).

infundō, īnfūdī, īnfūsum 3. I pour on (227).

ingēns, ingentis huge (94).

ingrātus, -a, -um ungrateful (121).

inhonestus, -a, -um shameful (82).

inimīcus 2. m. enemy (84).

inīquus, -a, -um unfair (134).

iniūria 1. f. wrong, injury (69).

innocēns, innocentis innocent (121).

inopia 1. f. scarcity, want (89).

inquit (defective verb) he says, he said (90).

īnscrībō, īnscrīpsī, īnscrīptum 3. I inscribe (168).

īnsequor, -cūtus 3. dep. I follow up, pursue (364).

īnsidiae 1. f. pl. ambush (95).

īnsigne, -is 3. n. insignia, indication of rank (128).

īnsignis, -is, -e distinguished, remarkable (174).

īnsiliō, -uī 4. I leap (155).

īnsolentia 1. f. insolence (220).

īnsolēns, īnsolentis insolent (134).

īnstituō, -uī, -ūtum 3. I train (161).

īnstruō, -xī, -ctum 3. I draw up (soldiers) (133).

īnsula 1. f. island (70).

intellegō, intellēxī, intellēctum 3. I understand (215).

inter (+acc.) among (26).

intercēdō, -cessī, -cessum (+dat.) 3. I veto (279).

intereā meanwhile (110).

interior, -or, -us inner (181).

interrogō 1. I ask (63).

intersum, -esse, -fuī (+dat.) I take part in (154).

intrā (+acc.) within (95).

intrepidus, -a, -um fearless (63).

intrō 1. I enter (63).

invādō, -sī, -sum 3. I make an attack (155).

inveniō, invēnī, inventum 4. I find (101).

investīgō 1. I search out (64).

invidia 1. f. envy (36).

invītō 1. I invite (136).

ipse, -a, -um himself, herself, itself (185).

īra 1. f. anger (63).

īrātus, -a, -um angry, in anger (128).

ita thus (122).

Ītalia 1. f. Italy (32).

itaque therefore (50).

iter, itineris 3. n. journey (181).

iterum again (36).

iubeō, iussī, iussum 2. I order (234).

iūcundus, -a, -um pleasant (215).

iūdex, -icis 3. c. judge (82).

iūdicium 2. n. judgment (318).

iūdicō 1. I judge (116).

iūgerum 2. n. acre (147).

iugum 2. n. yoke (101).

Iūlius, -iī 2. m. The nomen (family name) of Gaius Julius Caesar (58).

iungō, iūnxī, iūnctum 3. I join; arātrō iungō I yoke (lit. I join to the plough) (135).

Iūnō, -ōnis 3. f. the goddess Juno (134).

Iuppiter, Iovis 3. m. king of the gods, Jupiter (198).

iūs, iūris 3. n. right, privilege, law, justice (89).

iūsiūrandum 2. n. oath (160).

iussum 2. n. order (135).

iussū by the order (141).

iūstē justly (45).

iūstitia, -ae 1. f. justice, fairness (45).

iūstus, -a, -um just (122).

iuvenca 1. f. heifer (221).

iuvenis, -is 3. m. young man (89).

iuvō, iūvī, iūtum 1. I help (352).

Labiēnus 2. m. Labienus, a Roman legate (42).

labor, -ōris 3. m. work, toil (90).

labōrō 1. I work (4).

labyrinthus 2. m. labyrinth (70).

Lacedaemonius, -a, -um Lacedaemonian (102).

lacrima 1. f. tear (83).

lacus 4. m. lake (129).

lānificus, -a, -um of wool-work, of weaving (228).

lapis, -dis 3. m. stone (208).

laqueus 2. m. halter, snare (228).

lātē far and wide (26).

latebrae 1. f. pl. hiding-place (64).

lateō 2. I lie hid (77).

Latīnī 2. m. pl. the Latin people (155).

lātor, -ōris 3. m. proposer (82).

latrō, -ōnis 3. m. robber (174).

latus, -eris 3. n. side; ā latere on the flank (240).

lātus, -a, -um adj. wide (159).

laudō 1. I praise (51).

laus, -dis 3. f. praise (226).

lavō, lāvī, lautum 1. I wash (174).

lectus 2. m, bed (174).

lēgātus 2. m. ambassador, envoy, governor (76).

legiō, -ōnis 3. f. legion (154).

leō, leōnis 3. m. lion (221).

lēx, lēgis 3. f. law (82).

libenter willingly (51).

līber, -era, -erum free (69).

liber, librī 2. m. book (57).

līberālitās, -ātis 3. f. generosity (115).

līberī 2. m. pl. children (220).

līberō 1. I set free (63).

lībra 1. f. a pound (in weight) (134).

licet 2. (impersonal), it is allowed (279).

ligneus, -a, -um wooden (77).

linter, -tris 3. f. boat (273).

liquescō 3. I melt (142).

littera 1. f. a letter (of the alphabet) (102). litterae 1. f. pl. literature, writing (44).

locus 2. m. place; n. pl. region (64).

longitūdō, -inis 3. f. length (174).

longus, -a, -um long; nāvis longa man-of-war (203).

lūdō, lūsī, lūsum 3. I play (102).

lūdus 2. m. game (57).

lūx, lūcis 3. f. light; prīmā lūce at daybreak (101).

magicus, -a, -um magic (135).

magis (comparative of adverb magnopere) more (227).

magister, magistrī 2. m. master, schoolmaster (57).

magister equitum Master of the
  Horse (115).
magistrātus 4. m. magistrate (128).
magnitūdō, -inis 3. f. size, great size
  (154).
magnopere greatly (273).
magnus, -a, -um great (62).
mālō, mālle, māluī I prefer (304).
malum 2. n. evil (188).
mandō 1. I entrust, commit (51).
maneō, mānsī, mānsum 2. I remain,
  wait for (90).
mānēs 3. m. pl. ghosts; dī mānēs
  the gods of the world below (155).
mansuescō, -suēvī, -suētum 3. I
  become tame (267).
manus 4. f. hand, band of men (128).
mare, -is 3. n. sea (120).
māter, mātris 3. f. mother (89).
mātrimōnium 2. n. marriage; in
  mātrimōnium dūcō I marry (148).
mātūrō 1. I hasten (4).
maximē adv. very greatly, chiefly
  (372).
maximus, -a, -um superl. adj. greatest
  (166).
mē me (121).
media turba the middle of the crowd
  (168).
medius, -a, -um middle (101).
melior, -or, -us compar. adj. better
  (337).
membrum 2. n. limb (109).
memorābilis, -is, -e memorable (227).
memoria 1. f. memory; memoriā
  teneō I hold in memory,
  remember (214).
mēns, mentis 3. f. mind (234).
mēnsis, -is 3. m. month (220).
mercātor, -ōris 3. m. merchant (272).
mercātūra 1. f. trade (69).
mercēnārius, -a, -um mercenary
  (193).
mercēs, -ēdis 3. f. reward (382).
Mercurius 2. m. the messenger of the
  gods, Mercury (181).
meus my (136).
mīles, -itis 3. m. soldier (81).
mīlitāris, -is, -e military (161).

mīlitia 1. f. warfare (43).
mīlle (pl. mīlia) thousand (134).
minae 1. f. pl. threats (63).
Minerva 1. f. the goddess Minerva
  (77).
minimus, -a, -um superl. adj. smallest
  (166).
minister, ministrī 2. m. attendant
  (63).
minor, -or, -us compar. adj. smaller
  (166).
minuō, -uī, -ūtum 3. I diminish (298).
mīrus, -a, -um strange, wonderful
  (96).
miser, -era, -erum wretched,
  unhappy (68).
misericordia 1. f. pity (141).
mittō, mīsī, missum 3. I send (76).
moneō 2. I advise, warn (115).
mōns, montis 3. m. mountain, mount
  (89).
monstrum 2. n. monster (64).
mora 1. f. delay (240).
morbus 2. m. illness (292).
morior, mortuus 3. deponent. I die
  (284).
moror 1. (dep.) I delay (297).
mors, mortis 3. f. death (82).
mortuus, -a, -um dead (102).
mōs, mōris 3. m. custom (197).
moveō, mōvī, mōtum 2. I move,
  provoke, rouse (63).
mox soon, later (77).
multitūdō, -inis 3. f. multitude (305).
multus, -a, -um much, many (63);
  multō by much; nec multō post
  and not long afterwards (214).
mūniō 4. I fortify (88).
mūnus, -eris 3. n. a gift (82).
mūrus 2. m. wall (43).
Mūsa 1. f. Muse (116).
mūtō 1. I change, exchange (107).

nam for (95).
nārrō 1. I narrate (76).
nātūra 1. f. nature, natural condition
  (221).
nātus, -a, -um born; novem annōs
  nātus nine years old (214).

nauta 1. m. sailor (372).

nāvigō 1. I sail (25).

nāvis, -is 3. f. ship (90).

-ne a particle showing that the sentence is interrogative; often joined with nōn making nōnne which introduces a question to which the answer "yes" is expected: e.g. nōnne monet? does he not advise? (327)

nē (with subjunctive), let ... not, may ... not, lest (312).

nec see neque

necō 1. I kill (43).

neglegō, neglēxī, neglēctum 3. I neglect (75).

nēmō (acc. nēminem) no one (43).

Neptūnus 2. m. god of the sea, Neptune (198).

neque (nec) nor, and not (50).

neque (nec) ... neque (nec) neither ... nor (50).

nihil nothing (63).

Nīlus 2. m. the Nile (96).

nimis too much (208).

nisi unless (76).

nix, nivis 3. f. snow (227).

nīxus, -a, -um resting on (with abl.) (134).

nō 1. I swim; nandō (gerund) by swimming (383).

nōbilis, -is, -e noble (272).

noctū by night (134).

nōlō, nōlle, nōluī I am unwilling (304).

nōmen, -inis 3. n. name (102).

nōn not (38).

nōndum not yet (69).

nōnne see -ne

nōnnullus, -a, -um some (181).

nōnus, -a, -um ninth (214).

nōs we, us (38).

noster, -tra, -trum our, ours (45).

nostrī our men (62).

notō 1. I mark (102).

nōtus, -a, -um known, well-known (76).

novem nine (214).

novus, -a, -um new (108).

nox, noctis 3. f. night; media nox midnight (101).

nūdō 1. I strip (122).

nūllus, -a, -um none, no (69).

num a particle introducing a question to which the answer "no" is expected: e.g. num monet does he really advise? (327)

numerus 2. m. number (153).

numquam adv. never (153).

nunc adv. now (348).

nūntiō 1. I announce, report, give information (24).

nūntius 2. m. messenger (101).

nūper lately (109).

nympha 1. f. nymph (254).

ō oh! (89)

ob (+acc.) on account of (203).

obligō 1. I bind (214).

obscūrus, -a, -um obscure (292).

obses, obsidis 3. c. hostage (122).

obsideō, obsēdī, obsessum 2. I besiege (77).

occīdō, -dī, -sum 3. I kill (155).

occupō 1. I seize (128).

occurrō, -rrī, -rsum 3. I run to meet (181).

octāvus, -a, -um eighth (227).

octingentī, -ae, -a eight hundred (203).

octō eight (220).

oculus 2. m. eye (64).

odium 2. n. hatred (253).

odor, odōris 3. m. smell (260).

officium 2. n. duty (84).

ōlim once upon a time, formerly, once (31).

omnīnō altogether, wholly (57).

omnis, -is, -e all (94).

onerārius, -a, -um of burden; nāvis onerāria transport ship (203).

onus, oneris 3. n. burden (100).

oppetō, -īvī, -ītum 3. I meet (82).

oppidum 2. n. town (49).

opprimō, -ressī, -ressum 3. I overwhelm (348).

oppugnō 1. I attack, assail (24).

ops, opis 3. f. help; pl. wealth (332).
optimē adv. best (235).
optimus, -a, -um superl. adj. best (167).
opus, operis 3. n. work (228).
ōra 1. f. shore (77).
ōrāculum 2. n. oracle (129).
ōrātiō, -ōnis 3. f. speech (328).
ōrātor, -ōris 3. m. orator (318).
ōrdō, -inis 3. m. rank (161).
orīgō, -inis 3. f. origin (286).
ornō 1. I adorn (180).
ōs, ōris 3. n. mouth, face (102).
ostendō, -dī, -tum 3. I show, set forth (77).
ovis, ovis 3. f. sheep (168).

palūs, -ūdis 3. f. marsh (247).
pānis, -is 3. m. bread (134).
pār, paris equal (272).
parātus, -a, -um prepared (128).
parcō, pepercī, parsum 3. I spare (383).
pāreō 2. (+dat.) I obey (69).
parō 1. I prepare (25).
pars, -tis 3. f. part (109).
partim partly (167).
parum insufficiently, not enough (57).
parvō at a small price (115).
parvus, -a, -um small (62).
pāscō, pāvī, pāstum 3. I feed (168).
pater, patris 3. m. father (120).
patria 1. f. fatherland, native land, own country (35).
patricius, -a, -um patrician (69).
patruus 2. m. uncle (135).
paucus, -a, -um few (100).
paulātim gradually (155).
paulum a little (adverb) (312).
pauper, -eris 3. poor, a poor man (82).
pāx, pācis 3. f. peace (122).
pectus, -oris 3. n. breast (141).
pecūnia 1. f. money (95).
pecus, -oris 3. n. herd, cattle (95).
pedes, -itis 3. m. foot-soldier; (pl.) infantry (227).
pellō, pepulī, pulsum 3. I drive (254).
Pelopidae 1. m. pl. descendants of Pelops (109).

Pelops, Pelopis 3. m. Pelops (109).
penes (+acc.) in the power of; **penes nōs victōria est** the victory rests with us (116).
per (+acc.) through (26).
per by means of (58).
peragō, -ēgī, -actum 3. I accomplish (234).
pereō, -iī, -itum 4. I perish (347).
perfidia 1. f. treachery (173).
perīculum 2. n. danger, risk (49).
perītē skillfully (228).
perītus, -a, -um skilled; (+gen.) skilled in (193).
permoveō, -mōvī, -mōtum 2. I move, stir (254).
permulceō, -sī, -sum 2. I stroke (128).
perpetuus, -a, -um perpetual, continuous (272).
Persae 1. m. pl. Persians (136).
persolvō, -vī, -ūtum 3. I pay (142).
pertinācia 1, f. obstinacy (266).
perturbō 1. I throw into confusion, disturb (147).
pessimus, -a, -um (superlative of malus) worst, very bad (323).
pēs, pedis 3. m. foot (135).
petō, -īvī (-iī), -ītum 3. I seek, ask for (83).
philosophia 1. f. philosophy (44).
pīrāta 1. m. pirate (70).
placeō 2. I please (+dat.) (63).
plānē clearly (378).
plēbēius, -a, -um plebeian (69).
plēbs, plēbis 3. f. the common people (141).
plūrēs, -ēs, -a pl. adj. more (167).
plūrimus, -a, -um superl. adj. most (166).
Plūtō, -ōnis 3. m. Pluto (the god of the lower world) (187).
poena 1. f. punishment; **poenās persolvō** (+ gen.) I pay the penalty of (142).
Poenī 2. m. pl. the Carthaginians (180).
poēta 1. m. poet (187).
pōmum 2. n. apple (168).
pondus, -eris 3. n. weight (134).

Latin-to-English Vocabulary

pōnō, posuī, positum 3. I place (95); pōnō castra I pitch camp (101).

pōns, pontis 3. m. bridge (368).

populāris, -is, -e of the people; populārēs 3. m. pl. the democrats (292).

populus 2. m. the people (50).

porcīnus, -a, -um of or belonging to a pig (96).

porcus 2. m. pig (96).

porta 1. f. gate (77).

portō 1. I carry (83).

portus -ūs 4. m. harbour (382).

possideō, -sēdī, -sessum 2. I own (147).

possum, posse, potuī I am able (297).

post (+acc.), after (43).

posteā afterwards (31).

postrīdiē on the following day (95).

postulātiō, -ōnis 3. f. demand (147).

postulō 1. I demand (70).

potēns, potentis powerful (180).

potentia 1. f. power (70).

potestās, -ātis 3. f. power (259).

potior 4. dep. I obtain, gain possession of (347).

praecipuē especially (57).

praeclārus, -a, -um eminent (162).

praeda 1. f. booty (95).

praeficiō, -fēcī, -fectum (+dat.) 2. I appoint to the command of (292).

praesidium 2. n. garrison, fort (357).

praestō, -itī, -ātum 1. I keep (a promise), fulfil (76).

praesum, -esse, -fuī (+dat.) I command (155).

praeter (+acc.) except, besides (95).

praetor, -ōris 3. m. praetor (147).

pretium 2. n. price, ransom (173).

prīmō at first (38).

prīmum for the first time (64).

prīmus, -a, -um first (69).

prīnceps, -ipis 3. m. chief man (122).

prior, -or, -us compar. adj. former (188).

priusquam before, until (348).

prīvō 1. (+abl.) I deprive (384).

prō (+abl.) for, on behalf of, instead of (50).

probō 1. I approve of (220).

prōcēdō, -cessī, -cessum 3. I advance (154).

procul, far (35).

prōditor, -ōris 3. m. betrayer, traitor (122).

proelium 2. n. battle (167).

proficīscor, profectus sum 3. (dep.) I set out (298).

prōmissum 2. n. promise (76).

prōmittō, -mīsī, -missum 3. I promise (83).

prope (+acc.) near (34).

prope (adv.) almost (33).

properō 1. I hasten (64).

propter (+acc.) on account of, because of (36).

prōrogō 1. I extend (353).

prōsum, -desse, -fuī (+dat.) I benefit; (impersonally) prōdest it is profitable (272).

prōvincia 1. f. province (343).

prōvocō 1. I challenge (116).

proximus, -a, -um next (233).

pūblicus, -a, -um public (82).

pudor, -ōris 3. m. shame (161).

puella 1. f. girl (70).

puer 2. m. boy (55).

pugna, -ae 1. f. battle, fight (24).

pugnātum est (impersonal) it was fought, a battle was fought (233).

pugnō 1. I fight (4).

pulcher, -chra, -chrum beautiful (68).

pulchritūdō, -inis 3. f. beauty (102).

pullus 2. m. chicken (203).

Pūnicus, -a, -um Punic, Carthaginian (186).

pūniō 4. I punish (89).

putō 1. I think (322).

quam than (162).

quam maximē as much as possible (246).

quamquam although (76).

quattuor four (202).

-que and (120).

quercus, -ūs 4. f. oak (382).

quī, quae, quod who, which (110).

quīdam, quaedam, quoddam a certain (193).
quidem indeed (221).
quiēs, -ētis 3. f. rest (372).
quīngentī, -ae, -a five hundred (147).
quīnquāgintā fifty (215).
quīnque five (202).
quīntus, -a, -um fifth (213).
quis, quis, quid who? what? (261).
quō whither (253).
quoad as far as (298).
quod because (50).
quoniam since (63).
quoque also (102).
quotannīs every year (70).
quotiēns as often as, whenever (186).

rādō, rāsī, rāsum 3. I shave (96).
recipiō, recēpī, receptum 3. I take back; mē recipiō I betake myself, go, retreat (298).
rectē adv. rightly, properly (136).
reddō, -idī, -itum 3. I give back, restore (83).
redeō, -īre, -iī, -itum (compound of eō) I return (311).
redimō, -ēmī, -emptum 3. I buy back, ransom (193).
redintegrō 1. I renew (155).
reditus 4. m. return (129).
redūcō, redūxī, reductum 3. I lead back (173).
Regillus Lacus the Lake Regillus (56).
rēgia 1. f. palace (215).
rēgīna 1. f. queen (267).
rēgius, -a, -um royal (148).
regnō 1. I reign (26).
regnum 2. n. royal power, kingdom (82).
regō, rēxī, rēctum 3. I rule (75).
relinquō, relīquī, relictum 3. I leave (76).
reliquus, -a, -um the remaining, the other (77).
remittō, -īsī, -issum 3. I send back, let go (174).
repellō, reppulī, repulsum 3. I drive back (186).
repente suddenly (77).

reportō 1. I carry back; victōriam reportō I win a victory (44).
repudiō 1. I reject (162).
rēs 5. f. thing, affair, matter (146).
rescindō, -cidī, -cissum 3. I break down (368).
reserō 1. I unlock (77).
resistō, restitī 3. (+dat.) I resist (147).
respondeō 2. I answer (63).
responsum 2. n. the answer (63).
rēspūblica, reīpūblicae 5+1. f. state, republic (147).
restinguō, -nxī, -nctum 3. I extinguish (358).
restituō, -uī, -ūtum 3. I restore (280).
rēte, -is 3. n. net (260).
retrō back, backwards (187).
reus 2. m. defendant (84).
revertī (perfect tense), 3. I returned (76).
revocō 1. I recall, summon back (38).
rēx, rēgis 3. m. king (82).
Rhēnus Rhine (300).
Rhodus 2. f. the island of Rhodes (207).
rīma 1. f. cleft (221).
rīpa 1. f. bank (96).
rixa 1. f. quarrel (83).
rogō 1. I ask; lēgem rogō I propose a law (82).
rogus 2. m. pyre (358).
Rōma 1. f. Rome (33).
Rōmānus 2. m. a Roman (42).
Rōmānus, -a, -um Roman (63).
rostrātus, -a, -um beaked (186).
rostrum 2. n. beak (154).
Rubicō, Rubicōnis the Rubicon (378).

saccus 2. m. bag (90).
sacer, sacra, sacrum sacred (89).
sacerdōs, -ōtis 3. m. priest (121).
saepe often (32).
saepiō, -psī, -ptum 4. I block up (160).
saevus, -a, -um fierce (64).
sagitta 1. f. arrow (36).
saltō 1. I jump (43).
saltus 4. m. pass (160).
salūs, -ūtis 3. f. safety (134).
salūtō 1. I greet (292).

sanguis, -inis 3. m. blood (102).
sapiēns, sapientis wise (122).
sapientia 1. f. wisdom (30).
satis enough, sufficiently (69).
saxum 2. n. rock, stone; saxum
    Tarpeium the Tarpeian rock
    (141).
scāla 1. f. ladder (261).
scelus, -eris 3. n. crime (109).
schola 1. f. school (57).
sciō, scīvī, scītum 4. I know (364).
scīpiō, -ōnis 3. m. staff (128).
scrība 1. m. secretary (63).
scrībō, -ipsī, -iptum 3. I write (383).
scrīpta 2. n. pl. writings (57).
scrīptus, -a, -um written (108).
scūtum 2. n. shield (68).
sē himself (reflexive) (174).
secundus, -a, -um second (353).
sed but (44).
sedeō, sēdī, sessum 2. I sit (128).
sella 1. f. chair (128).
semel once (109).
semper always, forever (31).
senātor, -ōris 3. m. senator (101).
senātus 4. m. senate (167).
senex, senis 3. m. old man (83).
sententia 1. f. opinion (337).
sentiō, sēnsī, sēnsum 4. I perceive
    (109).
sepeliō, -elīvī, -ultum 4. I bury (247).
septem seven (70).
septimus, -a, -um seventh (215).
sequor, secūtus sum 3. dep. I follow
    (286).
sermō, -ōnis 3. m. conversation (129).
serō, sēvī, satum 3. I sow (135).
serpēns, serpentis 3. f. serpent (208).
serviō 4. I serve; (+dat) I serve for
    (342).
servō 1. I preserve, save (30).
servus 2. m. slave (57).
sevērus, -a, -um severe (161).
sex six (202).
sextus, -a, -um adj. sixth (357).
sexāgintā sixty (253).
sexiēs adv. six times (363).
sī if (38).
sīc thus (82).

sīcut just as (57).
silva 1. f. wood (77).
similis, -is, -e like (162).
simul at the same time (109).
sine (+abl.), without (141).
singulī, -ae, -a one by one, singly (63).
sinister, -tra, -trum left, on the left
    hand; sinistrum cornū the left
    wing (of an army); sinistrō cornū
    on the left wing (155).
sinō, sīvī, situm 3. I allow (384).
sinus 4. m. fold (220).
sistrum 2. n. rattle (254).
situs 4. m. position, situation (280).
socius 2. m. ally (56).
sōl, sōlis the sun (142).
soleō, solitus sum 2. I am accustomed
    (253).
sōlum (adv.) only (44).
sōlus, -a, -um only, alone (69).
somnium 2. n. dream (155).
sonus 2. m. sound (116).
sōpiō 4. I put to sleep (187).
sordidātus, -a, -um dressed in
    mourning (141).
soror, -ōris 3. f. sister (142).
sors, sortis 3. f. lot (198).
sortītus chosen by lot (71).
Spartānus 2. m. Spartan (57).
spectāculum 2. n. sight, show (128).
spectō 1. I watch (102).
speculum 2. n. mirror (208).
spēlunca 1. f. cave (64).
spēs, speī 5. f. hope (246).
spīrō 1. I breathe (64).
spoliō 1. I despoil (161).
spolium 2. n. spoil (usually pl. spoils)
    (161).
stadium 2. n. stadium (221).
statim at once (63).
statiō, -ōnis 3. f. outpost (154).
statua 1. f, statue (383).
stīpes, -itis 3. m. stake (299).
stō, stetī, statum 1. I stand (352).
sub (+acc. or +abl.) under (101).
subveniō, -vēnī, -ventum 4. (+dat.)
    I come to the help of (247).
succēdō, -cessī, -cessum 3. (+dat.) I
    succeed. (149)

succendō, -dī, -sum 3. I set fire to, kindle (358).

suffrāgium 2. n. vote (89).

sum, esse, fuī I am (153).

summus, -a, -um highest, utmost (193); summus mōns the top of the mountain (227).

sūmō, sūmpsī, sūmptum 3. I take, take up (83).

sunt are, there are (122).

super (+acc. or +abl.) above, over (220).

superbia 1. f. pride (89).

superbus, -a, -um proud, haughty (266).

supercilium 2. n. eyebrow (96).

superō 1. I overcome, defeat (26).

supersum, -esse, -fuī (+dat.) I survive (155).

supplicium 2. n. punishment (63).

surgō, surrēxī, surrēctum 3. I rise (102).

sūs, suis 3. c. pig (181).

suspīciō, -ōnis 3. f. suspicion (82).

sustineō 2. I endure (69).

suus, -a, -um his, her, their (reflexive) (179).

Syracusae 1. f. pl. Syracuse (180).

tabernāculum 2. n. tent (83).

tabula 1. f. tablet (108).

taceō 2. I am silent, say nothing (63).

taeda 1. f. torch (186).

talentum 2. n. a talent (a unit of weight around 30 kg, or that amount of silver, worth about $15,000 in today's money) (203).

tam so (63).

tamen however (38).

tandem at last (26).

tangō, tetigī, tāctum 3. I touch (116).

tantus, -a, -um so great (228).

tardē slowly (233).

taurus 2. m. bull (64).

tēla 1. f. web (228).

tēlum 2. n. weapon (49).

templum 2. n. temple (50).

temptō 1. I attempt, test (63).

tempus, -oris 3. n. time (188).

tendō, tetendī, tentum 3. I stretch (174).

teneō, tenuī, tentum 2. I hold, keep (63).

ter three times, thrice (83).

tergum 2. n. back; ā tergō in the rear (240).

terra 1. f. land, country (36).

terreō 2. I frighten (62).

tertius, -a, -um third (226).

testis, -is 3. c. witness (338).

texō, -uī, -tum 3. I weave (228).

Thetis, (acc. Thetin), Thetidis 3. f. Thetis (168).

tībia 1. f. flute; tībiā lūdō I play on the flute (116).

tībīcen, -inis 3. m. flute-player (186).

timeō 2. I fear, am afraid of (62).

timor, -ōris 3. m. fear (101).

toga 1. f. toga (101).

tot (indecl.) so many (69).

tōtus, -a, -um whole (77).

tractō 1. I drag (64).

trādō, -didī, -ditum 3. I hand over (122).

trahō, trāxī, tractum 3. I drag (77).

trānō I swim across (123).

trāns (+acc.) over, across (43).

transeō, -īre, -īvī (-iī), -itum (compound of eō) I cross (311).

transfīgō, -fīxī, -fīxum 3. I pierce (383).

transfuga 1. c. deserter (173).

trēs, trēs, tria three (202).

tribūnātus 4. m. tribunate, office of tribune (279).

tribūnus 2. m. tribune (76).

tribūtum 2. n. tribute (70).

trīgintā thirty (266).

trīstis, -is, -e sad (161).

triumphus 2. m. triumphal procession (101).

Trōia 1. f. Troy (25).

Trōianus, -a, -um Trojan (77).

trucīdō 1. I massacre (128).

truncus 2. m. trunk (174).

tum then (56).

tumulus 2. m. tomb, mound (83).

turba 1. f. crowd (69).

turpis, -is, -e disgraceful (233).
turris, -is 3. f. tower (140).
tūtus, -a, -um safe (271).
tuus thy, your (136).
tyrannus 2. m. tyrant (50).

ubi when, where (37).
ubique everywhere (51).
Ulixēs the hero Ulysses, known to the Greeks as Odysseus (77).
ūllus, -a, -um any (227).
ultimus, -a, -um last (299).
ultrō of one's own accord, voluntarily (121).
ūnā together (273).
unde whence (227).
undique on all sides (95).
ūnus, -a, -um one (64).
urbs, urbis 3. f. city; often "the city" (i.e. Rome) (89).
ut (with indicative) as (254).
ut (with subjunctive) that, in order that (expressing a purpose) (279).
ut (with subjunctive) that, so that (as a consequence) (272).
uter, utra, utrum which of two (220).
uterque, utraque, utrumque each (of two) (240).
ūtilis, -is, -e useful (161).
ūtor, ūtī, ūsus 3. deponent (+abl.) I use (284).
utrimque on both sides (101).
uxor, uxōris 3. f. wife (89); uxōrī nūntium mittere (+dat.) to send a message (i.e. of divorce) to a wife, i.e. to divorce a wife (328).

vacca 1. f. cow (286).
vae woe!, alas! (134)
vallis, -is 3. f. valley (241).
vastō 1. I lay waste (55).
Veiens, Veientis of, or belonging to Veii, Veientian (95).
vel even, or (96).
vel ... vel either ... or (161).
vellus, -eris 3. n. fleece (135).
velut as if (109).
vendō, -didī, -ditum 3. I sell (272).
venēnātus, -a, -um poisoned (260).

venēnum 2. n. poison (173).
venia 1. f. permission (154).
veniō, vēnī, ventum 4. I come (90).
venter, -tris 3. m. belly (306).
ventus 2. m. wind (90).
verberō 1. I thrash (57).
verbum 2. n. word (101).
vertex, -icis 3. m. top (174).
vertō, -tī, -sum 3. I turn (181).
vester, -tra, -trum you (pl.) (220).
vestīgium 2. n. footprint (64).
vexō 1. I annoy, harass (57).
via 1. f. street, road (96).
viātor, -ōris 3. m. traveller (174).
victor, -ōris 3. m. victor (101).
victōria, -ae 1. f. victory (24).
victus, -a, -um conquered (116).
videō, vīdī, vīsum 2. I see (116).
videor (passive of videō) I seem (240).
vīgintī twenty (203).
vinciō, vīnxī, vīnctum 4. I bind (90).
vincō, vīcī, victum 3. I conquer, defeat (148).
vindex, -icis 3. c. champion (141).
Vindobona 1. f. Vienna (107).
vīnum 2. n. wine (260).
vir 2. m. man, hero (70).
virga 1. f. wand (181).
virtūs, -ūtis 3. f. valour, courage (83).
vīs, vīs (pl. vīrēs, -ium) 3. f. force, violence (141).
vīta 1. f. life (51).
vitium, -i 2. n. vice (384).
vītō 1. I avoid (49).
vīvō, vīxī, victum 3. I live (215).
vīvus, -a, -um living, alive (96).
vix scarcely (128).
vocō 1. I call (148).
volō 1. I fly (142).
volō, velle, voluī I wish (297).
Volscī 2. m. pl. the Volsci, an ancient Italic people.
voluptās, -ātis 3. f. pleasure (215).
volvō, -vī, -ūtum 3. I roll (transitive); (in passive) I roll (intransitive) (323).
vorō 1. I devour (70).
vōs you (38).
vōx, vōcis 3. f. voice (140).

vulnerō 1. I wound (36).
vulnus, -eris 3. n. wound (141).

Zephyrus 2. m. Zephyr (the god of the West Wind) (90).
zōna 1. f. girdle (267).

GRAMMAR NOTES

LETTERS AND LAWS OF SOUND

1 The Latin Alphabet—The Latin Alphabet contains twenty-three letters, with the following signs:—

A B C D E F G H I (J) K L M N O P Q R S T U (V) X Y Z
a b c d e f g h i (j) k l m n o p q r s t u (v) x y z

The letters are divided into:
    1. Vowels (sounding by themselves);
    2. Consonants (sounding with a vowel).

Vowels

2 The pure vowels are a, e, o; i and u are classed as vowels and also as consonants (represented by the signs j and v), because they have both vowel and consonant sound.

3   **Quantity of Vowels**—Each of the five vowels can be either short or long: short when pronounced quickly, like English a in *man*; long when the voice dwells on the sound, as in *far*. A short sound is distinguished by the sign ˘, a long one by the sign ¯: ămō. Thus the five vowels stand for ten different sounds:

ă, ā, ĕ, ē, ĭ, ī, ŏ, ō, ŭ, ū,

The following five words may give an approximate idea of their pronunciation.

quĭnīne, dĕmēsne, păpā, prŏpōse, Zŭlū

A vowel before two consonants is said to be long 'by position.' A vowel before another vowel, or before h followed by a vowel, is nearly always short.

4 Diphthongs—A Diphthong (double sound) is formed by two vowels meeting in one syllable. The diphthongs commonly found in Latin are ae, oe, au; more rarely eu: Caesar moenis, laus, heu. The Diphthongs are always long.

CONSONANTS

5 Mutes (closed sounds)
   Gutturals (throat sounds) { hard, c, (k), qu,
{ soft, g
   Dentals (teeth sounds) { hard, t
{ soft, d
   Labials (lip sounds) { hard, p
{ soft, b
x is really a double letter, standing for cs, gs
y, z and the three Greek aspirates, ch, ph, th, are only found in Greek words as zōna, chlamys, phalanx, theātrum.

Syllables—A syllable consists of one or more letters which can be sounded with a single accent or tone of the voice: ī-lex.

FLEXION

6 Flexion is a change made in the form of a word to show differences of meaning and use.

   The **Stem** is the simplest form of a word in any language before it undergoes changes of Flexion.

   The **Character** is the final letter of the stem.

   The **Root** is the primitive element which the word has in common with kindred words in the same or in other languages.

PARTS OF SPEECH

8 Words are divided into:

Nouns: which are of three kinds:

Substantives, names of persons, places, or things:
Caesar, Caesar; Rōma, Rome; sōl, sun; virtūs, virtue.

Adjectives, which which express the qualities of Substantives:
Rōma antīqua, ancient Rome, sōl clārus, the bright sun.

Pronouns, which stand for a Substantive or Adjective:
ĕgo, I; illĕ, that, he; mĕŭs, my, mine.

Verbs: which express an action or a state:
sōl dat lūcem, the son gives light; Rōma manet, Rome remains.

Particles: which are of four kinds:

Adverbs, which qualify and limit Verbs, Adjectives, and sometimes other Adverbs:
Rōma diū flōruit: nunc minus potēns est.
Rome flourished long; now it is less powerful

Prepositions, which denote the relation of a Noun to other words
in the sentence:
per Rōmam errō, I wander through Rome.

Conjunctions, which connect words, phrases and sentences:
caelum suspiciō ut lūnam et sīdera videam.
I look up to the sky that I may see the moon and stars.

Interjections: words of exclamation: heu, ēheu, alas!

The Parts of Speech are therefore eight:

1. Substantives
2. Adjectives
3. Pronouns
4. Verbs
Which have Flexion.

5. Adverbs
6. Prepositions
7. Conjunctions
8. Interjections
Which are without Flexion except the comparison of Adverbs.

9 The flexion of Nouns is called Declension; that of Verbs, Conjugation.

There is no Article in Latin: lūx may stand for a light, the light, or simply light.

10 Substantives are (a) Concrete: vir, man; mēnsa, table. (b) Abstract: virtūs, virtue. Proper names are names of persons or places: Caesar, Rōma. A Collective Substantive includes many persons or things of the same kind: turba, crowd.

11 Numerals are words which express Number. They are Adjectives, as ūnus, one, duo, two; or Adverbs, as semel, once; bis, twice.

DECLENSION

12 Declension is the change of form which Nouns undergo to show changes of Number and Case.

13 The Numbers are two:
Singular for one person or thing: mēnsa, a table; gēns, a nation.
Plural for more than one: mēnsae, tables; gentēs, nations.

14 The Cases are six:

Nominative, the Subject Case, answering the question Who? or What?

Vocative, the Case of one Addressed.

Accusative, the Object Case, answering the question Whom? or What?

Genitive, answering the question Of whom? or Of what?

Dative, answering the question To whom? or To what?

Ablative, answering the question From whom? or From what?

Examples of the Cases:

Nominative	**sōl lūcet,**	*the sun shines.*
Vocative	**sōl** *or* **ō sōl,**	*o sun.*
Accusative	**sōlem lūcēre videō,**	*I see the sun shine.*
Genitive	**sōlis lūx,**	*the sun's light or the light of the sun.*
Dative	**sōlī lūx additur,**	*light is added to the sun.*
Ablative	**sōle lūx ēditur,**	*light issues from the sun.*

There was in the earliest Latin another Case, called the Locative, answering the question Where?

15   **GENDER**

The Genders are three:

1. Masculine; 2. Feminine; 3. Neuter (neither).

Gender is shown by the form of the word and by its meaning.

Nouns which include both Masculine and Feminine are said to be of Common Gender: cīvis, citizen; auctor, author.

(For Memorial Lines on Gender, see Appendix.)

DECLENSION OF SUBSTANTIVES

16

Substantives are grouped in Declensions according to the Character or final letter of the Stem as follows:

1. First Declension: A-Stems.
2. Second Declension: O-Stems.
3. Third Declension: Consonant Stems and I-Stems.
4. Fourth Declension: U-Stems.
5. Fifth Declension: E-Stems.

17

The Character of the Stem is most clearly seen before the ending -um or -rum of the Genitive Plural.

The Nominative, masculine and feminine, takes s, except in a-Stems, some stems in ro- of the Second Declension, and Stems in s, l, r, n of the Third. The Vocative is like the Nominative, except in the singular of Nouns in -us of the Second Declension.

Neuters have the Accusative like the Nominative in both singular and plural; the plural always ends in a.

FIRST DECLENSION

18

A-Stems.

The Nominative Singular is the same as the Stem.

| | Stem | mēnsă- |
| | | *table, f.* |

	SING.			PLUR.	
Nom.	**mēnsă,**	*a table.*	**mēnsae,**	*tables.*
Voc.	**mēnsă,**	*o table.*	**mēnsae,**	*o tables.*
Acc.	**mēnsam,**	*a table.*	**mēnsās,**	*tables.*
Gen.	**mēnsae,**	*of a table.*	**mēnsārum,**	*of tables.*
Dat.	**mēnsae,**	*to a table.*	**mēnsīs,**	*to tables.*
Abl.	**mēnsā,**	*from a table.*	**mēnsīs,**	*from tables.*

Decline like mēnsa: aquilla; lūna, moon; rēgīna, queen; stella, star.

dea, goddess. filia, daughter, have Dative and Ablative Plural, deābus, filiābus.

Note:—The Locative sing. ends in -ae; the plur. in -īs: Rōmae, at Rome; terrae, on the ground; mīlitae, at the war: Athēnīs, at Athens; forīs, abroad.

19 SECOND DECLENSION.

O-Stems.

The Nominative is formed from the Stem by adding **s**; in neuter nouns, **m**; the Character **ŏ** being weakened to **ŭ**.

In the greater number of nouns whose Stem ends in **ero**, or in **ro** preceded by a mute, the **o** is dropped, and the Nom. ends in **-er**.

Stem	annŏ- *year, m.*		puĕrŏ- *boy, m.*	măgistrŏ- *master, m.*	bellŏ- *war, n.*
SING.					
Nom.	**annŭs,**	*a year.*	**puĕr,**	**magistĕr**	**bellum**
Voc.	**annĕ,**	*o year.*	**puĕr,**	**magistĕr**	**bellum**
Acc.	**annum,**	*a year.*	**puerum**	**magistrum**	**bellum**
Gen.	**annī,**	*of a year.*	**puerī**	**magistrī**	**bellī**
Dat.	**annō,**	*to a year.*	**puerō**	**magistrō**	**bellō**
Abl.	**annō,**	*from a year.*	**puerō**	**magistrō**	**bellō**
PLUR.					
Nom.	**annī,**	*years.*	**puerī**	**magistrī**	**bellă**
Voc.	**annī,**	*o years.*	**puerī**	**magistrī**	**bellă**
Acc.	**annōs,**	*years.*	**puerōs**	**magistrōs**	**bellă**
Gen.	**annōrum,**	*of years.*	**puerōrum**	**magistrōrum**	**bellōrum**
Dat.	**annīs,**	*to years.*	**puerīs**	**magistrīs**	**bellīs**
Abl.	**annīs,**	*from years.*	**puerīs**	**magistrīs**	**bellīs**

Decline like **annus**: amīcus, *friend*; dominus, *lord*; servus, *slave*.

Decline like **puer**: gener, *son-in-law*; socer, *father-in-law*; līberī (plur.) *children*; lūcifer, *light-bringer*; armiger, *armour-bearer*.

Decline like **magister**: ager, *field*; cancer, *crab*; līber, *book*.

Decline like **bellum**: regnum, *kingdom*; verbum, *word*.

The following have some exceptional forms:—

Stem	fīlĭŏ- *son, m.*	vĭrŏ- *man, m.*	deŏ- *god, m.*
SING.			
Nom.	**fīliŭs**	**vĭr**	**deŭs**
Voc.	**fīlī**	**vir**	**deus**
Acc.	**fīlium**	**virum**	**deum**
Gen.	**fīliī** *or* **fīlī**	**virī**	**deī**
D. Abl.	**fīliō**	**virō**	**deō**
PLUR.			
N. V.	**fīliī**	**virī**	**dī (deī)**
Acc.	**fīliōs**	**virōs**	**deōs**
Gen.	**fīliōrum**	**virōrum** *or* **virum**	**deōrum** *or* **deum**
D. Abl.	**fīliīs**	**virīs**	**dīs (deīs)**

Decline like fīlius: Claudius, Vergilius, and many other proper names.

Note.—The Locative singular ends in ī; the plural in īs: humī, on the ground; bellī, at the war; Milētī, at Milētus; Philippīs, at Philippi.

20   THIRD DECLENSION.

Consonant and I- Stems.

The Third Declension contains—
A. Consonant Stems.
Mutes—
(1) Gutturals, c, g.
(2) Dentals, t, d.
(3) Labials, p, b.
Spirant s.
Nasals, n, m.
Liquids, l, r.
B. I- stems.

21 *Syllabus of Consonant Substantives, showing Stem-ending with Nominative and Genitive Singular.*

Stems in Gutturals with x in Nom. for cs or gs.

STEM	NOM. SING.	GEN. SING.	ENGLISH
ăc-	fax, f.	făcĭs	*torch*
āc-	pāx, f.	pācis	*peace*
ĕc-	nex, f.	nĕcis	*death*
ĕc- ĭc-	apex, m.	apĭcis	*peak*
ēc-	vervex, m.	vervēcis	*castrated ram*
ĭc-	fornix, m.	fornĭcis	*arch*
ĭc-	iūdex, c.	iūdĭcis	*judge*
īc-	rādīx, f.	rādīcis	*root*
ōc-	vōx, f.	vōcis	*voice*
ŭc-	dux, c.	dŭcis	*leader*
ūc-	lūx, f.	lūcis	*light*
ĕg-	grex, m.	grĕgis	*flock*
ēg-	rēx, m.	rēgis	*king*
ĕg- ĭg-	rēmex, m.	remĭgis	*rower*
ĭg-	strix, f.	strĭgis	*screech-owl*
ŭg-	coniunx, c.	coniŭgis	*wife* or *husband*
ūg-	wanting	frūgis, f.	*fruit*
ĭv-	nix, f.	nĭvis	*snow*

Stems in Dentals drop t, d, before s in the Nom.

STEM	NOM. SING.	GEN. SING.	ENGLISH
ăt-	ănăs, f.	anătĭs	*duck*
āt-	aetās, f.	aetātis	*age*
ĕt-	sĕgĕs, f.	segĕtis	*corn-crop*
ĕt-	pariēs, m.	pariĕtis	*room-wall*
ēt-	quiēs, f.	quiētis	*rest*
ĕt- ĭt-	mīlĕs, c.	mīlĭtis	*soldier*
ĭt-	căpŭt, n.	capĭtis	*head*
ōt-	nĕpōs, m.	nepōtis	*grandson*
ūt-	virtūs, f.	virtūtis	*virtue*
ct-	lac, n.	lactis	*milk*
ad-	vās, m.	vădis	*surety*
ĕd-	pēs, m.	pĕdis	*foot*
ēd-	mercēs, f.	mercēdis	*hire*
aed-	praes, m.	praedis	*bondsman*
ĕd- ĭd-	obsĕs, c.	obsĭdis	*hostage*
ĭd-	lăpĭs, m.	lapĭdis	*stone*
ōd-	custōs, c.	custōdis	*guardian*
ŭd-	pĕcus, f.	pecŭdis	*beast*
ūd-	incūs, f.	incūdis	*anvil*
aud-	laus, f.	laudis	*praise*
rd-	cŏr, n.	cordis	*heart*

Stems in Labials form Nom. regularly with s.

STEM	NOM. SING.	GEN. SING.	ENGLISH
ăp-	*wanting*	dăpĭs, f.	*banquet*
ĕp- ip-	princeps, c.	princĭpis	*chief*
ĭp-	*wanting*	stĭpis, f.	*dole (a small coin)*
ŏp-	*wanting*	ŏpis, f.	*help*
ĕp- ŭp-	auceps, m.	aucŭpis	*fowler*

Stems in the Spirant s, which, except in vās, becomes r.

STEM	NOM. SING.	GEN. SING.	ENGLISH
ās-	vās, n.	vāsis	*vessel*
aes- aer-	aes, n.	aeris	*copper, bronze*
ēs- ĕr-	Cerēs, f.	Cĕrĕris	*Ceres*
ĭs- ĕr-	cinis, m.	cĭnĕris	*cinder*
ōs- ōr-	honōs, m.	honōris	*honour*
ŏs- ŏr-	tempŭs, n.	tempŏris	*time*
ŭs- ĕr-	opŭs, n.	opĕris	*work*
ūs- ūr-	crūs, n.	crūris	*leg*

Stems in Liquids.

STEM	NOM. SING.	GEN. SING.	ENGLISH
ăl-	sal, m.	sălĭs	*salt*
ell-	mel, n.	mellis	*honey*
ĭl-	mūgil, m.	mūgĭlis	*mullet*
ōl-	sōl, m.	sōlis	*sun*
ŭl-	cōnsŭl, m.	cōnsŭlis	*consul*
ăr-	iubăr, n.	iubăris	*sunbeam*
arr-	far, n.	farris	*flour*
ĕr-	ansĕr, m.	ansĕris	*goose*
ēr-	vēr, n.	vēris	*spring*
ter- tr-	māter, f.	mātris	*mother*
ŏr-	aequŏr, n.	aequŏris	*sea*
ŏr-	ĕbŭr, n.	ebŏris	*ivory*
ōr-	sorŏr, f.	sorōris	*sister*
ŭr-	vultŭr, m.	vultŭris	*vulture*
ūr-	fūr, m.	fūris	*thief*

Stems in Nasals.

STEM	NOM. SING.	GEN. SING.	ENGLISH
ăn-	cănĭs, c.	canis	*dog*
ĕn-	iuvenis, c.	iuvenis	*young person*
ĕn- ĭn-	nōmĕn, n.	nomĭnis	*name*
ŏn- ĭn-	hŏmō, m.	homĭnis	*man*
ōn-	leō, m.	leōnis	*lion*
iōn-	rătiō, f.	ratiōnis	*reason*
rn-	carō, f.	carnis	*flesh*
ĕm-	hiems, f.	hiĕmis	*winter*

A. Consonant Stems

22
(1) Stems in **Gutturals: c, g.**

Stem	iūdĭc- *judge, c.*	rādīc- *root, f.*	rēg- *king, m.*	
SING.				
N. V.	**iūdĕx,**	*a judge*	**rādīx**	**rēx**
Acc.	**iūdĭcem,**	*a judge*	**rādīcem**	**rēgem**
Gen.	**iūdĭcĭs,**	*of a judge*	**rādīcĭs**	**rēgĭs**
Dat.	**iūdĭcī,**	*to a judge*	**rādīcī**	**rēgī**
Abl.	**iūdĭcĕ,**	*from a judge*	**rādīcĕ**	**rēgĕ**
PLUR.				
N. V.	**iūdĭcēs,**	*judges*	**rādīcēs**	**rēgēs**
Acc.	**iūdĭcēs,**	*judges*	**rādīcēs**	**rēgēs**
Gen.	**iūdĭcum,**	*of judges*	**rādīcum**	**rēgum**
Dat.	**iūdĭcĭbŭs,**	*to judges*	**rādīcĭbŭs**	**rēgĭbŭs**
Abl.	**iūdĭcĭbŭs,**	*from judges*	**rādīcĭbŭs**	**rēgĭbŭs**

Decline also: f. vōx, **vōc-**, voice; c. dux, **duc-**, leader; m. grex, **greg-**, flock.

23
(2) Stems in **Dentals: t, d.**

Stem	aetāt- *age, f.*	pĕd- *foot, m.*	căpĭt- *head, n.*
SING.			
N. V.	**aetās**	**pēs**	**căpŭt**
Acc.	**aetātem**	**pĕdem**	**căpŭt**
Gen.	**aetātĭs**	**pĕdĭs**	**căpĭtĭs**
Dat.	**aetātī**	**pĕdī**	**căpĭtī**
Abl.	**aetātĕ**	**pĕdĕ**	**căpĭtĕ**
PLUR.			
N. V.	**aetātēs**	**pĕdēs**	**căpĭtă**
Acc.	**aetātēs**	**pĕdēs**	**căpĭtă**
Gen.	**aetātum**	**pĕdum**	**căpĭtum**
Dat.	**aetātĭbŭs**	**pĕdĭbŭs**	**căpĭtĭbŭs**
Abl.	**aetātĭbŭs**	**pĕdĭbŭs**	**căpĭtĭbŭs**

Decline also: f, virtūs, **virtūt-**, virtue; c. mīles, **mīlit-**, soldier; m. lapis, **lapid-**, stone; f. laus, **laud-**, praise.

24   (3) Stems in **Labials: p, b.**

	Stem	princĕp- princĭp- *chief, c.*

	SING.	PLUR.
N. V.	princĕps	princĭpēs
Acc.	princĭpem	princĭpēs
Gen.	princĭpis	princĭpum
Dat.	princĭpī	princĭpĭbŭs
Abl.	princĭpĕ	princĭpĭbŭs

Decline also: c. forceps, **forcip-**, tongs; m. auceps, **aucip-**, fowler.

25   Stems in the **Spirant s.**

Stems in s do not add s in the Nominative Singular, and generally they change s into r in the other cases.

Stem	flōs- flōr- *flower, m.*	opŭs- opĕr- *work, n.*	crūs- crūr *leg, n.*
SING.			
N. V.	flōs	opŭs	crūs
Acc.	flōrem	opŭs	crūs
Gen.	flōrĭs	opĕrĭs	crūrĭs
Dat.	flōrī	opĕrī	crūrī
Abl.	flōrĕ	opĕrĕ	crūrĕ
PLUR.			
N. V.	flōrēs	opĕrēs	crūră
Acc.	flōrēs	opĕrēs	crūră
Gen.	flōrum	opĕrum	crūrum
Dat.	flōrĭbŭs	opĕrĭbŭs	crūrĭbŭs
Abl.	flōrĭbŭs	opĕrĭbŭs	crūrĭbŭs

Decline also: m. honōs, **honōr-**, honour; n. tempus, **tempor-**, time; n. corpus, **corpor-**, body; n. genus, **gener-**, race; n. iūs, **iūr-**, law.

26   Stems in the **Liquids: l, r.**

Stems in **l, r,** do not take **s** in the Nominative Singular.

Stem	cōnsŭl-	ămŏr-	pătĕr- pătr-	aequŏr-
	consul, m.	*love, m.*	*father, m.*	*sea, n.*
SING.				
N. V.	**cōnsŭl**	**ămŏr**	**pătĕr**	**aequŏr**
Acc.	**cōnsŭlem**	**ămŏrem**	**pătrem**	**aequŏr**
Gen.	**cōnsŭlĭs**	**ămŏrĭs**	**pătrĭs**	**aequŏrĭs**
Dat.	**cōnsŭlī**	**ămŏrī**	**pătrī**	**aequŏrī**
Abl.	**cōnsŭlĕ**	**ămŏrĕ**	**pătrĕ**	**aequŏrĕ**
PLUR.				
N. V.	**cōnsŭlēs**	**ămŏrēs**	**pătrēs**	**aequŏră**
Acc.	**cōnsŭlēs**	**ămŏrēs**	**pătrēs**	**aequŏră**
Gen.	**cōnsŭlum**	**ămŏrum**	**pătrum**	**aequŏrum**
Dat.	**cōnsŭlĭbŭs**	**ămŏrĭbŭs**	**pătrĭbŭs**	**aequŏrĭbŭs**
Abl.	**cōnsŭlĭbŭs**	**ămŏrĭbŭs**	**pătrĭbŭs**	**aequŏrĭbŭs**

Decline also: m. sōl, **sōl-,** sun; m. ōrātor, **ōrātōr-,** speaker; m. carcer, **carcer-,** prison; m. frāter, **frātr-,** brother; n. ebur, **ebor-,** ivory.

27   Stems in the **Nasals: n, m.**

Stems in n do not take s in the Nominative Singular. Stems in ōn, ŏn, drop the **n.**

Stem	leōn-	virgŏn- virgĭn-	nōmĕn- nōmĭn-
	lion, m.	*virgin, f.*	*name, n.*
SING.			
N. V.	**flōs**	**opŭs**	**nōmĕn**
Acc.	**flōrem**	**opŭs**	**nōmĕn**
Gen.	**flōrĭs**	**opĕrĭs**	**nōmĭnĭs**
Dat.	**flōrī**	**opĕrī**	**nōmĭnī**
Abl.	**flōrĕ**	**opĕrĕ**	**nōmĭnĕ**
PLUR.			
N. V.	**flōrēs**	**opĕrēs**	**nōmĭnă**
Acc.	**flōrēs**	**opĕrēs**	**nōmĭnă**
Gen.	**flōrum**	**opĕrum**	**nōmĭnum**
Dat.	**flōrĭbŭs**	**opĕrĭbŭs**	**nōmĭnĭbŭs**
Abl.	**flōrĭbŭs**	**opĕrĭbŭs**	**nōmĭnĭbŭs**

Decline also: m. latrō, **latrōn-,** robber; f. ratiō, **ratiōn-,** reason; m, ordō, **ordin-,** order; c. homō, **homin-,** man; n. carmen, **carmin-,** song.

There is only one Stem in **m**: hiems, -mis, f. winter.

B. I- Stems.

28   (1) Stems with Nom. Sing. in -**is** and in -**er** from Stem **ri**-

Stem	clāvĭ-	cīvĭ-	imbrĭ-
	key, f.	citizen, c.	shower, m.
SING.			
N. V.	**clāvĭs**	**cīvĭs**	**imbĕr**
Acc.	**clāvim, em**	**cīvem**	**imbrem**
Gen.	**clāvĭs**	**cīvĭs**	**imbrĭs**
Dat.	**clāvī**	**cīvī**	**imbrī**
Abl.	**clāvī, ĕ**	**cīvĕ, ī**	**imbrī, ĕ**
PLUR.			
N. V.	**clāvēs**	**cīvēs**	**imbrēs**
Acc.	**clāvīs, ēs**	**cīvīs, ēs**	**imbrīs, ēs**
Gen.	**clāvium**	**cīvium**	**imbrium**
Dat.	**clāvĭbŭs**	**cīvĭbŭs**	**imbrĭbŭs**
Abl.	**clāvĭbŭs**	**cīvĭbŭs**	**imbrĭbŭs**

Decline like **clāvis**: f. **classis**, fleet; f. **nāvis**, ship.

Decline like **cīvis**: m. **amnis**, river; m. **collis**, hill; m. **ignis**, fire; f. **ovis**, sheep; m. **canālis**, canal; m. **aedīlis**, aedile.

Decline like **imber**: f. **linter**, boat; m, **ūter**, leather bottle.

Note.—**vīs**, f., force, Stem **vī**-, is thus declined:

	SING.	PLUR.
N. V.	**vīs**	**vĭrēs**
Acc.	**vim**	**vīrēs**
Gen.	—	**vīrium**
Dat.	—	**vīribŭs**
Abl.	**vī**	**vīribŭs**

29   (2) Stems with Nom. Sing. in -**ēs**:

Stem	nūbĭ-, cloud, f.	
	SING.	PLUR.
N. V.	**nūbēs**	**nūbēs**
Acc.	**nūbem**	**nūbēs, īs**
Gen.	**nūbĭs**	**nūbium**
Dat.	**nūbī**	**nūbĭbŭs**
Abl.	**nūbĕ**	**nūbĭbŭs**

Decline also: f. **mōlēs**, pile; f. **rūpēs**, crag.

30   (3) Stems which have two consonants (a liquid or nasal and a mute) before **i**, and drop **i** before the **s** in the Nom. Sing: :

Stem	montĭ-	urbĭ-
	mountain, m.	*city, f.*
SING.		
N. V.	**mons**	**urbs**
Acc.	**montem**	**urbem**
Gen.	**montĭs**	**urbĭs**
Dat.	**montī**	**urbī**
Abl.	**montĕ**	**urbĕ**
PLUR.		
N. V.	**montēs**	**urbēs**
Acc.	**montēs, īs**	**urbēs, īs**
Gen.	**montium**	**urbium**
Dat.	**montĭbŭs**	**urbĭbŭs**
Abl.	**montĭbŭs**	**urbĭbŭs**

Decline also: m. dens, **denti**-, tooth; f. arx, **arci**-, citadel; f. ars, **arti**-, art; f. stirps, **stirpi**-, stem; f. frons, **fronti**-, forehead; f. frons, **frondi**-, leaf; f. bidens, **bidenti**-, sheep, but m. fork; c. parens, **parenti**-, parent.

31   (4) Neuter Stems with Nom. Sing. in -**ĕ**, -**ăl**, -**ăr**:

These either change **ĭ** into **ĕ** in the Nom. Sing. or drop the vowel and shorten the final syllable.

Stem	mărĭ-	ănĭmālĭ-	calcārĭ-
	sea, n.	*animal, n.*	*spur, n.*
SING.			
N. V. Acc.	**mărĕ**	**ănĭmăl**	**calcăr**
Gen.	**mărĭs**	**ănĭmālĭs**	**calcārĭs**
Dat. Abl.	**mărī**	**ănĭmālī**	**calcārī**
PLUR.			
N. V. Acc.	**mărĭă**	**ănĭmālĭă**	**calcārĭă**
Gen.	**mărium**	**ănĭmālium**	**calcārium**
Dat. Abl.	**mărĭbŭs**	**ănĭmālĭbŭs**	**calcārĭbŭs**

Decline also: conclāve, *room*; cubīle, *couch*; rētĕ, *net* (abl. sing. ĕ); tribūnal, *tribunal*; exemplar, *pattern*.

Note.—The Locative sing. ends in -ī or -ĕ; the plural in -ĭbus: rūrī or rūrĕ, *in the country*; vespĕrī or vespĕrĕ, *in the evening*; Carthăginī or Carthăginĕ, *at Carthage*; Gādibus, *at Cádiz*.

The following have exceptional forms:—Iuppiter, *Jupiter*; and sĕnex, *old man*.

		SING.	PLUR.
N. V.	**Iuppiter**	**sĕnex**	**sĕnēs**
Acc.	**Iŏvem**	**sĕnem**	**sĕnēs**
Gen.	**Iŏvĭs**	**sĕnĭs**	**sĕnum**
Dat.	**Iŏvī**	**sĕnī**	**sĕnĭbŭs**
Abl.	**Iŏvĕ**	**sĕnĕ**	**sĕnĭbŭs**

FOURTH DECLENSION.

33

U- Stems.

The Nominative of masculine and feminine nouns is formed by adding **s**; neuters have the plain Stem with **ū** (long).

	Stem	**grădŭ-** step, m.		**gĕnū-** knee, n.
SING.				
Nom.		**grădus**	*a step*	**gĕnū**
Voc.		**grădus**	*o step*	**gĕnū**
Acc.		**grădum**	*a step*	**gĕnū**
Gen.		**grădūs**	*of a step*	**gĕnūs**
Dat.		**grăduī**	*to a step*	**gĕnū**
Abl.		**grădū**	*from a step*	**gĕnū**
PLUR.				
Nom.		**grădūs**	*steps*	**gĕnŭă**
Voc.		**grădūs**	*o steps*	**gĕnŭă**
Acc.		**grădūs**	*steps*	**gĕnŭă**
Gen.		**grăduum**	*of steps*	**gĕnuum**
Dat.		**grădĭbŭs**	*to steps*	**gĕnĭbŭs**
Abl.		**grădĭbŭs**	*from steps*	**gĕnĭbŭs**

Decline like **gradus**: fructus, *fruit*; senātus, *senate*; manus, f., *hand*.
Decline like **genū**: cornū, *horn*; verū, *spit* (dat. abl. plur. -ŭbus).

‎‎

34 Domus, f., is thus declined:

	SINGULAR.	PLURAL.
N. V.	dŏmŭs	dŏmūs
Acc.	dŏmum	dŏmūs *or* dŏmōs
Gen.	dŏmūs	dŏmōrum *or* dŏmuum
Dat.	dŏmuī *or* dŏmō	dŏmĭbŭs
Abl.	dŏmō	dŏmĭbŭs

The Locative domī, *at home*, is often used.

FIFTH DECLENSION.

35 ## E- Stems.

The Nominative Singular is formed by adding **s** to the Stem.

Stem   rē-, *thing*, f.

	SINGULAR.		PLURAL.	
Nom.	rēs	*a thing*	rēs	*things*
Voc.	rēs	*o thing*	rēs	*o things*
Acc.	rem	*a thing*	rēs	*things*
Gen.	rĕī	*of a thing*	rērum	*of things*
Dat.	rĕī	*to a thing*	rēbŭs	*to things*
Abl.	rē	*from a thing*	rēbŭs	*from things*

Decline like **rēs**: diēs, *day* (gen. dat., diēī); aciēs, *line of battle*; faciēs, *face*; seriēs, *series*; speciēs, *form*; spēs, *hope*; fidēs, *faith*; glaciēs, *ice*; merīdiēs, *noon*.

Rēs and diēs are the only nouns used in the Gen., Dat., and Abl. Plural. Fidēs, glaciēs, merīdiēs, are singular only.

Note.—The Locative ends in -ē.

Rēspublica, *the public interest, the republic, the State*, is declined in both its parts:

	SINGULAR.	PLURAL.
N. V.	rēspublică	rēspublicae
Acc.	rempublicam	rēspublicās
Gen.	reipublicae	rērumpublicārum
Dat.	reipublicae	rēbŭspublicīs
Abl.	rēpublică	rēbŭspublicīs

FIFTH DECLENSION.

36 Many nouns are found only in the Singular; these are chiefly proper names and words of general meaning: as

iūstitia,	*justice.*	humus,	*ground.*
vesper,	*evening.*	aurum,	*gold.*

37 Many nouns are used only in the Plural:

arma,	*arms.*	īnsidiae,	*ambush.*
artūs,	*limbs.*	līberī,	*children.*
cūnae,	*cradle.*	mānēs,	*departed spirits.*
dīvitiae,	*riches.*	moenia,	*town walls.*
fastī,	*annals.*	nūgae,	*trifles.*
fēriae,	*holidays.*	penātēs,	*household gods.*
indūtiae,	*truce.*	tenebrae,	*darkness.*

And names of towns, days, festivals: Athēnae, Delphī, calendae, Bacchānālia.

38 Some words have a different meaning in Singular and Plural:

SINGULAR		PLURAL	
aedēs,	*temple.*	aedēs,	*house.*
auxilium,	*help.*	auxilia,	*allied forces.*
carbasus, f.,	*linen.*	carbasa, n.	*sails.*
castrum,	*fort.*	castra,	*camp.*
cēra,	*wax.*	cērae,	*wax tablet.*
cōpia,	*plenty.*	cōpiae,	*forces.*
fīnis,	*end.*	fīnēs,	*boundaries.*
grātia,	*favour.*	grātiae,	*thanks.*
impendīmentum,	*hindrance.*	impedīmenta,	*baggage.*
littera,	*letter of the alphabet.*	litterae,	*epistle, literature.*
lūdus,	*play.*	lūdī,	*public games.*
opem (acc.),	*help.*	opēs,	*wealth.*
opera,	*labour.*	operae,	*work-people.*
sāl,	*salt.*	salēs,	*wit.*

39 Some nouns have two forms of Declension:

pecus, pecǒris, n., *cattle*; pecus, pecǔdis, f., *a single head of cattle.*
plebs, plēbis, 3. f.; plēbēs, plēbeī, 5. f., *the common people.*

40 In many nouns some of the cases are wanting; thus:

	feast, f.	*fruit, f.*	*help, f.*	*prayer, f.*	*change, f.*
N. V.	—	—	—	—	—
Acc.	dăpem	frūgem	ŏpem	prĕcem	vĭcem
Gen.	dăpĭs	frūgĭs	ŏpĭs	—	vĭcĭs
Dat.	dăpī	frūgī	—	prĕ	—
Abl.	dăpĕ	frūgĕ	ŏpĕ	prĕcĕ	vĭcĕ

These have full plural -ēs, -um, -ibus, except Gen. vicium.

41 Some have only Nom. Acc. S.: fās, *right*, nĕfās, *wrong*, instar, *likeness, size*, opus, *need*, nihil, *nothing*.

DECLENSION OF ADJECTIVES

42 Adjectives are declined by Gender, Number and Case.

43 Adjectives of three endings in -us, -a, -um or -er, -a, -um are declined like Substantives of the Second and First Declension, O- and A- Stems.

Stem	bŏnŏ-	bŏnă- *good.*	bŏnŏ-
SING.			
Nom.	**bŏnŭs**	**bŏnă**	**bŏnum**
Voc.	**bŏnĕ**	**bŏnă**	**bŏnum**
Acc.	**bŏnum**	**bŏnam**	**bŏnum**
Gen.	**bŏnī**	**bŏnae**	**bŏnī**
Dat.	**bŏnō**	**bŏnae**	**bŏnō**
Abl.	**bŏnō**	**bŏnā**	**bŏnō**
PLURAL.			
Nom.	**bŏnī**	**bŏnae**	**bŏnă**
Voc.	**bŏnī**	**bŏnae**	**bŏnă**
Acc.	**bŏnōs**	**bŏnās**	**bŏnă**
Gen.	**bŏnōrum**	**bŏnārum**	**bŏnōrum**
Dat.	**bŏnīs**	**bŏnīs**	**bŏnīs**
Abl.	**bŏnīs**	**bŏnīs**	**bŏnīs**

Decline also: cārus, *dear*; dūrus, *hard*; malus, *bad*; magnus, *great*; parvus, *small*; dubius, *doubtful*.

Stem	tĕnĕrŏ-	tĕnĕră- *tender.*	tĕnĕrŏ-
SING.			
Nom.	tĕnĕr	tĕnĕră	tĕnĕrum
Voc.	tĕnĕr	tĕnĕră	tĕnĕrum
Acc.	tĕnĕrum	tĕnĕram	tĕnĕrum
Gen.	tĕnĕrī	tĕnĕrae	tĕnĕrī
Dat.	tĕnĕrō	tĕnĕrae	tĕnĕrō
Abl.	tĕnĕrō	tĕnĕrā	tĕnĕrō
PLURAL.			
Nom.	tĕnĕrī	tĕnĕrae	tĕnĕră
Voc.	tĕnĕrī	tĕnĕrae	tĕnĕră
Acc.	tĕnĕrōs	tĕnĕrās	tĕnĕră
Gen.	tĕnĕrōrum	tĕnĕrārum	tĕnĕrōrum
Dat.	tĕnĕrīs	tĕnĕrīs	tĕnĕrīs
Abl.	tĕnĕrīs	tĕnĕrīs	tĕnĕrīs

Decline also: asper, *rough*; lacer, *torn*; līber, *free*; miser, *wretched*; prosper, *prosperous*; frūgifer, *fruit-bearing*; plūmiger, *feathered*, and other compunds of ferō and gerō; also satur, satūra, satūrum, *full.*

Stem	nĭgrŏ-	nĭgră- *black.*	nĭgrŏ-
SING.			
Nom.	nĭger	nĭgră	nĭgrum
Voc.	nĭger	nĭgră	nĭgrum
Acc.	nĭgrum	nĭgram	nĭgrum
Gen.	nĭgrī	nĭgrae	nĭgrī
Dat.	nĭgrō	nĭgrae	nĭgrō
Abl.	nĭgrō	nĭgrā	nĭgrō
PLURAL.			
Nom.	nĭgrī	nĭgrae	nĭgră
Voc.	nĭgrī	nĭgrae	nĭgră
Acc.	nĭgrōs	nĭgrās	nĭgră
Gen.	nĭgrōrum	nĭgrārum	nĭgrōrum
Dat.	nĭgrīs	nĭgrīs	nĭgrīs
Abl.	nĭgrīs	nĭgrīs	nĭgrīs

Decline also: aeger, *sick*; āter, *jet-black*; pulcher, *beautiful*; ruber, *red*; sacer, *sacred.*

44 Adjectives of two endings and of one ending in the Nominative Singular are declined like Substantives of the Third Declension.

45 (1) Adjectives with Nominative Singular in -is, Masc. and Fem.; in -e Neuter: I- stems.

Stem   trīstĭ-, *sad.*

	SINGULAR.		PLURAL.	
	M. F.	N.	M. F.	N.
N. V.	trīstĭs	trīstĕ	trīstēs	trīstiă
Acc.	trīstem	trīstĕ	trīstēs, -īs	trīstiă
Gen.	trīstĭs	trīstĭs	trīstium	trīstium
D., Abl.	trīstī	trīstī	trīstĭbŭs	trīstĭbŭs

Decline also: brevis, *short*; omnis, *all*; aequālis, *equal*; hostīlis, *hostile*; facilis, *easy*; illustris, *illustrious*; lūgubris, *mournful.*

Some stems in ri-, form the Masc. Nom. Sing. in -er:

Stem   ācrĭ-, *keen.*

SING.	M.	F.	N.
N. V.	ācer	ācrĭs	ācrĕ
Acc.	ācrem	ācrem	ācrĕ
Gen.	ācrĭs	ācrĭs	ācrĭs
Dat.	ācrī	ācrī	ācrī
Abl.	ācrī	ācrī	ācrī

PLUR.	M.	F.	N.
N. V.	ācrēs	ācrēs	ācriă
Acc.	ācrēs, -īs	ācrēs, -īs	ācriă
Gen.	ācrium	ācrium	ācrium
D., Abl.	ācrĭbŭs	ācrĭbŭs	ācrĭbŭs

Decline like acer the following: celeber, *famous*; salūber, *healthy*; alacer, *brisk*; volucer, *winged*; campester, *level*; equester, *equestrian*; pedester, *pedestrian*; paluster, *marshy*; puter, *crumbling*; with September, Octōber November, December, masculine only.

(2) Adjectives with Nom. Sing. the same for all genders:

46 (a) I- Stems.

Stem   fēlĭcĭ-, *happy.*

	SINGULAR.		PLURAL.	
	M. F.	N.	M. F.	N.
N. V.	fēlix	fēlix	fēlīcēs	fēlīciă
Acc.	fēlīcem	fēlix	fēlīcēs, -īs	fēlīciă
Gen.	fēlīcĭs	fēlīcĭs	fēlīcium	fēlīcium
Dat.	fēlīcī	fēlīcī	fēlīcĭbŭs	fēlīcĭbŭs
Abl.	fēlīcī, -ĕ	fēlīcī, -ĕ	fēlīcĭbŭs	fēlīcĭbŭs

Stem   ingentĭ-, *huge.*

	SINGULAR.		PLURAL.	
	M. F.	N.	M. F.	N.
N. V.	ingēns	ingēns	ingentēs	ingentiă
Acc.	ingentem	ingēns	ingentēs, -īs	ingentiă
Gen.	ingentĭs		ingentium	
Dat.	ingentī		ingentĭbŭs	
Abl.	ingentī, -ĕ		ingentĭbŭs	

Decline like **fēlix**: audax, audāci-, *bold*; duplex, duplici-, *double*; vēlox, velōci-, *swift.*

Decline like **ingēns**: amans, amanti-, *loving*; sapiens, sapienti-, *wise*; concors, concordi-, *agreeing*; par, pari-, *like.*

47 (b) Consonant Stems, except pauper, form the Nominative Singular in **s**.

Stem   dīvĭt-, *happy.*

	SINGULAR.	PLURAL.
N. V.	dīvĕs	dīvĭtēs
Acc.	dīvĭtem	dīvĭtēs
Gen.	dīvĭtĭs	dīvĭtum
Dat.	dīvĭtī	dīvĭtĭbŭs
Abl.	dīvĭtĕ	dīvĭtĭbŭs

Decline like **dīves**: pauper, pauper-, *poor*; sospes, sospit-, *safe*; superstes, superstit-, *surviving*; deses, desid-, *slothful*; reses, resid-, *reposing*; compos, compot-, *possessing*; caelebs, caelib-, *unmarried*; pubes, puber-, *full-grown*; vetus, veter-, *old.*

Dīves has a contracted form dis, acc. ditem, etc.; with abl. sing. diti and neut. plur. dītia; gen. plur. ditium. Dīves and vetus are used as net. acc. sing. Vetus has neut. plur. vetera. The rest have no neuter forms.

Comparison of Adjectives

48 Adjectives are compared in three degrees.

    (1) Positive: **dūrus**, *hard.*   **trīstis**, *sad.*
    (2) Comparative: **dūriŏr**, *harder.*   **trīstiŏr**, *sadder.*
    (3) Superlative: **dūrissimus**, *hardest.* **trīstissimus**, *saddest.*

The Positive is the adjective itself expressing the quality; the Comparative expresses a greater degree; the Superlative expresses a very great, or the greatest, degree of the quality.

The Comparative is formed from the Positive by adding the suffix **-ior** to the last consonant of the Stem; the Superlative generally by adding **-issimus** to the last consonant of the Stem.

Stem	Positive	Comparative	Superlative
dūr-o-	dūrus	dūr-iŏr	dūr-issimus
trīst-i-	trīstis	trīst-iŏr	trīst-issimus
audāc-i-	audax, *bold*	audāc-iŏr	audāc-issimus

49 The Comparative is declined as follows:

	SINGULAR.		PLURAL.	
	M. F.	N.	M. F.	N.
N. V.	**trīstior**	**trīstius**	**trīstiŏrēs**	**trīstiŏră**
Acc.	**trīstiŏrem**	**trīstius**	**trīstiŏrēs**	**trīstiŏră**
Gen.	**trīstiŏrĭs**		**trīstiŏrum**	
Dat.	**trīstiŏrī**		**trīstiŏrĭbŭs**	
Abl.	**trīstiŏrě, -ī***		**trīstiŏrĭbŭs**	

*The Ablative in -ī is rare.

50 The Superlative is declined from o- and a- Stems, like bonus.
    Adjectives with Stems in ro-, ri-, form the Superlative by doubling the last consonant of the Stem and adding -imus. Words like niger insert e before r in the Superlative.

Stem	Positive	Comparative	Superlative
tener-o-	tener	tenerior	tenerrimus
nigr-o-	niger	nigrior	nigerrimus
celer-i-	celer	celerior	celerrimus
veter-i-	vetus (veter)	vetustior (veterior)	veterrimus

Six adjectives with Stems in **ĭli-** also form the Superlative by dou-
bling the last consonant of the Stem and adding -**imus**.

facilis, *easy.*	similis, *like.*	gacilis, *slender.*
difficilis, *difficult.*	dissimilis, *unlike.*	humilis, *lowly.*

facil-i-	facilis	facilior	facillimus

Irregular Comparison

51 (1) Some Comparatives and Superlatives are formed from Stems
distinct from that of the Positive:

Positive		Comparative		Superlative	
bonus,	*good.*	melior,	*better.*	optimus,	*best.*
malus,	*bad.*	pēior,	*worse.*	pessimus,	*worst.*
parvus,	*small.*	minor,	*less.*	minimus,	*least.*
multus,	*much.*	plūs,	*more.*	plūrimus,	*most.*
magnus,	*great.*	māior,	*greater.*	maximus,	*greatest.*

Plūs in the Sing. is neut. only; Gen. plūris. Its Plural is: Nom. Acc.
plūrēs (m. f.), plūra (n.); Gen. plūrium; D. Abl. plūribus.

Senex, *old,* has Comp. senior *or* nātu māior; Superl. nātu
maximus.

Iuvenis, *young,* has Comp. iūnior *or* nātu minor; Superl. nātu
minimus.

Note:—senior, iūnior are not used as true comparatives of senex,
iuvenis, but with the meaning old rather than young, and young,
rather than old.

52 (2) Adjectives compounded with -**dĭcus**, -**fĭcus**, -**vŏlus** (from
dīcō, faciō, volō), form the Comparative and Superlative as if from
participles in -**ens**.

Positive	Comparative	Superlative
maledicus, *evil-speaking.*	maledīcentior	maledīcentissimus
beneficus, *beneficent.*	beneficentior	beneficentissimus
benevolus, *well-wishing.*	benevolentior	benevolentissimus

53 (2) Adjectives in **-eus**, **-ius**, **-uus** are generally compared by using the adverbs magis, *more*, maxime, *most*, with the Positive: dubius, *doubtful*, magis dubius, *more doubtful*, maxime dubius, *most doubtful*.

54 Some Comparatives and Superlatives denoting relations of place have no Positive, but correspond to Adverbs from the same Stem.

	Comparative	Superlative
extrā (adv.), *outside.*	extĕrior	extrēmus, extimus
intrā (adv.), *within.*	intĕrior	intimus
suprā (adv.), *above.*	supĕrior	suprēmus, summus
infrā (adv.), *below.*	infĕrior	infimus, īmus
citrā (adv.), *on this side.*	citĕrior	citimus
ultrā (adv.), *beyond.*	ultĕrior	ultimus
prae (prep.), *before.*	prior	prīmus, *first.*
post (prep.), *after.*	postĕrior	postrēmus, *last.*
prope (adv.), *near.*	propior	proximus

Comparison of Adverbs

55 Adverbs derived from adjectives and ending in -ē, -ō, -ter, and rarely -ĕ, form Comparative in **-ius**, Superlative in **-issimē**.

Adjective	Adverb	Comparative	Superlative
dignus, *worthy.*	dignē, *worthily.*	dignius	dignissimē
tūtus, *safe.*	tūtō, *safely.*	tutius	tutissimē
fortis, *brave.*	fortiter, *bravely.*	fortius	fortissimē
facilis, *easy.*	facilĕ, *easily.*	facilius	facillimē

56 Irregular Comparison has corresponding forms in Adverbs.

Adverb	Comparative	Superlative
benĕ, *well.*	melius	optimē
malĕ, *ill.*	peïus	pessimē
paullum, *little.*	minus	minimē
multum, *much.*	plūs	plūrimum
magnŏpĕre, *greatly.*	magis	maximē
diū, *long.*	diutius	diutissimē
intus, *within.*	intĕrius	intimē

Magis means *more* in degree; plūs, *more* in quantity.

NUMERALS

57 Numeral Adjectives are of three kinds:
1. Cardinals; answering the question, *How many?*
2. Ordinals; answering the question, *Which in order of number?*
3. Distributives; answering the question, *How many each?*

58 Numeral Adverbs answer the question, *How many times?*

Unus, from **o-** and **a-** Stems, is declined as follows:

	SING.				PLUR.	
Nom.	ūnus	ūna	ūnum	ūni	ūnae	ūnă
Acc.	ūnum	ūnam	ūnum	ūnōs	ūnās	ūnă
Gen.	ūnius	ūnius	ūnius	ūnōrum	ūnārum	ūnōrum
Dat.	ūnī	ūnī	ūnī	ūnīs	ūnīs	ūnīs
Abl.	ūnō	ūnā	ūnō	ūnīs	ūnīs	ūnīs

Duo is an o- Stem, and trēs an i- Stem.

	M.	F.	N.	M. F.	N.
Nom.	duŏ	duae	duŏ	trēs	tria
Acc.	duōs	duās	duŏ	trēs	tria
Gen.	duōrum	duārum	duōrum	tria	tria
D. Abl.	duōbŭs	duābŭs	duōbŭs	trĭbŭs	trĭbŭs

Decline like **duŏ**: ambō, *both*.

The Cardinals from quattuor to centum are indeclinable. Hundreds from *two to nine hundred* are **o-** and **a-** Stems, ducentī, ducentae, ducenta. Mille (*a thousand*) is indeclinable; but mīlia (*thousands*) is declined like tria.

In Compound Numbers above twenty, the order is the same as in English. Either the smaller number with **et** comes first, or the larger without **et**: septem et trīginta, *seven and thirty*, or trīginta septem, *thirty-seven*. Ūnus usually stands first: ūnus et vīgintī, *twenty-one*. In numbers above a hundred the larger comes first, with or without **et**.

Thousands are expressed by putting (1) the numeral adverbs bis, ter, etc., before mille, which is used as an adjective: bis mille; or (2) cardinal numbers before mīlia: duo mīlia.

Mīlia is used as a neuter substantive, and followed by a gentive: duo mīlia hominum, *two thousand men*.

59

Arabic Numerals	Roman Numerals	Cardinals; answering the question Quot? *how many?*	Ordinals; answering the question Quotus? *which in order of number?* m. -us, f. -a, n. -um.	Distributives; answering the question Quotēnī? *how many each?* m. -ī, f. -ae, n. -ă.	Numeral Adverbs; answering the question Quotiens? *how many times?*
1	I	ūnus	primus (prior), *first*	singŭlī, *one each*	semel, *once*
2	II	duo	secundus (alter), *second*	bīnī, *two each*	bis, *twice*
3	III	trēs	tertius, *third*, etc.	ternī, or trīnī, *three each*, etc.	ter, *three times, etc.*
4	IIII or IV	quattuor	quartus	quaternī	quater
5	V	quinque	quintus	quīnī	quinquiens
6	VI	sex	sextus	sēnī	sexiens
7	VII	septem	septimus	septēnī	septiens
8	VIII or IIX	octo	octāvus	octōnī	octiens
9	VIIII or IX	nŏvem	nōnus	novēnī	noviens
10	X	dĕcem	decimus	dēnī	deciens
11	XI	undĕcim	undecimus	undēnī	undeciens
12	XII	duodecim	duodecimus	duodēnī	duodeciens
13	XIII	tredecim	tertius decimus	ternī dēnī	tredeciens
14	XIIII or XIV	quattuordecim	quartus decimus	quaternī dēnī	quattuordeciens
15	XV	quindecim	quintus decimus	quīnī dēnī	quindeciens
16	XVI	sēdecim	sextus decimus	sēnī dēnī	sēdeciens
17	XVII	septemdecim	septimus decimus	septēnī dēnī	septiesdeciens
18	XVIII or XIIX	{ duŏdēvigintī octodecim	duodēvicensimus	duodēvīcēnī	duodēviciens

316

19	XVIIII or XIX	{ ūndēvīgintī { novendecim	ūndēvīcēnsimus	ūndēvīcēnī	ūndēvīciens
20	XX	vīgintī	vīcēnsimus	vīcēnī	vīciens
21	XXI	ūnus et vīgintī	ūnus et vīcēnsimus	vīcēnī singulī	semel et vīciens
22	XXII	duo et vīgintī	alter et vīcēnsimus	vīcēnī bīnī	bis et vīciens
30	XXX	trīginta	trīgēnsimus	trīcēnī	trīciens
40	XXXX or XL	quadrāginta	quadrāgēnsimus	quadrāgēnī	quadrāgiens
50	L	quīnquāginta	quīnquāgēnsimus	quīnquāgēnī	quīnquāgiens
60	LX	sexāginta	sexāgēnsimus	sexāgēnī	sexāgiens
70	LXX	septuāginta	septuāgēnsimus	septuāgēnī	septuāgiens
80	LXXX or XXC	octōginta	octōgēnsimus	octōgēnī	octōgiens
90	LXXXX or XC	nōnāginta	nōnāgēnsimus	nōnāgēnī	nōnāgiens
100	C	centum	centēnsimus	centēnī	centiens
101	CI	centum et ūnus	centēnsimus prīmus	centēnī singulī	centiens semel
200	CC	ducentī, -ae, -a	ducentēnsimus	ducēnī	ducentiens
300	CCC	trecentī	trecentēnsimus	trecēnī	trecentiens
400	CCCC	quadringentī	quadringentēnsimus	quadringēnī	quadringentiens
500	Iɔ or D	quīngentī	quīngentēnsimus	quīngēnī	quīngentiens
600	Iɔc	sexcentī	sexcentēnsimus	sēcēnī	sexcentiens
700	Iɔcc	septingentī	septingentēnsimus	septingēnī	septingentiens
800	Iɔccc	octingentī	octingentēnsimus	octingēnī	octingentiens
900	Iɔcccc	nongentī, nōning-	nongentēnsimus	nongēnī	nongentiens
1,000	cIɔ or M	mīllē	mīllēnsimus	singula mīlia	mīliens
2,000	cIɔcIɔ or MM	duo mīlia	bis-mīllēnsimus	bīna mīlia	bis mīliens

PRONOUNS.

60 Pronouns either stand in the place of Substantives, or stand in the place of Adjectives, to define or point out Substantives.

There are three Persons:

First: The person speaking: *I* or *we*.

Second: The person spoken to: *you* (sing. or plur.).

Third: The person or thing spoken of: *he, she, it, they*.

Personal Pronouns stand only in place of Substantives. Possessive Pronouns, as meus, *my*, stand only for Adjectives. Most of the others can stand for Substantives or Adjectives.

61 PERSONAL AND REFLEXIVE.

SINGULAR.

	1st Person		2nd Person	
Nom.	**ĕgŏ,**	*I.*	**tū,**	*you* (also Voc.)
Acc.	**mē,**	*me.*	**tē,**	*you.*
Gen.	**meī,**	*of me.*	**tuī,**	*of you.*
Dat.	**mĭhĭ,**	*to me.*	**tĭbĭ,**	*to you.*
Abl.	**mē,**	*from me.*	**tē,**	*from you.*

PLURAL.

	1st Person		2nd Person	
Nom.	**nōs,**	*we.*	**vōs,**	*you* (also Voc.)
Acc.	**nōs,**	*us.*	**vōs,**	*you.*
Gen.	{ **nostrī** / **nostrum** }	*of us.*	{ **vestrī** / **vestrum** }	*of you.*
Dat.	**nōbīs,**	*to us.*	**vōbīs,**	*to you.*
Abl.	**nōbīs,**	*from us.*	**vōbīs,**	*from you.*

Relexive pronoun.

Nom.	—	
Acc.	**sē** or **sēsē,**	*himself, herself, itself, or themselves.*
Gen.	**suī,**	*of himself, etc.*
Dat.	**sĭbĭ,**	*to himself, etc.*
Abl.	**sē or sēsē,**	*from himself, etc.*

For the Personal Pronoun of the 3rd Person, he, she, it, the Demonstrative **is**, **ea**, **id**, is used.

62
POSSESSIVE.

SING.	1st Person:	**mĕus,**	**meă,**	**meum,**	*my.*
	2nd Person:	**tuŭs,**	**tuă,**	**tuum,**	*your.*
PLUR.	1st Person:	**nostĕr,**	**nostră,**	**nostrum,**	*our*
	2nd Person:	**vestĕr,**	**vestră,**	**vestrum,**	*your.*

Suus, sua, suum, *his, her, its, their,* is the Possessive Pronoun of the Reflexive.

Meus, tuus, suus are declined like bonus: noster, vester, like niger. Meus has Voc. Sing. masc. **mī.** The other Possessives, except noster, have no Vocative.

63
DEMONSTRATIVE.

is, *that,* or *he, she, it.*

	SINGULAR.			PLURAL.		
	M.	F.	N.	M.	F.	N.
Nom.	ĭs	eă	ĭd	iī *or* eī	eae	eă
Acc.	eum	eam	id	eōs	eās	eă
Gen.	ēiŭs	ēiŭs	ēiŭs	eōrum	eārum	eōrum
Dat.	eī	eī	eī	iīs (eīs)	iīs (eīs)	iīs (eīs)
Abl.	eō	eā	eō	iīs (eīs)	iīs (eīs)	iīs (eīs)

hic, *this (near me),* or *he, she, it.*

	SINGULAR.			PLURAL.		
	M.	F.	N.	M.	F.	N.
Nom.	hīc	haec	hōc	hī	hae	haec
Acc.	hunc	hanc	hoc	hōs	hās	haec
Gen.	hūius	hūius	hūius	hōrum	hārum	hōrum
Dat.	huic	huic	huic	hīs	hīs	hīs
Abl.	hōc	hāc	hōc	hīs	hīs	hīs

ille, *that (over there),* or *he, she, it.*

	SINGULAR.			PLURAL.		
	M.	F.	N.	M.	F.	N.
Nom.	illĕ	illă	illŭd	illiī	illae	illă
Acc.	illum	illam	illŭd	illōs	illās	illă
Gen.	illĭus	illĭus	illĭus	illōrum	illārum	illōrum
Dat.	illī	illī	illī	illīs	illīs	illīs
Abl.	illō	illā	illō	illīs	illīs	illīs

Istĕ, *that (over there),* is declined like ille.

64

DEFINITIVE.

īdem, *same.*

SINGULAR.

	M.	F.	N.
	M.	F.	N.
Nom.	īdem	eădem	ĭdem
Acc.	eundem	eandem	ĭdem
Gen.	ēiusdem	ēiusdem	ēiusdem
Dat.	eīdem	eīdem	eīdem
Abl.	eōdem	eădem	eōdem

PLURAL.

	M.	F.	N.
Nom.	eīdem *or* īdem	eaedem	eădem
Acc.	eosdem	easdem	eădem
Gen.	eōrundem	eārundem	eōrundem
Dat.	eīsdem *or* īsdem		
Abl.	eīsdem *or* īsdem		

ipse, *self.*

	SINGULAR.			PLURAL.		
	M.	F.	N.	M.	F.	N.
Nom.	ipsĕ	ipsă	ipsum	ipsī	ipsae	ipsă
Acc.	ipsum	ipsam	ipsum	ipsōs	ipsas	ipsă
Gen.	ipsĭus	ipsĭus	ipsĭus	ipsōrum	ipsārum	ipsōrum
Dat.	ipsī	ipsī	ipsī	ipsīs	ipsīs	ipsīs
Abl.	ipsō	ipsā	ipsō	ipsīs	ipsīs	ipsīs

65

RELATIVE.

quī, *who, which.*

	SINGULAR.			PLURAL.		
	M.	F.	N.	M.	F.	N.
Nom.	quī	quae	quŏd	quī	quae	quae
Acc.	quem	quam	quŏd	quōs	quās	quae
Gen.	cūiŭs	cūiŭs	cūiŭs	quōrum	quārum	quōrum
Dat.	cuī	cuī	cuī	quĭbŭs *or* quīs		
Abl.	quō	quā	quō	quĭbŭs *or* quīs		

66

INTERROGATIVE.

quis, *who? what?*

	M.	F.	N.		M.	F.	N.
Nom. {	quĭs	(quĭs)	quĭd	*Acc.* {	quem	quam	quĭd
	quī	quae	quŏd		quem	quam	quŏd

In all other Cases sing. and plur., Interrogative is like the Relative quī.

67   INDEFINITE.

quis, *anyone or anything.*

	M.	F.	N.		M.	F.	N.
Nom.	**quĭs**	**quă**	**quĭd**	*Acc.*	**quem**	**quam**	**quĭd**
	quī	**quae**	**quŏd**		**quem**	**quam**	**quŏd**

In all other Cases, the Indefinite is like the Relative, except that quă or quae may be used in the neut. nom. and acc. plural.

Quis, both Interrogative and Indefinite, and its compounds, are used **chiefly** as Substantives; **quī** and its compounds **chiefly** as Adjectives.

    Quid and its compounds are used **only** as Substantives; **quod** and its compounds **only** as Adjectives.

    Examples:

homō quī venit,	*The man who comes.*	(quī, relative.)
quis venit?	*Who comes?*	(quis, interrogative.)
quī homō venit?	*What man comes?*	(quī, interrogative.)
aliquid amārī,	*Something bitter.*	
aliquod verbum,	*Some word.*	

68   COMPOUND PRONOUNS.

MASC.	FEM.	NEUT.	
quīcumquĕ	quaecumquĕ	quodcumquĕ	} *whosoever, or*
quisquĭs	quisquĭs	quisquĭd (quicquĭd)	} *whatsoever.*
quīdam	quaedam	quiddam (quoddam)	{ *a certain person or thing.*
ălĭquĭs	ălĭquă	ălĭquĭd	} *someone or*
aliquī	aliquă	aliquod	} *something.*
quisquam	—	quidquam (quicquam)	*anyone at all.*
quisquĕ	quaequĕ	quidquĕ (quodquĕ)	{ *each one severally.*
ŭterquĕ	utraquĕ	utrumquĕ	*each of two.*

Quisquam is used as a Substantive, sing. only, chiefly in negative sentences; and the Adjective which belongs to it is ūllus: haud quisquam, *not anyone.*

69 The following Pronomial Adjectives form the Gen. Sing. in **-ius** and the Dat. Sing. in **-ī** like ille: **alius**, *other, another*; **ūllus**, *any*; **nūllus**, *none*; **sōlus**, *sole*; **tōtus**, *whole*; **ŭter**, *which of two*; **alter**, *one of two, the other*; **neuter**, *neither*.

	SINGULAR.			PLURAL.		
	M.	F.	N.	M.	F.	N.
Nom.	ălĭŭs	ălĭă	ălĭŭd	ălĭī	ălĭae	ălĭa
Acc.	alium	aliam	alĭŭd	aliōs	aliās	alia
Gen.	alīŭs	alīŭs	alīŭs	aliōrum	aliārum	aliōrum
Dat.	aliī	aliī	aliī	aliīs	aliīs	aliīs
Abl.	aliō	aliā	aliō	aliīs	aliīs	aliīs

Note.—In alius the **i** of the Gen. Sing. is always long. In the Gen. of words declined like it the quantity of the **i** is doubtful; also in the Gen. of ŭter, neuter.

Like alius, but with Neuter Singular in **-um**, are declined ūllus, nūllus, sōlus, tōtus.

	SINGULAR.		
	M.	F.	N.
Nom.	altĕr	altĕră	altĕrum
Acc.	altĕrum	altĕram	altĕrum
Gen.	alterĭŭs	alterĭŭs	alterĭŭs
Dat.	alterī	alterī	alterī
Abl.	alterō	alterā	alterō

	PLURAL.		
	M.	F.	N.
Nom.	altĕrī	altĕrae	altĕră
Acc.	alterōs	alterās	altĕră
Gen.	alterōrum	alterārum	alterōrum
Dat.	alterīs	alterīs	alterīs
Abl.	alterīs	alterīs	alterīs

Like alter, but casting out **e** before **r** in all cases except the Nom. Sing. Masculine, are defined,—

ŭter, utra, utrum, *which (of two)*. neuter, neutra, neutrum, *neither*. These are seldom used in the plural.

70   VERBS.

The **Verb** has:

The Three Persons—First, Second, Third.
The Two Numbers—Singular and Plural.
Six Tenses:
    (1) Present, (2) Future Simple, (3) Past
    Imperfect, (4) Perfect or Aorist,   The Verb Finite.
    (5) Future Perfect, (6) Pluperfect.
Three Moods:
    (1) Indicative, (2) Imperative,
    (3) Conjunctive.

The **Infinitive** (Verbal Substantive).
Three **Participles** (Verbal Adjectives).
The **Gerund** and **Gerundive** (Verbal   The Verb Infinite.
    Substantive and Adjective).
Two Supines (Verbal Substantives).

Two Voices:
    (1) Active, (2) Passive.

The Verb Finite is so called because it is limited by Mood and
Persons; while the Verb Infinite is not so limited.

71   PERSON AND NUMBER.

In English, Pronouns are used with Verbs to express the three
Persons Singular and Plural: *I am, We are.* But in Latin the Pronouns are expressed by personal suffixes.

su-**m**,	*I am,* am-**ō**, *I love.*	su-**mus**,	*we are.*
e-**s**,	*you are.*	es-**tis**,	*you are.*
es-**t**,	*he (she, it) is.*	su-**nt**,	*they are.*

The Imperative Mood has only the Second and Third Person Singular and Plural, not the First.

72   TENSES.

Tenses express the time of the action or state denoted by the
Verb, as being:

    (1) Present, Past, or Future;
    (2) Complete or Incomplete;
    (3) Momentary or Continuous.

In English, by means of auxiliary Verbs, differences of time can
be more accurately expressed than in Latin; so that one tense om
Latin may correspond to two tenses in English. Thus, rogō, *I ask*,
has the following tenses:

Present	Present	*incomplete*	rogō	*I ask* / *I am asking*
	Perfect	*complete*	rogāvī	*I have asked* / *I have been asking*
Future	Fut. Simple	*incomplete*	rogābo	*I shall ask* / *I shall be asking*
	Fut. Perfect	*complete*	rogāverō	*I shall have asked* / *I shall have been asking*
Past	Perfect / Imperfect	*incomplete*	rogāvī / rogābam	*I had asked* / *I was asking*
	Pluperf.	*complete*	rogāveram	*I had asked* / *I had been asking*

The Present, the Future Simple, and the Future Perfect are called
Primary Tenses. The Imperfect and the Pluperfect are called
Historic Tenses. The Perfect in the sense of *I have loved* is **Pri-
mary**; in the sense of *I loved* it is **Historic**.

73   MOOD.

Moods are the forms in which the idea contained in the Verb is presented.

The **Indicative** is the mood which states a fact: amō, *I love*.

The **Imperative** is the mood of command: amā: *love*.

The **Subjunctive** is the mood which represents something as thought of as dependent: ut amem, *that I may love*; sī amārem, *if I were to love*.* It has no Future tense forms, but its other tenses can be used with future meaning.

74   THE VERB INFINITE

The **Infinitive** is a Verb Noun expressing action or state in general, without limit of person or number: amāre, *to love*.

The **Gerund** is a Verbal Substantive declined like neuters of the Second Declension. It supplies Cases to the Infinitive: as amandī, *of loving*.

The **Gerundive** is a Participle, or Verbal Adjective: amandus, -a, -um, *fit to be loved*.

The **Supines** are Cases of a Verbal Substantive: amātum, *in order to love*; amātū, *in or for loving*.

The **Participles** are so called because they have partly the properties of Verbs and partly those of Adjectives; there are three besides the Gerundive:

(a)   Act. Pres.   amāns,   *loving* (declined like ingēns).
(b)   Act. Fut.   amātūrus,   *about to love* }   (declined like
(c)   Pass. Perf.   amātus,   *loved*   }   bonus).

---

*In the Paradigms the tenses of the Subjunctive are given without any English translation, because their meaning varies so much according to the context that it is impossible to convey it by any one rendering.

75 VOICE.

The **Active Voice** expresses what the Subject of a Verb is or does:

sum, *I am*; valeō, *I am well*; amō, *I love*; regō, *I rule.*

The **Passive Voice** expresses what is done to the Subject of the Verb:

amor, *I am loved*; regor, *I am ruled.*

76 Deponent Verbs are Verbs which have chiefly the forms of the Passive Voice with the meaning of the Active Voice.

77 Verbs in the Active Voice and Deponent Verbs are,

(a) Transitive, acting on an object:
amō eum, *I love him*; hortor vōs, *I exhort you.*

(b) Intransitive, not acting on an object: stō, *I stand*; loquor, *I speak.*

Only Transitive Verbs have the full Passive Voice.

78 THE CONJUGATIONS.

Verbs are generally arranged according to the Character of the Present Stem in four Conjugations.

The Character is most clearly seen before the suffix **-re** (or **-ĕre**) of the Infinitive Present Active. It is either one of the vowels **a, e, i, u,** or a Consonant.

First Conjugation,	**A- Stems.**
Second Conjugation,	**E- Stems.**
Third Conjugation,	**Consonant and U- Stems.**
Fourth Conjugation,	**I- Stems.**

Deponent Verbs are also divided into four Conjugations with the same Stem endings.

79 The following forms must be known in order to give the full Conjugation.

	A- Stems.	E- Stems.	Consonant and U- Stems.	I- Stems.
Active Voice.				
1 Pers. Pres. Indic.	amō	moneō	regō	audiō
Infin. Pres.	amāre	monēre	regere	audīre
Perfect.	amāvī	monuī	rēxī	audīvī
Supine in -um.	amātum	monitum	rēctum	audītum
Passive Voice.				
1 Pers. Pres. Indic.	amor	moneor	regor	audior
Infin. Pres.	amārī	monērī	regī	audīrī
Partic. Perf.	amātus	monitus	rēctus	audītus
Gerundive.	amandus	monendus	regendus	audiendus

When the Perfect ends in -vī, a shortnened for is often used: amāvistī becomes amāstī; amāvērunt, amārunt; audīvī, audiī; audīvērunt, audiērunt.

For -ērunt (3rd pers. pl. Perf. Indic.) -ēre is often written: amāvēre, audīvēre.

The 2nd pers. sing. ends in -ris or -re in the Passive: amābāris, amābāre; but usually -ris in the Pres. Indic.

80 PERIPHRASTIC CONJUGATION.

The Active Future Participle and the Gerundive may be used with all the Tenses of the Verb sum:

amātūrus, -a sum,	*I am about to love.*
amātūrus, -a es,	*you are about to love.*
amātūrus, -a est,	*he (she) is about to love.*
amātūrī, -ae sumus,	*we are about to love.*
etc.	
amandus, -a sum,	*I am fit to be loved.*
etc.	

In the same way the Participle futūrus may be used with the tenses of sum: futūrus sum, *I am about to be.*

The Active Future Participle with fuisse forms an Imperfect Future Infinitive, which is only used occasionally: amātūrus fuisse, *to have been about to love.*

81. THE VERB **SUM** – I AM (SUM, FUĪ, ESSE, FUTŪRUS).

TENSE	INDICATIVE	
Present	sum	*I am*
	es	*you (s.) are*
	est	*he is*
	sumus	*we are*
	estis	*you (pl.) are*
	sunt	*they are*
Future Simple	erō	*I shall be*
	eris	*you (s.) will be*
	erit	*he will be*
	erimus	*we shall be*
	eritis	*you (pl.) will be*
	erunt	*they will be*
Imperfect	eram	*I was*
	erās	*you (s.) were*
	erat	*he was*
	erāmus	*we were*
	erātis	*you (pl.) were*
	erant	*they were*
Perfect	fuī	*I have been* or *I was*
	fuistī	*you (s.) have been* or *you (s.) were*
	fuit	*he has been* or *he was*
	fuimus	*we have been* or *we were*
	fuistis	*you (pl.) have been* or *you (pl.) were*
	fuērunt	*they have been* or *they were*
Future Perfect	fuerō	*I shall have been*
	fueris	*you (s.) will have been*
	fuerit	*he will have been*
	fuerimus	*we shall have been*
	fueritis	*you (pl.) will have been*
	fuerint	*they will have been*
Pluperfect	fueram	*I had been*
	fuerās	*you (s.) had been*
	fuerat	*he had been*
	fuerāmus	*we had been*
	fuerātis	*you (pl.) had been*
	fuerant	*they had been*

Subjunctive	Imperative
sim sīs sit sīmus sītis sint	es, estō, *be* (s.) estō, *let him be* este, estōte, *be* (pl.) suntō, *let them be*

	The Verb Infinitive
essem essēs esset essēmus essētis essent	*Infinitives* Present esse, *to be* Perfect fuisse, *to have been* Future $\left\{ \begin{array}{l} \text{futūrus esse} \\ \text{fore} \end{array} \right\}$ *to be about to be*
fuerim fuerīs fuerit fuerīmus fuerītis fuerint	*Participles* Present (*none*) Future futūrus, *about to be* Gerunds and Supines (*none*)
fuissem fuissēs fuisset fuissēmus fuissētis fuissent	Like Sum are conjugated its compounds: absum, *am absent*; adsum, *am present*; dēsum, *am wanting*; insum, *am in or among*; intersum, *am among*; obsum, *hinder*; praesum, *am set over*; ;prōsum, *am of use*; subsum, *am under*; supersum, *survive*. In prōsum the final **d** of the old preposition is kept before **e**: prodes

82. ACTIVE VOICE – FIRST CONJUGATION Ā-STEMS

TENSE		INDICATIVE
Present	amō	I love or I am loving
	amās	you (s.) love or you are loving
	amat	he loves or he is loving
	amāmus	we love or we are loving
	amātis	you (pl.) love or you (pl.) are loving
	amant	they love or they are loving
Future Simple	amābō	I shall love
	amābis	you (s.) will love
	amābit	he will love
	amābimus	we shall love
	amābitis	you (pl.) will love
	amābunt	they will love
Imperfect	amābam	I was loving
	amābās	you (s.) were loving
	amābat	he was loving
	amābāmus	we were loving
	amābātis	you (pl.) were loving
	amābant	they were loving
Perfect	amāvī	I have loved or I loved
	amāvistī	you (s.) have loved or you (s.) loved
	amāvit	he has loved or he loved
	amāvimus	we have loved or we loved
	amāvistis	you (pl.) have loved or you (pl.) loved
	amāvērunt	they have loved or they loved
Future Perfect	amāverō	I shall have loved
	amāveris	you (s.) will have loved
	amāverit	he will have loved
	amāverimus	we shall have loved
	amāveritis	you (pl.) will have loved
	amāverint	they will have loved
Pluperfect	amāveram	I had loved
	amāverās	you (s.) had loved
	amāverat	he had loved
	amāverāmus	we had loved
	amāverātis	you (pl.) had loved
	amāverant	they had loved

SUBJUNCTIVE	IMPERATIVE
amam amēs amet amēmus amētis ament	amā, amātō, *love* (s.) amātō, *let him love* amāte, amātōte, *love* (pl.) amantō, *let them love*

THE VERB INFINITIVE

SUBJUNCTIVE	
amārem amārēs amāret amārēmus amārētis amārent	*Infinitives* Present amāre, *to love* Perfect amāvisse, *to have loved* Future amātūrus esse, *to be about to love*
amāverim amāverīs amāverit amāverīmus amāverītis amāverint	*Gerund* amandum, *the loving*
	Supines amātum, *in order to love* amātū, *in* or *for loving*
	Participles
amāvissem amāvissēs amāvisset amāvissēmus amāvissētis amāvissent	Present amāns, *loving* Future amātūrus, *about to love*

83. ACTIVE VOICE – SECOND CONJUGATION Ē-STEMS

TENSE	INDICATIVE	
Present	moneō	*I advise* or *I am advising*
	monēs	*you (s.) advise* or *you are advising*
	monet	*he loves* or *he is advising*
	monēmus	*we advise* or *we are advising*
	monētis	*you (pl.) advise* or *you (pl.) are advising*
	monent	*they advise* or *they are advising*
Future Simple	monēbō	*I shall advise*
	monēbis	*you (s.) will advise*
	monēbit	*he will advise*
	monēbimus	*we shall advise*
	monēbitis	*you (pl.) will advise*
	monēbunt	*they will advise*
Imperfect	monēbam	*I was advising*
	monēbās	*you (s.) were advising*
	monēbat	*he was advising*
	monēbāmus	*we were advising*
	monēbātis	*you (pl.) were advising*
	monēbant	*they were advising*
Perfect	monuī	*I have advised* or *I advised*
	monuistī	*you (s.) have advised* or *you (s.) advised*
	monuit	*he has advised* or *he advised*
	monuimus	*we have advised* or *we advised*
	monuistis	*you (pl.) have advised* or *you (pl.) advised*
	monuērunt	*they have advised* or *they advised*
Future Perfect	monuerō	*I shall have advised*
	monueris	*you (s.) will have advised*
	monuerit	*he will have advised*
	monuerimus	*we shall have advised*
	monueritis	*you (pl.) will have advised*
	monuerint	*they will have advised*
Pluperfect	monueram	*I had advised*
	monuerās	*you (s.) had advised*
	monuerat	*he had advised*
	monuerāmus	*we had advised*
	monuerātis	*you (pl.) had advised*
	monuerant	*they had advised*

Subjunctive	Imperative
moneam moneās moneat moneāmus moneātis moneant	monē, monētō, *advise* (s.) monētō, *let him advise* monēte, monētōte, *advise* (pl.) monentō, *let them advise*

The Verb Infinitive

Infinitives

Present	monēre,	*to advise*
Perfect	monuisse,	*to have advised*
Future	monitūrus esse,	*to be about to advise*

Gerund

monendum, *the advising*

Supines

monitum, *in order to advise*
monitū, *in or for advising*

Participles

Present	monēns,	*advise*
Future	monitūrus,	*about to advise*

The subjunctive column (continued):

monērem
monērēs
monēret
monērēmus
monērētis
monērent

monuerim
monuerīs
monuerit
monuerīmus
monuerītis
monuerint

monuissem
monuissēs
monuisset
monuissēmus
monuissētis
monuissent

84. ACTIVE VOICE – THIRD CONJUGATION CONSONANT (AND U) STEMS

TENSE	INDICATIVE	
Present	regō	*I rule or I am ruling*
	regis	*you (s.) rule or you are ruling*
	regit	*he rules or he is ruling*
	regimus	*we rule or we are ruling*
	regitis	*you (pl.) rule or you (pl.) are ruling*
	regunt	*they rule or they are ruling*
Future Simple	regam	*I shall rule*
	regēs	*you (s.) will rule*
	reget	*he will rule*
	regēmus	*we shall rule*
	regētis	*you (pl.) will rule*
	regent	*they will rule*
Imperfect	regēbam	*I was ruling*
	regēbās	*you (s.) were ruling*
	regēbat	*he was ruling*
	regēbāmus	*we were ruling*
	regēbātis	*you (pl.) were ruling*
	regēbant	*they were ruling*
Perfect	rēxī	*I have ruled or I ruled*
	rēxistī	*you (s.) have ruled or you (s.) ruled*
	rēxit	*he has ruled or he ruled*
	rēximus	*we have ruled or we ruled*
	rēxistis	*you (pl.) have ruled or you (pl.) ruled*
	rēxērunt	*they have ruled or they ruled*
Future Perfect	rēxerō	*I shall have ruled*
	rēxeris	*you (s.) will have ruled*
	rēxerit	*he will have ruled*
	rēxerimus	*we shall have ruled*
	rēxeritis	*you (pl.) will have ruled*
	rēxerint	*they will have ruled*
Pluperfect	rēxeram	*I had ruled*
	rēxerās	*you (s.) had ruled*
	rēxerat	*he had ruled*
	rēxerāmus	*we had ruled*
	rēxerātis	*you (pl.) had ruled*
	rēxerant	*they had ruled*

Subjunctive	Imperative
regam regēs regat regāmus regātis regant	rege, regitō, *rule* (s.) regitō, *let him rule* regite, regitōte, *rule* (pl.) reguntō, *let them rule*

The Verb Infinitive

Subjunctive	
regerem regerēs regeret regerēmus regerētis regerent	*Infinitives* Present regere, *to rule* Perfect rēxisse, *to have ruled* Future rēctūrus esse, *to be about to rule*
rēxerim rēxerīs rēxerit rēxerīmus rēxerītis rēxerint	*Gerund* regendum, *the ruling* *Supines* rēctum, *in order to rule* rēctū, *in* or *for ruling* *Participles*
rēxissem rēxissēs rēxisset rēxissēmus rēxissētis rēxissent	Present regēns, *ruling* Future rēctūrus, *about to rule*

85. ACTIVE VOICE – FOURTH CONJUGATION Ī-STEMS

TENSE		INDICATIVE
Present	audiō	*I hear* or *I am hearing*
	audīs	*you (s.) hear* or *you are hearing*
	audit	*he hears* or *he is hearing*
	audīmus	*we hear* or *we are hearing*
	audītis	*you (pl.) hear* or *you (pl.) are hearing*
	audiunt	*they hear* or *they are hearing*
Future Simple	audiam	*I shall hear*
	audiēs	*you (s.) will hear*
	audiet	*he will hear*
	audiēmus	*we shall hear*
	audiētis	*you (pl.) will hear*
	audient	*they will hear*
Imperfect	audiēbam	*I was hearing*
	audiēbās	*you (s.) were hearing*
	audiēbat	*he was hearing*
	audiēbāmus	*we were hearing*
	audiēbātis	*you (pl.) were hearing*
	audiēbant	*they were hearing*
Perfect	audīvī	*I have heard* or *I heard*
	audīvistī	*you (s.) have heard* or *you (s.) heard*
	audīvit	*he has heard* or *he heard*
	audīvimus	*we have heard* or *we heard*
	audīvistis	*you (pl.) have heard* or *you (pl.) heard*
	audīvērunt	*they have heard* or *they heard*
Future Perfect	audīverō	*I shall have heard*
	audīveris	*you (s.) will have heard*
	audīverit	*he will have heard*
	audīverimus	*we shall have heard*
	audīveritis	*you (pl.) will have heard*
	audīverint	*they will have heard*
Pluperfect	audīveram	*I had heard*
	audīverās	*you (s.) had heard*
	audīverat	*he had heard*
	audīverāmus	*we had heard*
	audīverātis	*you (pl.) had heard*
	audīverant	*they had heard*

SUBJUNCTIVE	IMPERATIVE
audiam audiās audiat audiāmus audiātis audiant	audī, audītō, *hear* (s.) audītō, *let him hear* audīte, audītōte, *hear* (pl.) audiuntō, *let them hear*

	THE VERB INFINITIVE
	Infinitives
audīrem audīrēs audīret audīrēmus audīrētis audīrent	Present audīre, *to hear* Perfect audīvisse, *to have heard* Future audītūrus esse, *to be about to hear*
audīverim audīverīs audīverit audīverīmus audīverītis audīverint	*Gerund* audiendum, *the hearing* *Supines* audītum, *in order to hear* audītū, *in* or *for hearing* *Participles*
audīvissem audīvissēs audīvisset audīvissēmus audīvissētis audīvissent	Present audiens, *hearing* Future audītūrus, *about to hear*

86. PASSIVE VOICE – FIRST CONJUGATION Ā-STEMS

TENSE		INDICATIVE
Present	amor	I am or I am being loved
	amāris	you (s.) are or you are being loved
	amātur	he is or he is being loved
	amāmur	we are or we are being loved
	amāminī	you (pl.) are or you (pl.) are being loved
	amantur	they are or they are being loved
Future Simple	amābor	I shall be loved
	amāberis (-re)	you (s.) will be loved
	amābitur	he will be loved
	amābimur	we shall be loved
	amābiminī	you (pl.) will be loved
	amābuntur	they will be loved
Imperfect	amābar	I was being loved
	amābāris (-re)	you (s.) were being loved
	amābātur	he was being loved
	amābāmur	we were being loved
	amābāminī	you (pl.) were being loved
	amābantur	they were being loved
Perfect	amātus sum	I have been or I was loved
	amātus es	you (s.) have been or you (s.) were loved
	amātus est	he has been or he was loved
	amātī sumus	we have been or we were loved
	amātī estis	you (pl.) have been or you (pl.) were loved
	amātī sunt	they have been or they were loved
Future Perfect	amātus erō	I shall have been loved
	amātus eris	you (s.) will have been loved
	amātus erit	he will have been loved
	amātī erimus	we shall have been loved
	amātī eritis	you (pl.) will have been loved
	amātī erunt	they will have been loved
Pluperfect	amātus eram	I had been loved
	amātus erās	you (s.) had been loved
	amātus erat	he had been loved
	amātī erāmus	we had been loved
	amātī erātis	you (pl.) had been loved
	amātī erant	they had been loved

Subjunctive	Imperative
amer amēris (-re) amētur amēmur amēminī amentur	amāre, amātor, *be loved* (s.) amātor, *let him be loved* amāminī, *be loved* (pl.) amantor, *let them be loved*

	The Verb Infinitive
amārer amārēris (-re) amārētur amārēmur amārēminī amārentur	*Infinitives* Present amārī, *to be loved* Perfect amātus esse, *to have been loved* Future amātum īrī
amātus sim amātus sīs amātus sit amātī sīmus amātī sītis amātī sint	*Participle* Perfect amātus, *loved* or *having been loved*
	Gerundive amandus, *fit to be loved*
amātus essem amātus essēs amātus esset amātī essēmus amātī essētis amātī essent	

87. PASSIVE VOICE – SECOND CONJUGATION Ē-STEMS

TENSE		INDICATIVE
Present	moneor	*I am* or *I am being advised*
	monēris	*you (s.) are* or *you are being advised*
	monētur	*he is* or *he is being advised*
	monēmur	*we are* or *we are being advised*
	monēminī	*you (pl.) are* or *you (pl.) are being advised*
	monentur	*they are* or *they are being advised*
Future Simple	monēbor	*I shall be advised*
	monēberis (-re)	*you (s.) will be advised*
	monēbitur	*he will be advised*
	monēbimur	*we shall be advised*
	monēbiminī	*you (pl.) will be advised*
	monēbuntur	*they will be advised*
Imperfect	monēbar	*I was being advised*
	monēbāris (-re)	*you (s.) were being advised*
	monēbātur	*he was being advised*
	monēbāmur	*we were being advised*
	monēbāminī	*you (pl.) were being advised*
	monēbantur	*they were being advised*
Perfect	monitus sum	*I have been* or *I was advised*
	monitus es	*you (s.) have been* or *you (s.) were advised*
	monitus est	*he has been* or *he was advised*
	monitī sumus	*we have been* or *we were advised*
	monitī estis	*you (pl.) have been* or *you (pl.) were advised*
	monitī sunt	*they have been* or *they were advised*
Future Perfect	monitus erō	*I shall have been advised*
	monitus eris	*you (s.) will have been advised*
	monitus erit	*he will have been advised*
	monitī erimus	*we shall have been advised*
	monitī eritis	*you (pl.) will have been advised*
	monitī erunt	*they will have been advised*
Pluperfect	monitus eram	*I had been advised*
	monitus erās	*you (s.) had been advised*
	monitus erat	*he had been advised*
	monitī erāmus	*we had been advised*
	monitī erātis	*you (pl.) had been advised*
	monitī erant	*they had been advised*

SUBJUNCTIVE	IMPERATIVE
monear moneāris (-re) moneātur moneāmur moneāminī moneantur	monēre, monētor, *be advised* (s.) monētor, *let him be advised* monēminī, *be advised* (pl.) monentor, *let them be advised*

	THE VERB INFINITIVE
monērer monērēris (-re) monērētur monērēmur monērēminī monērentur	*Infinitives* Present monērī, *to be advised* Perfect monitus esse, *to have been advised* Future monitum īrī
monitus sim monitus sīs monitus sit monitī sīmus monitī sītis monitī sint	*Participle* Perfect monitus, *advised* or *having been advised* *Gerundive* monendus, *fit to be advised*
monitus essem monitus essēs monitus esset monitī essēmus monitī essētis monitī essent	

88. Passive Voice – Third Conjugation Consonant (and U) Stems

Tense		Indicative
Present	regor	I am or I am being ruled
	regeris	you (s.) are or you are being ruled
	regitur	he is or he is being ruled
	regimur	we are or we are being ruled
	regiminī	you (pl.) are or you (pl.) are being ruled
	reguntur	they are or they are being ruled
Future Simple	regar	I shall be ruled
	rēgēris (-re)	you (s.) will be ruled
	regētur	he will be ruled
	regēmur	we shall be ruled
	regēminī	you (pl.) will be ruled
	regentur	they will be ruled
Imperfect	regēbar	I was being ruled
	regēbāris (-re)	you (s.) were being ruled
	regēbātur	he was being ruled
	regēbāmur	we were being ruled
	regēbāminī	you (pl.) were being ruled
	regēbantur	they were being ruled
Perfect	rēctus sum	I have been or I was ruled
	rēctus es	you (s.) have been or you (s.) were ruled
	rēctus est	he has been or he was ruled
	rēctī sumus	we have been or we were ruled
	rēctī estis	you (pl.) have been or you (pl.) were ruled
	rēctī sunt	they have been or they were ruled
Future Perfect	rēctus erō	I shall have been ruled
	rēctus eris	you (s.) will have been ruled
	rēctus erit	he will have been ruled
	rēctī erimus	we shall have been ruled
	rēctī eritis	you (pl.) will have been ruled
	rēctī erunt	they will have been ruled
Pluperfect	rēctus eram	I had been ruled
	rēctus erās	you (s.) had been ruled
	rēctus erat	he had been ruled
	rēctī erāmus	we had been ruled
	rēctī erātis	you (pl.) had been ruled
	rēctī erant	they had been ruled

Subjunctive	Imperative
regar regāris (-re) regātur regāmur regāminī regantur	regere, regitor, *be ruled* (s.) regitor, *let him be ruled* regiminī, *be ruled* (pl.) reguntor, *let them be ruled*
	The Verb Infinitive
regerer regerēris (-re) regerētur regerēmur regerēminī regerentur	*Infinitives* Present regī, *to be ruled* Perfect rēctus esse, *to have been ruled* Future rēctum īrī
rēctus sim rēctus sīs rēctus sit rēctī sīmus rēctī sītis rēctī sint	*Participle* Perfect rēctus, *ruled* or *having been ruled*
	Gerundive regendus, *fit to be ruled*
rēctus essem rēctus essēs rēctus esset rēctī essēmus rēctī essētis rēctī essent	

89. PASSIVE VOICE – FOURTH CONJUGATION Ĭ-STEMS

TENSE	INDICATIVE	
Present	audior	I am or I am being heard
	audīris	you (s.) are or you are being heard
	audītur	he is or he is being heard
	audīmur	we are or we are being heard
	audīminī	you (pl.) are or you (pl.) are being heard
	audiuntur	they are or they are being heard
Future Simple	audiar	I shall be heard
	audiēris (-re)	you (s.) will be heard
	audiētur	he will be heard
	audiēmur	we shall be heard
	audiēminī	you (pl.) will be heard
	audientur	they will be heard
Imperfect	audiēbar	I was being heard
	audiēbāris (-re)	you (s.) were being heard
	audiēbātur	he was being heard
	audiēbāmur	we were being heard
	audiēbāminī	you (pl.) were being heard
	audiēbantur	they were being heard
Perfect	audītus sum	I have been or I was heard
	audītus es	you (s.) have been or you (s.) were heard
	audītus est	he has been or he was heard
	audītī sumus	we have been or we were heard
	audītī estis	you (pl.) have been or you (pl.) were heard
	audītī sunt	they have been or they were heard
Future Perfect	audītus erō	I shall have been heard
	audītus eris	you (s.) will have been heard
	audītus erit	he will have been heard
	audītī erimus	we shall have been heard
	audītī eritis	you (pl.) will have been heard
	audītī erunt	they will have been heard
Pluperfect	audītus eram	I had been heard
	audītus erās	you (s.) had been heard
	audītus erat	he had been heard
	audītī erāmus	we had been heard
	audītī erātis	you (pl.) had been heard
	audītī erant	they had been heard

SUBJUNCTIVE	IMPERATIVE
audiar audiāris (-re) audiātur audiāmur audiāminī audiantur	audīre, audītor, *be heard* (s.) audītor, *let him be heard* audīminī, *be heard* (pl.) audiuntor, *let them be heard*
	THE VERB INFINITIVE
audīrer audīrēris (-re) audīrētur audīrēmur audīrēminī audīrentur	*Infinitives* Present audīrī, *to be heard* Perfect audītus esse, *to have been heard* Future audītum īrī
audītus sim audītus sīs audītus sit audītī sīmus audītī sītis audītī sint	*Participle* Perfect audītus, *heard* or *having been heard* *Gerundive* audiendus, *fit to be heard*
audītus essem audītus essēs audītus esset audītī essēmus audītī essētis audītī essent	

90. DEPONENT VERB – ŪTOR, ŪTĪ, ŪSUS, USE (THIRD DECLENSION)

TENSE	INDICATIVE	
Present	ūtor	*I use or I am using*
	ūteris	*you (s.) use or you are using*
	ūtitur	*he uses or he is using*
	ūtimur	*we use or we are using*
	ūtiminī	*you (pl.) use or you (pl.) are using*
	ūtuntur	*they use or they are using*
Future Simple	ūtar	*I shall use*
	ūtēris (-re)	*you (s.) will use*
	ūtētur	*he will use*
	ūtēmur	*we shall use*
	ūtēminī	*you (pl.) will use*
	ūtentur	*they will use*
Imperfect	ūtēbar	*I was using*
	ūtēbāris (-re)	*you (s.) were using*
	ūtēbātur	*he was using*
	ūtēbāmur	*we were using*
	ūtēbāminī	*you (pl.) were using*
	ūtēbantur	*they were using*
Perfect	ūsus sum	*I have used or I used*
	ūsus es	*you (s.) have used or you (s.) used*
	ūsus est	*he has used or he used*
	ūsī sumus	*we have used or we used*
	ūsī estis	*you (pl.) have used or you (pl.) used*
	ūsī sunt	*they have used or they used*
Future Perfect	ūsus erō	*I shall have used*
	ūsus eris	*you (s.) will have used*
	ūsus erit	*he will have used*
	ūsī erimus	*we shall have used*
	ūsī eritis	*you (pl.) will have used*
	ūsī erunt	*they will have used*
Pluperfect	ūsus eram	*I had used*
	ūsus erās	*you (s.) had used*
	ūsus erat	*he had used*
	ūsī erāmus	*we had used*
	ūsī erātis	*you (pl.) had used*
	ūsī erant	*they had used*

SUBJUNCTIVE	IMPERATIVE
ūtar ūtāris (-re) ūtātur ūtāmur ūtāminī ūtantur	ūtere, ūtitor, *use* (s.) ūtitor, *let him use* ūtiminī, *use* (pl.) ūtuntor, *let them use*

THE VERB INFINITIVE

Infinitives

Present ūtī, *to use*

ūterer
ūterēris (-re)
ūterētur
ūterēmur
ūterēminī
ūterentur

Perfect ūsus esse, *to have used*
Future ūsūrus esse, *to be about to use*

Gerund

ūtendum, *using*

ūsus sim
ūsus sīs
ūsus sit
ūsī sīmus
ūsī sītis
ūsī sint

Supines

ūsum, *in order to use*
ūsū, *in* or *for using*

Participles

Present ūtēns, *using*
Future ūsūrus, *about to use*
Perfect ūsus, *having used*

ūsus essem
ūsus essēs
ūsus esset
ūsī essēmus
ūsī essētis
ūsī essent

Gerundive

ūtendus, *fit to be used*

91 Many Perf. Participles of Deponent Verbs are used passively as well as actively: as confessus from confiteor, *confess*; imitātus from imitor, *imitate*; meritus from mereor, *deserve*; policitus from po-liceor, *promise*.

92 Some Verbs have a Perfect of Passive form with a Present of Active form; they are called **Semi-deponents**:

audeō, *dare*   ausus sum, *I have dared* or *I dared*.
gaudeō, *rejoice* gāvisus sum, *I have rejoiced* or *I rejoiced*.
soleō, *am wont* solitus sum, *I have been wont* or *I was wont*.
fīdō, *trust*   fīsus sum, *I have trusted* or *I trusted*.

93 Some Verbs have an Active form with a Passive meaning; they are called **Quasi-Passive**:

exulō, *am banished*.   liceō, *am put up for sale*.
vāpulō, *am beaten*.   vēneō, *am on sale*.
fīō, *am made*.

94 Some Verbs have Perfect Participles with Active meaning, like the Deponent Verbs:

iūrō, *swear*   iūrāvī, *I swore*   iūrātus, *having sworn*.
cēnō, *sup*   cēnāvī, *I supped* cēnātus, *having supped*.
prandeō, *dine* prandī, *I dined*   pransus, *having dined*.

95 Inceptive Verbs, with Present Stem in **-sco** (Third Conjugation), express beginning of action, and are derived from the Verb-Stems or from Nouns:

pallescō,   *turn pale*,   from palleō.
nigrescō,   *turn black*,   from niger.

96 Frequentative Verbs (First Conj.) express repeated or intenser action, and are formed from Supine Stems:

rogitō, *ask repeatedly* (rogō); cantō, *sing with energy* (canō).

97 Desiderative Verbs (Fourth Conj.) express desire of action, and are formed from Supine Stem:

ēsuriō, *am hungry* (edō, ēsurus).

98   VERBS IN -IO (THIRD CONJUGATION).

Forms from Present Stem, cap-i-, *take*.

		ACTIVE VOICE			PASSIVE VOICE	
		INDIC.	SUBJUNC.		INDIC.	SUBJUNC.
Present		capiō capis capit capimus capitis capiunt	capiam capiās capiat capiāmus capiātis capiant	Present	capior caperis capitur capimur capiminī capiuntur	capiar capiāris (-re) capiātur capiāmur capiāminī capiantur
Future Simple		capiam capiēs capiet capiēmus capiētis capient		Future Simple	capiar capiēris (-re) capiētur capiēmur capiēminī capientur	
Imperfect		capiēbam capiēbās capiēbat capiēbāmus capiēbātis capiēbant	caperem caperēs caperet caperēmus caperētis caperent	Imperfect	capiēbar capiēbāris (-re) capiēbātur capiēbāmur capiēbāminī capiēbantur	caperer caperēris (-re) caperētur caperēmur caperēminī caperentur
Imperative	Sing.	2. cape		2. capere		
	Plur.	2. capite		2. capiminī		

Infin. Pres. capere	Infin. Pres. capī
Gerund capiendum	Gerundive capiendus
Pres. Partic. capiēns	

The Verbs whose Present stem is conjugated like capiō are:

capiō, cupiō *and* faciō,	and their	*take, desire, make*
fodiō, fugiō *and* iaciō,	compounds,	*dig, fly, throw,*
pariō, rapiō, sapiō, quatiō		*bring forth, seize, know, shake,*
Compounds of speciō *and* laciō	obsolete Verbs,	*look at, entice,*
Deponents: gradior, patior, morior,		*step, suffer, die,*
And in some tenses, potior, orior.		*get possession of, arise.*

99 Verbs are called irregular:

(1) Because they are formed from more than one root, as **sum**.

(2) Because their tense-forms differ from those of regular verbs.

100   **Possum**, *I can*, **potuī, posse**.

The Presesnt Indicative possum is compounded of sum, *I am*, and the adjective potis or potī, *able*.

	ACTIVE VOICE			PASSIVE VOICE	
	INDIC.	SUBJUNC.		INDIC.	SUBJUNC.
Present	possum potes potest possumus potestis possunt	possim possīs possit possīmus possītis possint	Present	potuī potuistī potuit potuimus potuistis potuērunt	potuerim potuerīs potuerit potuerīmus potuerītis potuerint
Future Simple	poterō poteris poterit poterimus poteritis poterunt		Future Simple	potuerō potueris potuerit potuerimus potueritis potuerint	
Imperfect	poteram poterās poterat poterāmus poterātis poterant	possem possēs posset possēmus possētis possent	Imperfect	potueram potuerās potuerat potuerāmus potuerātis potuerant	potuissem potuissēs potuisset potuissēmus potuissētis potuissent

Infinitive Present, posse (pot-esse); Perfect, potuisse.

Potēns is used as an adjective, *powerful, able,* never as a Participle.

101   **Ferō**, *bear*, **ferre, tulī, lātum**.

	ACTIVE VOICE			PASSIVE VOICE	
	INDIC.	SUBJUNC.		INDIC.	SUBJUNC.
Present	ferō fers fert ferimus fertis ferunt	feram ferās ferat ferāmus ferātis ferant	**Present**	feror ferris fertur ferimur feriminī feruntur	ferar ferāris (-re) ferātur ferāmur ferāminī ferantur
Future Simple	feram ferēs feret ferēmus ferētis ferent		**Future Simple**	ferar ferēris (-re) ferētur ferēmur ferēminī ferentur	
Imperfect	ferēbam ferēbās ferēbat ferēbāmus ferēbātis ferēbant	ferrem ferrēs ferret ferrēmus ferrētis ferrent	**Imperfect**	ferēbar ferēbāris (-re) ferēbātur ferēbāmur ferēbāminī ferēbantur	ferrer ferrēris (-re) ferrētur ferrēmur ferrēminī ferrentur
Imperative Sing.	2. fer, fertō 3. fertō			2. ferre, fertor 3. fertor	
Imperative Plural	2. ferte, fertōte 3. feruntō			2. feriminī 3. feruntur	
Infin. Pres. ferre Gerund ferendum Pres. Partic. ferēns			Infin. Pres. ferrī Gerundive ferrendus		

The Perfect-Stem forms are regular:

tul-ī,   -erō   -eram   -erim   -issem

Also the Supine-Stem forms:

Supines $\begin{cases} \text{lātum} \\ \text{lātū} \end{cases}$ Participles $\begin{cases} \text{lātus} \\ \text{lātūrus} \end{cases}$ Infin. $\begin{cases} \text{tulisse} \\ \text{lātus esse} \\ \text{lātum īrī} \end{cases}$

lātus sum, erō, eram, sim, essem.

102   **Eō** (for **eiō**), *go*, **īre, iī, itum**.

	Indic.	Subjunc.	Imperative
Present	eō īs it īmus ītis eunt	eam eās eat eāmus eātis eant	ī, ītō ītō īte, ītōte euntō
Future Simple	ībō ībis ībit ībimus ībitis ībunt		THE VERB INFINITE. *Infinitive* Present īre Perfect īsse, īvisse Future itūrus esse
Imperfect	ībam ībās ībat ībāmus ībātis ībant	īrem īrēs īret īrēmus īrētis īrent	*Gerund* eundum *Supines* itum itū
Perfect	iī īstī iit iimus īstis iērunt	ierim ierīs ierit ierīmus ierītis ierint	*Participles* Present iēns (Acc. euntem) Future itūrus

In the Perfect Tense of eō the forms iī, īstī etc. are more usual than īvī etc.; also in the compounds rediī, redīstī, etc.

The Impersonal Passive, ītur, itum est, is often used.

103 **Queō**, *can*, **nequeō**, *cannot*, are conjugated like eō in the forms which are found, but many are wanting; they have no Imperative and no Gerunds.

Ambiō, *go round*, canvass, is conjugated like audiō.

104

Volō, *am willing, wish.*
Nōlō, *am unwilling, do not wish.*
Mālō, *prefer, wish rather.*

	INDICATIVE			IMPERATIVE
Present	volō	nōlō	mālō	nōlī, nōlītō
	vīs	nōn vīs	māvīs	nōlītō
	vult	nōn vult	māvult	
	volumus	nōlumus	mālumus	nōlite, nōlītōte
	vultis	nōn vultis	māvultis	nōluntō
	volunt	nōlunt	mālunt	
Future Simple	volam	(nōlam)	(mālam)	Volō and mālō have no Imperative.
	volēs	nōlēs	(mālēs)	
	volet	nōlet	mālet	
	volēmus	(nōlēmus)	(mālēmus)	THE VERB INFINITE
	volētis	(nōlētis)	(mālētis)	
	volent	(nōlent)	mālent	*Infinitive*
Imperf.	volēbam	nōlēbam	mālēbam	Present { velle, nōlle, mālle
	volēbās	nōlēbās	mālēbās	
	etc.	*etc.*	*etc.*	*Gerunds*
	SUBJUNCTIVE			(volendum) (nōlendum)
Present	velim	nōlim	mālim	—
	velīs	nōlīs	mālīs	*Supines*
	velit	nōlit	mālit	*None*
	velīmus	nōlīmus	mālīmus	
	velītis	nōlītis	mālītis	*Participles*
	velint	nōlint	mālint	
Imerfect	vellem	nōllem	māllem	Present { volēns, (nōlēns), —
	vellēs	nōllēs	māllēs	
	vellet	nōllet	māllet	
	vellēmus	nōllēmus	māllēmus	
	vellētis	nōllētis	māllētis	
	vellent	nōllent	māllent	

The Perfect-Stem forms are regular:

Volu-ī	-erō	-eram	-erim	-issem		voluisse
Nōlu-ī	-erō	-eram	-erim	-issem	Infin. {	nōluisse
Mālu-ī	-erō	-eram	-erim	-issem		māluisse

105   **Fīō**, *am made, become*, **fierī, factus sum**.

The Present-Stem tenses of **fīō** supply a Passive to the Active verb **faciō**, *make*. The Perfect tenses are borrowed from the Perfect Passive of faciō formed from the Supine-Stem **facto-**.

	INDIC.	SUBJUNC.	IMPERATIVE
Present	fīō fīs fit (fīmus) (fītis) fiunt	fīam fīās fīat fīāmus fīātis fīant	(fī) (fīte)
Future Simple	fīam fīēs fīet fīēmus fīētis fīent		THE VERB INFINITE. *Infinitive* Present fierī Perfect factus esse Future factum īrī *Participles* Perfect factus
Imperfect	fīēbam fīēbās fīēbat fīēbāmus fīēbātis fīēbant	fierem fierēs fieret fierēmus fierētis fierent	*Gerundive* faciendus
Perf.	factus sum *etc.*	factus sim *etc.*	

106   DEFECTIVE VERBS

Defective verbs are those which lack a considerable number of forms.

Coepī, *I have begun, I began*, **Meminī**, *I remember*, **Ōdī**, *I hate*, are limited mainly to Perfect-Stem forms. Meminī and ōdī, though Perfect in form, are Present in meaning.

Indicative

Perfect	coepī	memīnī	ōdī
Fut. Perfect	coeperō	meminerō	ōderō
Pluperfect	coeperam	mimineram	ōderam

Subjunctive

Perfect	coeperim	meminerim	ōderim
Pluperfect	coepissem	meminissem	ōdissem

Infinitive, Imperative, Participles

Perfect Infinitive	coepisse	meminisse	ōdisse
Fut. Infinitive	coeptūrus esse	*none*	ōsūrus esse
Imperative	*none*	{ mementō mementōte	*none*
Perfect Participle	coeptus	*none*	ōsus, *hating*
Fut. Participle	coeptūrus	*none*	ōsūrus

Note 1.—Coepī has also Pef. Passive forms: coeptus sum, etc., which are used mainly when coepī governs a passive infinitive, as: urbs aedificārī coepta est, the city began to be built.

Note 2.—Incipiō, I begin, supplies the present-stem forms which coepī lacks.

Note 3.—The participle ōsus is active and present in meaning.

Nōvī (Perfect of nōscō, *I get to know*) means *I have got to know, I know*; nōverō, *I shall know*; nōveram (nōram), *I knew*; nōvisse (nōsse), *to know*, etc.

Aiō, *I say or affirm*:

Ind. Pres.	**aiō**	**ais**	**ait**	—	—	**aiunt**
Imperf.	**aiēbam**	**aiēbās**	**aiēbat**	**aiēbāmus**	**aiēbātis**	**aiēbant**
Subj. Pres.	—	—	**aiat**	—	—	**aiant**
Participle **aiēns**						

Inquam, *I say*:

Ind. Pres.	**inquam**	**inquis**	**inquit**	**inquimus**	**inquitis**	**inquiunt**
Imperf.	—	—	**inquiēbat**	—	—	**inquiēbant**
Fut. Simple	—	**inquiēs, inquiet**	—	—	—	—
Perf.	—	**inquīstī, inquit**	—	—	—	—
Imper.		**inque**				

IMPERSONAL VERBS

Impersonal Verbs have only the Third Person Singular of each tense, an Infinitive, and a Gerund. They do not have a personal Subject in the Nominative.

The principal are the following:

Present		Perfect	Infinitive
miseret	*it moves to pity*	mieruit	miserēre
piget	*it vexes*	piguit	pigēre
paenitet	*it repents*	paenituit	paenitēre
pudet	*it shames*	puduit	pudēre
taedet	*it wearies*	taeduit	taedēre
decet	*it is becoming*	decuit	decēre
dēdecet	*it is unbecoming*	dēdecuit	dēdecēre
libet	*it pleases*	libuit	libēre
licet	*it is lawful*	licuit	licēre
oportet	*it behoves*	oportuit	oportēre
rēfert	*it concerns*	rētulit	rēferre

108 Some Impersonals express change of weather and time:

fulgurat	*it lightens*	**tonat**	*it thunders*
ningit	*it snows*	**lūcēscit**	*it dawns*
pluit	*it rains*	**vesperāscit**	*it grows late*

Interest, *it concerns*, is used impersonally (**190–193**), though intersum also has all the personal forms.

Intransitive Verbs also are used impersonally in the Passive: **ītur** , *one goes, a journey is made.*

109   TABLE OF PRINCIPAL PARTS OF VERBS*

Present	Infin.	Perfect	Supine	

First Conjugation: Ā- Stems
USUAL FORM

amō	amāre	amāvī	amātum	*love*

EXCEPTIONS
Perfect in -uī

secō	-āre	secuī	sectum	*cut*
sonō	-āre	sonuī	—	*sound*
vetō	-āre	vetuī	vetitum	*forbid*

Perfect with Reduplication:

stō	-āre	stetī -stitī*	statum	*stand*

Perfect with Lengthened Vowel:

iuvō	-āre	iūvī	iūtum	*help*

110 Second Conjugation: Ē- Stems
USUAL FORM

moneō	monēre	monuī	monitum	*advise*

EXCEPTIONS
Perfect in -uī; but Supine in -tum or -sum:

cēnseō	-ēre	cēnsuī	cēnsum	*deem, vote*
doceō	-ēre	docuī	doctum	*teach*

Perfect in -vī:

fleō	-ēre	flēvī	flētum	*weep*

Perfect in -sī:

ardeō	-ēre	arsī	—	*burn (intr.)*
augeō	-ēre	auxī	auctum	*increase (tr.)*
fulgeō	-ēre	fulsī	—	*shine*
haereō	-ēre	haesī	—	*stick*
iubeō	-ēre	iussī	iussum	*command*
maneō	-ēre	mānsī	mānsum	*remain*
rīdeō	-ēre	rīsī	rīsum	*laugh*
suādeō	-ēre	suāsī	suāsum	*advise*

Perfect with Reduplication

mordeō	-ēre	momordī	morsum	*bite*
pendeō	-ēre	pependī	—	*hang*

*Forms printed with a hyphen, as -stitī, are used only in compounds.

Present	Infin.	Perfect	Supine	

Reduplicated Perfect with Supine in -sum:

| pendeō | -ēre | pependī | pensum | *hang* |
| mordeō | -ēre | momordī | morsum | *bite* |

Perfect in -i with Supine in -sum:

| sedeō | -ēre | sēdī | sessum | *sit* |
| videō | -ēre | vīdī | vīsum | *see* |

111 Third Conjugation: Consonant and U- Stems

CONSONANT STEMS

Perfect in -sī or -xī with Supine in -tum:

regō	regere	rēxī	rēctum	*rule*
dīcō	-ere	dīxī	dictum	*say*
dūcō	-ere	dūxī	ductum	*lead*
intellegō	-ere	intellēxī	intellēctum	*understand*
surgō	-ere	surrēxī	surrēctum	*arise*
tegō	-ere	tēxī	tēctum	*cover*
trahō	-ere	trāxī	tractum	*draw*
vehō	-ere	vēxī	vectum	*carry*
vīvō	-ere	vīxī	victum	*live*
strūo	-ere	struxī	structum	*build*
nūbō	-ere	nūpsī	nūptum	*marry*
scrībō	-ere	scrīpsī	scrīptum	*write*
gerō	-ere	gessī	gestum	*carry on*
sūmō	-ere	sūmpsī	sūmptum	*take*
cingō	-ere	cīnxī	cīnctum	*surround*
iungō	-ere	iūnxī	iūnctum	*join, attach*

Perfect in -sī or -xī with Supine in -sum:

fīgō	-ere	fīxī	fixum	*fix*
spargō	-ere	sparsī	sparsum	*sprinkle*
cēdō	-ere	cessī	cessum	*yield*
claudō	-ere	clausī	clausum	*shut*
dīvidō	-ere	dīvīsī	dīvīsum	*divide*
lūdō	-ere	lūsī	lūsum	*play*
mittō	-ere	mīsī	missum	*send*
premō	-ere	pressī	pressum	*press (tr.)*
concutiō	-ere	concussī	concussum	*shake together*

Perfect in -vī with Supine in -tum:

serō	-ere	sēvī	satum	*sow*
spernō	-ere	sprēvī	sprētum	*despise*
cognōscō	-ere	cognōvī	cognitum	*get to know*
crēscō	-ere	crēvī	crētum	*grow*
nōscō	-ere	nōvī	nōtum	*get to know*

Perfect in -īvī with Supine in -ītum:

| quaerō | -ere | quaesīvī | quaesītum | *seek* |

Present	Infin.	Perfect	Supine	
Perfect in -ui with Supine in -tum:				
colō	-ere	coluī	cultum	*till, worship*
rapiō	-ere	rapuī	raptum	*seize*
pōnō	-ere	posuī	positum	*place*
Reduplicated Perfect with Supine in -tum:				
canō	-ere	cecinī	cantum	*sing*
tangō	-ere	tetigī	tāctum	*touch*
tendō	-ere	tetendī	tentum(tēnsum)	*stretch*
discō	-ere	didicī	—	*learn*
pariō	-ere	peperī	partum	*bring forth*
Reduplicated Perfect with Supine in -sum:				
cadō	-ere	cecidī	cāsum	*fall*
caedō	-ere	cecīdī	caesum	*beat, kill*
currō	-ere	cucurrī	cursum	*run*
fallō	-ere	fefellī	falsum	*deceive*
parcō	-ere	pepercī	—	*spare*
pellō	-ere	pepulī	pulsum	*drive*
pendō	-ere	pependī	pēnsum	*hang*
Compounds of dō:				
addō	-ere	additī	additum	*add*
condō	-ere	condidī	conditum	*found, hide*
crēdō	-ere	crēdidī	crēditum	*believe*
ēdō	-ere	ēdidī	ēditum	*give forth*
perdō	-ere	perdidī	perditum	*lose*
reddō	-ere	reddidī	redditum	*restore*
vēndō	-ere	vēndidī	vēnditum	*sell*
Lengthened stem in Perfect with Supine in -tum:				
emō	-ere	ēmī	ēmptum	*buy*
legō	-ere	lēgī	lēctum	*choose, read*
rumpō	-ere	rūpī	ruptum	*break*
fugiō	-ere	fūgī	fugitum	*fly*
agō	-ere	ēgī	āctum	*do*
frangō	-ere	frēgī	frāctum	*break*
faciō	-ere	fēcī	factum	*make*
iaciō	-ere	iēcī	iactum	*throw*
fundō	-ere	fūdī	fūsum	*pour*
edō	-ere	ēdō	ēsum	*eat*
Perfect in -ī:				
bibō	-ere	bibī	bibitum	*drink*
vertō	-ere	vertī	versum	*turn*
U- STEMS				
induō	-ere	induī	indūtum	*put on*
statuō	-ere	statuō	statūtum	*set up*
solvō	-ere	solvī	solūtum	*loosen, pay*
volvō	-ere	volvī	volūtum	*roll*

Present	Infin.	Perfect	Supine	

112 Fourth Conjugation: I- Stems
USUAL FORM

audiō	audīre	audīvī	audītum	*hear*

EXCEPTIONS

Perfect in -ivī with Supine in -tum:

sciō	-īre	scīvī	scītum	*know*

Perfect in -uī with Supine in -tum:

aperiō	-īre	aperuī	apertum	*open*

Perfect in -sī with Supine in -tum:

hauriō	-īre	hausī	haustum	*drain*
vinciō	-īre	vinxī	vinctum	*bind*

Perfect in -sī with Supine in -sum:

sentiō	-īre	sēnsī	sēnsum	*feel*

Perfect in -ī with Supine in -tum:

veniō	-īre	vēnī	ventum	*come*
repēriō	-īre	repperī	repertum	*discover*

Deponent Verbs
113 E- Stems *(Perfect -itus sum)*:

vereor	verērī	veritus sum		*fear*
reor	rērī	ratus sum		*think*

114 *Semi-Deponent Verbs:*

audeō	audēre	ausus sum	—	*dare*
soleō	solēre	solitus sum	—	*be wont*

115 *Consonant and U- Stems (Perfect -tus or -sus sum):*

fungor	fungī	fūnctus sum	*perform*
īrāscor	īrāscī	īrātus sum	*be angry*
morior	morī	mortuus sum	*die*
nāscor	nāscī	nātus sum	*be born*
patior	patī	passus sum	*suffer*
proficīscor	proficīscī	profectus sum	*set out*
queror	querī	questus sum	*complain*
ūtor	ūtī	ūsus sum	*use*
loquor	loquī	locūtus sum	*speak*
sequor			

116 *I-Stems (Perfect -ītus, -tus, or -sus sum)*

experior	experīrī	expertus sum	*try*
orior	orīrī	ortus sum	*arise*
ōrdior	ōrdīrī	ōrsus sum	*begin*
potior	potītī	potītus sum	*acquire*

SYNTAX

THE SIMPLE SENTENCE

Introductory Outline

117 SYNTAX teaches how **Sentences** are made.
Sentences are **Simple** or **Compound**.

118 A Simple Sentence has two parts:
1. The **Subject**: the person or thing spoken about;
2. The **Predicate**: that which is said about the Subject.

119 The **Subject** must be a **Substantive**, or some word or words taking the place of a Substantive:

A **Substantive**: lēx, *the law*.
A **Substantive Pronoun**: ego, *I*.
An **Adjective, Participle**, or **Adjectival Pronoun**:
Rōmānus, *a Roman*; īrātus, *an angry man*; ille, *that (man)*.
A **Verb Noun Infinitive**: nāvigāre, *to sail or sailing*.

120 The **Predicate** must either be a **Verb** or contain a Verb, because it makes a statement or assertion about the Subject; and it is usually a Verb Finite, which alone has the power of making direct statements.

EXAMPLE OF THE SIMPLE SENTENCE.

Subject.	Predicate.	Subject.	Predicate.
lēx	iubet.	nōs	pārēmus.
Law	*commands.*	*We*	*obey.*

A single Verb may be a sentence. Vēnī, vīdī, vīcī, *I came, I saw, I conquered*, comprises three sentences.

121 Some Verbs cannot by themselves form complete Predicates. The Verb sum is a complete Predicate only when it implies mere existence:

serges	est	ubī	Trōia	fuit.
Corn	*is*	*where*	*Troy*	*was.*

It more often links the Subject with the **Complement**, which completes what is said about it.

122 Verbs which link a Subject and Complement are called **Copulative Verbs**. Others besides sum are:

appāreō, *appear*;   audiō, *am called*;   maneō, *remain*;
ēvādō, exsistō, *turn out*;   videor, *seem*.

The Passives of Verbs of making, saying, thinking (**Factitive** Verbs [**134**]) are also used as Copulative Verbs:

fīō (faciō), *become* or *am made*;   feror, *am reported*;
appellor, *am called*;   legor, *am chosen*;
creor, *am created*;   putor, *am thought*;
dēclāror, *am declared*;   vocor, *am called*.

Copulative Verbs have the same case after them as before them.

123 The Complement may be—
An **Adjective**, or a Participle or Pronoun as an Adjective.
A **Substantive**.

	Subject	Predicate	
		Copulative Verb	Complement
1.	leō	est	validus.
	The lion	*is*	*strong.*
2.	illī	appellantur	philiosophī.
	They	*are called*	*philosophers.*

124 Many Verbs usually require another Verb in the Infinitive to carry on their construction: as soleō, *am wont*; possum, *am able*; queō, *can*; dēbeō, *ought*; volō, *wish*; cōnor, *try*.

solet legere.   possum īre.
He is wont to read.   *I am able to go.*

These Verbs are called **Indeterminate**, and the Infinitive following them is called **Prolative**, because it carries on (prōfert) their construction.

AGREEMENT

RULES OF THE FOUR CONCORDS

125 I. A Verb agrees with its Subject in Number and Person:

> tempus fugit.   lībrī leguntur.
> *Time flies.*   *Books are read.*

126 II. An Adjective agrees in Gender, Number and Case with the Substantive it qualifies:

> vir bonus bonam uxorem habet.
> *The good man has a good wife.*

> verae amicitiae sempiternae sunt.   CICERO.
> *True friendships are everlasting.*

127 III. When a Substantive or Pronoun is followed by another Substantive, so that the second explains or describes the first, and has the same relation to the rest of the sentence, the second Noun agrees in Case with the first, and is said to be in Apposition:

> Procas rēx Albanōrum, duōs filiōs, Numitōrem et Amulium, habuit.   LIVY.
> Procas, king of the Albans, had two sons, Numitor and Amulius.

128 IV. The Relative **quī**, **quae**, **quod**, agrees with its Antecedent in Gender, Number and Person; in Case it takes its construction from its own clause:

> amō te, mater, quae me amās.
> *I love you, mother, who love me.*

> quis hic est homo quem aedes videō?   PLAUTUS.
> *Who is this man whom I see before the house?*

> arborēs multās serit agricola, quārum fructus nōn adspiciet.
> *The farmer plants many trees, of which he will not see the fruit.*
> CICERO.

129   Composite Subject

1. When two or more Nouns are united as the Subject, the Verb and Adjectives are usually in the Plural:

> venēnō ambsūmpti sunt Hannibal et Philopoemen.   Livy
> *Hannibal and Philopoemen were cut off by poison.*

2. If the Persons of a Composite Subject are different, the Verb agrees with the first person rather than the second; with the second rather than the third:

> sī tū et Tullia valētis, ego et Cicerō valēmus.   Cicero
> *If you and Tullia e well, I and Cicero are well.*

3. When the Genders are different, Adjectives agree with the Masculine rather than the Feminine:

> rēx rēgiaque classis ūnā prōfectī.   Livy
> *The king and the royal fleet set out together.*

4. If the things expressed are without life, the Adjectives are generally Neuter:

> rēgna, honōrēs, dīvitiae, cadūca et incerta sunt.   Cicero
> *Kingdoms, honours, riches, are frail and fickle things.*

THE CASES
The Nominative and Vocative Cases

130 The Subject of a Finite Verb is in the Nominative Case:

> annī fugiunt.   labitur aetas.   Ovid
> *Years flee.*   *Time glides away.*

131 The Complement of a Finite Copulative Verb is in the Nominative Case:

> Cicerō dēclārātus est cōnsul.   Cicero
> *Cicero was declared consul.*

132 The Vocative is used with or without an Interjection (**233**):

> ō sōl pulcher! *O beauteous sun!*   Pompēi! *O Pompeius!*

THE ACCUSATIVE CASE

Accusative of Direct Object

133 The Direct Object of a Transitive Verb is in the Accusative Case:

agricola colit agrōs; uxor domum tuētur.
The farmer tills the fields; his wife takes care of the house.

134 Factitive Verbs (verbs of *making, saying, thinking*) have a second Accusative, in agreement with the Object:

Cicerōnem cōnsulem dēclārāvit.   SALLUST
The people declared Cicero consul.

Note.—The Accusative is used as the Subject of the Infinitive to form a Clause (240).

sōlem fulgere vidēmus.
We see that the sun shines.

135 Some Verbs of *teaching, asking, concealing* (doceō, *teach*, flāgitō, *demand*, rogō, *ask*, ōrō, *pray*, cēlō, *conceal*) take two Accusatives, one of the Person, the other of the Thing:

Racilius prīmum mē sententiam rogāvit.   CICERO
Racilius asked me first my opinion.

In the Passive they keep the Accusative of the Thing:

prīmus ā Reciliō sententiam rogātus sum.
I was asked my opinion first by Recilius.

136 Place to which Motion is directed is in the Accusative:

eō Rōmam, *I go to Rome* (**179**, **181**b).

Cognate Accusative

137 Many Intransitive Verbs take an Accusative containing the same idea as the Verb:

fontūna lūdum īnsoltentem lūdit.   HORACE
Fortune plays an insolent game

Adverbial Accusative

138 The Accusative of Respect is joined to Verbs and Adjectives, especially in poetry:

tremit artūs. VERGIL	naudae lacertōs. TACITUS
He trembles in his limbs.	*Bare as to the arms.*

(For Accusative of Extent, see **185**, **186**, **187**.)

THE DATIVE CASE

139 The Dative is the Case of the Person or Thing *to* or *for* whom or which something is done.

Dative of the Indirect Object

The Dative of the Indirect Object is used:

140 (1) With Transitive Verbs of *giving, telling, showing, promising;* which take also an Accusative of the Direct Object:

> tibi librum sollicitō damus aut fessō.   HORACE
> *We give you a book when you are anxious or weary.*

> saepe tibi meum somnium nārrāvī.   CICERO
> *I have often told you my dream.*

141 (2) With Intransitive Verbs of *pleasing, helping, sparing, appearing, believing, obeying,* and their opposites:

> imperiō pārent. CAESAR   parce piō generī. VERGIL
> *They obey the command.*   *Spare a pious race.*

Note.—These Verbs contain the ideas of *being pleased to, helpful to, obedient to,* etc.

142 Note.—Delectō, iuvō, *delight,* laedō, *hurt,* gubernō, *govern,* regō, *rule,* iubeō, *command,* take an accusative:

> multōs castra iuvant. HORACE   animum rege. HORACE
> *The camp delights many.*   *Rule the temper.*

Temperō, moderor, *govern, restrain,* take sometimes the accusative, sometimes the dative:

> hic moderātur equōs quī nōn moderābitur īrae.   HORACE
> *This man controls horses who will not restrain his anger.*

143 (3) With Adjectives implying *nearness, fitness, likeness, help, kindness, trust, obedience,* or any opposite idea:

> quis amīcior quam frāter frātrī? SALLUST
> *Who (is) more friendly than a brother to a brother?*

> hominī fidēlissimī sunt equus et canis. PLINY
> *The horse and the dog are the most faithful to man.*

144 The Dative of the Indirect Object is used with Compound Verbs formed with the following Prepositions:

> ad, ante, ab, sub, super, ob,
> in, inter, dē, con, post, *and* prae

And with the Adverbs bene, male, satis.

(a) Transitive:

> gigantēs bellum dīs intulērunt.   Cicero
> *The giants waged war against the gods.*

(b) Intransitive:

> his negotiīs nōn interfuit solum sed praefuit.   Cicero
> *He not only took part in these affairs, but directed them.*

> ceteris satisfaciō semper, mihi numquam.   Cicero
> *I always satisfy others, myself never.*

Dative of Advantage

145 The person or thing for whose advantage or disadvantage something is done is in the Dative Case:

> tibi arās, tibi seris, tibi eidem metis.   Plautus
> *For yourself you plough, your yourself you sow,*
> *for the same self you reap.*

> nōn sōlum nōbis dīvitēs esse volumus.   Cicero
> *We do not wish to be rich for ourselves alone.*

146 Dative of the Possessor, with esse:

> est mihī plēnus Albānī cadus.   Horace
> *I have a cask full of Alban wine. (lit. there is to me.)*

147 A **Dative** is used to express the **Results** or **Purpose** of action:

> exemplō est magnī formīca labōris.   Horace
> *The ant affords an example of great labour.*

> equitātum auxiliō Caesarī mīserunt.   Caesar
> *They set the cavalry as a help to Caesar.*

THE ABLATIVE CASE

148 The Ablative is the Case which defines circumstances; it is rendered by many prepositions, *from with, by, in.*

Ablative of Separation

149 The **Ablative of Separation** is used with Verbs meaning to *remove, release, deprive, want* (**169**); with Adjectives such as līber, *free*; also with the Adverb, *far from*:

> populus Athēniēnsis Phōciōnem patriā pepulit.   NEPOS
> *The Athenian people drove Phocion from his country.*

150 The **Ablative of Comparison** (expressing Difference) is used with Comparative Adjectives and Adverbs:

> nihil est amābilius virtūte.   CICERO
> *Nothing is more amiable than virtue.*

Note.—This construction is equivalent to quam, *than*, with the Nominative or Accusative. 'Virtute' equals 'quam virtus.'
(For **Place Whence** see **180**, **181**c.)

Ablative of Association

151 The **Ablative of Association** is used with Verbs and Adjectives denoting *plenty, fullness, possession*: abundō, *abound*, dōnō, *present*, praeditus, *endowed with* (**169**):

> villa abundat porcō, gallīnā, lacte, cāseō, melle.   CICERO
> *The farm abounds in pork, poultry, milk, cheese, honey.*

> iuvenam praestantī mūnere dōnat.   VERGIL
> *He presents the youth with a noble gift.*

152 The **Ablative of Quality** is used with an Adjective in Agreement (**171**):

> senex prōmissā barbā, horrentī capillō.   PLINY
> *An old man with long beard and rough hair.*

153 **Ablative of Respect**:
> paucī numerō.   nātiaone Mēdus.
> *Few in number.*   *By birth a Mede.*

154 The **Ablative of Manner** in which something happens or is done has an Adjective in agreement with it; or it follows the Preposition **cum**, *with*:

> iam veniet tacitō curva senecta pede.   OVID
> *Presently bent old age will come with silent foot.*

> magnā cum cūrā atque dīligentiā scrīpsit.   CICERO
> *He wrote with great care and attention.*

155 The **Ablative Absolute** is a phrase consisting of a Noun in the Ablative Case and a Participle, or another Noun, in agreement with it: it is called Absolute because its construction is independent of the rest of the Sentence:

> rēgibus exāctīs cōnsulēs creātī sunt.   LIVY
> *Kings having been abolished, consuls were elected.*

> nīl dēspērandum Teucrō duce.   HORACE
> *There must be no despair, Teucer being leader.*

Instrumental Ablative

156 The **Agent**, by whom something is done, is in the Ablative, with the Preposition **ā**, **ab**, after a Passive Verb (**194**).

The **Instrument** by means of which something is done is in the Ablative Case without a Preposition:

> hī iaculīs, illī certant dēfendere saxīs.   VERGIL
> *These strive to defend with javelins, those with stones.*

157 The **Ablative of the Cause** is used with Adjectives, Passive Participles, and Verbs:

> ōdērunt peccāre malī formīdine poenae.   HORACE
> *The bad hate to sin through fear of punishment.*

158 The Deponent Verbs fungor, *perform*, fruor, *enjoy*, vescor, *feed on*, utor, *use*, potior, *possess oneself of* (**169**), take an Ablative:

> Numidae ferīna carne vēscēbantur.   SALLUST
> *The Numidians used to feed on the flesh of wild animals.*

159 The Adjectives dignus, *worthy*, indignus, *unworthy*, and the Transitive Verb dignor, *deem worthy*, also contentus, *contented*, and fretus, *relying on*, take an Ablative:

> dīgnum laude virum Mūsa vetat morī.   HORACE
> *A man worthy of praise the Muse forbids to die.*

161 An **Ablative of the Measure of difference** is joined with Comparatives and Superlatives, and, rarely, with Verbs:

> Hibernia dīmidiō minor est quam Britannia. CAESAR
> *Ireland is smaller by half than Britain.*

162 The **Ablative of Price** is used with Verbs and Adjectives of *buying* and *selling*:

> vēndidit hic aurō patriam. VERGIL
> *This man sold his country for gold.*

The Locative Ablative

163 The **Locative** is the Case of the **Place at which** something is or happens. Its distinct forms remain in the Singular in names of towns and small islands: Romae, *at Rome*; Corcyrae, *at Corcyra*; and in a few other words, as domī, *at home*. For the most part its uses have passed to the Ablative, and it is often difficult to distinguish between the two Cases, especially in the Plural, here their forms are identical. (For **Place where**, see **178**, **181**a.)

THE GENITIVE CASE

164 The Genitive is used to define or complete the meaning of another Noun on which it depends. It also follows certain Verbs.

165 The **Genitive of Definition** follows the Noun on which it depends:

> vōx voluptātis. nōmen rēgis.
> *The word pleasure.* *The name of king.*

Note.—But the name of a city is always placed in Apposition: urbs Roma, the city of Rome.

166 The **Attributive Genitive** defines the Noun on which it depends like an Adjective:

> lūx sōlis. annī labor.
> *The light of the sun.* *A year's toil.*

167 The **Genitive of the Author**:

> ea statua dīcēbātur esse Myrōnis. CICERO
> *That statue was said to be Myro's.*

168 Verbs and Adjectives of accusing, *condemning, convicting,* or *acquitting* take a Genitive of the fault or crime:

> alter latrōciniī reus, alter caedis convictus est.   CICERO
> *The one was accused of robbery, the other was convicted of murder.*

169 Verbs and Adjectives implying *want* and *fullness,* especially egeō, indigeo, *want,* impleō, *fill,* potior, *get possession of* (**159**), plenus, *full,* often take a Genitive:

> indigeō tuī cōnsiliī.   CICERO   acerra turis plena. HORACE
> *I need your advice.*   *A pan full incense.*

> signōrum potitī sunt. SALLUST
> *They got possession of the standards.*

170 **Possessive Genitive:**

> rēgis cōpiae.   Contempsi Catilinae gladios. CICERO
> *The king' forces.*   *I have braved the swords of Catiline.*

171 The **Genitive of Quantity** has an Adjective in agreement:

> ingenuī vultūs puer ingenuīque pudōris.   JUVENAL
> *A boy of noble countenance and noble modesty.*

172 **Genitives of Value**, magnī, parvī, plurimī, minimī, nihilī, are used with verbs of *valuing* and *weighing*:

> voluptātem virtus minimī facit.   CICERO
> *Virtue accounts pleasure of very little value.*

Partitive Genitive

173 The Genitive of a Noun which is distributed into parts is called a Partitive Genitive.

> Sulla centum vīgintī suōrum āmīsit.   EUTROPIUS
> *Sulla lost a hundred and twenty of his men.*

> multae hārum arborum meā manū sunt satae.   CICERO
> *Many of these trees were planted by my hand.*

The Objective Genitive

174 Note.—The terms Subjective and Objective Genitive are used to express different relations of the Genitive to the Noun on which it depends. Thus amor patris, *the love of a father*, may mean either 'the love felt *by* a father' (where patris is a Subjective Genitive), or 'the love felt *for* a father' (where patris is an Objective Genitive).

175 An Objective Genitive is used with Verbal Substantives, Adjectives, and Participles which have the meaning of *love, desire, hope, fear, care, knowledge, skill, power*:

With Substantives:
> erat īnsitus mentī cognitiōnis amor.   CICERO
> *Love of knowledge had been implanted in the mind.*

With Adjectives and Participles:
> avida est perīculī virtūs.   SENECA
> *Valour is greedy of danger.*

> quis famulus amantior dominī quam canis?   COLUMELLA
> *What servant is fonder of his master than the dog is?*

176 Most Verbs of *remembering, forgetting, reminding*, meminī, reminīscor, oblīvīscor, usually take the Genitive, sometimes the Accusative. Recordor almost always takes the Accusative, rarely the Genitive:
> animus meminit praeteritōrum.   CICERO
> *The mind remembers past things.*

> nam modō vōs animō dulcēs reminīscor, amīcī.   OVID
> *For now I remember you, O friends, dear to my soul.*

177 The Adjectives corresponding to these Verbs, memor, ammemor, always take a Genitive:
> omnēs immemorem beneficiī ōdērunt.   CICERO
> *All hate one who is forgetful of a kindness.*

Verbs of *pitying*, misereor, miserēscō, take a Genitive:
> nīl nostrī miserēre.   VERGIL
> *You pity me not at all.*

> Arcadiī, quaesō, miserēscite rēgis.   VERGIL
> *Take pity, I entreat, on the Arcadian king.*

Note.—Miseror, commiseror take an Accusative.

PLACE, TIME, AND SPACE

Place

178 **Place where** anything is or happens is generally in the Ablative Case with a Preposition; sometimes without a Preposition (especially in poetry), an Adjective of place being attached to the Substantive:

> castra sunt in Ītaliā contrā rempūblicam collocāta.   CICERO
> *A camp has been formed in Italy against the republic.*

> mediō sedet īnsula pontō.   OVID
> *The island lies in mid ocean.*

179 **Place whither** is in the Accusative with a Preposition:

> Caesar in Ītaliam magnīs itineribus contendit.   CAESAR
> *Caesar hastened into Italy with long marches.*

180 **Place whence** is in the Ablative with **ab**, **ex**, or **dē**:

> ex Āsiā trānsīs in Eurōpam.   CURTIUS
> *Out of Asia you cross into Europe.*

181 In names of **towns** and **small islands**, also in **domus**, and **rus**, **Place where**, **whither**, or **whence** is expressed by the Case without a Preposition:

(a) **Place where**, by the Locative:

> quid Rōmae faciam? JUVENAL   is habitat Miletī. TERENCE
> *What am I to do at Rome?*   *He lives at Miletus.*

> Philippis Neāpolī est, Lentulus Puteolīs.   CICERO
> *Philip is at Naples, Lentulus at Puteoli.*

> est mihi namque domī pater, est iniusta noverca.   VERGIL
> *I have at home a father and an unjust stepmother.*

(b) **Place whither**, by the Accusative:

> Rēgulus Carthāgine rediit.   CICERO
> *Regulus returned to Carthage.*

> vōs īte domum; ego rūs ībō.
> *Go ye home; I will go into the country.*

(c) **Place whence**, by the Ablative:

> Dēmarātus fūgit Tarquiniōs Corinthō.   CICERO
> *Demaratus fled from Corinth to Tarquinii.*

182 The road by which one goes is in the Ablative:

> ībam forte Viā Sacrā.   HORACE
> *I was going by chance along the Sacred Way.*

Time

183 **Time at which**, in answer to the question *When?* is expressed by the Ablative: hieme, *in winter*, sōlis occāsū, *at sunset*:

> ego Capuam vēnī eō ipsō diē.   CICERO
> *I came to Capua on that very day.*

184 **Time within which**, generally by the Ablative:

> quicquid est bīduō sciēmus.   CICERO
> *Whatever it is, we shall know in two days.*

185 **Time during which**, generally by the Accusative:

> Perīclēs quadrāgintā annōs praefuit Athēnīs.   CICERO
> *Pericles was leader of Athens forty years.*

Space

186 **Space over which** motion takes place is in the Accusative:

> mīlia tum prānsī tria rēpimus.   HORACE
> *Then having had luncheon we crawl three miles.*

187 **Space of measurement**, answering the questions *How high? How deep? How broad? How long?* is generally in the Accusative:

> erant mūrī Babylōnis ducēnōs pedēs altī.   PLINY
> *The walls of Babylon were two hundred feet high.*

PREPOSITIONS

188 With **Accusative**:

ante, apud, ad, adversus,
circum, circā, citrā, cis,
contrā, inter, ergā, extrā,
īnfrā, intrā, iuxtā, ob,
penes, pōne, post, and praeter,
prope, propter, per, secundum,
suprā, versus, ultrā, trāns;
Add super, subter, sub and in,
When 'motion' 'tis, not 'state',
 they mean.

before, near, to, towards,
around, about, on this side of,
against, between, towards, outside of,
beneath, within, beside, on account of,
in the power of, behind, after, along,
near, on account of, through, next to,
above, towards, beyond, across;
Add *over, underneath, under, into,*
When they mean 'motion', not 'state'.

189 With **Ablative**:

ā, ab, absque, cōram, dē,
palam, clam, cum, ex, and ē,
sine, tenus, prō, and prae:
Add super, subter, sub and in,
When 'state' not 'motion', 'tis
 they mean.

by, from, without, in the presence of, from,
in sight of, unknown to, with, out of,
without, as far as, for, before;
Add *over, underneath, under, in,*
When they mean 'state', not 'motion'.

IMPERSONAL VERBS

Case Construction

190 The following Verbs of *feeling* take an Accusative of the person with a Genitive of the of the cause: **miseret**, **piget**, **paenitet**, **pudet**, **paedet**:

miseret tē aliōrum, tuī tē nec miseret nec pudet.   PLAUTUS
You pity others, for yourself you have neither pity nor shame.

191 **Libet**, **licet** take a Dative:

nē libeat tibi quod nōn licet.   CICERO
Let not that please you which is not lawful.

192 Interest, *it is of importance*, *it concerns*, is used with the Genitive of the person or thing concerned, but with the feminine Ablatives meā, tuā, suā, nostrā, vestrā or the Possessive Pronouns:

> interest omnium rēctē facere.　Cicero
> *It is for the good of all to do right.*

> et tuā et meā interest tē valēre.　Cicero
> *It is of importance to you and to me that you should be well.*

193 Rēfert, *it concerns*, *it matters*, is also used with the feminine Ablatives of the Possessive Pronouns:

> quid meā rēfert cui serviam?　Phaedrus
> *What does it matter to me whom I serve?*

PASSIVE CONSTRUCTION

194 When a sentence is changed from the Active to the Passive form:

The Object of a Transitive Verb becomes the Subject; the Subject becomes Agent in the Ablative with the Preposition ā or ab:

Numa lēgēs dedit.	Numa gave laws.
ā Numā lēgēs datae sunt.	Laws were given by Numa.

195 Intransitive Verbs are used impersonally in the Passive:

nōs currimus.	*We run.*
ā nōbīs curritur.	lit. *There is running (done) by us.*

or the Agent may be omitted:

sīc īmus ad astra. ⎫
sīc ītur ad astra. ⎬　*Thus we go to the stars.*

PRONOUNS

196 The Reflexive Pronoun, **sē, sēsē, suī, sibi**, of the Third Person, refers to the Subject in a Simple Sentence:

> fūr tēlō sē dēfendit.   CICERO
> *The thief defends himself with a weapon.*

> īra suī impotēns est.   SENECA
> *Anger is not master of itself.*

197 The Possessive **suus**, formed from the Reflexive, is used to express *his own, their own*, when emphasis is required, and usually refers to the Subject of the Verb:

> nēmō rem suam emit.
> *No one buys what is his own.*

sometimes to other cases if the context shows that it cannot be referred to the Subject:

> apibus fructum restituō suum.   PHAEDRUS
> *I restore to the bees their own produce.*

198 **Eius** is the Possessive used of the Third Person where no emphasis is required and it does not refer to the Subject:

> Chīlius tē rogat, et ego eius rogātū.   CICERO
> *Chilius asks you, and I (ask you) at his request.*

199 **Hic**, **ille** are often used in contrast: **hic** usually means *the latter*, **ille** *the former*:

> quōcumque adspiciō, nihil est nisi pontus et āēr,
> nubibus hic tumidus, flūctibus ille mināx.   OVID

> *Whithersoever I look, there is naught but sea and sky,*
> *the latter heaped with clouds, the former threatening with billows.*

200 **Ipse**, *self*, is used of all the three Persons, with or without a Personal Pronoun: ipse ībō, *I will go myself*.

Indefinite Pronouns

201 **Aliquis** means *some one*: dīcat aliquis, *suppose some one to say*.

202 Quīdam means *a certain person* (known but not named):
vir quīdam, *a certain man.*

203 Quisquam (Substantive) ⎫
Ūllus (Adjective) ⎭ *any at all*

are used after a negative word, or a question expecting a negative
answer:

nec amet quemquam nec amētur ab ūllō.   JUVENAL
Let him not love anyone or be loved by any.

nōn ūllus arātrō dignus honōs.   VERGIL
Not any due honour to the plough.

204 Quīvīs, **quīlibet**, *any you like*:

nōn cuivīs hominī contingit adīre Corinthum.   HORACE
It does not happen to every man to go to Corinth.

205 Quisque, *each* (severally), is often used with sē, suus:

sibi quisque habeant quod suum est.   PLAUTUS
Let them have each for himself what is his own.

206 Uterque, *each* (of two), *both*, can be used with the Genitive of
Pronouns; but with Substantives it agrees in case:

uterque parēns. OVID   utrōque vestrum dēlector. CICERO
Both father and mother.   *I am delighted with both of you.*

207 Uter, *which* (of two), is Interrogative: uter melior? *which is the
better?*

uter utrī īnsidiās fēcit?
Which laid an ambush for which?

208 Alter, *the one, the other* (of two), *the second*, is the Demonstrative
of uter: alter ego, alter idem, *a second self*:

quicquid negat alter, et alter.   HORACE
Whatever the one denies, so does the other.

209 Alius, *another* (of any number), *different*:

Fortūna nunc mihi, nunc aliī benigna.   HORACE
Fortune, kind now to me, now to another.

THE VERB INFINITE

210 The parts of the Verb Infinite have some of the uses of Verbs, some of the uses of Nouns,

211 The **Infinitive** as a Verb has Tenses, Present, Past, or Future, it governs Cases and is qualified by Adverbs; as a Noun it is neuter, indeclinable, used only as Nominative or Accusative.

212 As Nominative:

> iuvat īre et Dōrica castra vīsere.   Vergil
> *To go and view the Doric camp is pleasant.*

> nōn vīvere bonum est sed bene vīvere.   Seneca
> *It is not living which is good, but living well.*

213 As Accusative:

> errāre, nescīre, dēcipī, et malum et turpe dūcimus.   Cicero
> *To err, to be ignorant, to be deceived, we deem both unfortunate and disgraceful.*

214 The Prolative Infinitive is often used to carry on the construction of Indeterminate and some other Verbs:

> solent diū cōgitāre quī magna volunt gerere.   Cicero
> *They are wont to reflect long who wish to do great things.*

Gerund and Gerundive

215 The Genitive, Dative, and Ablative of the **Gerund**, and the Accusative with a Preposition, are used as Cases of the Infinitive.

216 The **Accusative** of the Gerund follows some Prepositions, especially ad, ob, inter:

> ad bene vīvendum breve tempus satis est longum.   Cicero
> *For living well a short time is long enough.*

> morēs puerōrum sē inter lūdendum dētegunt.   Quintilian
> *The characters of boys show themselves in their play.*

217 The **Genitive** of the Gerund is used after Substantives and Adjectives:

> ars scrībendī discitur. cupidus te audiendī sum. Cicero
> *The art of writing is learnt. I am desirous of hearing you.*

218 The **Dative** of the Gerund follows a few Verbs, Adjectives, and Substantives:

> pār est disserendō. Cicero dat operam legendō.
> *He is equal to arguing.* *He gives attention to reading.*

219 The **Ablative** of the Gerund expresses Cause or Manner, or it follows a Preposition:

> fugiendō vincimus. dē pugnandō dēlīberant.
> *We conquer by flying.* *They deliberate about fighting.*

220 If the Verb is Transitive, the **Gerundive** is more often used than the Gerund, agreeing with the Object as an Adjective. It takes the Gender and Number of the Object, but the Object is drawn into the Case of the Gerundive.

The following examples show how the Gerundive takes the place of the Gerund:

Gerund		Gerundive	
ad petendum pācem		ad petendam pācem	*in order to seek peace.*
petendī pācem		petendae pācis	*of seeking peace.*
petendō pācem	becomes	petendae pācī	*for seeking peace.*
petendō pācem		petendā pāce	*by seeking peace.*
ad mūtandum lēgēs		ad mūtandās lēgum	*in order to change laws.*
mūtandī lēgēs		mūtandārum lēgum	*of changing laws.*
mūtandō lēgēs		mūtandīs lēgibus	*for or by changing laws.*

221 The Gerund and Gerundive are often used to express that something out or is to be done; the Dative of the Agent being expressed or understood.

222 If the Verb is **Intransitive** the Gerund is used impersonally:

> eudum est mihi eundum est
> *One must go.* *I must go.*

223 If the Verb is **Transitive** the Gerundive is used in agreement:

> Caesarī omnia ūnō tempore erant agenda. Caesar
> *All things had to be done by Caesar at one time.*

SUPINES

224 The Supines are also used as Cases of the Infinitive:

225 The **Supine** in -**um** is an Accusative after Verbs of motion, expressing the purpose:

> lūsum it Maecēnās, dormītum ego.   HORACE
> *Maecenas goes to play, I to sleep.*

with the Infinitive **īrī**, used impersonally, it forms a Future Passive Infinitive:

> aiunt urbem captum īrī.
> *They say that the city will be taken.*

Note.—Literally, *they say there is a going to take the city.*

226 The **Supine** in -**ū** (Dative and Ablative) is used with some Adjectives, such as facilis, dulcis, turpis, and the Substantives fās, nefās:
turpe factu, *disgraceful to do.*

> hoc fās est dictū.   lībertās, dulce audītū nōmen.   LIVY
> *It is lawful to say this.   Freedom, a name sweet to hear.*

ADVERBS

227 **Adverbs** show how, when, and where the action of the Verb takes place; they also qualify Adjectives or other Adverbs: rēctē facere, *to do rightly*; hūc nunc venīre, *to come hither now*; facile prīmus, *easily first*; valdē celeriter, *very swiftly*.

228 **Negative Adverbs** are **nōn**, **haud**, **nē**:

Nōn, *not*, is simply negative:

> nivēs in altō marī nōn cadunt.   PLINY
> *No snow falls on the high seas.*

Haud, *not*, is used with Adjectives and with other Adverbs:

> rēs haud dubia.   haud aliter.
> *No doubtful matter.   Not otherwise.*

Nē is used with the second person of the Perfect Subjunctive for prohibitions: nē trānsierīs Hibērum (LIVY), *do not cross the Ebro*; with the second person of the Present Subjunctive **nē** often means *lest*: nē fôrte creda (HORACE), *lest by chance you believe* or *that you may not by chance believe.*

CONJUNCTIONS

229 **Conjunctions** connect words, sentences, and clauses, and are **Co-ordinative** or **Subordinative**.

230 **Co-ordinative Conjunctions** connect two or more Nouns in the same Case:

> mīrātur portās, strepitumque et strāta viārum.   VERGIL
> *He marvels at the gates and the noise and the pavements.*

> aut Caesar, aut nūllus.
> *Either Caesar or nobody.*

231 **Subordinate Conjunctions** join Dependent Clauses to the Principal Sentence. (See Compound Sentence.)

Co-ordination

232 When two or more sentences are joined together by Co-ordinative Conjunctions, so as to form parts of one sentence, they are said to be **Co-ordinate Sentences**, and each is independent in its construction:

> et mihi sunt vīrēs et mea tēla nocent.   OVID
> *I too am not powerless, and my weapons hurt.*

> Gygēs ā nūllō vidēbātur, ipse autem omnia vidēbat.   CICERO
> *Gyges was seen by no one, while he himself saw all things.*

INTERJECTIONS

233 **Interjections** are apart from the construction of the sentence
Ō, ah, ēheu, heu, prō, are used with the Vocative, Nominative or Accusative; ēn, ecce, with the Nominative or Accusative; ei, vae, with the Dative only:

> ō fōrmōse puer! VERGIL   ō fortūnātem Rōmam! CICERO
> *O beautiful boy!*   *O fortunate Rome!*

> ēn ego vester Ascanius!   VERGIL
> *Lo here I am your Ascanius!*

> vae victīs!   VERGIL
> *Woe to the vanquished!*

QUESTIONS

234 Single Questions are asked by

> nōnne, expecting the answer *yes*.
> num, expecting the answer *no*.
> -ne, expecting either answer.
> an, expressing surprise and expecting answer *no*.

> canis nōnne similis lupō est?   CICERO
> *Is not a dog like a wolf?*

> num negāre audēs?   Cicero   potesne dīcere?   CICERO
> *Do you venture to deny? Can you say?*

> an tū mē trīstem esse putās?   PLAUTUS
> *Do you think I am sad?*

235 Alternative Questions are most often asked by:

> utrum…an (*or*).
> -ne…an (*or*).

> utrum ea vestra an nostra culpa est?   CICERO
> *Is that your fault or ours?*

> Rōmamne veniō, an hīc maneō, an Arpīnum fugiō?   CICERO
> *Do I come to Rome, or stay her, or flee to Arpinum?*

THE COMPOUND SENTENCE

236 A **Compound Sentence** consists of a Principal Sentence with one or more Subordinate Clauses.

237 Subordinate Clauses depend in their construction on the Principal Sentence. They are:

I. Substantival.　II. Adverbial.　III. Adjectival.

I. Subtantival Clauses.

238 A **Substantival Clause** stands like a Substantive, as Subject or Object of a Verb, or in Apposition.

239 Substantival Clauses have three forms, corresponding to the three Direct forms of the Simple Sentence.

(1) Indirect Statement; (2) Indirect Command or Request; (3) Indirect Question.

240　　　　　　　　　　**(1) Indirect Statement**

The **Accusative with Infinitive** is the most usual form of Indirect Statement:

valeō.	} Direct	scis me valere.	} Indirect
I am well.	} Statement	*You know that I am well.*	} Statement

nūntiātum est Scipiōnem adesse.　Caesar
It was announced that Scipio was at hand.

Dēmocritus dīcit innumerābilēs esse mundōs.　Cicero
Democritus says that there are countless worlds.

illud temerē dictum, sapientēs omnēs esse bonōs.　Cicero
It was rashly said that all wise men are good.

A Clause formed by **ut with the Subjunctive** is sometimes used in Indirect Statement:

expedit ut cīvitātēs sua iūra habeant.　Livy
That states should have their own laws is expedient.

Sometimes a Clause formed by **Quod** with the Indicative is used instead of the Accusative with Infinitive, especially with Verbs of rejoicing and grieving:

dolet mihi quod tū stomachāris.　Cicero
It grieves me that you were angry.

241   **(2) Indirect Command or Request**

A Clause depending on a Verb of *commanding, wishing, exhorting, entreating*, is in the **Subjunctive**: if positive, with **ut**; if negative, with **nē**.

valē. } Direct   cūrā ut valeās.   } Indirect
Farewell. } Command   *Take care that you keep well.* } Command

postulātur ab amīcō ut sit sincērus.   CICERO
It is required of a friend that he be sincere.

mihi nē abscēdam imperat.   TERENCE
He commands me not to go away.

242   **(3) Indirect Question**

Indirect Question is formed by a dependent Interrogative Pronoun or Particle with a Verb in the Subjunctive:

valēsne?   } Direct   quaerō valēsne.   } Indirect
Are you well? } Question   *I ask if you are well.* } Question

nesciō quid faciās.
I do not know what you are doing.

fac mē certiōrem quandō adfutūrus sīs.   CICERO
Let me know when you are coming.

243   **II. ADVERBIAL CLAUSES**

Adverbial Clauses qualify like an Adverb, answering the questions *how, why, when*, and are joined to the Principal Sentence by Conjunctions. They are:

1. Consecutive, expressing *consequence*, joined by **ut**, *so that*, **ut nōn**, *so that...not*, with the **Subjunctive**:

nōn sum ita hebes ut istud dīcam.   CICERO
I am not so stupid as to say that.

2. Final, expressing *purpose*, joined by **ut**, *in order that*, **nē**, *in order that...not*, with the **Subjunctive**:

veniō ut videam.   abiī ne videram.
I came that I may see.   *I went away that I might not see.*

3. Causal, giving a *reason*, joined by **quod, quia**, *because*, **quoniam, quandō**, *since*, with the **Indicative**:

ego prīmam tollō nōminor quia Leō.   PHAEDRUS
I take the first (share) because my name is Lion.

or by **cum**, *since*, with the **Subjunctive**:

> quae cum ita sint, ab Iove veniam petō.   CICERO
> *Since these things are so, I seek pardon of Jupiter.*

4. Temporal, showing the *time*, joined by **ubī**, **ut**, **cum**, **quandō**, *when*, **quotiēns**, *as often as*, **dum**, **dōnec**, *while, until*, generally with the Indicative:

> lituō Rōmulus regiōnēs dīxerit tum cum urbem condidit.   CICERO
> *Romulus marked out the districts with a staff at the time when he founded the city.*

But in narrative **cum** is often used with the Imperfect or Pluperfect Subjunctive:

> cum ad oppidum vēnisset oppugnāre instituit.   CAESAR
> *When he had come to the town, he began to attack it.*

5. Conditional, expressing a *condition*, joined by **sī**, *if*, **nisi**, *unless*. If the condition is regarded as relating to an actual fact, the Indicative is used; if to what is only possible or imaginary, the Subjunctive:

> sī valēs, bene est.   CICERO
> *If you are in good health, all is well.*

> sī veniās, gaudeam.
> *If you were to come, I should rejoice.*

> sī vēnissēs, gāvīsus essem.
> *If you had come, I should have rejoiced.*

6. Concessive, making a *concession*, joined by **etsī**, **etiamsī**, *even if, although*, **quamquam**, *although*, with the Indicative if something is granted as being true, with the Subjunctive if it is only granted for the sake of argument:

> etiamsī tacent, satis dīcunt.   CICERO
> *Although they are silent, they say enough.*

> etiamsī tacērent, satis dīcerent.
> *Even if the were to be silent, they would say enough.*

7. Comparative, making an imaginary *comparison*, joined by **quasi**, **tamquam**, **sī**, **ut sī**, **velut sī**, *as if*, with the Subjunctive:

> tamquam sī claudus sim, cum fūstī est ambulandum.
> *I must walk with a stick as if I were lame.*   PLAUTUS

244 III. Adjectival Clauses

Adjectival Clauses qualify like an Adjective, and are joined to the Principal Sentence by the Relative **quī**, **quae**, **quod**, or by a Relative Participle with the Verb in the Indicative:

> est in Britanniā flūmen, quod appellātur Tamesis.   CAESAR
> *There is in Britain a river which is called the Thames.*

But the Relative often forms a Clause Consecutive, Final or Causal, with the Subjunctive, corresponding to the Adverbial Clauses of similar meaning:

> lēgātōs mīsit quī pācem peterent.
> *He sent ambassadors to seek peace.*

> nē illī sit cēra ubī facere possit litterās.   PLAUTUS
> *Let him not have any wax on which to write.*

245 Sequence of Tenses

The general rule for the Sequence of Tenses is that a Primary Tense in the Principal Sentence is followed by a Primary Tense in the Clause, a Historic Tense by a Historic Tense.

246 RULES FOR THE CHANGE OF DIRECT SPEECH INTO INDIRECT SPEECH (ŌRĀTIŌ OBLĪQUA)

Ōrātiō Oblīqua is used in reports, whether short or long, of speeches, letters, etc.

247 In **Indirect Statement** the Principal Verbs are changed from the Indicative to the Infinitive in the same tense:

Direct	Indirect
Rōmulus urbem condidit.	nārrant Rōmulum urbem condidisse.
Romulus founded the city.	*They say that Romulus founded the city.*

Note.—If the actual words of the speaker or writer are quoted, they are often introduced with inquit, *he says*, following the first word:

> Rōmulus haec precātus. "hinc," inquit, "Rōmānī, Iuppiter
>   iterāre pugnam iubet."   LIVY
> *When Romulus had thus prayed, "Hence," he says, "Romans,*
>   *Jupiter commands (you) to renew the battle."*

248 In **Indirect Commands** the Subjunctive (most commonly in the Imperfect, but sometimes in the Present Tense) takes the place of the of the Imperative in Direct Commands:

īte, inquit, creāte cōnsulēs ex plēbe.	(hortātus est:) īrent, creārent cōnsulēs ex plēbe.
Go, he says, and elect consuls from the plebs.	*He exhorted them to go and elect consuls from the plebs*

249 In **Indirect Questions** the Verbs are in the Subjunctive (usually in the Imperfect or Pluperfect Tense, but sometimes in the Present or Perfect):

quid agis? inquit.	rogāvit cum quid ageret.
He says, 'What are you doing?'	*He asked him what he was doing.*
clāmāvit 'quid ēgistī?'	quaesīvit quid ēgisset.
He exclaimed, 'What have you done?'	*He asked what he had done.*

250 The Pronoun which refers to the Subject of the Verb is the Reflexive **sē**; the Pronoun which refers generally to the Person spoken to is **ille**:

dicit Caesarī Ariovistus nisi dēcēdet sese illum nōn prō amīcō, sed prō hoste habitūrum.   CAESAR

Ariovistus says to Caesar that 'unless he departs he (Ariovistus) shall consider him (Caesar) not as a friend by as an enemy.'

Sometimes **ipse** is used for the sake of clear distinction:

dicit Ariovistus trānsisse Rhēnum sese nōn sua sponte sed rogātum ā Gallīs; sēdēs habēre in Galliā ab ipsīs concessās.

Ariovistus says that he had crossed the Rhine, not of his own accord, but when asked by the Gauls; that he had settlements in Gaul granted by themselves (the Gauls).

251 In any Clause dependent on a Clause in Ōrātiō Oblīqua, the Verb must be in the Subjunctive:

Rōmulus urbem condidit quae Rōma appellātur.	nārrātur Rōmulum urbem condidisse quae Rōma appēlletur.
Romulus founded the city which is called Rome.	*It is related that Romulus founded the city which is called Rome.*
Titum amō quia bonus est.	dicit sē Titum amāre quia bonus sit.
I love Titus because he is good.	*He says that he loves Titus because he is good.*

252

Direct Statement	Indirect Statement

cum Germānis Haeduī semel atque iterum armīs contendērunt; magnam calamitātem pulsī accēpērunt, omnem nōbilitātem, omnem equitātum āmisērunt. sed peius victōribus Sēquanis quam Haeduīs victīs accidit; proptereā quod Ariovistus, rēx Germānōrum, in eōrum fīnibus cōnsēdit, tertiamque partem agrī Sēquanī, quī est optimus tōtius Galliae, occupāvit. Ariovistus barbarus, īrācundus est, nōn possunt eius imperia diūtius sustinērī.

The Haeduans have repeatedly fought with the Germans; they have been defeated and suffered great misfortune; they have lost all their nobles and all their cavalry. But worse has befallen the conquering Sequani than the conquered Haeduans, for Ariovistus, king of the Germans, has settled in their dominions and occupied a third part of their territory, which is the best in all Gaul. Ariovistus is barbarous and passionate; his commands can no longer be endured.

Locūtus est prō Haeduīs Divitiacus: cum Germānis Haeduōs semel atque iterum armais contendisse; magnam calamitātem pulsōs accēpisse, omnem nōbilitātem, omnem equitātum āmisisse. sed peius victōribus Sēquanis quam Haeduīs victīs accidisse; proptereā quod Ariovistus, rēx Germānōrum, in eōrum fīnibus cōnsēdisset, tertiamque partem agrī Sēquanī, quī esset optimus tōtius Galliae, occupāvisset, Ariovistum esse barbarōrum, īrācundum, nōn posse eius imperia diūtius sustinērī.

Divitiacus said on behalf of the Haedui: "That the Haedui had fought repeatedly with the Germans; that, having been defeated, they had suffered great misfortune (and) had lost all their nobles, all their cavalry. But that worse had befallen the conquering Sequani than the conquered Haeduans, for Ariovistus, king of the Germans, had settled in their dominions and had occupied a third part of their territory, which was the best in all Gaul. That Ariovistus was barbarous, passionate; and that his commands could no longer be endured.

253

Direct Command	Indirect Command

vestrae prīstinae virtūtis et tot secundissimōrum proeliōrum retinēte memoriam, atque ipsum Caesarem, cuius ductū saepenumerō hostēs superāvistis, praesentem adesse exīstimāte.

Keep in mind your former valour and your many successful battles, and imagine that Caesar, under whose leadership you so often overcame your foes, is himself present.

Labiēnus militēs cohortātus ut suae prīstinae virtūtis et tot secundissimōrum proeliōrum retinērent memoriam, atque ipsum Caesarem, cuius ductū saepenumerō hostēs superāssent, praesentem adesse exīstimārent, dat sīgnum proeliī.

Labienus, having exhorted the soldiers to keep in mind their former valour and their many successful battles, and to imagine that Caesar, under whose leadership they had so often overcome their foes, was himself present, gives the signal for battle.

254 RULES OF QUANTITY

I. General Rules

1. A syllable is short when it contains a short vowel followed by a simple consonant or by another vowel: as pater, deus.
2. A syllable is long when it contains a long vowel or diphthong: frāter,- cāedēs, nēmo.
3. A vowel short by nature becomes long by position when it is followed by two consonants, or by x or z: cānto, sīmplēx, orўza.
   Exception.—A short vowel before a mute followed by a liquid becomes doubtful: lugubre, tenebrae, trīplex.
4. A long vowel or diphthong becomes short before another vowel, or before h followed by a vowel: proavus, trahō, praeesse.
   But in Greek words the vowel or diphthong keeps its length: āer, Aenēas, Enÿo, Meliboeus.
   Exceptions.—In fīo, Gāius, Pompēi, dīus, diēi, Rhēa (Silvia), the vowel remains long.
   Note.—Prae in compounds is the only Latin word in which a diphthong occurs before a vowel.
5. A syllable is called doubtful when it is found in poetry to be sometimes long, sometimes short: Diana, fidei, rei, and the genitives in -ius, as illius, except alīus, alterius.
6. The quantity of a stem syllable is kept, as a rule, in compounds and derivatives: cado occido, ratus irritus, flūmen flūmineus.
   Exceptions to this are numerous:—lūceō, lucerna.

255 II. Rules for Monosyllables

Most monosyllables are long: dā, dēs, mē, vēr, sī, sīs, sōl, nōs, tū, mūs.
Exceptions:

Substantives:	cor, fel, mel, os (bone), vir.
Pronouns:	is, id, qua (any), quis, quid, quod, quot, tot.
Verbs:	dat, det, it, scit, sit, stat, stet, fac, fer, es (from sum).
Particles:	ab, ad, an, at, bis, cis, et, in, nec, ob, per, pol, sat, sed, sub, ut, vel, and the enclitics -ne, -que, -ve.

256 III. Rules for Final Syllables

1. **A final** is short.
   Exceptions.—Ablatives of decl. 1. mēnsā, bonā; Vocative of Greek names in **as**, Aenēā; and of some in ēs, Anchīsā; Indeclinable Numerals, trīgintā; Imperatives of conj. 1. amā (but puta); most Particles in **a**; frūstrā, intereā (but ita, quia, short).

2. **E final** is short: lege, timēte, carēre.

   Exceptions.—Ablatives of declension 5. rē, diē, with the derivatives quārē, hodiē. Cases of many Greek nouns; also famē. Adverbs formed from Adjectives; miserē; also ferē, fermē (but bene, male, facile, impūne, temere, short). Imperatives of conj. 2. monē (but cave is doubtful). Also the interjection ohē.

3. **I final** is long: dīcī, plēbī, dolī.

   Exceptions.—Vocatives and Datives of Greek nouns; Chlōri, Thyrsidi; but Datives sometimes long: Paridī. Particles; sīcubi, nēcubi, nisi, quasi. Mihi, tibi, sibi, ubi, and ibi are doubtful.

4. **O final** is long: virgō, multō, iuvō.

   Exceptions.—Duo, octo, ego, modo, cito, and a few verbs: puto, scio. In the Silver age, o was often shortened in Verbs and Nouns.

5. **U final** is long: cantū, dictū, diū.

6. **Finals in c** are long: illīc; except nec and dōnec.

7. **Finals in l, d, t** are short: Hannibal, illud, amāvit.

8. **Finals in n** are short: Īlion, agmen.

   Exceptions.—Many Greek words: Hymēn, Ammōn.

9. **Finals in r** are short: calcar, amābitur, Hector.

   Exceptions.—Many Greek words: āēr, crātēr; and compounds of pār: dispār, impār.

10. **Finals in as** are long: terrās, Menalcās.

    Exceptions.—Greek nouns of decl. 3. Arcas (gen. -adis), and acc. pl. lampadas; anas, a duck.

11. **Finals in es** are long: nūbēs, vidērēs.

    Exceptions.—Cases of Greek nouns: Arcades, Nāiades. Nominatives of a few substantives and adjectives with dental stems in et, it, or id: seges, pedes, obses; also penes. Compounds of es; ades, potes.

12. **Finals in is** are short: dīceris, ūtilis, ēnsis.

    Exceptions.—Datives and Ablatives in īs, including grātīs, forīs. Accusatives in īs: nāvīs; some Greek Nouns in īs: Salamīs. Sanguis, pulvis, doubtful. 2nd Pers. Sing. Pres. Ind. conjugation 4. audīs; compounds of vīs, sīs; also velīs , mālīs, nōlīs. 2nd Pers. Sing. Perf. Subj. amāverīs.

13. **Finals in os** are long: ventōs, custōs, sacerdōs.

    Exceptions.—Greek words in os: Dēlos, Acardos; also compos, impos, exos.

14. **Finals in us** are short: holus, intus, amāmus.

    Exceptions.—Nominatives from long stems of decl. 3. are long: virtūs, tellūs, incūs, iuventūs; the contracted cases of del. 4.: artūs, gradūs; and a few Greek words: Dīdūs, Sapphūs (genitive).

15. The Greek words chelys, Tiphys, Erīnys have the final syllable short and the vocative ending y.

APPENDIX

Memorial Lines on the Gender of Latin Substantives

I. General Rules.
The Gender of a Latin Noun
by meaning, form, or use is shown.

1. A Man, Month, Mountain, River, Wind,
and People **Masculine** we find:
Rōmulus, Octōber, Pindus, Padus, Eurus, Achīvī.

2. A Woman, Island, Country, Tree,
and City, **Feminine** we see:
Pēnelopē, Cȳprus, Germānia, laurus, Athēnae.

3. To Nouns that cannot be declined
The **Neuter** Gender is assigned:
Examples fās and nefās give
And the Verb–Noun Infinitive
Est summum nefās fallere:
Deceit is gross impiety.

Common are: sacerdōs, dux,	*priest (priestess), leader*
vātēs, parēns et coniūnx,	*seer, parent, wife (husband)*
cīvis, comes, custōs, vindex,	*citizen, companion, guard, avenger*
adulēscēns, infāns, index,	*youth (maid), infant, informer*
iūdex, testis, artifex,	*judge, witness, artist*
praesul, exsul, opifex,	*director, exile, worker*
hērēs, mīles, incola,	*heir (heiress), soldier, inhabitant*
auctor, augur, advena,	*author, augur, new-comer*
hostis, obses, praeses, ālēs,	*enemy, hostage, president, bird*
patruēlis et satelles	*cousin, attendant*
mūniceps et interpres,	*burgess, interpreter*
iuvenis et antistes	*young person, overseer*
aurīga, prīnceps: add to these	*charioteer, chief*
bōs, damma, talpa, serpēns, sūs,	*ox (cow), deer, mole, serpent, swine*
camēlus, canis, tīgris, perdix, grūs.	*camel, dog, tiger, partridge, crane.*

II.   Special Rules for the Declensions.

First Declension (Ā-Stems).

Rule.   Feminine in First *a, ē*,
Masculine *ās, ēs* will be.

Exc.   Nouns denoting Males in *a*
are by meaning *Māscula*:
and Masculine is found to be
Hadria, *the Adriatic Sea*.

Second Declension (O-Stems).

Rule.   O-Nouns in *us* and *er* become
Masculine, but Neuter *um*.

Exc.   Feminine are found in *us*,
alvus, Arctus, carbasus,   *paunch, Great Bear, linen*
colus, humus, pampinus,   *distaff, ground, vine-leaf*
vannus: also trees, as pirus;   *winnowing-fan, pear-tree*
with some jewels, as sapphīrus;   *sapphire*
Neuter pelagus and vīrus.   *sea, poison*
Vulgus Neuter commonly,   *common people*
rarely masculine we see.

Third Declension (Consonant and I-Stems).

Rule 1.   Third-Nouns Masculine prefer
endings *ō, or, ŏs*, and *er*;
add to which the ending *ĕs*,
if its Cases have increase.

Exc. (a)   Feminine exceptions show
Substantives in *dō* and *gō*.
But ligō, ōrdō, praedō, cardō,   *spade, order, pirate, hinge*
Masculine, and Common margō.   *margin*

(b)   Abstract Nouns in *iō* call
Fēminīna, one and all:
Masculine will only be
things that you may touch or see,
(as curculiō, vespertīliō,   *weevil, bat*
pugiō, scīpiō, and pāpiliō)   *dagger, staff, butterfly*
with the Nouns that number show;
such as terniō, sēnio.   *3, 6*

(c)   Ēchō Feminine we name: *echo*
carō (carnis) is the same.   *flesh*

(d) Aequor, marmor, cor decline   *sea, marble, heart*
    Neuter; arbor Feminine.   *tree*

(e) Of the Substantives in ŏs,
    Feminine are cōs and dōs;   *whetstone, dowry*
    while, of Latin Nouns, alone
    Neuter are os (ossis), *bone*,
    and ōs (ōris), *mouth*: a few
    Greek in *os* are Neuter too.*

(f) Many Neuters end in *er*,
    siler, acer, verber, vēr,   *withy, maple, stripe, spring*
    tūber, ūber, and cadāver,   *hump, udder, carcase*
    piper, iter, and papāver   *pepper, journey, poppy*

(g) Feminine are compēs, teges,   *fetter, mat*
    mercēs, merges, quiēs, seges,   *fee, sheaf, rest, corn*
    though their Cases have increase:
    with the Neuters reckon aes.   *copper*

Rule 2.   Third-Nouns Feminine we class
    ending *is*, *x*, *aus*, and *ās*,
    s to consonant appended,
    ēs in flexion unextended.

Exc. (a) Many Nouns in *is* we find
    to the Masculine assigned:
    amnis, axis, caulis, collis,   *river, axle, stalk, hill*
    clūnis, crīni, fascis, follis,   *hind-leg, hair, bundle, bellows*
    fūstis, ignis, orbis, ēnsis,   *bludgeon, fire, orb, sword*
    pānis, piscis, postis, mēnsis,   *bread, fish, post, month*
    torris, unguis, and canālis,   *stake, nail, canal*
    vectis, vermis, and nātālis,   *lever, worm, birthday*
    sanguis, pulvis, cucumis,   *blood, dust, cucumber*
    lapis, cassēs, Mānēs, glīs.   *stone, nets, ghosts, dormouse*

(b) Chiefly Masculine we find,
    sometimes Feminine declined,
    callis, sentis, fūnis, finis,   *path, thorn, rope, end*
    and in poets torquis, cinis.   *necklace, cinder*

(c) Masculine are most in *ex*:
    Feminine are forfex, lēx,   *shears, law*
    nex, supellex: Common, pūmex   *death, furniture, pumice*
    imbrex, ōbex, silex, rumex.   *tile, bold, flint, sorrel.*

*As melos, *melody*; epos, *epic poem*.

(d) Add to Masculines in *ix*,
fornix, phoenix, and calix.   *arch, —, cup*

(e) Masculine are adamās,   *adamant*
elephās, mās, gigās, ās   *elephant, male, giant, as*
vas (vadis) Masculine is known,   *surety*
vās (vāsis) is a Neuter Noun.   *vessel*

(f) Masculine are fōns and mōns,   *fountain, mountain*
chalybs, hydrōps, gryps, and pōns,   *iron, dropsy, griffin, bridge*
rudēns, torrēns, dēns, and cliēns,   *cable, torrent, tooth, client*
fractions of the ās, as triēns.   *four ounces*
Add to Masculines tridēns,   *trident*
oriēns, and occidēns,   *east, west*
bidēns (*fork*); but bidēns (*sheep*),
with the Feminines we keep.

(g) Masculine are found in *ēs*
verrēs and acīnacēs.   *boar, scimitar*

Rule 3.   Third-Nouns Neuter end *a, e,*
ar, ur, us, c, l, n, and *t.*

Exc. (a) Masculine are found in *ur*
furfur, turtur, vultur, fūr.   *bran, turtle-dove, vulture, thief*

(b) Feminine in *ūs* a few
keep, as virtūs, the long *ū*:   *virtue*
servitūs, iuventūs, salūs,   *slavery, youth, safety*
senectūs, tellūs, incūs, palūs.   *old-age, east, anvil, marsh*

(c) Also pecus (pecudis)   *beast*
Feminine is Gender is.

(d) Masculine appears in *us*
lepus (leporis) and mūs   *hare, mouse*

(e) Masculines in *l* are mūgil,   *mullet*
cōnsul, sāl, and sōl, with pugil.   *consul, salt, sun, boxer*

(f) Masculines are rēn and splēn,   *kidney, spleen*
pecten, delphīn, attagēn   *comb, dolphin, grouse*

(g) Feminine are found in *ōn*
Gorgōn, sindōn, halcyōn   *Gorgon, muslin, kingfisher*

Fourth Declension (U-Stems)

Rule. Masculines end in *us*: a few
are Neuter nouns that end in *ū*.

Exc. Women and trees are Feminine,
with acus, domus, and manus,   needle, house, hand
tribus, Īdūs, porticus.   tribe, the Ides, porch

Fifth Declension (Ē-Stems)

Rule. Feminine are Fifth in ēs,
Except merīdiēs and diēs.   noon, day

Exc. Diēs in the Singular
Common we define;
But its Plural cases are
always Masculine.

17515511R00231

Printed in Great Britain
by Amazon